Also by Susan Kelly

The Gemini Man

The Summertime Soldiers

Trail of the Dragon

Until Proven Innocent

And Soon I'll Come to Kill You

Out of the Darkness

THE
BOSTON
STRANGLERS

Susan Kelly

PINNACLE BOOKS
Kensington Publishing Corp.

http://www.kensingtonbooks.com

Some names have been changed to protect the privacy of individuals connected to this story.

PINNACLE BOOKS are published by

Kensington Publishing Corp.
119 West 40th Street
New York, NY 10018

Copyright © 1995, 2002, 2013 by Susan Kelly
Previously published as a hardcover edition by Birch Lane Press

All Kensington Titles, Imprints, and Distributed Lines are available at special quantity discounts for bulk purchases for sales promotions, premiums, fund-raising, and educational or institutional use. Special book excerpts or customized printings can also be created to fit specific needs. For details, write or phone the office of the Kensington special sales manager: Kensington Publishing Corp., 119 West 40th Street, New York, NY 10018, attn: Special Sales Department, Phone: 1-800-221-2647.

Pinnacle and the P logo Reg. U.S. Pat. & TM Off.

ISBN-13: 978-0-7860-3251-8
ISBN-10: 0-7860-3251-0

First Pinnacle Mass Market Printing: March 2002
10 9 8 7 6 5

Printed in the United States of America

ACKNOWLEDGMENTS

Since it was members past and present of the Cambridge (Massachusetts) Police Department who put me onto this story, I owe them my first and greatest thanks for all their help, in particular, Superintendent Walter L. Boyle; retired Captain William R. Burke, Jr.; retired Detective Sergeant Fidele Centrella; the late Detective Louise Darling; Lieutenant Michael D. Giacoppo; former Detective M. Michael Giacoppo, now a private investigator; Detective Joseph McCarthy; retired Detective James Roscoe; and Crime Analyst Richard Sevieri. Several other officers contributed to this book; they have requested that their names not be used for reasons of privacy and personal safety, and I respect their wishes. They know who they are and I thank them.

I am more than grateful to Massachusetts Attorney General Scott Harshbarger and former Assistant Attorney General Thomas Samoluk, who dug up and put at my disposal more than twenty-five cartons of material relating to the Strangler case—material that until now has never been made public. Without Mr. Harshbarger and Mr. Samoluk, I would not have a book.

My deep thanks also to former United States Senator Edward Brooke; former Governor of Massachusetts Endicott Peabody; and former United States Attorney General Elliot Richardson.

Richard and Rosalie DeSalvo, brother and sister-in-law of the late Albert DeSalvo, offered me not only their help but their kind hospitality while I was gathering information for this book.

Francis C. Newton, Jr., Esq., and Thomas Troy, Esq., counsel for the late Albert DeSalvo, provided me with much important information about their famous and ill-starred client (and wasted a lot of billable hours doing it!). I can say the same of Dr. Ames Robey, whose mordant observations on the criminal justice system may merit a book in themselves.

Former Boston Police Commissioner Edmund McNamara and former Boston Police Department Detective Sergeant James McDonald were kind enough to share with me their invaluable recollections.

Former Lieutenant John Moran of the Salem (Massachusetts) Police Department, who knows more about the murder of Evelyn Corbin than anyone else alive—except for the perpetrator—helped immeasurably, not the least in giving me a guided tour of the murder site.

Novelists and former crime reporters George V. Higgins and Andrew Coburn had riveting reminiscences of the major players in the Strangler drama—and recounted them in fascinating detail. Professor William Russo of Curry College provided valuable information about the making of the movie *The Boston Strangler.*

Michael Brady, Ann Marie Barr, Franco Davoli, Bill Martin, Howard Hock, and Winston Alves of the Massachusetts State Record Office made my research there a pleasure.

Middlesex County Courthouse Librarian Sandra Lindheimer went above and beyond the call of bibliographic duty in helping me track down trial manuscripts and appeals briefs. I received similar excellent help from Jeannette Ramos at the United States District Court in Boston.

Jack Reilly, Joy Pratt, and novelist Lee Grove provided me with vivid memories of—and sharp observations about—the Harvard Square scene in the early 1960s.

Gordon Parry, who would have been a great stand-up comic but probably made a better forensic investigator, was enormously helpful to me in re-creating some of the crime scenes.

Reporters William Davis and Stephen Kurkjian of the *Boston Globe* were more than professionally courteous in helping me run down some suspects. Without John Cronin of the *Boston Herald,* this book would lack most of its wonderful illustrations.

I thank Gerold Frank for his kindness in answering my questions.

Diane Sullivan Dodd and Casey Sherman: thanks.

This book grew out of an article of mine published in the April 1992 issue of *Boston Magazine;* for this, I thank former editor Michael Roberts, who knows a thing or two about a hot crime story himself.

I appreciate the kindness of Jack Barry, Dan Doherty, John Donovan, Bill O'Donnell, Kathleen Rogers, Andrew Tuney, James Ward, and Roger Woodworth in sharing with me their memories of the Strangler investigation and its principals.

Thanks to Officers Richard Aumais and David St. Jean of the Andover (Massachusetts) Police Department for their help.

Jeff Klein of Pip Printing in Cambridge did a great job reproducing old photographs.

The following people, who figure prominently in this book, are deceased:

John Bottomly
Donald Conn
Phillip DiNatale
George McGrath
Cornelius Moynihan
P. J. Piscitelli

Robert Sheinfeld
Edward Sherry

The following people either declined to be interviewed or did not respond to requests for interviews:

Charles Burnim
John Collins
George Nassar
Juris Slesers

I also interviewed F. Lee Bailey, Esq., and Jon Asgeirsson, Esq., two other of Albert DeSalvo's attorneys. They stopped speaking to me after a while; nonetheless, I appreciate their initial input.

And thanks to those of you who requested anonymity: Your reasons for doing so make a great deal of sense.

CONTENTS

Preface

November 8, 1981, was one of those lead-gray days when the sky seems very close to the earth. I was visiting the Cambridge, Massachusetts, Police Department to do research for what would become my first published novel, *The Gemini Man*, a story about a serial killer.

I was sitting in the reception area outside the chief's office, waiting to speak to a lieutenant, a homicide specialist working out of the Criminal Investigation Division. Side by side on a bench diagonally across the room from me were two cops, both white-haired, both in their late fifties or early sixties, both in plain clothes. They introduced themselves as "the two Billies" * and asked me who I was. I gave my name and added that I was doing research on crime and police work. I did not have the nerve to identify myself as a writer: At that point, my only publications were three brief scholarly articles on medieval literature.

The two Billies had been detectives for the past thirty years, the first said. If I wanted some good stories, I should ask them.

"We been around the block a few times," the second said.

I smiled and said I'd look forward to hearing about

---

* Neither wishes to be further identified.

that. Then I added, "At the moment, I'm trying to find information about serial killers."

The two Billies looked at each other.

"Like Ted Bundy," I said.

"How about the Boston Strangler?" the first Billy said.

"Him, too," I replied.

The two glanced at each other again. Their faces wore the slightest of grins.

"We can tell you a lot about that," the second Billy said.

Something was going on here. I studied the two men. "I'd love to hear it," I said.

The first Billy gazed at me, still with that odd little smile. "Lemme ask you a question."

"Sure."

"Who do *you* think the Boston Strangler was?"

It seemed like a strange question. Sort of like asking who was buried in Grant's Tomb.

"Albert DeSalvo," I said.

Everybody knew that. All the newspapers had proclaimed DeSalvo the Strangler. A best-selling book by a famous writer had said so. Ditto a major movie. History's only more notorious serial killer was Jack the Ripper.

The two laughed.

"Albert DeSalvo was the Boston Strangler like my dog was the Boston Strangler," the second Billy said.

I stared at him. Then I said, "Tell me."

"You first, Billy," the second said.

I went on to write *The Gemini Man* (in which I made a passing reference to the two Billies' story) and five more crime novels. The research for those books required frequent contact with law enforcement officials. Every once in a while, in conversation with one or another of these people, I'd mention what I'd been told that November day in 1981. To my initial surprise and then increasing fascination, almost all the cops, lawyers, and prosecutors concurred with the two Billies. Some had different theories about who the Boston Strangler—or Stranglers—might have been. But they all agreed on one point: Albert DeSalvo, a construction worker with a long record of convictions for breaking and entering, armed robbery, and sex offenses, was not the killer of the eleven women who died terrible deaths between June 1962 and January 1964.

If DeSalvo wasn't, who was?

I decided to try to find out.

In the autumn of 1964, thirty-three-year-old Malden, Massachusetts, resident Albert Henry DeSalvo, loving husband and devoted father of two, was arrested and charged with numerous counts of armed robbery, unnatural acts, and rape, offenses that had been committed in various suburban communities in the greater Boston area. In the summer of 1965, after several months' incarceration in a state facility for the criminally insane and sexually dangerous, DeSalvo confessed to being the Boston Strangler. He claimed, moreover, responsibility not just for eleven of the killings the press ascribed to what it liked to call "the Phantom Fiend," but for two others. His descriptions of these thirteen murders were graphic. So much so that it took DeSalvo two months to recite all the details.

The only problem was—a great many of those details were wildly inaccurate. And DeSalvo was ignorant of facts the killer would have known.

DeSalvo's confession was a phony from beginning to end. The individual who conducted the interrogation and tape-recorded it, one of the top law enforcement officials of the Commonwealth of Massachusetts, was quite aware of that. Still, he permitted the confession to stand unchallenged. A few years later, this individual would profit handsomely from the sale to the movies of the rights to DeSalvo's story and the part he himself played in it.

Albert DeSalvo was never charged with, much less tried or convicted for, being the Boston Strangler. He couldn't be. Not one shred of physical evidence connected him to any of the murders. Nor could any eyewitness place him at or even near any of the crime scenes.

No police officer from any of the towns and cities in which the stranglings occurred was ever permitted to question De-Salvo.

Why did the Office of the Attorney General of the Commonwealth of Massachusetts—or at least one of its top representatives—accept DeSalvo's confession, knowing full well that it was phony? Simply because this was the quickest and easiest way to close the books on eleven gruesome murders.

Of course, there was also the money. The individual from the attorney general's office was not the only person whose bank account would be fattened by De-Salvo's confession.

Albert DeSalvo went to trial in January 1967 on the rape, armed robbery, and unnatural acts charges lodged against him in the fall of 1964. At the trial his attorney, F. Lee Bailey, identified his client as the Boston Strangler. Bailey's strategy—one he had used successfully at an earlier court proceeding to determine DeSalvo's competence—was based on the belief that if DeSalvo was branded the killer of thirteen women in an open forum, a jury would have to find him not guilty by reason of insanity of the armed robbery and sexual assault charges. Bailey further reasoned that De-Salvo would be committed by the judge to a mental institution rather than a state prison, since he was clearly a very sick man in desperate need of treatment.

Bailey's strategy failed the second time around. The jury found DeSalvo guilty of armed robbery and sexual assault. The judge, apparently convinced by Bailey that DeSalvo was an appalling menace to society, sentenced him to life in prison. Afterward Bailey bitterly declared that Massachusetts had just burned another witch.

DeSalvo was stabbed to death in prison in 1973. His murder—just like those of the eleven strangling* victims—is officially considered unsolved.

Two questions remain. The first, of course, is—why did Albert DeSalvo confess to a string of murders he never committed?

He had four reasons, all of which must have seemed to him quite valid. First, his attorney, in whom he reposed complete faith, was erroneously convinced that the 1964 rape and armed robbery charges would put DeSalvo in prison for life. (According to other legal authorities, it was very unlikely Albert would have received such a stiff sentence.) Second, DeSalvo was told that the sale of his life story and confession would make him a great deal of money, which could be given to his beloved wife and children for their support. Third, his attorney convinced him that he would be confined to a posh mental hospital—Johns Hopkins, Albert claimed—if he identified himself as the Strangler. Fourth, in branding himself a serial killer, Albert would become world-famous, something he dearly wanted to be.

He achieved this last goal, but surely not in the manner he'd intended.

If the previous question has four answers, the final question has two parts. The first: If Albert DeSalvo wasn't the Boston Strangler, who was? The second: Why, then, wasn't the real Strangler—or Stranglers— ever arrested and prosecuted?

I am convinced that there was not one Boston

---

* The two other murders to which DeSalvo confessed are also considered unsolved.

Stranger, but rather a bare minimum of six and much more likely eight or nine. The Boston Stranglings were not eleven serial killings—at least six of them were one-on-one murders committed for motives as individual as were the killers.

And why were these killers never charged, but permitted to get away with their crimes? No blame can be attached to the police for this. In one case, the principal suspect died. In two others, the suspects left the state and vanished. In other cases, the suspects were incarcerated on other charges (some of them still are). In still another case, a piece of conclusive evidence was never obtained. In another case, the Suffolk County District Attorney's office was ready to seek an indictment. The indictment was postponed, and later dropped, because of a squabble over jurisdictional rights.

In a final instance, the excellent case being prepared against a particular suspect by the attorney general's office was abruptly abandoned by that office. This was shortly before Albert DeSalvo began suggesting that *he* was the killer.

In 1966, Gerold Frank wrote that "the story of the Boston stranglings has ended."

He was wrong. In some ways, it had just begun.

"What is truth?" said jesting Pilate; and did not stay for an answer.

—Francis Bacon, 1625

It isn't really justice; it's the way you play the game.

—F. Lee Bailey, 1976

PART ONE

1

A Time of Terror

The first one to die was Anna Slesers.

Slesers, a fifty-six-year-old Latvian immigrant, lived at 77 Gainsborough Street in Boston. On the evening of June 14, 1962, she was due to attend a memorial service for the victims of the Russian invasion of Latvia during World War II. Her son Juris would escort her.

Juris knocked on the door of Apartment 3-F a little before 7:00 P.M. No answer. No sound of movement from within the apartment, either. Thinking his mother might have gone to the store, Juris went downstairs to the foyer to await her.

She did not appear.

Juris went back upstairs and knocked again at the apartment door. No response. He returned to the foyer. It was then he noticed that his mother had forgotten to retrieve her mail.

At a quarter to eight, there was still no sign of Mrs. Slesers. Juris, probably now very worried, decided to break into her apartment.

His mother was at home. She had been at home the whole time.

Her body lay in the hall leading from the bathroom to the kitchen. The blue housecoat she'd worn had been ripped open to leave her torso nude. Her left leg was out straight, her right, the knee bent, at a nearly forty-five-degree angle.

She had been strangled with the cord of the housecoat, which had been drawn very tightly around her neck and tied under her chin in a sort of bow. There was blood in her right ear and a gaping laceration on the back of her skull. Her neck was scratched and abraded and her chin contused.

The blood in her vagina indicated that she had been sexually assaulted, probably with an object.

Except for a small amount of blood on the kitchen floor and an overturned wastebasket, there was no sign that a struggle had taken place in the apartment. It had apparently been searched. For a reason no one could guess, a chair had been placed in the front hallway just inside the door.

The following day, the Boston *Traveler* carried a story with the headline MOM FOUND STRANGLED IN BACK BAY. The *Boston Globe* story on the murder described the victim as "an attractive divorcée."

Slightly over two weeks later, on June 30, the body of Nina Nichols, sixty-eight, was found on the bedroom floor of her apartment at 1940 Commonwealth Avenue in the Brighton section of Boston.

The pink housecoat she wore was open. Her bra had been yanked up above her breasts. Her slip had been pushed up to her waist. On her feet were blue tennis shoes. She lay on her back.

The two nylon stockings around her neck had been tied and knotted very tightly. There was blood in and around both ears, and a small abrasion on the lower right side of her face.

Her external genitalia had been lacerated and there was blood and mucus in her vagina.

One of the Boston police detectives called to the crime scene took from it an empty wine bottle, a woman's black plastic purse, and a small cardboard box. These were brought to headquarters for further examination.

That same day in Lynn, a small industrial city fifteen miles northeast of Boston, Helen Blake met a terrible death. According to the autopsy report, "this sixty-five-year-old white female was found by her housekeeper about 6 P.M., July 2, 1962, lying upon her bed within her ransacked apartment. The housekeeper had last conversed with the victim at 4:30 P.M., June 29, 1962 . . . Decedent was lying prone on her bed, clad in pajama tops, with legs equally abducted [pulled apart] and face turned toward the left." There was dried blood in both ears and on the outer part of the left one. The two stockings around her neck were knotted at the nape. Over the stockings was wrapped a bra, tied in front below the chin.

Her pajama top, which had been pushed up over her shoulders, bore reddish-brown stains. So did her pajama pants and the bed sheets.

Her vagina and anus had been lacerated, although the medical examiner found no spermatozoa in either.

ANOTHER SILK STOCKING MURDER was how the next day's edition of the *Globe* described the crime.

On Tuesday morning, July 11, 1962, a chambermaid named Eva Day entered Room 7 on the second floor of the Hotel Roosevelt, a now no longer extant fleabag on lower Washington Street in Boston.

Eva Day retreated shrieking from the room she had intended to clean. On the bed lay an elderly woman, naked and dead. An autopsy would establish that she had been manually strangled.

Accompanied by a man, she had checked into the hotel the previous night. They gave their names as Mr. and Mrs. Byron Spinney. The address the man wrote on the registration card was as phony as the names he and the victim had assumed.

The dead woman was identified first as Ethel Johnson, wife of one Johnny Johnson. Someone else identified her as Anne Cunningham, alias Annie Oakley. She was known to a third party as Winnie Hughes, and to a fourth as simply Tobey. Ultimately she was correctly identified as Margaret Davis, age sixty, by her nephew Daniel O'Leary. She was an alcoholic who had been treated, apparently with little success, at City Hospital. She had also been a patient at the House of the Good Shepherd in the Jamaica Plain section of Boston, where she had worked as a domestic until the beginning of June.

At 7:47 P.M. on August 21, 1962, the Boston police arrived at 7 Grove Street, at the bottom of Beacon Hill, to find the body of a woman who had been more grotesquely done to death than any of the previous victims.

Seventy-five-year-old Ida Irga had actually died on August 19. She lay on her back on the living room floor of Apartment 10. She wore, according to the police report, "a light brown nightdress which was torn, completely exposing her body. There was a pillowcase wrapped tightly around her neck, her legs were propped up on individual chairs, and were spread approximately four to five feet from heel to heel, and a standard bed pillow, less the cover, was placed under her buttocks; there was dried blood both under her body and covering the entire head, mouth, and ears."

The police also "found the [bed]room light burning; and on the floor was a sheet and blanket and a pair of women's underpants and a quantity of dried blood and two brown hair combs. Also a trail of blood leading from where she was apparently attacked in the bedroom, and then apparently carried or dragged out into the living room."

There were slight injuries to her external genitalia. No spermatozoa were found in her vagina. She had died of manual strangulation and strangulation by ligature.

Her body had been positioned so that her pubic area

faced the front door of the apartment. It was this sight that greeted the person who found her, her younger brother Harry Halpern.

On August 22, the *Globe* ran a front-page article about Ida's death headlined WIDOW 5TH VICTIM OF STRANGLER.

Sixty-seven-year-old Jane Sullivan had moved to 435 Columbia Road in the Dorchester area of Boston on July 1, 1962. She died there on August 21, 1962.

Her body was not found until ten days later. The discovery was made by her nephew, forty-four-year-old Dennis Mahoney, at 3:10 P.M. His mother, Jane's sister, had been worried about Jane because she hadn't heard from her in a while. Dennis's mother asked him to check up on his aunt.

He found her on her knees in the bathtub, partially submerged in six inches of water. Her feet were up over the back end of the tub, her buttocks thrust into the air. Her head was beneath the faucet. A housecoat covered the upper part of her body; her underpants were pulled down on her legs.

Although the corpse was badly decomposed, the autopsy found no evidence of trauma to the vagina or anus. There was matted blood on the right side of Jane's scalp. Two stockings were twined around her neck and knotted, and the right side of the hyoid bone had been fractured. Her bra was on the bathroom floor.

There was no evidence of forcible entry to the apartment (nor had there been in any of the previous cases), but there was blood on the floors of the kitchen, hall, and bathroom. Jane's handbag was open on the living room sofa. There was no evidence that the apartment had been ransacked.

A partial fingerprint was found at the scene. It could not be identified.

There were also bloodstains on the handle of a corn broom.

About 6:35 A.M. on October 13, 1962, Violet Prioleau of 618 Columbus Avenue in Boston happened to glance out her apartment window at the rear of 791 Tremont Street. She saw in the ward what appeared to be a body. She caught the attention of John Reese, who worked at 791 Tremont. He investigated and confirmed that what Violet Prioleau had spotted was indeed a corpse. It was that of thirty-seven-year-old Modeste Freeman.

Reese called the police. They arrived five minutes later.

Modeste, who had lived at 394 Northampton Street in Boston, was not only far younger than the previous murder victims, but of a different race—black—as well.

If Ida Irga's slaying had been the most grotesque to date, Modeste Freeman's was surely the most barbaric. Her body was nude except for a piece of clothing wrapped around her neck. What had been a beautiful face was now a distorted pulp, the nose virtually flattened. Her skull was battered into a lump. She had died of strangulation by ligature and multiple blunt force trauma.

Her blood alcohol level was staggeringly high, something not found in any of the other victims.

A wooden stick had been shoved up her vagina.

At five-thirty in the afternoon of December 5, 1962, a student at the Carnegie Institute of Medical Technology, Gloria Todd, returned to the apartment at 315 Huntington Avenue in Boston that she shared with two fellow students, Audri Adams and Sophie Clark. What confronted her when she opened the door made her turn and rush headlong back down the building stairway. In her flight she encountered a neighbor, Anthony Riley of 313 Huntington Avenue. Later that evening, at police headquarters, Gloria told investigators, "He [Riley] spoke to me and I said, 'Hi, Tony.' I stopped, and he said, 'What's the matter?' and I said, 'I don't know what to do,' and I felt as if I was going to faint, and he said 'What's the matter?' and I told him what I had saw [*sic*]."

What she had seen was the body of twenty-year-old Sophie Clark.

Sophie lay on her back, legs apart, partially dressed in a print housecoat, a garter belt, black stockings, and black tie shoes. Beneath the garter belt she wore a menstrual harness with a fragment of the tab of a sanitary napkin attached to the metal clasp. Around her neck was a half-slip, and beneath that, a nylon stocking tied very tightly. Near her body were a ripped bra, bloodstained pink flowered underpants, and the sanitary napkin that had clearly been torn from her.

Gloria and Riley, accompanied by Nat Nelson, the janitor of the building, went back to Apartment 4-C. Riley, a nurse, felt Sophie for a pulse. There was none. With a surgical scissors, he removed a gag from her mouth. He attempted resuscitation.

A male friend of the victim arrived at the apartment nearly simultaneously with Gloria, Riley and Nelson.

The nurse's effort to revive Sophie failed. He called the police.

Sophie had suffered no external genital injuries, nor was there any trauma to her scalp, skull, or brain. Smears taken from her vagina and rectum showed no fresh blood, nor was there any menstrual discharge. She had died of strangulation by ligature.

A Salem cigarette butt was found in the toilet. The roommates smoked Salems, Newports, Pall Malls, and Marlboros.

A seminal stain was found on the rug in the living room near where Sophie lay.

And also among the effects in the apartment was discovered a typed document headed " 'Silk Stockings' From an Old Story Entitled, 'The New Look' Or 'Mother Should Have Stayed At Home.' " It was an adolescent, quasi-literate fragment of pornography that told from the woman's point of view the tale of her seduction—which took place all because she wore silk stockings.

Like Modeste Freeman, Sophie Clark was black, although of mixed-race ancestry. Her lovely features, reproduced in newspaper photographs the day following the murder, had an almost Polynesian cast.

In six months, eight women had been savagely murdered. Six were white and late middle-aged to elderly (although Anna Slesers had looked somewhat younger than she was). The two most recent victims were young, black, and beautiful.

What were the other differences?

Modeste Freeman had been killed on the street, unlike any of the others. Anna Slesers, Nina Nichols, Helen Blake, Ida Irga, and Jane Sullivan, all widowed, divorced, or never married, had lived alone. Sophie Clark, engaged to a young man from her home state of New Jersey, had not. Margaret Davis, a street person, had lived wherever she could find shelter.

If there was any sort of pattern to these crimes, the next murder would introduce a further aberration to it.

Twenty-three-year-old Patricia Bissette, a secretary at the Boston firm of Engineering Systems Incorporated, was supposed to get a ride to work from her boss on the morning of December 31, 1962. When he knocked on her apartment door a little before 8:00 A.M., though, she didn't answer. He left for work. The phone calls he placed to Patricia from there went unanswered as well. Finally he became worried enough about his secretary to return to her apartment at 515 Park Drive in Boston. With the help of the building's custodian, Pat's boss climbed through a window into her living room.

The young woman lay in bed, the sheet and blankets pulled to her chin. She looked peacefully asleep, according to one of the forensic investigators called to the scene. She was not asleep; she was dead. Around her neck, concealed by the bedclothes, had been tightly knotted a white blouse, a single stocking, and two other stockings wound together. All were tied in front, extremely tightly.

She had had sexual intercourse very shortly before her death, and there was some injury to her rectum.

She was not married, nor ever had been. She lived alone, although she had previously shared apartments elsewhere in Boston and New York. The owner of 515 Park Drive sometimes used Pat's living room to conduct rental business.

At the time of her death, she was one month pregnant.

Lawrence, Massachusetts, lies twenty-five miles northwest of Boston. A mill and factory city incorporated in the mid-nineteenth century, its principal enterprises today are arson and the sale of illegal drugs. For a city of seventy thousand, it has a very high rate of violent crime. Thirty years ago, however, it was a far safer place in which to live or work.

Unless you were Mary Brown. At 8:15 P.M. on March 6, 1963, she was found dead in the living room of her apartment at 319 Park Street. She was white, sixty-eight years old, and lived alone.

She had been bludgeoned over the head, stabbed, and strangled. It was the beating that caused her death.

The abundance of partially degenerated spermatozoa in her vagina indicated that she had also been raped. What the Lawrence Police Department found when some of its members entered her apartment was a "body on the floor with her head about a foot from the south wall of the room and the rest of her body facing in a direct northerly direction. She was nude and her girdle was pulled down to her left foot. Her rubber overshoes and stockings were still on and a black dress and other articles of clothing were pulled up over her head. Her throat was badly bruised and the floor in the vicinity of her head was covered with blood. What appeared to be a knife or a fork was stuck in her left breast up to the handle."

CAMBRIDGE GIRL, 26, STRANGLED read the headline of the May 9, 1963, editions of Boston's tabloid *Record American*.

In fact, Beverly Samans had been stabbed to death—seventeen times in and around the left breast, according to the autopsy report. Her neck bore four horizontal incised wounds, two on the right side, two on the left, almost like parallel gill slits.

Although the body was nude, the victim had neither been raped nor sexually assaulted by means of an object. No injuries were found to her genitalia, nor were any spermatozoa found in either her vagina or rectum.

Beverly was found dead by a friend, Oliver Chamberlain, at 7:00 P.M. on May 8. She lay on her back on a studio bed. A white scarf had been tied around her neck. Beneath this were two nylon stockings. Her hands were bound behind her back with a multicolored scarf. Each wrist was individually tied. There were no ligature marks on her neck.

Beverly had been an accomplished singer, a part-time counselor to the mentally disturbed, and a graduate student at Boston University. Among her possessions the Cambridge police found a wirebound notebook she used for her course in educational research. The last entry in the book was dated May 4. Above the notes she had taken on that day's lecture, Beverly printed her exasperated reaction to what was evidently a colossally boring professorial discourse. The comment read: "What sins in my life did I ever commit to deserve this?"

Evelyn Corbin, who was fifty-one years old according to the Essex County Medical Examiner and fifty-eight years old according to the Massachusetts State Police, lived northeast of Boston in Salem. Whatever her true age was—and it was most likely fifty-eight, given the chronology of her life—she seemed to have been remarkably youthful in appearance and manner. Or so those who knew her in life reported. Salem Police Inspector John Moran, who knew Evelyn only in death, said, "She looked about 110 to me. But death will do that to you."

The last time anyone except her killer saw Evelyn alive was at 10:30 on the morning of September 8, 1963.

A few hours later one of her neighbors in the apartment building at 225 Lafayette Street, Flora Manchester, grew concerned that she hadn't heard from Evelyn, who was supposed to have Sunday dinner with Mrs. Manchester and her son Robert. A little after 1:00 P.M., Mrs. Manchester used the key given her by Evelyn to unlock the Corbin apartment door. What she saw within made her scream, "My God, she's been attacked." Another neighbor, Marie L'Horty, went to call the police.

Robert Manchester went into Evelyn's apartment. A few minutes later he emerged, his hands to his head, saying, "She's gone."

The forty-one-year-old Manchester and Evelyn had been lovers.

Evelyn lay faceup on her bed, her left leg hanging toward the floor. The upper left corner of the spread covered her trunk. There was blood in both her ears, and a bloodstain on the bed cover beneath her head. Her right hand and forearm were beneath her body.

She was dressed in a housecoat, nightgown, and white ankle socks. Three buttons were missing from the robe, and the nightgown was torn. Her pubic area was partly exposed.

One stocking was tied around her left ankle. Two were tied around her neck. On the bedroom floor lay a pair of women's underpants, blood- and lipstick-stained above the crotch. The bed and floor were littered with crumpled tissues similarly lipstick-smeared. They were later found to bear traces of dried semen as well.

The autopsy revealed spermatozoa in the victim's mouth, although not in her vagina. The newspapers would say that the killer had indulged "an unnatural appetite." The euphemism was transparent to any adult reader.

On November 25, 1963, Massachusetts was still reeling from the shock of the assassination of its favorite son, John Fitzgerald Kennedy. How many people on that Monday attended to an article on the very last page of the *Boston Herald,* the one entitled LAWRENCE WOMAN FOUND STRANGLED?

Twenty-three-year-old Joann Graff, a University of Chicago graduate and an industrial designer for Bolta Products in Lawrence, had been murdered just over twenty-four hours after the president of the United States had been pronounced dead of a gunshot wound to the head at Parkland Hospital, Dallas. Of the two killings, Kennedy's was the quicker and more merciful.

Joann's body was found at noon on Sunday by her landlord, Sebastian Corzo, and a Lawrence police officer, F.T. O'Connor. They had gone to Joann's apartment at the request of Mr. and Mrs. John Johnson, friends who had been trying unsuccessfully to get in touch with the young woman since the previous afternoon. Joann had accepted their dinner invitation for Saturday evening, but had failed to come to her apartment door when Mr. Johnson arrived to pick her up at 4:30 P.M. that day. Nor did she appear at the Lutheran Redeemer Church the following morning to teach her Sunday school class, a sin of omission this devoutly religious young woman would seem to be incapable of committing. The Johnsons were very worried.

Their worst fears were realized when Corzo and O'Connor walked into Joann's place at 54 Essex Street. "Oh, my God," Corzo exclaimed.

Joann lay diagonally supine on the bed, her right leg dangling down over the side. Her left foot rested near the pillow. Her arms were crooked, and her right hand, lying on her midriff, was curled into a loose fist, as if in death she was still trying to fend off her assailant.

She was naked but for an opened blouse and the three ligatures around her neck: two brown nylon stockings and the leg of a black leotard. The latter was tied with a square knot with an extra turn. One stocking had a granny knot with an additional turn, the other a bowed surgeon's knot.

Her external vaginal area was lacerated and bloody; there were two half-moon contusions below her right nipple and two abrasions above and to the left of it. Her right thigh was contused. The autopsy would show that she had been raped.

Beneath her body was a torn and bloody white bra. Her slacks and underpants, inside out, had been dropped or thrown to the floor. Her eyeglasses lay beside her head, one earpiece beneath her neck. The bedspread, like the bra, was bloodstained.

On New Year's Day, 1964, nineteen-year-old Patricia Delmore and eighteen-year-old Pamela Parker of 44A Charles Street in Boston acquired a roommate to share their three-room apartment. Her name was Mary Sullivan,* and her twentieth birthday was upcoming that month. She didn't live to celebrate it.

On January 4, at 6:20 P.M., Boston police officers arrived at 44A Charles Street. They had been summoned there by a stunned and hysterical Patricia and Pamela, who had come home from work only twenty minutes earlier. They had found Mary in the bedroom.

She was in a sitting position on the bed, her back against the headboard, a pillow beneath her buttocks. Although her bra had not been removed, it had been loosened to bare her breasts. Over her shoulders she

---

* No relation to Jane Sullivan.

wore an opened yellow-and-beige-striped blouse. Around her neck she wore a triple ligature consisting of a charcoal nylon stocking, a pink silk scarf, and a pink-and-white scarf with a floral design.

Mary's knees were flexed and her thighs were spread apart. A broom handle had been pushed three and a half inches into her vagina. Both breasts were mauled. A trail of a sticky substance resembling semen had dripped from her mouth to her right chest.

Propped up against her left foot was a greeting card that read "Happy New Year!"

2

Police Under Fire

The period beginning with the death of Anna Slesers and ending with that of Mary Sullivan was not a good time for the Boston Police Department and its brand-new commissioner, Edmund McNamara. For despite the best efforts of McNamara and his detectives, not a single one of the nine homicides committed within their jurisdiction could be solved.

"If this rampant crime wave keeps up, the mayor [John Collins] will fire McNamara as quickly as he'd fire anyone else," thundered Boston City Councilor William J. Foley.

Foley's colleague Patrick F. McDonough, an ex-cop, weighed in with a further denunciation of the commissioner and his administration of the force, zeroing in on McNamara's recently announced plan to reduce the department's size.

And State Legislator Perlie Dyar Chase, who represented the Back Bay district in which Anna Slesers, Sophie Clark, and Patricia Bissette had been murdered, tossed a bombshell of his own onto the House floor: a demand that the Boston Police Department and its investigators be investigated themselves.

This political volcano of discontent with the force

erupted just two weeks after the death of Patricia Bissette. In the intervening time, a sixteen-year-old high school girl named Daniela (Donna) Saunders had been dragged into an alley near her home, choked, and then thrown to the ice-slick pavement. Although she had not been raped, the brutality with which this pretty, intelligent member of the Jeremiah Burke High School glee and math clubs, active in Junior Achievement and Saint Hugh's Catholic Youth Organization, had been done to death sent shock waves not only through her Roxbury neighborhood but through Boston at large. And even though the police fairly quickly closed the books on Donna's murder—her killer turned out to be a boy whom she had refused to kiss— the volcano kept bubbling.

It would explode with the violence of Krakatoa in the aftermath of Mary Sullivan's slaying.

Edmund McNamara, the man standing hip-deep in the lava flow, was no career Boston cop risen from the ranks but an ex-FBI agent. A graduate of the College of the Holy Cross, where he had played football, he had given sixteen years' service to the Bureau. Fourteen of them were spent in the Boston area. At the time McNamara became commissioner of the BPD, the relationship between the city law enforcement agency and its federal counterpart was one of mutual loathing, a hostility dating back to the Brink's Robbery in 1950 when both departments had raced each other to crack the case.

The irony was that in April of 1962 McNamara had ridden into town like Shane. A man of impeccable personal and professional repute, he had been appointed to clean up corruption in the BPD. (A lethally embarrassing documentary showing members of the force taking bribes from bookies had been aired on CBS, resulting in the resignation of McNamara's predecessor.) Even more ironically, the ex-FBI man had been charged with trimming the fat from the department.

Thus what he had been mandated to do in the late spring of 1962 he would be damned for attempting in the early winter of 1963.

Not only the politicians but the press were after McNamara and his police. The *Record American,* which had long since decreed that the murders in Brighton, Dorchester, Beacon Hill, Lawrence, Lynn, and the Back Bay were the work of the same person—"the Phantom Strangler"—immediately designated Donna Saunders as the Phantom's latest victim. That she was shortly proven not to have been anything of the sort did not noticeably abash the paper. "Cop Laxity Charged in Slain Girl Case," the *Record* stated on January 9, 1963. RAP COPS AT STRANGLE PROTEST blared the headline.

Nor was the *Globe,* the only one of the broadsheets of that era in existence today, any more circumspect. B.U. COED SLAIN BY KNIFE FIEND, its front page proclaimed the day after the discovery of Beverly Samans's body. Even the *Herald,* the most conservative (in both senses of the word) daily, was not immune to the occasional bout of sensationalism, although its preeminent columnist, George Frazier, wrote a scathing commentary about the *Record* and its "sob sister" reportage of the murders.

Speaking today, Edmund McNamara offers a pungent assessment of the Fourth Estate of three decades past: "The papers sent all their drunks to cover the police department."

Whether written by lushes or teetotalers, the news accounts of the murders had a punch and power that was undeniable. And they generated a whirlwind of hysteria, at least in certain segments of the population of eastern Massachusetts.

In *The Boston Strangler,* Gerold Frank wrote that "women all but barricaded themselves in their apartments." He went on to describe the measures they took to prevent a home invasion by a homicidal sex pervert: "There were runs on door locks and lock-smiths; the demand for watchdogs, for dogs of any kind, cleaned out the Animal Rescue League pound minutes after it opened each morning. Elderly widows living alone arranged for their married children to phone them three times a day,"*

The newspapers published advice to women living by themselves, including tips from Commissioner McNamara himself:

- Make sure all doors are locked and if possible have a safety lock put on doors. Also check all windows to ascertain they are safely locked.
- Have superintendent or janitor in building make sure entrance door is securely locked.
- Let no one into an apartment until positive identification is established.
- Notify Police Department immediately if you see anyone in the neighborhood acting suspiciously.
- Remember the Police Department wants all information which may have a connection to any of those crimes.

These suggestions, made in the wake of Ida Irga's murder, were good counsel at any time, in any city. And thousands of urban women hastened to adopt them.

A retired metropolitan-area police detective, looking back on the eighteen bloody months between June 14, 1962, and January 4, 1964, says, "There was such a furor, such an uproar. Everybody was scared stiff."

"Oh, my God," recalls an eighty-year-old East Cambridge woman. "That was a terrible time. The priests were warning all the women not to leave their doors unlocked." A Cape Cod resident remembers that her

---

* Frank, p. 40.

grandmother would hide all the stockings in the house before going to bed. Another local woman says flatly, "It was as if Jack the Ripper had come back from the dead to stalk Boston."

The demonic tread of the Phantom Strangler fell only lightly, if not inaudibly, however, in the affluent suburbs. A woman living in Andover, barely three miles from the murder scenes of Joann Graff and Mary Brown, shrugs when asked for recollections of the period: "It was something that happened in Boston."

The Andover woman's sentiments were shared even by some Bostonians. The granddaughter-in-law of a well-to-do and socially prominent Beacon Hill resident whose townhouse was only blocks from where Mary Sullivan and Ida Irga had been killed maintains that the dowager had no fear she might fall prey to a murderous intruder. And if the women of East Cambridge, a blue-collar ethnic community, were frightened, their white-collar and largely WASP sisters in West Cambridge and Harvard Square (where Beverly Samans died) harbored no such anxiety. "The hysteria passed over us," the wife of a Harvard Business School professor remarks. Jack Reilly, bartender at the Casablanca in Harvard Square in the early sixties, adds, "People were too busy having fun to be scared."

Edmund McNamara, now in his seventies and long retired from law enforcement work, still retains the imposing physical presence of the fullback he once was. He also retains a vivid memory of what it was like to be a cop in the line of fire during the strangling investigations. "Boston homicide was under tremendous pressure. They were being called stupid and incompetent every day. They were hugely frustrated."

Two of the most frustrated of McNamara's detectives were Edward Sherry and John Donovan. Donovan, formerly chief of the homicide squad and later director of security at Holy Cross, says, "I lived with this thing night and day for four years." According to sources outside as well as inside the BPD, he and Sherry (who died a number of years ago) ran the homicide unit very well. And despite the accusations by the press and politicians, the fact that by mid-January of 1964 the police had failed to solve the killings of Anna Slesers, Nina Nichols, Margaret Davis, Ida Irga, Jane Sullivan, Modeste Freeman, Sophie Clark, Patricia Bissette, and Mary Sullivan was in no way the result of carelessness or sloth. In any event, the BPD's colleagues in Cambridge, Lynn, Lawrence, and Salem weren't having any better luck tracking down the murderers of Beverly Samans, Helen Blake, Joann Graff, Mary Brown, and Evelyn Corbin.

Unlike the *Record American,* the BPD was sure it was looking for multiple killers rather than one single Phantom Fiend, a conviction again widely shared in the Cambridge, Lawrence, Lynn, and Salem departments. A number of very strong suspects were indeed identified. That none of them panned out was due mostly, says former Boston Detective Sergeant James McDonald, to an absence of physical evidence to link the suspects to the crimes. McNamara concurs: "In a premeditated murder, the murderer doesn't intend to leave evidence." Thus, "premeditated murders are very rarely solved."

This depressing reality was suspended for twenty-four hours in March of 1963, when two Cambridge police officers arrested Roy Smith of Boston on suspicion of homicide.

Shortly before 4:00 P.M. on March 11, Israel Goldberg let himself into his home at 14 Scott Road, Belmont, a suburb about seven miles west of Boston. On the floor of the living room lay his sixty-two-year-old wife, Bessie. One of her stockings had been removed and used to strangle her. The rest of her clothing was in disarray; the position in which her body had been left suggested she had been raped. (This was later borne out by microscopic investigation.)

Most of the living room furniture had been pulled to the center of the room. The vacuum cleaner also stood in the middle of the floor. Ornaments and knick-knacks from the living room had been placed on the dining room table.

Roy Smith, an itinerant handyman and ex-convict whom Mrs. Goldberg had hired to help her clean house that day, was the immediate suspect for her murder. Wanted posters bearing his likeness were circulated by the thousand through area law enforcement agencies.

The hunt for the alleged killer was a brief one. On March 12, the two Cambridge police officers, William Coughlin and Michael Giacoppo, ran Smith to ground at his girlfriend's house near Central Square in Cambridge.

That night Chet Huntley and David Brinkley reported that the Boston Strangler, in the person of Roy Smith, had been captured. And indeed Smith, with his history of violence against women, made an outstanding suspect for at least some of the Boston murders. Unfortunately, as the police shortly discovered, he had been incarcerated from April to September of 1962 and thus rendered incapable of murdering anyone outside the prison walls. Certainly he had not killed Anna Slesers, Nina Nichols, Margaret Davis, Helen Blake, Ida Irga, or Jane Sullivan.

But the address Smith called home at the time of his arrest was 175 Northampton in Boston, the same street on which Modeste Freeman had lived only a few blocks down. She had died the month after Smith's release from prison.

Roy Smith was tried and convicted of the murder of Bessie Goldberg. He was sentenced to life in prison.

The Phantom Fiend roamed free.

3

The State Takes Over

On January 17, 1964, Massachusetts Attorney General Edward Brooke announced that as the highest-ranking law enforcement official in the Commonwealth, he would take over the investigation of all fourteen of the strangling homicides. His action was, as Brooke himself noted, an unprecedented one. But as he further pointed out, desperate times demanded desperate measures. And the press was getting out of control.

A Republican who had pulled off the considerable feat of being elected in an overwhelmingly Democratic state, Brooke was handsome, dignified, charismatic, and an extremely astute and able politician. He was a husband and father of two daughters, a World War II veteran and combat hero, and a lawyer with a flourishing private practice. He was also something else—the most prominent African-American holder of public office in the entire country. There were rumors that he might soon become its first black governor.

Brooke had his sights set on higher things.

There is no reason to doubt that humanitarian considerations as well as a desire to see justice done were prime factors in Brooke's decision to intervene in the Strangler case. His public statements about it leave no doubt that the string of murders caused him sorrow and concern. But for a man in his position the issue had a greater complexity than simply catching a killer or killers.

It was a tremendous risk for the attorney general to preempt the authority of the various municipal police departments. The maneuver would backfire if the fourteen murders remained unsolved. And if despite his intervention women continued to die in various horrible ways, Brooke could probably kiss his political career good-bye.

But—if under his stewardship the cops nabbed the Strangler or Stranglers, what public office might he not aspire to afterward? With his eye on that glittering prize, Brooke took the gamble and took command.

His decision made pragmatic as well as political sense. The murders had occurred in Suffolk (Boston), Middlesex (Cambridge), and Essex (Lawrence, Lynn, and Salem) counties, so there were not only five city police forces involved but three district attorneys' offices as well. The potential for jurisdictional wrangles was enormous. To consolidate the various independent murder investigations would eliminate a great deal of this worry. It would also provide a clearinghouse for information that might lead to the quicker solution of one, some, or ideally all of the homicides. And it would reduce, if not eliminate, duplication of investigative effort.

A further advantage to Brooke's plan was that it would enable whatever detectives he appointed to devote their time and energies solely to the strangling murders. This was not the case with the municipal and state police agencies, which had not only other past and present felonies and misdemeanors to investigate, but new ones coming in all the time. Even if every cop in Cambridge wanted to spend eight hours a day every day tracking down the killer of Beverly Samans, the workload wouldn't have permitted it.

And Brooke's move would also pacify the media, which was surely one of his goals. Two extraordinarily resourceful and tenacious reporters for the *Record-American*, Loretta McLaughlin and Jean Cole, had written a series of articles on the murders (it was these that drew the critical fire of their colleague at the *Herald*, George Frazier) in which they not only reconstructed the crimes themselves but dissected the police investigations as well. In a meeting with three representatives of the attorney general's staff, McLaughlin and Cole charged the BPD with negligence and gross inefficiency: failing to exchange names of suspects with other law enforcement agencies; refusing to acknowledge the similarities between the crimes; failing to assemble complete autopsy reports and photos of the victims; feeding false information to the press; and not cooperating with Suffolk District Attorney Garrett Byrne, among other derelictions.

Perhaps most important, Brooke's action would assure the public that finding the perpetrator or perpetrators of the stranglings was still the top priority of Massachusetts law enforcement.

So on the chilly morning of January 17, the attorney general invited to his office the commissioner of public safety; the captain of the state police detectives; the district attorneys of Essex, Middlesex, and Suffolk counties; and the chiefs of the Cambridge, Lawrence, Lynn, and Salem police departments. The gathering reviewed the situation that had evolved over the past eighteen months. Then Brooke announced that he was appointing as coordinator of what would become known as the Strangler Task Force, or the Strangler Bureau, Assistant Attorney General John S. Bottomly.

Bottomly and Brooke went way, way back together. It was in fact Bottomly who, while he and Brooke were law students at Boston University, had introduced the latter to Republican party politics. Other than this ideological bond, the two had in common their military experience during World War II, although Captain Bottomly had spent his tour of duty in the office of the secretary to the General Staff rather than in slogging up a fortified hill in Italy as had Brooke. Beyond that they were opposites. Bottomly was an independently wealthy Yankee blueblood who came to the law only after deciding not to take up medicine, divinity, or teaching as a career. His avocations were eclectic: ship salvage, investment, mining, and sports. Most of all, he professed an interest in reforming "the system."

When Brooke chose him as the Strangler Bureau Coordinator, Bottomly was chief of Eminent Domain. Why did the attorney general not reach out for an assistant attorney general who had a background in the investigation and prosecution of murder cases? This was the biggest case of all. Why hand it to a man whose expertise lay in government-enforced real-estate buys?

"Mostly because of his organizational skills," Brooke says today. "He was a good administrator."

Bottomly was also "unimpeachably honest," according to Roger Woodworth, another of Brooke's assistant attorney generals. And, "Jack bubbled over with enthusiasm." Woodworth cites an example of Bottomly's effervescence: When he'd concluded an especially advantageous land deal, Bottomly would request his staff to leap up from behind their desks and cheer.

In addition to these credentials, Bottomly had another sterling qualification for his new job: "Jack had no experience in criminal law per se, so he was the perfect guy."

When asked to clarify this statement, Woodworth replies that the fourteen murders were "nontraditional," and Bottomly was given to "nontraditional methods."

Perhaps it was another incidence of desperate times requiring desperate remedies. In any event, the ensuing months would underscore the truth of Woodworth's comment.

Other people who came in contact with Bottomly during his tenure as task force coordinator did not share Woodworth's high opinion of the man and his capabilities.

Says Edmund McNamara: "Holy Jesus, what a nutcake."

Says a former Cambridge detective: "He was an idiot."

Novelist George V. Higgins, who reported on the stranglings for the Associated Press, remarks that he never heard a reference to Bottomly without the word *asshole* attached to it "as either a suffix or a prefix. I started to think maybe it was part of the guy's name. That Asshole John Bottomly."

Dr. Ames Robey, the forensic psychiatrist who helped the Strangler Bureau screen possible suspects, merely sighs: "Bottomly. Oh, God, Bottomly."

For better or worse, this was the man now overseeing one of the biggest criminal investigations—and most intensive manhunts—in the history of jurisprudence.

Working directly for Bottomly were four men: State Police Detective Lieutenant Andrew Tuney; Metropolitan Police Officer Stephen Delaney; and Detective Phillip DiNatale and Special Officer James Mellon of the Boston Police Department. They were given administrative and clerical assistance by Jane Downey and Sandra Irizarry. A medical-psychiatric committee, formed at the instigation of Brooke, worked in conjunction with the Task Force. Headed by Dr. Donald Kenefick of Boston University's Law-Medicine Research Institute, the committee included Michael Luongo, a Suffolk County medical examiner; James Brussel, associate commissioner of mental health for the State of New York (Brussel was famous for helping to track down George Metesky, the "Mad Bomber" who terrorized New York City from the early 1940s to the mid-1950s);

Massachusetts State Police Chemist Arthur J. McBay; Carola Blume, graphologist for the Massachusetts Department of Mental Health; two psychiatrists, Leo Alexander and Max Rinkel; and a clinical anthropologist, plus several other psychiatrists who did not wish to be publicly identified.

On March 23, 1964, Governor Endicott Peabody invoked the authority vested in him by the General Laws of the Commonwealth to offer a reward of ten thousand dollars to any person who could furnish information leading to the arrest and conviction of the person or persons who had committed the murders of Anna Slesers, Nina Nichols, Helen Blake, Margaret Davis, Ida Irga, Jane Sullivan, Sophie Clark, Patricia Bissette, Beverly Samans, Evelyn Corbin, Joann Graff, and Mary Sullivan.

The first duty—and it was a daunting one—facing the Task Force was to copy the reports made by the municipal police departments and district attorneys' offices on the murders that had taken place in each of their jurisdictions. The Xerox Corporation was commissioned to reproduce the over 37,500 pages of material that began pouring into the attorney general's office. These duplicated reports were then divided into casebooks—one for each victim, five copies of those—chronologically arranged and fully indexed. One set of casebooks went to the Medical-Psychiatric Committee, a second to the Massachusetts Bureau of Identification, and a third to Boston Homicide. The two left over stayed with the Strangler Bureau, housed in offices on the second floor of the State House.

A local computer firm offered to collate free of charge the ton of data being fed to the Task Force. The offer was gratefully accepted.

The Strangler Bureau actively solicited the help of local private detective agencies. It was Brooke's feeling that the promise of the reward money would encourage offers of such help.

The general public was also asked to come forward with "any and all information which might be considered to have any relationship to the crimes. To facilitate that, a special Post Office Box, No. 1193, was rented in the main Post Office in Boston. The telephone number, 227-4600, Ext. 271, of the office of the Coordinator was also widely publicized."*

As of mid-August 1964 the Strangler Bureau had received a thousand letters and phone calls from people the world over who wanted to help solve the murders. The correspondence is on file today in the Massachusetts State Record Office.

Many of these letters were written by intelligent and conscientious individuals with potentially useful insights and information to offer. Others were clearly the products of crackpots as sincerely committed to their beliefs as were their more rational (and literate) counterparts. Reading some of them was like trying to read *Finnegans Wake* without the key. A man from Meriden (or, as he spelled it, Meridin), Connecticut, laboriously outlined a theory that the Strangler was a sort of Frankenstein monster created by a terrorist cabal. This "crew of orgy sex crazed 'Red hitlers' " had implanted bugging devices in the bloodstreams of the population of the New Haven jail, turning the inmates into homicidal electronic zombies.

Some of the crackpots were mercenary. A woman from Leominster, Massachusetts, staked a claim to the reward money posted by Governor Peabody in exchange for her theory that the Strangler had magical

---

* *Report of Attorney General Edward W. Brooke: Coordination of Investigations of Stranglings,* August 18, 1964, p. 8.

powers that enabled him to pass through locked doors
and to vanish into thin air at will. She ended her letter
on a becomingly modest note: "Please do not broadcast or advertise my name concerning the above theory. Thank you!" The attorney general's office was
more than happy to comply with her request.

An elderly Canadian man offered not a solution to
the murders but a suggestion as to how the women of
Boston might protect themselves from further harm.
"Get the Ladies Aid to warn young and old to grab
the tough guy by the balls or testicles as some call,"
the self-described old age pensioner advised. "Squeeze
good and hard and that's all is necessary."

A Boston woman opined that the Strangler had
taken the inspiration for his crimes from a television
broadcast of the movie *Dial M for Murder.* "You people
should look into these pictures before they are put on
the air," the letter-writer scolded.

There was a constant flow of correspondence from
people who maintained that the stranglings might be
solved most quickly by a psychic. These writers fell into
two categories: the apparently rational and the obviously demented. The essence of lunatic rambling on
the subject of extrasensory perception and its value to
criminal investigation is embodied in two letters directed to the attorney general of "Massachesetts," sent
by a Detroit man. In the first letter, heavily studded
with ellipses and exclamation points, the author claims
not only to have foreseen the murder of Mary Sullivan
but to have had a vision of its perpetrator: a bespec-
tacled, dark-skinned, muscular but effeminate transves-
tite "messenger of God."

When the attorney general did not reply, the Detroit
man shot off a second letter even less lucid than the
first. Paragraph after paragraph was filled with dis-
jointed and completely incomprehensible references
to Chou En-lai, Charles "degualle," Cassius Clay, Clare
Boothe Luce, Robert Kennedy, and "Hoofa," presum-

ably Jimmy Hoffa. These were followed by reflections
on the sad lot of the psychic, who had to choose between going public with his visions and being thought
crazy or suppressing all telepathic knowledge—an effort, the writer claimed, that made him "Heave ho *ho
ho ho R E G U R G I T A T E !*"

The letter ends with a request for maps of the Boston area.

The Strangler Bureau also received tart complaints
about the inefficiency of the Boston Police Department. One addressed to Bottomly stated that it was
about time the assistant attorney general had stepped
in to oversee the investigation. Why, the woman asked,
was the Boston force so helpless to catch the killer?

In an effort to shield her identity, the writer signed
herself "A Fellow Trinity Church Member." But the
effort to preserve her anonymity was sabotaged by the
fact that she typed the letter on notepaper engraved
with her full name.

And so it went. The only consolation for the Task
Force was that while as of mid-August 1964 it hadn't
solved any of the murders, at least no new ones had
been committed.

The police departments of Boston, Cambridge,
Lawrence, Lynn, and Salem continued with their own
investigations.

4

Psychiatrists and Psychics

A prime directive of the Medical-Psychiatric Committee headed by Donald Kenefick was to draw up a profile of the kind of individual who might be responsible for the stranglings.

Not that anybody on the Task Force believed that a single person had committed all fourteen of the murders. (This was probably its sole area of accord with the outside law enforcement agencies.) A progress report issued by Brooke's office on August 18, 1964, makes that much clear:

> At an early stage of the coordinated deliberations it was concluded that certain homicides bore little relationship to the so-called "Stranglings" or to each other. Among other things the conclusions were based on the manner in which the victims met their deaths, the condition of the area where the victims' bodies were found and the habits of the victims . . . Margaret Davis' . . . death appears to be the result of a fight with her male

companion. Modeste Freeman, whose body was found in a vacant lot off Columbus Avenue, was also subjected to a vicious beating. Mary Brown was another unfortunate victim of a savage beating in her home probably by a sneak thief who ransacked her apartment . . . There remain eleven homicides which are the object of continued police investigations and intensive study by medical doctors, psychiatrists, a medical anthropologist, chemists, and a graphologist using to the fullest possible extent the most modern techniques and equipment available . . . Beginning with the death of Sophie Clark on December 5, 1962, almost four months after the murder of Jane Sullivan, subsequent murders are dissimilar in important respects to the homicides of the older women in the summer of 1962. Considered in this latter group of homicides are the murders of Sophie Clark, Patricia Bissette, Beverly Samens [sic], Evelyn Corbin, Joanne[sic] Graff and on January 4, 1964, Mary A. Sullivan. With one exception these victims were between the ages of 19 and 26 at the time of their deaths . . . The backgrounds and personal habits of the victims beginning with the murder on December 5, 1962, are so different from those of the earlier and older victims that the strong probability is the psycopathic [sic] killer of the older women would not have considered the younger victims suitable objects for the release of his hate and frustrations. For the reasons set forth below it is also probable that the homicides on and after December 5, 1962 were not committed by one person.

As noted above all of the older victims lived alone. Miss Clark had two roommates. The physical evidence at the scene of the crime and on the body of the victim indicate that this homicide has many of the characteristics of a rape which may have unintentionally become murder . . . In some respects it appears that the murderer of Patricia Bissette was guided in his arrangement of the scene and the manner of his crime by what had been printed in the newspapers about Sophie Clark just 26 days before. There is a strong possibility in this case that the murderer was known to the victim and his presence in her apartment was readily accepted by her . . . Of all the victims still classified in the "Stranglings" [Beverly Samans] was the only one who was stabbed . . . The ligatures in this case apparently were applied for "decorative" purposes and undoubtedly in an attempt to imitate the "Stranglings" which had received considerable publicity as such by May 8, 1963. The strong possibilities in this case are that it is a homicide quite separate from the others being considered in this report . . . details of the murder of [Evelyn Corbin] and the scene of the crime suggest the strong possibility that the imitation factor was again dominant in the mind of the murderer. However, his knowledge of the details of earlier crimes was sufficiently incomplete to frustrate the total success of his plan. [Mary Sullivan's] death was caused by strangulation. In many ways it was by far the most elaborate of all the murders considered in this report. For that and other significant reasons it appears to have no probable relationship to its predecessors . . . The details of this murder indicate that the criminal was strongly influenced by the desire to imitate previous "Stranglings" as he understood them from newspaper accounts.

What kind of man would commit such atrocities? Donald Kenefick and his team of consultants thought it might be an individual "at least 30, and probably a good deal older. He is neat, orderly, and punctual. He either works with his hands, or has a hobby involving handi-work. He most probably is single, separated or divorced. He would not impress the average observer as crazy . . . He has no close friends of either sex (and this includes a wife, if he had one.) . . . What kind of a mother would he have?' A sweet, orderly, neat, compulsive, seductive, punitive, overwhelming woman. She might go about half exposed in their apartment but punish him severely for any sexual curiousity [sic], and so on. What kind of father would he have? I am afraid none. No mere male would be good enough for such a woman, anyhow, and once he had fulfilled his biological functions, the mother would dispose of him. I would imagine that [the mur-derer] was an only child, or one with at most one sibling (probably an older sister)."

Kenefick referred to this hypothetical sexual sadist and killer as "Mr. S." He too was fairly positive there had to be more than one of them operating. He ended his report to the Task Force by wishing them "Good hunting!"

Not only did the Medical-Psychiatric Committee at-tempt to probe the mind-set of a pathological killer, it also set out to probe the psyches of his victims. Carola Blume, the resident graphologist, analyzed the hand-writing of the murdered women in the hope that some character trait revealed by it might provide the expla-nation for the victims' dreadful fates.

Would any of this help solve the killings? The Task Force could only hope so. With every passing day the trail of Mr. S. was growing colder and colder.

Brooke had vowed "to leave no stone unturned" in the search for the killers. It was for this reason, he said, that he ultimately consented to do what so many letters and phone calls to the attorney general's office had been urging: bring in a psychic.

According to Gerold Frank, Bottomly was the prime

mover behind this decision "because he had long been intrigued by telepathic experiments conducted by friends in the National Aeronautic and Space Administration Laboratories in Cambridge."*

Ames Robey has a slightly different perspective on the situation: "Bottomly's mother was fascinated by ESP and psychic phenomena. And she kept bugging him to get a seer, get a seer, it's the only way you'll ever catch the Strangler. He finally said yes just to shut her up."

Edmund McNamara reacted to the proposal with outraged disgust: "I said, 'Fine. Why don't I just fire all my detectives and hire a bunch of gypsies with crystal balls to solve crimes?' " He forbade his two principal investigators, John Donovan and Edward Sherry, to have anything to do with any seers the Strangler Bureau might retain.

Brooke left it to Bottomly to choose a suitable psychic, and the one Bottomly chose was Peter Hurkos, whose biography Bottomly had read in Jess Stearn's book about the paranormal, *Door to the Future*. Hurkos was a Dutch housepainter who, at the age of thirty-five, had fractured his skull and emerged from the resultant coma a telepath. The Task Force coordinator put out the word to his assistants: Find me this man. They did, in Hollywood, where he was prepping actor Glenn Ford to play him in a movie.

Hurkos accepted Bottomly's offer and arrangements were made to bring him to Boston. Under cover of night, he flew into the Providence, Rhode Island, airport rather than to Logan International. He had insisted on that condition in order to minimize the chance of a Boston reporter spotting him and spreading the word that the famed "psychic detective" was in town. Such publicity would, Hurkos maintained, interfere with his concentration. Accompanying the in-

---

* Frank, p. 100.

cognito seer was a six-foot-eight-inch-tall armed body-
guard in full cowboy regalia who left a trail of bug-eyed
and slack-jawed airport personnel in the wake of his
John Wayne swagger.

To give Hurkos his due, he did actually seem to have
some kind of telepathic ability. And to give Bottomly *his*
due, the taxpayers of Massachusetts didn't have to foot
the bill for Hurkos's services, either. "It didn't cost the
Commonwealth anything," says Roger Woodworth, adding that Hurkos's fee was paid by two private citizens'
groups.

Brooke was as eager to avoid publicity as was Hurkos.
To this end, he requested from the press—and got—a
voluntary embargo on news coverage of the Dutch
seer's trip to Boston. "This unselfish action," Brooke
later wrote, "was an extraordinary example of cooperation in a most highly competitive industry." It must
have been a relief to Attorney General Brooke as well.

Hurkos was not the world's easiest guest. He was put
up for a while—a *short* while—at the Commander Hotel in Cambridge, and a city detective was assigned to
babysit him for the duration. The cop had his work
cut out for him. In the middle of the night the detective was roused from sleep by a frantic phone call from
Hurkos, who demanded to be removed from the hotel
immediately. He was unable to rest, the psychic
claimed, because the ghosts in the Revolutionary War
cemetery near the Commander were screaming at him.
Mindful of his duty, the detective climbed out of bed,
pulled on his clothes, and drove to the hotel to pick
up Hurkos. Not knowing what else to do, he then
brought Hurkos back to his own home. Once inside
the cop's house, however, Hurkos refused to stay. It
was the presence of the detective's children that disturbed him. Their innocent aura would prevent him
from picking up the evil vibrations of the Strangler.

It says a great deal about the Cambridge detective's

powers of self-control that there wasn't a male strangling victim.

Less than forty-eight hours after the psychic hit
town, the Boston police officers assigned by Bottomly
to work with him were pleading to be let off the hook.

"Nobody particularly wanted to be with him," comments former Inspector John Moran, in a classic understatement. Moran looks thoughtful. Then he
remarks, "They should have taken him down to the
track and let him pick the horses."

Even Bottomly seems to have entertained second
thoughts about Hurkos. Two days after the seer arrived
in Boston, Bottomly received a confidential report that
Hurkos was the defendant in a breach of contract suit
in Wisconsin. He was also an adulterer. "That is conduct," Bottomly wrote frostily, "of which I personally
do not approve."

Hurkos did identify a Strangler suspect, and it was
one whom the Task Force had already seriously considered. This individual, a shoe salesman, was as innocuous in manner and appearance as Donald
Kenefick had predicted (a loaded word, in this context) he might be. Six months later Brooke wrote that
this suspect was "a lifetime celibate with a history of
mental illness [who] inexplicably joined three marriage clubs." The man's brothers had been trying to
persuade him to seek professional help for some time
before he came to the attention of the Task Force.
Recent bizarre changes in his behavior had them worried. These changes had also worried the police in the
town where the man lived.

Hurkos was convinced of this suspect's guilt. His mis-
sion in Boston complete, he left town assuring his hosts
that in the person of the shoe salesman they had their
man. They didn't; there was no physical evidence nor
any eyewitness to connect the man to any of the murders. He ended up voluntarily committing himself to
a mental institution.

Despite the departure of Hurkos, the Strangler Bureau hadn't concluded its dealings with him. As a parting gift, someone in the office had given him a card identifying the bearer as "a special honorary assistant attorney general," a title as high-sounding as it was meaningless. That piece of paper and a nickel would buy Hurkos a cup of coffee, but he was an avid collector of law enforcement memorabilia and added the card to his considerable store of toy credentials and badges.

The gift would come back to haunt, so to speak, its giver.

All the while Hurkos had been in Boston sniffing out the psychic spoor of the Strangler, the FBI had been looking for him. Not because it wanted his help in solving a case; it wanted to arrest him. For impersonating one of its agents at a gas station in Milwaukee.

Hurkos was taken into custody in New York City.

On February 10, 1964, a story by Bill Norton and Bob Castricone entitled HURKOS FRAMED—BROOKE AIDE appeared on page one of the *Globe*. In it the two reporters described Hurkos's arrest and arraignment and then went on to quote a "spokesman" for Attorney General Brooke as saying, "I think the charges [against Hurkos] are as phony as a $3 bill." The speaker then went on to characterize the arrest as a deliberate attempt on the part of the FBI to discredit the Strangler Task Force. And, finally, the spokesman indulged in a bit of nose-thumbing: "It took us two hours to discover him [Hurkos] in an actor's home in California. Yet, it took the FBI almost two months to find their man."

This spokesman, or at least the person whom the article purported to quote, was Bottomly.

On Valentine's Day the Task Force coordinator fired off a four-page, single-spaced typed letter to James Handley, special agent-in-charge of the Boston FBI office, denying that he had made the statements attributed him by Norton and Castricone—*except* for the jibe about the FBI's dragged-out pursuit of Hurkos. Bottomly should have left bad enough alone at that point. Instead, he went on to write: "As a result of our conversation on February 12, 1964, I am of the opinion that regardless of the exact words I used on February 10, 1964 you and those you represent consider it not only irresponsible for me ever to imply criticism of the FBI, but that it is wrong for me to criticize and I should not do it. In addition to correcting the record, this letter is written to inform you and those you represent that I disagree strongly with that position. I believe criticism has value. It is my hope and expectation that the FBI can survive criticism. In some cases, I would suggest that the FBI might be improved by listening to it rather than attempting to stifle or suppress it. Finally, I happen to be proud of the political society in which I live and the heritage of which we are beneficiaries, and I resent strongly any attempt by you or those you represent to restrict my voicing or writing my opinions freely . . . In closing, I reiterate my sincere wish that the FBI in the future advise the Department of the Attorney General of any investigation or impending arrest of any consultant which this Department is planning to retain or has retained. I share with you the desire for cooperation. However, I value criticism and accept it in the spirit in which it is given in the hope that I may learn therefrom and improve myself thereby."

At that point, Edward Brooke was probably devoutly wishing he'd never heard of Hurkos, and maybe not of Bottomly, either. Of course the matter didn't end there. The incorporeal presence of Hurkos would linger, like the bad smell emitted by a clogged drain. Brooke was still deflecting media queries about the incident a month later.

Did the Hurkos affair hurt the image of the Strangler Bureau?

"It made it a laughingstock," snorts Gordon Parry, a forensics expert who investigated the deaths of Patricia Bissette and Mary Sullivan.

One year later, the point was moot, because in March

of 1965 an inmate of Massachusetts Correctional Institution–Bridgewater, a state facility for the sexually dangerous and criminally insane, confessed to being the Phantom Fiend, Mr. S., murderer of thirteen women.

His name was Albert Henry DeSalvo.

PART TWO

PART TWO

5

The Measuring Man

Who was the man who claimed to be the Boston Strangler?

Albert Henry DeSalvo, the third of six children, was born in Chelsea, Massachusetts, on September 3, 1931, to Charlotte and Frank DeSalvo, natives of Newfoundland. In today's jargon, the family would be described as dysfunctional. The reality was far worse than this euphemism could ever encompass. Frank DeSalvo, a fisherman and a skilled machinist, was arrested repeatedly for refusing to support his wife and children. It would have been much better for them had he committed the kind of crime that would have kept him in prison for a long stretch and out of their lives. He was a monster of abuse to Charlotte and the four boys and two girls, beating them regularly with fists, belts, and pipes. On one occasion he pulled a gun on Charlotte; on another he broke her fingers, serially snapping them like dry twigs. According to Albert, Frank had once *sold* him and his sisters to a Maine farmer for nine dollars. He also brought home prostitutes and had intercourse with them in front of the children. Albert also claimed that his father taught him how to shoplift.

Richard DeSalvo, Albert's younger brother by five years, confirms the stories of Frank DeSalvo's sadistic, almost insane, brutality: "I recall being under the bed a lot, because that was where I was safe." Richard tells a story of how Frank, in an alcohol-fueled rage, began pummeling Charlotte. "He pushed her into the washing machine—it was the old-fashioned kind with a wringer—and she got cut badly and bruised." Albert tried to intervene to protect his mother. "My father picked him up by the throat and shook him in the air."

Albert started grade school in September 1937 and in September 1943 was enrolled in a special class at the Williams School in Chelsea. Two months later had had racked up his first arrest—for assault and battery with intent to commit robbery. The take was $2.85. His victim was a boy approximately his own age.

Albert was given a suspended sentence to the Lyman School, a reformatory for delinquent boys. He continued on at Williams, working after classes as a florist's delivery boy, a shoeshine boy, and a dishwasher. He also got a paper route. He liked going to the movies, he told his social worker, although he didn't "love" them.

He feared walking alone at night. Dark streets held a special terror for him.

Although Christmas that year was a good one for Albert (Santa was generous), four days afterward he was arrested again by the Chelsea police. Once more the charge was assault and battery and larceny. This time Albert's sentence to the Lyman School was enforced.

By September of 1944 the fortunes of Charlotte DeSalvo and her six children had improved measurably. Separated repeatedly, she and Frank had finally divorced, the decree becoming final that year. Charlotte, legally released from her bondage to the man who had made her so miserable for so long, became a new woman. A social worker who visited the divorcée and her children at 353 Broadway saw someone who "has taken renewed vigor in the bettering of her home and all that goes with it. She is receiving $31.31 from the mother's aid program and, in addition, she has been working each morning for half a day at the Slade's Photo Shop in Chelsea. Observation indicates that she is putting her resources to good use. She has not been bothered by her husband for a long time and seems considerably relieved because of former pressure. She is still keeping company with one Paul Kinosian and anticipates marriage in August of 1945. Mr. Kinosian has been exceptionally kind to the children, and she vows that the present affair is on the level. She feels that Albert should be with her."

The social worker and the trustees of the Lyman School agreed with Charlotte's self-assessment. On October 26, 1944, Albert was paroled.

He was thrilled to be back at home. He resumed his job as a florist's delivery boy, and attended classes regularly at Williams. His first report card in 1945 was a very good one. He was enthusiastic about sports. Says Richard DeSalvo: "We used to go an hour or an hour and a half early to school so we could play softball or touch football, depending on the season."

All throughout 1945 and half of the following year Albert kept out of trouble. He left his after-school job at the florist's to take another at the Gold Medal Tonic Company in Chelsea. He joined the Boys' Town Club and hoped to go to summer camp. He worked for his stepfather Paul (whom Charlotte had indeed married on schedule in August 1945) at Shaffer's Junk Shop in Chelsea.

All this success his social worker attributed to a better home life. And it is true that Paul Kinosian, unlike Frank DeSalvo, worked hard to support his new family. But circumstances otherwise were not entirely rosy. Kinosian, according to Richard DeSalvo, was given to bursts of temper he directed at his stepchildren and the daughter he and Charlotte had together. As punishment for disobedience or insolence, Richard recalls, Kinosian would "take two cans of fruit from the cupboard and make me stand on them. Then I had to hold out my hands and balance a hairbrush on one of them. If my hand started to shake, Paul would belt me." When Richard was sixteen, Kinosian picked him up, threw him physically out of the house and onto the porch; he landed on his head and split his scalp. Richard left home thereafter. He paid one return visit and Kinosian went after him with a hammer.

Still, Richard recalls, there were a lot of good times—many more and much better than with Frank. Kinosian would play ball or horseshoes with the boys, or take them fishing. And when he worked as a trucker, he would sometimes bring Richard on trips. "He was ignorant," Richard says. "He could have been a hell of a lot nicer person. He didn't know he wasn't supposed to be violent."

Albert, Richard says, joined the service to escape from Paul.

But before that, there was more trouble with the law. At the end of August 1946, Albert was sent back to Lyman. The charge: unlawful use of an automobile. On September 9, at 6:00 A.M., he and two other boys ran from Lyman. Albert was probably talked into the flight by one of the others. Picked up by the authorities and returned to custody, he was required to earn three thousand merits before the trustees would consider parole. They did not hold out much hope for him.

Nonetheless, he was freed on probation in early 1947 and sent home. He went back to school. On Saturdays he worked for a fruit peddler. His dearest wish, he confided to a social worker, was to earn and save enough money to buy Charlotte a Mother's Day present. Years later, he would be arrested for committing a burglary in order to buy his wife and daughter Valentine's Day candy and cards.

All throughout 1947 and 1948 Albert kept up his studies and kept out of trouble. He joined the YMCA, went to dances there, and took various other odd jobs—shining shoes again and working on a pickle truck. His behavior at home was helpful and cooperative. His goal was to graduate from the ninth grade at Williams and enlist in the military.

He did indeed fulfill the former ambition, and spent the summer of 1948 working as a waiter in a sandwich shop in Harwich on Cape Cod. But the application to join the army he made in early September was rejected because he was still on parole from Lyman. Instead, he took a job with a laundry in Chelsea. It turned out to be very temporary; the army reconsidered its initial decision and took him as a recruit in the middle of the month.

Albert had two periods of active duty, the first lasting from September 16, 1948, to June 25, 1951, the second from June 26, 1951, to February 15, 1956. Both times he received an honorable discharge. From basic training at Fort Dix and Camp Kilmer in New Jersey he was sent to Germany, where, in 1949, he met a young woman named Irmgard Beck. Albert attained the rank of Specialist E-5 and served as a colonel's orderly. In July 1951 he was reassigned to Camp Kilmer. One month later he managed again to run afoul of the law, this time the military rather than the civil. In August he was court-martialed for failing to obey an order and busted back to private.

The next accusation against him would be far graver.

On December 5, 1953, Albert married his love of four years, Irmgard Beck. Five months later he was posted to Fort Hamilton, New York, and from there to Fort Dix. On January 5, 1955, Albert was arrested in Mount Holly, New Jersey, for carnal abuse of a child. A little over two months later, he was taken into custody in Wrightstown for loitering. He was fined and released.

The carnal abuse charge was nol-prossed that December.

Nineteen fifty-five also saw the birth of Albert and Irmgard's daughter, Judy. What should have been a joyous occasion for the young couple in an otherwise bleak year was marred by the fact that the child was born with a pelvic disease. And Irmgard began to turn away from Albert. He was later to say that her fear of becoming pregnant with another child who might suffer a mental or physical handicap worse than Judy's curtailed their sex life.

In 1956 Albert left the army, and he and Irmgard moved to Albert's hometown of Chelsea. He got a job. In September he was arrested for running a traffic light in East Boston. In the spring of 1957 he spent two months in the Veterans Administration Hospital being treated for a problem with his left shoulder. Upon his release, he resumed work.

On January 8, 1958, Albert was arrested by the Boston Police Department. The charge was suspicion of breaking and entering in the nighttime; he was found guilty and given a suspended sentence. The Chelsea police picked him up on February 15, this time for staging two daytime breaks. (These burglaries were the ones he told the judge he had committed to underwrite his Valentine's Day gifts to Irmgard and Judy.) Again, he was found guilty, and again, his sentence to the house of correction was suspended. A third arrest in Boston on a similar count on April 18 had the same result.

In June of 1959, Albert took a leave of absence from work so that he and Irmgard could travel to Germany. Their visit lasted two months, and on their return to the United States in mid-August, Albert went back to his old job. And his old tricks. On October 26, he was arrested in Boston. The charge was the usual: breaking and entering and larceny in the nighttime. For this latest peccadillo Albert received yet another suspended sentence.

Because the 1950s was an era in which the concept of revolving-door justice was relatively unknown, the question arises: How did Albert, with his record of repeat offenses, escape even a minimal prison term? It is possible that his defense attorney, Robert Sheinfeld, was unusually talented. It is also possible that Albert was lucky enough to appear before a string of very lenient judges. Then again, perhaps all the charges against him were flimsy. There is no way to be sure today.

During 1960, Albert managed to stay on the right side of the law, or at least nobody caught him violating it. That year was a good one for other reasons for him and Irmgard: It saw the birth of their son, Michael. The baby was robustly healthy; a happy contradiction of Irmgard's fears.

Whatever peace and stability the family achieved with the arrival of Michael was shattered less than seven months later. On March 17, 1961, Albert was taken into custody by the Cambridge police. He had been interrupted in the process of trying to break into a house on Broadway in that city. A chase ensued, during which one of the pursuing officers fired a warning shot. Albert surrendered. At the police station he readily admitted to the breaking and entering charge, and also to possession of burglar's tools. And then he began confessing to activities far more disturbing.

Cambridge had been the locale of a series of bizarre sexual assaults. A man calling himself Johnson, purporting to represent the Black and White Modeling Agency, would appear at the homes of attractive young women, compliment them on their looks, and ask to take their measurements. Flattered, many of the women complied. Before departing, "Johnson" would assure them that someone from the agency would be in touch. That never happened. Some of the women subsequently called the police.

Now Albert was claiming to be this Johnson, otherwise referred to by the Cambridge police as "the Measuring Man." The court had him shipped off for a psychiatric examination at Westborough State Hospital, where he was diagnosed as a sociopath.

On May 3, 1961, Albert went to trial in Cambridge on several counts of assault and battery, lewdness, and breaking and entering in the daytime. Judge Edward Viola found him not guilty on the lewdness complaints, guilty on the others. For each count Albert received a two-year sentence, all of them to be served concurrently. He was remanded to the Billerica House of Correction. In September, Viola, feeling the sentence was too harsh, reduced it. Albert was a free man as of April 1962.

Two months later Anna Slesers was murdered.

6

The Green Man

Those who knew Albert DeSalvo remember his smile more vividly than anything else about him. Wide and sunny, it lit his face and warmed all who saw it, including hardened cops. There was nothing otherwise extraordinary about Albert's appearance: He was a man of medium height with powerful shoulders (he had boxed in the army), thick chestnut hair combed back in a modified pompadour, hazel eyes, and a protuberant nose. His voice was a soft, rapid tenor. His demeanor could be boyish and open or sullen and withdrawn, depending on the circumstances. He knew how to charm and disarm, the chief reason why his Measuring Man masquerade was so successful.

Despite his frequent arrests, he was regularly employed, although he tended to shift from place to place. Prior to his March 1961 arrest he had worked as a press operator for American Biltrite Rubber Company in Everett, the city next door to Chelsea. Upon his release from the Billerica House of Correction, he took a job with the Monroe shipyard of Chelsea. After a few months he went to work for general contractor C. Russell Blomerth of Malden, where he and his wife and children now lived, and finally for

Highland Contractors of Wakefield, for whom he was a construction maintenance man. Years later, after Albert had confessed to being the Strangler, Russell Blomerth would register his horrified disbelief at Albert's self-indictment and extol his former employee as a good, decent, and kindly man who betrayed no psychological abnormality.

First and foremost, Albert was a dedicated family man, a loving and involved father to Judy and Michael. To his nieces and nephews he was a devoted uncle; Richard DeSalvo's son Timothy possesses an elaborate wooden fort Albert built him, plus a collection of letters enjoining the boy to be an obedient son and attentive student. To his sister-in-law Rosalie, Albert maintained a jaunty affection. He occupied an equal space in their hearts, and still does.

It was as if in the area of family relationships and obligations, at least, Albert had set out to be the exact opposite of his own father.

He treated his wife Irmgard as if she were a goddess, which indeed she was to him. Despite this, the marriage was not a particularly happy one. The sexual hiatus following Judy's birth had put an enormous strain on it. And Albert perceived Irmgard as being cold emotionally as well as physically to him. It is obvious now that they were temperamentally unsuited to each other, Albert always needing and wanting more love than Irmgard could ever give. Perhaps no amount would have been sufficient for him. Long after their divorce, Albert would write a painful and bitter reminiscence of their life together.

> Irm when I came out of jail made me feel like nothing. In front of people she would scold me. Then she would say after wards don't lie or say something thats not true and don't make something bigger than what it is. Instead of saying nothing or agreeing with me—she would throw me

down in front of people and when I would tell her
about it she would say next time you will no better.
She told me she wasted one year of her life—and
if I ever hurt her again she would leave me and
take the children far away. She told me I would
have to learn to control myself and when she
wanted it she would let me know—many nights I
was so hot I wanted to be loved. She would say
maybe tomorrow night—and I would wait in till
she was a sleep. And then I would take her legs
and open her legs and make love to her. And some
nights she would make believe she was asleep.
Then she would say I'm dirty and sickening doing
that to her. She called me an animal . . . I loved
her so much. She made me scared to make love
to her. I felt unclean and less than a man in bed
with her. She herself will tell you. She made me
feel low and unlike a man. I stoped in the middle
of trying to make love to her. I told her I could
jerk off and get better thrill. Many many nights I
layed in bed next to her. And bad as I wanted to
make love. I was so hot. I didn't dare ask her because I knew what her answer would be. I hated
her so bad but I loved her so. I was burning up . . .
New Year Eve we went out and I felt different with
her. She danced with me and put her hand in
back of my head and put her fingers thru my hair
and kissed me and held me close. And she said
she was happy things are getting better. We had a
nice XMASS. This is when I felt a big change in
her to me. She started treating me better. That
night we made real love together. It wasn't till
about the last two months before Nov. 64 that she
made me feel like a man. She gave me love that
I never dreamed she could give me . . . I felt like
a real man for the first time. She to me was always
pure and could do no wrong. There wasn't a thing
in this world I wouldn't try doing for her. No mat-

ter how bad she hurt me I could never stay mad
at her and yet at times I hated her so bad I held
it in. I felt all fluid and like I was going to burst.
Not knowing what to do. That feeling would only
come so often. Feeling less than a man. Being hurt
so deep by her.

Irmgard, of course, saw their relationship differently.
She was fully aware and appreciative of Albert's best
qualities: his tenderness toward her and the children
and his concern for their well-being, his desire to give
them the best life possible. But his incessant sexual
demands wore her down; he wanted, she claimed, to
make love six times a day. Even if she had been similarly inclined, Irmgard had a household to run and
two children to tend, one of whom was chronically ill
and needed special care. How could she do all that
and still meet Albert's demands? There weren't
enough hours in the day.

Albert and Irmgard: a doomed and tragic *folie à deux.*

If Albert's most compelling physical feature was his
delightful smile, his least attractive personality trait was
his compulsion toward braggadocio. "He always had
to be the biggest and the best," says a Cambridge detective who came to know him well and who grew fond
of him despite all the trouble Albert was to cause the
CPD. "He was the kind of guy who, if you said to him,
'Hey, I did twenty burglaries,' he'd say, 'That's nothing,
I did two hundred.'" James Ward, an orderly at
Bridgewater while Albert was incarcerated there, says
of Albert that "he loved to toot his own horn." He
even annoyed the other inmates with his incessant
boasting.

"A blowhard," Edmund McNamara says.

Albert had another notable personal characteristic.
According to one of his attorneys, Francis C. Newton,

Jr., "Albert was the type of guy who didn't seem to be a leader, but more the type who was easily led."

Albert's willingness to submit himself to a stronger personality, coupled with his irresistible urge toward self-aggrandizement, would seal his fate.

At approximately 9:15 on the morning of May 29, 1964, Geraldine Surette was asleep in the bedroom of her apartment in Wakefield, a town about ten miles north of Boston. She may have been awakened by some noise or movement. At any rate, when she opened her eyes, she found herself looking at a man, a total stranger, sitting on the bed. He pulled back the covers, lifted Mrs. Surette's nightgown, and began fondling her body. He told her that he had just gotten out of the service and that he knew her husband.

In the same room the Surettes' baby slept in a crib. The man ceased fondling Mrs. Surette, rose, and walked over to where the child lay. He reached into the crib and picked up the baby. Mrs. Surette got out of bed and retrieved her child from the intruder. The three of them moved to the kitchen. There the man reached under Mrs. Surette's nightgown and again caressed her breasts; she was still cradling the baby in her arms. She glanced at the clock and said, "Jeez, I didn't realize it was so late." She added that her friend Jean was coming to take photographs. The man replied, "Oh, you wear glasses; we couldn't use you. I have the wrong Surette." He ran out the door.

This surreal and frightening incident had lasted perhaps ten to fifteen minutes. Mrs. Surette later discovered twenty-five dollars missing from the budget book in which she kept the apartment rent money.

Virginia Thorner lived alone in Melrose, a town bordering Wakefield. Shortly before 8:00 A.M. on June 8, 1964, she heard a knock on her front door. She admitted the caller when he told her there was a leak in her apartment.

As he was walking toward the bathroom, ostensibly to check the plumbing there, the man said, "Are you tired, Virginia?" She confessed that she was, and asked the time. "Quarter of eight," the man informed her.

The man found no leak in the bathroom. "I think it must be the bedroom," he said.

Mrs. Thorner was examining the windows for a possible leak there when the man came up behind her, encircling her body with one arm and crooking the other over her face.

He ordered her onto the bed and then blindfolded her with her shortie pajama bottoms. Then he gagged her and blindfolded her again with a kerchief. He began kissing her breasts and pubic area.

"Give me twenty dollars and I'll leave," he said.

"I don't have twenty dollars," Mrs. Thorner said. "I only have one."

They got up, and the man forced her to lead him to the living room, where the money lay on the coffee table. The kerchief over Mrs. Thorner's eyes had dropped to her chin, enabling her to glimpse the knife her attacker was holding to her side.

"Turn around, go back to the bedroom," the man said. He told her he'd kill her if she screamed. Mrs. Thorner would in 1967 testify that he added, "Do what I say or I will kill you. I have killed before and I will do it again. I have even got an old lady but they don't know it. I don't want to hurt you."

He pushed her down on the bed and had her fellate him.

He tied her up and then departed, saying, "Don't scream. You remember what I said. Give me five minutes."

Despite the fact that her hands were tied behind her back, Mrs. Thorner was able to telephone the Melrose police. They had to cut her free, so secure were the knots binding her.

Around her neck were draped four scarves. They would be entered as evidence at her assailant's trial.

At 9:00 A.M. on September 29, 1964, Muriel LeBlanc heard a knock on the front door of her apartment in Arlington, a suburb of Boston. Dressed in underwear, a housecoat, and slippers, Mrs. LeBlanc went to the door but didn't open it right away. She asked who was there. A voice on the other side of the door replied, "There's a leak in the basement. The basement is half-full of water and I have to get in and shut off all the pipes, the water pipes." Mrs. LeBlanc answered that her apartment had no leaks.

The person on the other side of the door kept rapping at it, and finally identified himself as Dave—the name of the person who was indeed the building superintendent. Mrs. LeBlanc opened the door. A man unknown to her stepped over the threshold.

In his hand was a gun. He raised it and pressed the barrel to Mrs. LeBlanc's forehead. "This is a holdup, lady," he said. "I want your money."

"Take it," replied Mrs. LeBlanc.

The man entered the apartment, shutting the door behind him. He asked her where the money was; she indicated her handbag on a chair. The man ordered her to go sit on the couch. She didn't move. Then she heard a click and felt something sharp pressing against her neck. "That's a knife at your throat, lady," the man said. She turned and he put the gun to the back of her head.

"Don't make a sound or yell," the intruder warned. "Because if you do, I'll cut your throat from ear to ear." He added that he wasn't kidding.

Mrs. LeBlanc would tell a judge and jury that the man had asserted that he had no fear of police or prison. The cops were looking for him anyway, he said, and had been for years. "You won't get a second chance, lady, I'll just cut your throat. So don't you yell or make a sound."

"Don't worry," said Mrs. LeBlanc. "I won't yell."

She sat on the couch as ordered. The man then tied her ankles together with a pair of pajama pants belonging to Mr. LeBlanc. Then he bound her hands behind her back with one of her husband's scarves.

"Why are you doing these terrible things?" Mrs. Le-Blanc asked.

"What terrible—?" The man faltered. "What things, what things?"

"Coming in here like this and tying me up," Mrs. LeBlanc, a woman of uncommon courage, replied. "Why are you doing these terrible things, coming in here like this?" she repeated. "What would your mother say if she could see you now?"

"She wouldn't like it," the man admitted. Nonetheless, he began to unbutton Mrs. LeBlanc's robe and to kiss her. Mrs. LeBlanc jerked her head aside and his mouth grazed her neck. He told her he wanted to feel her breasts.

"I'm an old woman and I don't want you bothering me," Mrs. LeBlanc snapped.

The man crossed the room and masturbated. Then he went into the bathroom. When he returned, he and Mrs. LeBlanc argued about whether there was any rent money in the apartment, she insisting there wasn't and he insisting that there had to be because it was the end of the month. All this time he held a gun to her ear, Mrs. LeBlanc recollected.

She won the argument about the rent money. The man took a diamond ring from her jewelry box and eleven dollars from her wallet. Then he said, "I'm going, lady," and left the apartment.

Mrs. LeBlanc wriggled free of her bonds and tried to call the police. When she lifted the telephone receiver, however, she got no dial tone. The wires had apparently been cut.

She told the court that at one point during her ordeal, the man had asked her where she kept her silk stockings. "I don't have any," she had answered. "I don't wear them this time of year."

She also told the court that she had never been so scared in her entire life.

At 9:45 on the morning of October 27, 1964, a twenty-year-old Cambridge woman named Suzanne Macht, a Boston University student and the wife of a local university instructor, woke up to find a man standing in her bedroom. As she would tell a packed courtroom two years and two months later, the intruder said, "You know me." She had never seen him before and replied, "No, I don't."

"I'm a police detective," the man stated, adding that he wanted to ask her a few questions. He began walking toward the bed. Then he told Mrs. Macht that he was in fact not one of the police but fleeing from them. They were surrounding the building at that moment.

Mrs. Macht screamed and rose from the bed. The man yanked out a knife and told her not to look at him. He assured her that he wouldn't hurt her. Then he bound her hands and gagged and blindfolded her.

He pulled up her nightgown and began to fondle and kiss her breasts and pubic area. She squirmed off the bed and struggled to her feet. The man kissed her again, lifted her in his arms, and placed her back on the bed. He did not rape her, nor did he strike or beat her.

He asked her to forgive him for what he had just done—and not to tell his mother about it. As he started to leave the room, Mrs. Macht asked him to loosen her bonds. He did so, and then he departed.

Mrs. Macht quickly freed herself and called her husband at work. A while later, she called the Cambridge police to report the assault.

She checked the two doors to the apartment, both of which had been locked by her husband when he'd left for school. Knife markings indicated that they had been jimmied.

Her final statement to the court was that the man had told her he'd kill her if she screamed.

Suzanne Macht recited the details of her sordid and terrifying experience to Detectives Duncan McNeill, James Galligan, and Louise Darling of the Cambridge police.

The description she offered of the clothing her attacker had worn had a familiar ring to Sergeant McNeill. Like other area police departments, the Cambridge force had been receiving Teletype messages about a distinctively clad man who'd committed a number of housebreaks and sexual assaults in Connecticut. This person invariably dressed in dark green shirt and pants; the costume was apparently some kind of work uniform. Its wearer had become known to law enforcement personnel as the Green Man.

Later that day a Massachusetts state police technician made a sketch of Suzanne Macht's assailant based on the information she gave him. One of the Cambridge detectives, Paul Cloran, thought that the finished portrait bore a strong resemblance to the Measuring Man they'd arrested in 1961.

The Measuring Man, Albert DeSalvo, was now living in Malden with Irmgard and the children. Duncan McNeill arranged with the police department of that city to have Albert brought in and put in a lineup.

Suzanne Macht, who had already identified Albert's photograph, picked him right out of an eight-man lineup. She asked to hear him speak, and claimed to recognize his voice—which was indeed a distinctive one.

Albert faced his accuser and calmly said, "I don't know the woman." When informed that she had positively identified him, he replied, "It couldn't be."

McNeill advised him of his rights. Albert asked permission to make a phone call. He also requested that his brothers, Frank, Joseph, and Richard, be summoned and allowed to join him while he was in custody.

McNeill told Albert the story that Suzanne Macht had related. "I don't know the woman," Albert reiterated, "and I didn't do it. How could I admit it?" Irmgard and Albert's sister Irene came to the Malden police station where Albert was being questioned. The three talked together for a while. McNeill said later that he overheard Irene say, "Al, tell them everything. Don't hold back."

Albert turned to McNeill. He said, "I've committed some breaks and I've been all around the area. Sergeant, you have a rape or a couple of rapes you don't know about."

Accompanied by Albert, McNeill drove back to Cambridge. Albert wanted to point out to McNeill the scene of one of his crimes. He was doing so, he remarked, in order that the Cambridge police might maintain jurisdiction over him. He had a specific reason for wanting it that way. "I *like* you guys," he confided to one of McNeill's colleagues. Years later he was still saying the same thing; he would always refer to Louise Darling as "that nice lady cop."

When McNeill and Albert drove past Suzanne Macht's apartment building, Albert said, "That's where the girl lived who looked at me the other night."

At the Cambridge station, Albert was handed over to law enforcement officials from the other New England states who wanted to question him about sex crimes committed within their bailiwicks. Some of them apparently came on like gangbusters. Albert, normally talkative and relaxed with his friends on the Cambridge force, shut down and refused to speak with the out-of-staters.

"Actually, I don't blame Al," says one ex-Cambridge

cop today. "There was some state police major from Rhode Island who was acting like a real asshole."

On November 3, 1964, Albert was arraigned at the Third District Court in Cambridge on charges of breaking and entering in the daytime to commit a felony; confining and putting in fear with intent to commit a felony; unnatural and lascivious acts on the person of Suzanne Macht; and assault and battery by means of a dangerous weapon. He entered a plea of not guilty. The case was continued to November 17 and bail was set at eight thousand dollars.

On November 6, Albert was brought back to district court. He was there charged with further complaints of breaking and entering in the daytime with intent to commit a felony; breaking and entering in the daytime with intent to commit larceny; and unnatural and lascivious acts on the persons of Geraldine Surette, Virginia Thorner, and Muriel LeBlanc.

Again, Albert pled not guilty. New complaints against him were continued until December 11. Judge Edward Viola ordered him to be confined at MCI-Bridgewater for observation.

7

A Murder in
the Suburbs

At 3:45 P.M. on September 29, 1964, Rita Buote and her fourteen-year-old daughter, Diane, both of Lawrence, were on their way to Boston. Driving along Route 125 in Andover, Mrs. Buote noticed that her car was running low on gas. She pulled into the Texaco station managed by Irvin Hilton. In the next instant, the quiet lives of the Buote women changed forever. And another quiet life ended horribly.

To quote from the police report: "As they approached the gasoline pumps, [the Buotes] observed a man on his knees in front of the lubritorium door and another man standing over him. They saw the man standing fire one shot into the body of the man on the ground and saw him fall over on his side and then heard three more shots fired from the assailant's weapon. They saw a small black firearm in the right hand of the assailant. At the time, they were about 25 to 30 feet from the victim both sitting in the front seat of their car. They observed the assailant then walk hurriedly towards their car and as he approached the driver's side, Mrs. Buote snapped the latch on the door from the inside, locking the door. Both the witnesses observed the assailant through the window on the front left side of the car. Upon finding the door locked, he pounded on the roof of the car and said, 'Open the door.' They both saw the small black gun in his right hand and he pointed it in their direction. Mrs. Buote heard the gun click twice and told her daughter to get down on the floor. She crouched down on the floor of the car on the driver's side." Mrs. Buote said later that she also told Diane to pray.

As Mrs. Buote was driving into the Texaco station from one side, a truck operated by William King of Andover pulled in on the other. With King was his friend Reginald Mortimer. King stopped the truck before the gas pumps, and he and Mortimer heard what sounded to them like exploding firecrackers. They saw a slim, dark-haired man of medium height, wearing a light tan trench coat or top coat, run toward the Buote vehicle. They then watched as the man ran toward another car parked near the pumps, leapt into it, and sped off in the direction of North Andover. They got the plate number and King went into the gas station to call the police.

The getaway car turned out to have been stolen earlier that day from near the Massachusetts Institute of Technology campus in Cambridge. It was found later that evening on a street in Andover adjacent to Phillips Academy. The car was registered to a navy lieutenant who was taking classes at MIT. Underneath the front seat the lieutenant had left a thirty-two-caliber nickel-plated Harrison and Richardson revolver and a twenty-two-caliber Astra semiautomatic pistol.

Sergeant Robert Deyermond of the Andover police found six twenty-two-caliber cartridge shells at the crime scene. The corresponding slugs were later dug out of the victim's body.

The dead man, Irvin Hilton, a forty-three-year-old

North Andover resident, was autopsied at Lawrence General Hospital. He had been shot six times at close range. He had also been stabbed in the back. If the bullets hadn't killed him, the knife would have. It was thought that the person responsible for Hilton's bloody execution may have forced the gas station manager to his knees and ordered him to beg for his life while simultaneously pumping bullets into him.

The viciousness of the murder curdled the blood of the investigating police officers.

Rita and Diane Buote looked at dozens of mug shots, but could not make an identification. They were, however, insistent that they would recognize Hilton's slayer if they saw him again. And their description of him was thorough enough to enable Andover police officer William Tammany to draw a composite. The sketch was given to the press for publication.

A Lawrence cop named Charles Keenan saw it in the local paper, the *Lawrence Eagle-Tribune,* and the man it portrayed looked very familiar to him. He checked his files and came up with a photograph of a former Lawrence resident who had in 1961 been paroled after serving sixteen years of a life sentence for second-degree murder. The photo was shown to Rita and Diane Buote. According to the police report, their identification of it was immediate—and positive. This was the man who had murdered Irvin Hilton.

The suspect was at present living in the Mattapan section of Boston. The Andover, Lawrence, and state police got in touch with the BPD and obtained a warrant at Dorchester District Court to search the suspect's car and his apartment at 51 Deering Road. When the police went into the apartment they found the suspect with a social worker, Francis Touchet, of the Medfield State Hospital. They also found a hunting knife, which they confiscated.

"Do you remember me?" Sergeant Keenan asked the suspect.

"I can't place you," the man replied.

"Do you remember sixteen years ago?" Keenan persisted.

"Oh, yes," the suspect said.

"Same thing as sixteen years ago," Keenan said.

The suspect nodded in apparent agreement.

He was put in a lineup and viewed first by Diane Buote and then by Rita.

"That's him," Diane exclaimed when it was the suspect's turn to step forward from the line.

"When and where did you see this man?" asked a police officer.

"Thursday afternoon at the gas station," Diane answered.

Was she positive?

"Yes, I'm sure," Diane said firmly.

That night the Andover police station, where the suspect was being confined, was under heavy guard.

On October 2, the suspect was charged with murder at the Lawrence District Court. His lawyer, Paul Smith, entered for him a plea of not guilty. Counsel also asked for and was granted a continuance to October 29. On that date the case was continued yet again to November 5. At that point, the suspect had retained a new lawyer.

The probable cause hearing on November 5 ended with the suspect being held without bail for the Essex County Grand Jury, sitting in Salem. He was remanded to the Lawrence jail.

On November 12, the *Lawrence Eagle-Tribune* reported that five Boston-area men, including a minister and WBZ-Radio talk show host Paul Benzaquin, had formed what they called a Committee for Reasonable Justice to raise seven thousand dollars to pay the suspect's legal fees.

On January 18, 1965, the suspect was sent to MCI-Bridgewater for a court-ordered psychiatric examination and observation. On February 10, his commitment there was extended another thirty-five days. He was initially diagnosed as a paranoid schizophrenic with an extremely severe sociopathic personality disorder.

The suspect's name was George Henry Nassar.

His new attorney was F. Lee Bailey.

8

Enter George Nassar . . . And F. Lee Bailey

Who was George Nassar?

According to F. Lee Bailey, he was a student of the Russian language planning to attend Northeastern University. He'd been a newspaper reporter and a hospital attendant. Most impressively, however, "he'd taught Sunday school and, a couple of times, had taken over the pulpit for one of his minister friends."*

According to Attorney Francis C. Newton, Jr., "If you met him at a party or on the street, you'd think he was the pleasantest person imaginable. Very bright, with impeccable manners. And yet he had the history of a mad dog."

According to George V. Higgins, "He was a vicious, unprincipled and crafty figure."

According to Ames Robey, medical director of Bridgewater, he was "a man of great anger." Also a busy one. "The information we had about Mr. Nassar

---

* Bailey, p. 144.

was that of the Charlestown [a section of Boston] gang wars that were going on in the early sixties, he was responsible for at least seventeen of the murders and maybe as many as thirty."

According to a retired Cambridge detective, "Nassar was the scariest guy I ever heard of."

Let former Inspector John Moran have the final word: "Guys like him, you shoot them first and *then* tell them to put their hands up."

Sunday school teacher or psychotic killer, George Nassar was born in Providence, Rhode Island, in June 1932. He was the eldest of two children of Henry Nassar and the former Helen George, both of Syrian descent. Henry had emigrated to the United States with his parents, and worked as a weaver in various mills in Lawrence. He died there in 1955. Helen, who had been born in Dover, New Hampshire, and worked also in the mills as a bobbin setter, had been previously married to a man named Lawrence Otis. She and Otis were divorced in 1931. They had one son, named after his father. Helen had no better luck with her second marriage; Henry abandoned her and the children long before his death.

George and his younger sister, Eileen, grew up in Lawrence and attended local schools. They were raised as Catholics. George played neighborhood sports and joined the Boy Scouts. Otherwise he was not the convivial type; his teachers found him quiet, reserved, and a poor mixer.

He was a sophomore in high school when he was arrested on a charge of second-degree murder.

Police would later characterize the crime as a thrill-killing. Nassar himself claimed to have done if "for excitement." In May of 1948, he and two companions, sixteen-year-old William Kenney and sixteen-year-old Gennaro Pullino, went on a robbery spree in Lawrence that netted them eighty dollars. They hit four establishments; at one of them, the female proprietor chased the three from her premises with a broom.

Dominic Kirmil, a shopkeeper at 99 Park Street, was not so lucky. When the trio held him up, he came at them brandishing a Coke bottle. Nassar withdrew from the pocket of his dark-colored trench coat (evidently trench coats were his garb of choice for the commission of homicides) a nickel-plated revolver and shot Kirmil four times. The shopkeeper died three hours later of massive blood loss.

There were a number of witnesses to the crime, all of whom could describe the youth in the dark trench coat.

On May 20, Nassar was cruising along Route 110 in Ayer, Massachusetts, in a stolen car. He lost control of the vehicle, hit a soft shoulder, and flipped four times. He emerged from the wreckage unscathed but for an abraded elbow.

Lawrence patrolmen Charles Keenan and Walter Sliva picked him up and brought him in on auto theft charges.

In his pocket Nassar had two thirty-eight-caliber bullets. Beside the wrecked car had been found a nickel-plated revolver. With this knowledge in mind, Keenan began questioning Nassar about the Kirmil slaying.

Nassar and his cohorts Kenney and Pullino were indicted and allowed to plead guilty to a second-degree murder charge. Nassar's lawyer, citing his client's youth and potential for rehabilitation, asked Judge Frank Smith of the Salem Superior Court to show mercy in his disposition of the case. Smith, who had allowed a plea of second- rather than first-degree murder to be entered because of the defendants' "tender age," sentenced the three boys to life in prison.

Nassar served his time at MCI-Norfolk in Dedham, Massachusetts. There he met Unitarian minister William Moors, an assistant to the prison chaplain. Moors and Nassar became "good friends," as Moors would tell the *Lawrence Eagle-Tribune* in the aftermath of Nassar's arrest for the murder of Irvin Hilton. Moors decried the press coverage of the Andover slaying as "inflammatory and suggestive," "calloused, immoral and unfair."

Nassar had in fact become the Willie Horton of his day. Francis X. McCann, a Democratic state senator from Cambridge, insisted that the parole board give a public accounting of the reasons it had granted Nassar early release in 1961. Representative Perlie Dyar Chase, he who had demanded an investigation of the Boston Police Department for its failure to solve the Strangler murders, maintained that the State Crime Commission ought to reexamine all pardons and paroles handed down during the previous decade.

Nassar's new attorney, F. Lee Bailey, unlike the Reverend Mr. Moors, claimed to be quite satisfied with the pretrial publicity accorded his client. In a speech entitled "Trial by Newspaper," given to the Greater Lawrence Men's Brotherhood of Temple Emmanuel on November 23, 1964, Bailey said he was confident that any negative effects of the media treatment of Nassar could be blunted.

Nassar himself seems to have had no problems with the Fourth Estate either. In an interview with Michael J. Carney of the *Lawrence Eagle-Tribune*, Nassar asked Carney, "What's my chance of getting into the newspaper business as a reporter?" He had, after all, experience in the field—he'd worked on the prison newsletter during his incarceration at Norfolk.

Nassar had interests other than the Russian language, theology, and journalism. When the cops searched his Mattapan apartment, they found among his effects a badly typed leaflet produced by an organization called the Guardians of Democracy. The group met every evening at a private home in Everett. Its membership drive appears to have been aimed at the previously institutionalized:

> MOST OF THE TROUBLES YOU SUFFER [the leaflet read] WITH RIGHT NOW STEM FROM THIS ENFORCED SOCIALISM AND NOT FROM ANY PRETENDED MENTAL ILLNESS. THE MENTAL HEALTH DEPT. IS NOTHING BUT ONE OF THE WEAPONS OF THE SOCIALISTS. UNLESS YOU GET BUSY IMMEDIATELY AND JOIN US, YOUR PROBLEMS ARE GOING TO GROW UNTIL YOU ARE THOROUGHLY FAMILIAR WITH THE HORRORS OF ALL OUT SLAVERY.

Perhaps over a decade and a half of imprisonment had created a joiner out of Nassar, the adolescent loner; the police also found in his apartment a copy of a letter addressed to "Dear Couple" and dated April 24, 1964. The letter is clearly a response to a solicitation for group sex. In it, Nassar furnishes a physical description of himself and a list of his interests: reading, writing, hosting parties, taking photographs, and going to the theater. "And, more and more lately," he adds, "exploring the bizarre, exciting and unexplored."

Nassar himself is part of a couple: "I have a girl-friend who is in many ways more unconventional than I am." [She must have been quite a gal.] He ends the letter with the hope that he and "dear couple" together can provide the woman with an opportunity to "blossom out."

The alleged contract killer had emerged from incarceration an aspiring swinger.

Who was F. Lee Bailey, Nassar's replacement for Paul Smith? In 1964, at the age of thirty-one, he was already a national figure on his way to becoming a legendary one like his brother defenders Edward Bennett Williams, Racehorse Haynes, Melvin Belli, and Percy Foreman. Perhaps he would someday attain the mythic stature of a Clarence Darrow. Alan M. Dershowitz, himself a major constellation in the legal firmament, who taught Bailey's younger brother Bill in one of his Harvard Law School classes and who ultimately represented the elder Bailey when he was charged in 1973 with conspiracy to commit mail fraud, has called his former client's cross-examination technique "masterful" and "spectacular." Ames Robey, a perpetual courtroom adversary, praises Bailey's summations as "brilliant."

Trial lawyers are a notoriously flamboyant and egotistical breed; Bailey extended the parameters of the stereotype. He carried enormous sums of money on his person (retainers, he told colleagues) and a gun to protect the wad. He once tried to pay an eighty-five-cent restaurant check with a one-thousand-dollar bill; with stunning aplomb, the coffee-shop waitress asked him if he had anything smaller. He blasted around Boston in a souped-up Pontiac GTO with the license plate TRIAL; he zoomed in and out of airports at the controls of his own twin-engine Cessna 310, single-engine Cessna 172, or Beechcraft Bonanza.

"A high, wide, and handsome kind of guy," comments Francis C. Newton, Jr.

Bailey was born in Waltham, Massachusetts, on June 10, 1933, the son of an advertising man and a nursery school founder. In 1943, his parents divorced. He attended good private schools, earning the scholarships to do so. In 1950 he matriculated at Harvard as an English major.

In his sophomore year, Bailey read *The Art of Advocacy*, by famed attorney Lloyd Paul Stryker. The book so impressed him that he changed his career plans—from writer to lawyer.

Bored with higher education, he dropped out of Harvard at the end of his second year and joined the Naval Flight Training program. A year and a half later he switched to the Marines and became a jet fighter pilot. He also volunteered for his group's legal staff. Very shortly afterward, the chief legal officer died in a plane crash and Bailey took over his position. The experience he garnered was invaluable. Upon leaving the Marines, Bailey was admitted to Boston University Law School (alma mater of John Bottomly and Edward Brooke), despite his lack of an undergraduate degree. He would graduate first in his class.

Just three months after passing the bar, Bailey took on and won his first sensational case—the Torso Murder. A Lowell, Massachusetts, auto mechanic had been accused of killing his wife and tossing her headless, dismembered body into the Merrimack River. Bailey obtained an acquittal for his client, George Edgerly, in part by suggesting to the jury that the prosecutor in the case was willing to send an innocent man to the electric chair just to insure his own reelection. The ploy worked.

(Several years later Edgerly was arrested again, this time on a charge of taking an ax to a Lawrence auto dealer. He was convicted—but this time he didn't have Bailey defending him.)

In 1964, Bailey would have an even more spectacular success representing another accused wife-killer, Cleveland osteopath Samuel Sheppard. Bailey contended that Dr. Sheppard, who had been convicted and imprisoned in 1954, had been the victim of a smear campaign conducted by the *Cleveland Press* and the *Cleveland Plain Dealer*. The adverse publicity, Bailey maintained, had made it impossible for Sheppard to get a fair trial. A decade later, Bailey got a judge to agree. Sheppard was freed from prison on ten thousand dollars' bond and tried two years later. Bailey represented him in this courtroom battle and Sheppard,

the second time around on the same charges, was acquitted.

If George Nassar had confidence in his new attorney,
it seemed well placed.

9

The Cuckoo's Nest

Albert DeSalvo hated Bridgewater, for which he can hardly be blamed, and was vocal about his discontent with the conditions of the place. Albert didn't much care for Ames Robey, Bridgewater's medical director, either. Robey, in his turn, found Albert, with his constant bragging and demands for attention, exasperating. Nonetheless, Robey, like some of the Cambridge police, would develop a grudging fondness for his troublesome patient. Maybe it was the Smile. Or maybe it was Albert's ability as a natural-born comedian with a flair for practical jokes.

Not that Albert had much occasion or, probably, inclination to be funny during his first sequestration in Bridgewater. He suffered through the court-ordered thirty-five days, during which he was diagnosed as having a sociopathic personality disorder with schizoid features. It was possible that he might become acutely psychotic. Nonetheless, Robey found Albert initially competent to stand trial for the various offenses with which he had been most recently charged. The doctor's diagnosis would change radically over the next few months.

On December 10, 1964, Albert was returned to the

East Cambridge jail, where he began behaving in a way that seemed to confirm Dr. Robey's worst fears of a psychotic breakdown. He claimed that he heard voices; he claimed that Irmgard had appeared in his cell and berated him for his misdeeds. He also became depressed and suicidal. He was sent back to Bridgewater on January 14, 1965.

Albert also had a new lawyer, Jon A. Asgeirsson, his previous attorney, Robert Sheinfeld, having given up in disgust. Sheinfeld, who had labored mightily on behalf of Albert for so many years, obtaining for him light or suspended sentences, threw in the towel after Albert was accused of assaulting Suzanne Macht, Muriel LeBlanc, Virginia Thorner, and Geraldine Surette. Albert understood Sheinfeld's point of view, and in fact thanked the attorney for his past efforts.

In any event, it was Asgeirsson who appeared on behalf of Albert at a hearing in the case of *Commonwealth v. DeSalvo* in Middlesex Superior Court on February 4. The sole witness was Ames Robey.

Asgeirsson told Judge Edward Pecce, "I have been connected with this case since last November, and I have been very disappointed with [Albert's] reaction to me—to my questions, I should say, not to me personally, but to my questions. He's been cooperative as much as to his ability as he can, but I question his stability and his ability to know what is going on around him." The judge asked if Asgeirsson was satisfied that Albert was mentally incompetent to stand trial. Asgeirsson replied that he was.

Ames Robey took the stand then and testified that his observations and those of other doctors at Bridgewater had indicated that Albert's illness had indeed grown worse. With medication he might be able to stand trial a few months from now. At the moment he was not competent to do so, although Robey felt that Albert was still able to comprehend the nature and severity of the crimes he had committed at the time he committed them. Robey declined to give a definitive opinion as to whether Albert had been driven by an irresistible impulse when he broke into the homes of Suzanne Macht, Muriel LeBlanc, Virginia Thorner, and Geraldine Surette.

The outlook for a complete remission of Albert's schizophrenic symptoms was not, according to Robey, very favorable: "The defendant is presently thirty-three, I believe, and this is getting into an age group that certainly causes the prognosis to be more guarded than if he were, for example, seventeen, twenty, twenty-two, or in this area."

Albert then asked to speak for himself. Judge Pecce granted him permission. Albert took the stand—and promptly contradicted Asgeirsson and Robey by stating that he was fully competent to stand trial. He talked about his previous incarceration at Westborough State Hospital, where he told the doctors that an irresistible impulse had indeed compelled him to act out the Measuring Man charade. He spoke of how he had hoped to be returned to Westborough in November of 1964, and that the Cambridge police had told him they'd make such a recommendation to the court. But a number of recent escapes from that institution had dashed Albert's hopes. He had to be sent to a more secure facility.

Albert then spoke bitterly about life in Bridgewater. There, he was sure, he would never receive proper treatment. Throughout his denunciation of the place ran a vein of prudish, almost puritanical horror at some of the things he'd heard and seen. It was an odd reaction on the part of someone who otherwise spoke in such frank terms of his own sexual desires and exploits:

> My first day I entered [Bridgewater] and first thing they do is rip off my ring, which is their procedure. Good. They use the words on you right away.

And that doctor that they have come to interview you, he sits down at a desk with a set of officers there and inmates all around like animals, and he in turn starts to interview about dirty words. The first thing he asks you. And I looked around. I ask, "This is a doctor interviewing me?" And all you see is these cells and these inmates jumping around and looking at you, and this doctor interviews you. Every second word is filth that he's talking about.

So to make a long story short, they then send you into the room for five days, twenty-four hours a day locked up. I came and I wanted to, as I read in the papers and told by officers, if a man is sick and is asking help, they'll help him. Well, if that is being helped, put him naked on the floor, which they do, throw him in the cell twenty-four hours for the next five days, and then throw him in a room afterwards, and then they let him outside for fifteen hours—he sits at a table, walking back and forth, and then the next thing he just goes to bed for eight hours. All right, that's their way of rehabilitation. You say okay.

And the next thing I go to staff the first time, which I talked to Dr. Robey. I walked in. Maybe five or ten minutes at the most. He says, "Well, we'll get you ready for staff. The trial as soon as possible." That's my first time. I see him two weeks later. He says, "Well, you are capable of going to trial now and we find you are an emotionally disturbed person," and that's it. As far as I was concerned I saw a psychiatrist there—which is a personality test that they take and this and that for about an hour and a half, but possibly two hours—but that is the only time I seen what they call a doctor on my first time.

So my second time coming there, where they have already found me sane they couldn't understand why I am back again, and I personally didn't want to go back . . . If they treated me as a person, not like an animal, then I would freely give what's inside me to let out, but myself, when I saw I was being brought in, I froze, I revealed nothing. What I really wanted to do—I just gave them the other things. What I am trying to say, I feel I am competent to stand trial. However, Your Honor, you think so or not, the doctors, that's entirely up to them. But on my second time *I was told by other people that if I am committed there to go ahead and play the game that I am depressed and seeing things in my room* [emphasis added], and if I was committed there I would probably get two or three years and be free. I found this to be untrue. And after such time, thinking of it here, I went and told Dr. [Samuel] Allen and in turn the other supervisor I had lied to them. *I did not see these things* [emphasis added], and I am willing and capable of standing trial and I made this all up to them.

Judge Pecce thanked Albert for his testimony. Then he informed Albert that he would be recommitted to Briegewater until further order of the court.

Albert was shipped back to the institution he so despised. And there he renewed his acquaintance with another recently arrived inmate: George Nassar.

10

Bailey Takes Action

In *The Boston Strangler,* Gerold Frank quotes a letter written on January 9, 1965, by Albert to his former attorney, Robert Sheinfeld. In the letter, Albert apologizes to Sheinfeld for having caused the lawyer so many headaches, and expresses his gratitude for Sheinfeld's representation. He speaks of his sexual offenses with considerable regret and shame. "But still," he adds, "thank God I neaver [sic] got to hurt anyone."*

At the same time Albert was writing to Sheinfeld of his relief at not seriously injuring any of his victims, and sitting in the East Cambridge jail conjuring up visions of a furious and reproachful Irmgard, he was, according to Gerold Frank, intimating to his new lawyer Jon Asgeirsson that he might be "the Boston 'S' man." But Albert, again according to Frank's version of the story, had to lead up to this revelation with a series of coy yet typically self-aggrandizing hints: The story he was about to tell Asgeirsson would be one bigger than that of the Brink's robbery. Asgeirsson asked him if by that he meant the recent Plymouth,

---

* Frank, p. 334.

102 THE BOSTON STRANGLERS

Massachusetts mail robbery (four suspects in that major heist were, coincidentally, successfully defended by F. Lee Bailey). Albert said no, his story wasn't like that at all, it was a bigger one even than the saga of Jack the Ripper. Asgeirsson, Frank relates, told his client to stop vamping around and spit out whatever it was he had on his mind. Then Albert blurted to his attorney that he had committed *all* of the Boston stranglings.*

What was Asgeirsson's reaction?

"I did do a lot of things involving lawyers," he says today. When asked to specify, he answers, "I don't want to tell you."

Whatever Asgeirsson did took place between January and the beginning of March 1965.

In *The Defense Never Rests,* an account of his greatest cases published in 1971, F. Lee Bailey writes of how his first meeting with Albert DeSalvo came to pass. He was sitting in the prisoners' waiting room of Essex County Superior Court in Salem with his client, George Nassar, when Nassar said to him, " 'If a man was the strangler, the guy who killed all those women, would it be possible for him to publish his story and make some money with it?'

"I had to smile [writes Bailey]. 'It's perfectly possible,' I said. 'But I wouldn't advise it. I suspect that a confession in book form would be judged completely voluntary and totally admissible. I also suspect that it would be the means by which the author would put himself in the electric chair.'

" 'I'll pass on the information,' said Nassar. 'I promised this guy at Bridgewater I'd ask you. He's been after me to have you come in and talk to him, but I know you're pretty busy.'

---

* Frank, p. 251.

"I was vaguely curious. 'What's the guy's name?'

" 'Albert DeSalvo,' Nassar said."*

On March 4, 1965, Bailey paid his first visit to Albert at Bridgewater.

That initial visit, according to Ames Robey, lasted a half hour. Bailey was asked to leave the premises because he wasn't Albert's attorney of record. Then Robey called Jon Asgeirsson, who *was* Albert's attorney of record and thus the only one permitted to visit him at Bridgewater. Robey asked Asgeirsson, "What the hell is going on?"

According to Robey, Asgeirsson replied, "I don't know."

According to Bailey, he had lunch with Robey a week or so *before* he paid his first visit to Albert.† In the course of the meal, Bailey asked Robey if he knew Albert. Robey laughed and replied that he certainly did, and furthermore that while the man claimed to have an ungovernable sex drive, he had probably fantasized most of his encounters with women. And he was by no means a killer, Robey commented.

Bailey adds that Albert's brother Joe called to tell him that Albert wished to consult him. The lawyer's next move, by his own account, was to get in touch with Lieutenant John Donovan, head of the Boston Police Department's homicide squad. "I told him I might be talking to a man who was likely to claim he had committed some of the stranglings. I needed a few clues—things known to the police but not to the general public that would help me judge the man's

---

* Bailey, p. 143.
† Bailey, pp. 144–45.

validity. Donovan sent his close assistant Lieutenant Edward Sherry to my office, and Sherry gave me a few leads."*

It was more than a few. Speaking today, Donovan characterizes what was provided Bailey as "a lot of information."

Armed with this data, Bailey went down to Bridgewater. Albert, who was polite and diffident during that brief meeting, answered all the questions the lawyer asked him promptly and apparently accurately. He also wanted to know if two things would be possible, says Bailey: whether he could be sent to a decent mental institution and whether the sale of his story would realize sufficient profits to make life financially comfortable for Irmgard and the children.†

One other person was present at this meeting: George Nassar.

Bailey informed Donovan and Sherry of what Albert had told him. Then he made the two detectives an offer: He would, he said, record his next question-and-answer session with Albert and allow them to listen to the tape. But nothing on it could be used against his client. Sherry and Donovan agreed to the proposal, furnished Bailey with more "secret" information about the murders, and left the lawyer's office.

Meanwhile, Ames Robey was still wondering what the hell was going on. He called Edward Brooke and said, "Something's up with the Strangler business."

Dictaphone in hand, Bailey returned to Bridgewater the following day. It was during this second meeting

---

* Bailey, p. 145.
† Bailey, pp. 144–45.

that the lawyer was convinced that Albert was the Strangler. "Anyone experienced in interrogation learns to recognize the difference between a man speaking from life and a man telling a story that he has either made up or gotten from another person," Bailey wrote in *The Defense Never Rests.* "DeSalvo gave every indication that he was speaking from life."*

As he had promised, Bailey played the tape for Donovan and Sherry. They, he writes, were as quickly and firmly convinced on the basis of what they heard in playback that Albert was the Phantom Fiend as Bailey himself was when he listened to Albert live.

Following this, Bailey says, "Boston Police Commissioner Edmund McNamara agreed to come to my office at once. As Donovan left to pick him up, I called Dr. Ames Robey and asked him to come over from Bridgewater."

McNamara and Robey appeared as requested. Bailey played the tape for them. When the last echoes of Albert's mechanically reproduced voice had died away, according to Bailey, the commissioner fired up a big cigar and asked his men for their recommendations.†

Of this story, McNamara says today, "Absolutely untrue." He never listened to the tape, he maintains, and in fact turned on his heel and walked out of Bailey's office as soon as the lawyer made it clear what he proposed to do. Right away, McNamara says, Bailey wanted to strike a deal—before telling McNamara who the suspect was or what this individual was supposed to have done. The commissioner, of course, knew precisely what Bailey had in mind.

"I said, 'Look, if you're talking about DeSalvo, forget it.' Bailey almost fell off his chair." Then McNamara

---

* Bailey, p. 151.
† Bailey, p. 153.

added, "You got the wrong guy. Go see the district attorney."

Before he left Bailey's office, McNamara noted that a large quantity of Chinese food had been brought in and dished out to Donovan and Sherry. They had also been offered and had accepted drinks.

Robey confirms that a considerable amount of liquor flowed during the meeting, although most of it went down the throats of the two cops rather than that of Bailey.

The commissioner took his leave. "I blasted John Donovan for even taking me there," he remarks today.

Despite his anger with Donovan and Sherry at having involved him in the incident, McNamara still maintains a high regard for the investigative abilities of his two lieutenants. They entered into the deal with Bailey out of sheer frustration at their failure to solve the strangling murders, he says. But: "You can fault my guys a little for being suckers."

Of the tape Bailey had played for the detectives, McNamara remarks, "Who knows how it was edited?"

Says Donovan today, "I'm sure it was legitimate, what we did."

Bailey wanted Albert to take a polygraph test. Donovan, he writes, agreed to the idea with alacrity. Robey objected; he wanted to give a physical examination to Albert first. Bailey fumed at the delay this would entail—he felt the examination wasn't necessary, because all anyone needed to submit to a lie detector test was a pulse and that Albert certainly had—but finally conceded to Robey's demand. First he counseled Albert to behave himself with Robey, whom he states his client disliked intensely.

The next day Robey pronounced Albert fit to take a polygraph.*

Bailey and Donovan agreed that the head of the Strangler Task Force, John Bottomly, should be apprised of what had transpired over the past few days. Bailey told Donovan to give Bottomly a call; he himself had to go to Springfield to give a speech.

Bailey and Bottomly spoke later that day. Bottomly, according to Bailey, mentioned that the Task Force had been just about to zero in on Albert themselves (Phillip DiNatale, one of the Task Force investigators, had in fact been sent down to Bridgewater to get Albert's palm print). Bottomly agreed that a lie detector test sounded useful and promising.

Bailey never got to administer the polygraph to Albert. When he turned up at Bridgewater the next day with the equipment, he was directed not to his client but to the office of Superintendent Charles Gaughan. Gaughan told Bailey that he had been instructed to deny the lawyer access not only to Albert but to George Nassar.

The order had come from the attorney general.

Bailey said to Gaughan that perhaps some legal action or the threat thereof might change his mind.† Today he says that Bottomly was behind the move to deny him contact with his clients because the Task Force chief wanted to take over the case. "He filed a series of lawsuits in federal court preventing me from seeing DeSalvo."

Edward Brooke, however, disputes this claim: "I issued that order myself."

Brooke was unhappy with Bailey's conduct in mak-

---

* Bailey, pp. 153–54.
† Bailey, pp. 155–56.

ing the initial visit to Bridgewater to see Albert without first informing Jon Asgeirsson of his intentions. "I was upset by the fact that F. Lee had done this," Brooke says today. "And I called the other lawyer [Asgeirsson]." What Bailey did was not technically illegal, Brooke comments, but the ethics of it were very questionable. "I even threatened to go to the Bar Association."

In short order, the *Record American* broke the news that the Boston Strangler was incarcerated at Bridgewater and that he was being represented by F. Lee Bailey. Today, Bailey says he isn't really sure how the *Record* obtained its information. He theorizes that a Boston police officer tipped off one of the reporters who were always hanging around the station.

When the *Record* hit the stands, Attorney General Brooke hit the roof. To add to his displeasure was the fact that a television crew had turned up at Bridgewater and was milling around outside the gates trying to get shots of the wing where DeSalvo was being held. Brooke went to the Supreme Judicial Court of Massachusetts and got an injunction preventing anyone involved in the Strangler case from speaking to the press.

A month or so before Albert had begun his confession, Irmgard had left Massachusetts with Judy and Michael. The stigma of her husband's arrest in Cambridge on sexual assault charges had been too painful to endure; she sought surcease as well as refuge with her sister in a western state where the name DeSalvo meant nothing to anyone. On March 7, whatever separate and fragile peace she had achieved was shattered. Bailey called her with the information that her husband's name and face would be on the front pages of tomorrow's newspapers in connection with a horrific story. He advised Irmgard to change her name (which she had already done) and go deeper into hiding. He would be flying out to speak with her immediately.

Gerold Frank reports that Irmgard received another telephone call, this one from an individual who spoke German, Irmgard's native language. He informed her that he was calling on behalf of F. Lee Bailey because Mr. Bailey feared his own phone might be tapped. Someone from Bailey's office was en route to see her as they talked, he said.*

Then Albert's brothers Frank and Joe came on the line. They confirmed the appalling news Bailey had so dramatically broken—that Albert had confessed to being the Boston Strangler. Irmgard must, they emphasized, do whatever Bailey's representative told her to do.

She heard, but she didn't believe. Ten days later she telephoned Albert at Bridgewater and told him that if he didn't stop spouting these monstrous lies, she would kill herself and Judy and Michael.

---

* Frank, p. 248.

11

Wheeling and Dealing

From Charles Gaughan's office at Bridgewater, Bailey writes, he went back to Boston and agonized over Albert's position as a pawn in Bottomly's power play. Attorney General Brooke had not accepted Bailey's phone calls. Was it possible, the lawyer mused, that Brooke too wanted to take credit for solving the stranglings? To further his own political aspirations? And could the same be said of Boston's Democratic mayor, John Collins? Collins would be the big winner if his police department rather than the attorney general's office got the laurels for cracking the Strangler case.

Bailey filed the legal papers necessary to overturn Brooke's ban on the lawyer's access to his client George Nassar. He did not file a similar petition with respect to Albert, he states, although he prepared the appropriate papers. By telegram, he notified Albert at Bridgewater of these recent developments—and cautioned him to watch out for those who might attempt to trick or manipulate him into unguarded speech.

Brooke also was eager to protect Albert's rights, reasoning that if the man were incompetent to stand trial, he might be equally incapable of picking his own lawyer. The attorney general therefore determined that a guardian be appointed to oversee Albert's affairs. He explained this to Bailey at a meeting in the attorney general's office. Bailey in his turn argued that the notion of the state choosing counsel for even an insane defendant violated the essence of the adversarial system. He and Brooke agreed to take the matter to court.

Bailey retained his own attorney to represent him in the upcoming battle with Brooke. It was Paul Smith, George Nassar's original counsel for the Irvin Hilton slaying.*

"Word of a possible break in the Strangler case had leaked out," Bailey writes in *The Defense Never Rests,* "and the Suffolk County Courthouse was filled with newsmen as I picked my way over cables and past cameras to the courtroom door."†

Ames Robey remembers this event well: "I almost couldn't get off the elevator. There were even representatives from Reuters and Tass. Every network, every Boston newspaper—the place was a *madhouse.* I managed to get off and wend my way to the courtroom door. Just as I was about to go into the courtroom, Bailey grabbed me. Dragged me into the little lawyers' anteroom there and said, 'Ames, you've got to say he [Albert] is competent.' Why would I have to say that? Because Lee had filed a charge against me for malpractice because I'd done a lumbar puncture on a [Bridgewater] patient we suspected of having syphilis, oh, some months before, and the patient claimed he was having headaches. Well, after a spinal tap, almost everyone has headaches if they don't lie flat and you

---

* Bailey, pp. 156–58.
† Bailey, p. 158.

remove some pressure. You're very likely to have a headache for three hours. And Bailey said, 'If you don't [find Albert competent], it will cost you everything.' I said, 'Lee.' He, by the way, had me by both lapels. I'm much taller than Lee. I said, 'Lee, let go of me or I'll back out of this room sobbing as I go. Don't ever threaten me again, Mr. Bailey.' He dropped me like a hot rock."

The inadvertent ringmaster of this media circus, Judge Arthur Whittemore, ruled that two state-appointed psychiatrists would decide the issue of Albert's competence.

Afterward Bailey phoned his own expert on mental health issues, Dr. Robert Ross Mezer, hypnoanalyst William Joseph Bryan III, and attorney Melvin Belli for advice and consultation.

Bailey has consistently and vigorously maintained that he originated and carried out the plan that Albert be allowed to confess to the stranglings in return for a grant of immunity from prosecution and an assurance of being given good psychiatric treatment at a decent facility. But certain records appear to contradict Bailey. In a memo to Brooke dated April 27, 1965, Bottomly mentions having proposed the same idea earlier to the attorney general. And was Bailey the major figure in all the negotiations and legal maneuverings on Albert's behalf as he presents himself as being in The Defense Never Rests? Or did Jon Asgeirsson, whom Bailey relegates to the background in his book, play a much more active role in these events? Very possibly the latter. At any rate, it was from Asgeirsson rather than Bailey that Bottomly sought approval of the idea he'd outlined to Brooke:

At the Friday hearing before Judge Whittemore, Bill Cowin [Assistant Attorney General William

Cowin] advises that it was learned that the state psychiatrist will testify that DeSalvo is not competent to stand trial and at best it is very doubtful that he is competent to make sound decisions in the management of his own affairs. After receiving that information I arranged for an appointment with Asgeirsson to explore the possibility of implementing the suggestion I made earlier to you [Brooke] to make a determination about DeSalvo one way or the other.

That meeting was held with Asgeirsson this morning [April 27, 1965] . . . I suggested one idea was to have the Attorney General after consultation with and the consent of the three District Attorneys involved agree to the permanent commitment of DeSalvo in a mental institution after interrogation convinces him that DeSalvo is the strangler. I advised him that this suggestion was made informally and no publicity could result, and that if it was publicized the idea must be withdrawn immediately. *He represented to me that he did not feel that it was necessary to consult with Bailey on this matter at this stage, and that he was genuinely concerned that if he did consult with him adverse publicity might well result. It is obvious that he is increasingly disenchanted with his relationship with Bailey.* [Emphasis added.]

If Asgeirsson was unhappy with his co-counsel (if that is indeed the role Bailey played), he apparently wasn't the only one. Bottomly noted to Brooke that Asgeirsson "advised that the members of DeSalvo's family, particularly Joseph, were becoming increasingly disenchanted with Bailey."

In the course of this meeting, Asgeirsson and Bottomly also took up the matter of Albert's guardianship. The Task Force chief proposed that Charles Gaughan, Superintendent of Bridgewater, assume that position.

Asgeirsson objected and counterproposed Joseph De-Salvo. He and Bottomly then agreed to confer with Joseph about the matter along with William Cowin, the assistant attorney general delegated to handle the filing of any guardianship petition.

On May 4, Bottomly penned another memo to Brooke in which he referred to his continuant conversations with Asgeirsson about Albert's fate within the judicial system. Bailey was not party to these talks—clearly very crucial ones—either.

On May 5, Brooke met with the district attorneys of Essex, Middlesex, and Suffolk counties to discuss how the investigation of Albert's alleged involvement in the stranglings ought to be pursued. If Bailey attended that meeting, there is no reference to his presence.

Although Bottomly was working with Asgeirsson on his own plan to have Albert indicted for at least one of the thirteen murders, he did not then believe that Asgeirsson's client was the Boston Strangler. "On that assumption," he remarked to Brooke, "I am strictly from Missouri."

On May 6, according to *The Defense Never Rests*, Bailey and the attorney general's office reached a decision concerning the matter of Albert's guardianship. The man chosen to assume it was George McGrath, a former corrections commissioner for the Commonwealth. Bailey was entirely satisfied with the choice; he thought highly of McGrath.*

But was he the architect of McGrath's appointment, as his book suggests? A message from William Cowin to Bottomly, dated May 6, 1965, gives a slightly differ-

---

* Bailey, p. 166.

ent version not only of how the guardianship agreement was struck, but of who the principals in it were:

> Judge McMenimen this morning appointed George McGrath temporary guardian of the person of Albert DeSalvo and Joseph DeSalvo temporary guardian of the estate of Albert DeSalvo. *The judge accepted Jon Asgeirsson's representation that he was satisfied with this arrangement* [emphasis added] and refused to set a date for a hearing on the permanent appointment at this time.
>
> McMenimen feels that since counsel have agreed there is no need for further proceedings yet. I imagine that if Bailey returns now and makes a commotion he will get a very cool reception from the Probate Court.

According to Cowin, then, not only was Bailey not in the attorney general's office engineering the guardianship agreement, he wasn't even in town.

In June of 1965 Bailey had to defend George Nassar, who was then being tried for the murder of Irvin Hilton. When the trial was well under way, Bailey says, Lieutenant Andrew Tuney ("a tall, handsome man") of the Strangler Task Force came to him to inquire about the possibility of interviewing Albert about the thirteen murders. Bailey consented, provided that George McGrath be present during the interrogation and that anything Albert said remain inadmissible as evidence. Tuney accepted the deal. John Donovan would be his co-interviewer.[*]

Whatever arrangement Bailey had made with Tuney, however, was anticipated by an agreement Bottomly

---

had long since struck with Asgeirsson. As Bottomly wrote Brooke on May 4, "I have indicated to Asgeirsson that [Albert's] interrogators would be me, Lt. Tuney and the head of the homicide bureau of the community when that particular crime was the subject of interrogation. Tapes would be made of the interrogations, transcriptions would then be prepared. The 'evidence' [note Bottomly's quote marks here] could then be thoroughly evaluated and compared with other information."

Interestingly, Bottomly was as of April 27 considering John Donovan as cointerrogator. A week later he seems to have changed his mind.

Meanwhile, Bailey was pursuing his own course. From *The Defense Never Rests:* "George McGrath and I met with Tuney and John Donovan to work out the arrangements for DeSalvo's interrogation. Tuney would question DeSalvo with McGrath present. DeSalvo would waive neither his right against self-incrimination nor his right to have counsel present. Whatever information the detectives obtained could only be used to help doctors involved in the case make their evaluations. The Boston Strangler would confess to police, but the confession would be inadmissible as legal evidence."

This meeting took place, according to Bailey, shortly after June 26, 1965.*

On that same day, in Essex Superior Court in Salem, George Nassar was convicted of first-degree murder and sentenced to die in the electric chair. Bailey vowed to appeal.

* * *

---

* Bailey, p. 167.

Whatever plans Bailey made concerning the interrogation of Albert went sadly awry. Ultimately it was Bottomly who, unaccompanied by Andrew Tuney, John Donovan, or any homicide detectives from Boston, Cambridge, Lawrence, Lynn, or Salem, took on that responsibility. The Task Force chief began his questioning in August and concluded it on September 29, 1965. George McGrath was present during some of these sessions. If anyone else was, his presence is not officially noted on the transcripts of the interrogation tapes.

Albert's confession to the murders of Anna Slesers, Nina Nichols, Helen Blake, Ida Irga, Jane Sullivan, Sophie Clark, Patricia Bissette, Mary Brown, Beverly Samans, Evelyn Corbin, Joann Graff, and Mary Sullivan* having been obtained, the problem now arose of what to do with this man. Certainly the self-proclaimed Strangler couldn't be released to prey on more women. Bailey thought it might be possible to have Albert tried but found not guilty by reason of insanity. But he foresaw problems with such a course of action. If, for example, the prosecutor at Albert's trial failed to call Ames Robey as a witness, Robey "might be on the major networks within hours, yelling 'fix.' " And Bailey was afraid for his own reputation, too, if despite all his efforts a jury found Albert guilty and *sane:* "I had an excellent change of being known as a lawyer

---

* He professed no knowledge of the slayings of Margaret Davis or Modeste Freeman. He did, however, claim to have caused the death of eighty-five-year-old Mary Mullen of Brighton on June 28, 1962. The story Albert allegedly told was that he'd broken into Mrs. Mullen's apartment and attempted to strangle her. But she died of a heart attack first. Mrs. Mullen's death had previously been attributed to natural causes. A very good suspect in the killing of Modeste Freeman was incarcerated in Bridgewater in 1964.

who'd taken a perfectly protected client and steered him into the electric chair."* He also fretted that some of his colleagues might label him a publicity seeker.

All that autumn of 1965 and winter and early spring of 1966 he and Brooke debated the next step, Bailey says. The former attorney general today recalls these discussions as having been more than heated and verging on the acrimonious.

"Oh, my goodness," Brooke laughs. "I had known F. Lee Bailey earlier. If you know what his personality is like, you know it was rocky. It was a tough negotiation; it didn't come off very easily."

"Ed and Lee crossed swords very vigorously," adds former Assistant Attorney General Roger Woodworth. They had "some sharp points of disagreement about the arrangement."

Before the matter of Albert's fate could be settled, however, a startling event took place, one that forced duelists Bailey and Brooke to sheath their rapiers momentarily. On April 8, 1966, John Bottomly abruptly resigned from the attorney general's office. No reason was publicly given for his action. Today Brooke cites an intraoffice quarrel as the cause of Bottomly's departure: "Jack had a rather short fuse." The blow-up, Brooke claims, had nothing to do with the Strangler case or its disposition.

William Cowin assumed Bottomly's duties. One of Cowin's first moves, according to Bailey, was to put in gear the machinery necessary to remove George McGrath as Albert's guardian—a move for which Bailey, despite his approval of McGrath, had been agitating recently. On April 12, a judge deemed Albert competent to handle his own affairs, legal and finan-

---

* Bailey, pp. 171–72. Bailey may have been overreacting here. There wasn't much chance Albert would be executed: no convicted felon had been in Massachusetts since 1948. Even Nassar would escape the chair.

cial. Within days of that decision, Bailey and Brooke reached their own agreement that Albert be brought to trial—not as the Boston Strangler but as the Green Man. Albert would plead not guilty by reason of insanity to the sexual assault charges filed against him in Cambridge. Bailey would then use the fact that Albert was really the Strangler to prove just how crazy his client was.

On June 7, 1966, the Supreme Judicial Court of Massachusetts ordered a new trial for George Nassar. The day before, the United States Supreme Court had made the same determination in the case of Samuel Sheppard.

F. Lee Bailey, attorney for both men, was on a roll. And in fine fettle. "I was on a dusty street in Dodge City," he writes, "and the bad guys were falling right and left."*

He didn't mean George Nassar and Sam Sheppard.

As a man now considered by the court capable of managing his own business, Albert entered a major contractual relationship on June 17, 1966. On that day, he signed a release to Gerold Frank granting the author "in perpetuity, throughout the world in all languages, the exclusive right to publish, sell, distribute, perform, or otherwise disseminate all my literary properties and rights to biographical material concerning me." In return Albert would receive from Frank an advance of fifteen thousand dollars against 10 percent of the first two hundred and 15 percent of any sums over that amount that Frank might earn from his book on the Boston Strangler.

---

* Bailey, p. 173.

Today Frank says he never asked for or received any such release from Albert for the book. But the document bearing Albert's signature and addressed to Frank is on file in the United States District Court in Boston.

It was witnessed by two individuals: F. Lee Bailey and Albert's former guardian, George McGrath.

Frank says that he believes Albert was supposed to be paid some release money for the movie that was made of Frank's book, but "he never got it." Frank adds, "I'm not sure why he didn't get it."

On June 30, 1966, Albert went before Judge Horace Cahill in the Middlesex Superior Court at a hearing to establish his competence to stand trial on the Green Man charges. The prosecutor was Assistant District Attorney Donald Conn.

Bailey's witnesses, Dr. Robert Ross Mezer and Dr. Samuel Tartakoff (one of the state-appointed psychiatrists who had examined DeSalvo), testified that Albert was competent to stand trial.

The prosecution witness, Dr. Ames Robey, testified the opposite. He says today that he did so because at that point "Albert so badly wanted to be the Strangler" that he had passed beyond rationality and was therefore incapable of participating in his own defense.

A few days later, Judge Cahill ruled that Albert was fit to stand trial on the Green Man charges.

The logic behind Bailey's winning argument was convoluted but clever: He did not label Albert the Strangler, but simply as someone responsible for "certain crimes." Of course, everyone in the courtroom knew exactly what those "certain crimes" were. At any rate, Bailey's contention was that while Albert had been insane when he committed his Green Man sexual assaults (and by implication insane also when he did the stranglings), he was now sufficiently mentally healthy to be tried for his lesser offenses.

Robey, who held the opposite view, did not prevail.

On July 4, 1966, Albert wrote Gerold Frank that he had appointed George McGrath as his "agent and fiduciary in certain business transactions specifically including those which now exist or may develop between yourself and me." Albert further requested that any monies owed him be sent to McGrath, who would be empowered to endorse and cash the checks. Those checks should, however, be made out to one "Robert McKay."

This statement was witnessed by F. Lee Bailey.

John Bottomly was not the only person to quit his job. So did Task Force members Sandra Irizarry and Andrew Tuney. Stephen Delaney, another member of the team, had returned to his old post at the Metropolitan District Commission in July of 1965. By late 1966, they had all found new employment.

Irizarry, Tuney, and Delaney now worked for F. Lee Bailey.

On July 24, 1966, Bailey undertook the defense of Carl Coppolino, an anesthesiologist indicted for killing his mistress's husband in New Jersey in 1963 and his own wife, Carmela, in Florida in 1965. Andrew Tuney acted as one of Bailey's investigators in the case.

On August 5, 1966, the William Morris Agency, representing Gerold Frank, sent George McGrath, now the Commissioner of Corrections for the City of New York, a check for fifteen thousand dollars. This check was made out to and endorsed by "Robert McKay," and made payable to the order of F. Lee Bailey.

In its August and September issues, *The Ladies' Home Journal* ran excerpts from Gerold Frank's *The Boston Strangler.* In October, New American Library published the book in hardcover. It became an immediate best-seller.

The book identified Albert DeSalvo by name as the Strangler—and further as the rapist of *over two thousand women.*

Ames Robey remembers hearing this claim and wondering how Albert had found the time.

The November 5, 1966, number of the *Saturday Evening Post* featured an article entitled "F. Lee Bailey: Renegade in the Courtroom." A long and flattering account of the lawyer's personal history and legal exploits (illustrated with photos of Bailey and his quondam secretary and second wife, Froma "Wicki" Bailey, relaxing aboard their sloop and lounging at their home wet bar), it again named Albert as the killer of thirteen women. "Bailey's tactic," author Edward Linn wrote, "has been to publicize as much as possible that DeSalvo is the Strangler, which has made the Boston Bar Association unhappy."

Just how unhappy the association was would become manifest in the spring of 1967.

In December of 1966, Bailey won another great legal battle. Carl Coppolino was found not guilty of having slain William Farber, the husband of Coppolino's ex-mistress Marge Farber. It was Marge Farber who had launched the original accusations of murder against

Coppolino. Bailey dismissed Mrs. Farber's statements to the authorities as the vendetta of a woman scorned.

Albert did not go to trial on the Green Man charges until January of 1967, well after he had already been convicted in the court of worldwide opinion as perhaps the most dangerous criminal in history. Why the delay?

Bailey writes that not only was his own court calendar full until then but that "Donald Conn and I agreed that there was nothing to be gained by trying an already sensational case on the eve of a senatorial election."*

Edward Brooke won that 1966 election. His opponent was Endicott Peabody, former Democratic governor of Massachusetts.

---

* Bailey, p. 178.

12

The Green Man Goes to Trial

Why did Albert DeSalvo, dedicated family man, want so much to be known as a killer more bloodthirsty than Jack the Ripper?

"He had a desperate need to be somebody important," says Ames Robey.

"He enjoyed the notoriety of the situation," says former Cambridge Police Detective Michael Giacoppo.

"He had a deep-rooted need to be famous," says Attorney Thomas Troy, who represented Albert after Bailey and Asgeirsson had passed from the picture.

Members of Albert's family confirm his tendency toward delusions of grandeur. Irmgard herself, according to Albert's own admission, constantly chided him for his self-promoting exaggerations, which acutely embarrassed her when he inflicted them on the couple's friends. Even Gerold Frank, who maintains today that he has no doubt Albert was the Strangler, reported in his book a number of occasions on which Albert spoke quite gleefully of all the fame that would come his way by virtue of his confession to being the murderer of thirteen women.

Beyond the fulfillment of a fantasy of celebrity, did Albert have a practical reason for proclaiming himself the Strangler? Everyone, including Bailey, agrees that he did—he believed he could sell his story for sufficient money to keep Irmgard, Judy, and Michael financially secure for the rest of their lives. And on top of that there was the reward money offered by Governor Peabody in 1964. Gerold Frank writes that Albert and George Nassar may have mistakenly believed that ten thousand dollars would be paid for information leading to the arrest and conviction of the murderer of *each* Strangler victim, a sum in excess of one hundred thousand dollars, which the two men could then split, Nassar presumably taking his cut as the agent who represented Albert's confession to Bailey.*

Although one hundred thousand dollars, even two hundred thousand dollars, was a lot more money in 1965 than it is today, how great a sum could it seem in exchange for a lifetime behind the bars of a maximum security prison or a state mental hospital? For this was precisely the trade Albert seemed ready to make.

He apparently felt that he had no freedom left to lose.

Even his lawyer maintained this view. In *The Defense Never Rests,* Bailey writes that he told Brooke and Bottomly, " 'Look, when I met Albert, there were enough indictments pending against him to pretty much insure that he'd never be walking the streets again.' "†

In fact, Bailey was being overly pessimistic. For all

---

* What Governor Peabody had in fact offered was ten thousand dollars total for a solution to any one or all of the killings. Albert's misapprehension would be confirmed at his 1967 trial.
† Bailey, p. 172.

his past adult offenses, sexual and otherwise, Albert
had served less than a year in jail. Admittedly, the
Green Man charges were more serious than anything
he'd faced previously. But even if Albert had been tried
and found guilty on all of them, according to several
legal authorities, he probably would have received a
maximum sentence of twenty-five years with an almost
certain parole after ten. This was not a pleasing prospect, certainly, but neither again was it a lifetime in
durance vile.

Albert, who was street-smart, could have figured this
out for himself. But here the street-smart Albert ran
up against the gullible and easily led Albert. Who can
say why it turned out that way? Perhaps the shock of
being sent to Bridgewater rather than to Westborough
State Hospital as he had hoped had caused something
in Albert to snap, sending his judgment into limbo.
The fact remains that sometime between November
1964 and the winter and early spring of 1965, someone
apparently convinced Albert that his most recent arrest
guaranteed him a permanent place on the guest rolls
of a state correctional facility.

The Commonwealth of Massachusetts fired its opening gun in the matter of Albert Henry DeSalvo on
January 10, 1967, in Middlesex Superior Court in Cambridge. Judge Cornelius Moynihan would preside. Assistant District Attorney Donald Conn would prosecute
the case. Albert would be represented by Bailey and
Asgeirsson, whose role as co-counsel seemed to have
slipped Bailey's mind by the time he came to write *The
Defense Never Rests.**

---

* Bailey suffered a similar odd lapse of memory in the fall
of 1968, when asked in U.S. District Court when he had
first met Albert. Bailey wasn't exactly sure; he thought it
might have been in February of 1965. In 1971, he was able

The process of jury selection began. Most of the women called declined to serve on the then judicially acceptable grounds that the testimony they would hear would be unfit for female ears. It was reported that counsel finally agreed that an all-male jury be empaneled. Some of the relatively few women spectators at the trial appeared unhappy with the decision.

Before the jury was chosen, however, Judge Moynihan held a preliminary hearing to determine whether Albert was competent to stand trial. The Commonwealth's first witness in this matter was Samuel Allen, a psychiatrist who had observed Albert at Bridgewater.* Allen's finding was that Albert was mentally capable of understanding the charges against him and the nature of the concomitant legal proceedings; he was also, in Allen's opinion, fit to participate in his own defense.

Bailey then called Albert to the stand. Albert testified that he had thoroughly consulted with his cocounsels Bailey and Asgeirsson and that he understood the nature of the defense they had prepared for him. He affirmed that he was fully cognizant that he might receive a heavy sentence if the jury found him guilty of the charges brought against him. He was aware of, and agreeable to, the fact that Bailey did not intend to argue any of the factual allegations made against him.

On January 10, Judge Moynihan wrote his decision: "I find that the Defendant is alert, intelligent, and is well able to understand questions put to him and to give rational and intelligent answers thereto. On the

---

to specify the date as March 4, 1965, citing the Bridgewater visitors' book as his source. The log does confirm that Bailey was at Bridgewater that day.

* And who was now its acting medical director, Robey having left to become director of the Center for Forensic Psychiatry in Ann Arbor, Michigan.

witness stand, he indicated adequate emotional control, despite a rather trying cross-examination.

"I conclude, therefore, that the defendant at the present time is not suffering from a mental disease, disorder, or defect to such an extent as to affect his capacity to understand the nature of the charges on which he is being tried, the nature and purpose of this criminal proceeding, the possible penalties and verdicts that may result from the trial and the nature of the defenses available to him. I further find that he does have the capacity to cooperate with and to assist his counsel in the defense."

Bailey's defense strategy was basically the same one he'd used at Albert's competency hearing in June 1966. Only this time he did not delicately allude to "certain crimes" his client had committed. Rather, Bailey openly referred to Albert as the Boston Strangler. It was the lawyer's reasoning that any man who would commit thirteen gruesome sex murders in the course of eighteen months was obviously hopelessly insane. And if this could be vividly demonstrated to a jury—which Bailey, armed with the knowledge of Albert's confession, had no doubt it could—that jury would surely find DeSalvo not guilty by reason of insanity on the lesser charges of rape and armed robbery.

In this order, Suzanne Macht, Geraldine Surette, Muriel LeBlanc, and Virginia Thorner took the stand to recount what Albert had done to them. DeSalvo stipulated to the identifications made of him by all four women. Sergeant Duncan McNeill of the Cambridge Police Department testified that Albert had described to him the defendant's rapid and noise-free method of housebreaking: DeSalvo had cut strips of plastic from detergent bottles and with these slipped locks.

McNeill informed the court that Albert had admitted to him robbing Mrs. LeBlanc, and that he had also committed another break-in in which he netted eight or nine dollars from a child's piggy bank. Albert told McNeill that the gun he'd held to Mrs. LeBlanc's head had been a toy one and that although he carried a knife, "I never killed anybody."

McNeill also testified that in the Malden police station he'd overheard Albert say to his sister Irene and to Irmgard, "Please, let me be a man just this once."

Albert had tried to evade the authorities on the morning of November 5, 1964.* When McNeill asked him why he'd done so, Albert had replied that he knew he was in trouble and wanted to settle his affairs, principally the sale of his car and house. He told McNeill that he wanted Irmgard to have the profits.

The suspect did have three hundred dollars on his person when taken into custody, McNeill recollected for the court. Albert claimed it was the proceeds from the sale of his car. And, McNeill added, a lawyer showed up at the police station that evening with a paper for Albert to sign regarding the sale of his house. McNeill said that he had advised Albert to consult Jon Asgeirsson, the attorney now representing him, before putting his signature on anything.

McNeill's final piece of direct testimony was to state that the defendant had remarked to him that the Malden police officer who'd arrested Albert had been an old man. "You know," Albert had commented, "I could have taken that gun from him and shot him. But what the hell."

On cross-examination, Sergeant McNeill revealed that Albert had asked McNeill to "help" him.

The defendant's psychiatric case was first stated by Dr. James A. Brussel, associate commissioner of the New

---

* Out on bail after his November 3 arraignment, he was being sought by police on November 5 for questioning on out-of-state assault charges.

York State Department of Mental Health. A former member of the Strangler Task Force's Medical-Psychiatric Committee, Dr. Brussel was now, like Sandra Irizarry, Andrew Tuney, and Stephen Delaney, in the employ of F. Lee Bailey. Dr. Brussel told the court that he had examined Albert for a total of four to five hours on October 16, 1965, and January 9, 1967. During those sessions Brussel interviewed the defendant about his life. Brussel said that Albert had given him an autobiography replete with anecdotes of "abnormal behavior with family, friends, and animals." Albert also, according to Brussel, had discussed his sexual activities with the wives of fellow officers while he was in the army and his exploits as the Measuring Man.

Brussel further told the court that Albert had admitted to him experiencing a "brain sensation" that would compel him to leave work and go looking for an apartment to break into and plunder.

Brussel went on to testify that in April 1964, as part of his duty to the Medical-Psychiatric Committee, he had profiled whomever the Strangler might be as a paranoid schizophrenic. During cross-examination he allowed that Albert in 1966 and 1967 did not quite fit this diagnosis, although Brussel did indeed find the defendant in 1966 suffering from a chronic undifferentiated type of schizophrenia with paranoid features. The doctor had also found that although Albert had been driven by an irresistible impulse to commit his Green Man crimes, he had been sufficiently *compos mentis* to take the precautions necessary to avoid detection by the police.

Brussel did not conduct a physical exam or any neurological testing of the defendant, nor did he inquire of the Bridgewater guards whether Albert had betrayed any symptoms of violence or disorder.

During redirect examination Brussel told the court that the defendant knew the difference between right and wrong under the dictates of law, religion, and morality, and that he was fully aware his actions were criminal. He was, however, Brussel reiterated, driven by an urge he could not control.

Brussel also said that Albert had never spoken to him of any ambition to make money by admitting to the stranglings. (Brussel may have been unique in this respect, since Albert broadcast the desire to profit from his crimes to virtually everyone else who came within earshot.) Nor did Brussel consider Albert a compulsive confessor.

Bailey's next hired psychiatric gun, Dr. Robert Ross Mezer, testified that Albert, whom he had seen four times during March 1965, three times during April 1965, and seven times the following year, was a long-term sexual psychopath who as a child had tortured dogs and cats and had once strangled another boy until his eyes had rolled back in his head.

Mezer also told Judge Moynihan and the jury that Albert had confessed to him the murders of thirteen women and provided the doctor with a complete account of his nonhomicidal sexual assaults.

Mezer further stated that Albert had told him he labored under an uncontrollable urge that forced him to wander various neighborhoods in search of an apartment he could break or talk his way into in order to have sex with the female occupant.

One of Mezer's most intriguing revelations was that Albert had told him he'd feigned the hallucinations he'd experienced in the house of correction—those of Irmgard furiously chastising him—for the purpose of *being sent back to Bridgewater.* Bailey, of course, had been maintaining all along that his client was desperate to get *out* of Bridgewater. And Albert himself was explicit about his hatred of the place.

The first witness called to the stand by the Commonwealth was Stanley Setterlund, a Bridgewater inmate who had, according to his own testimony, become one of Albert's confidants. Setterlund told the court that Albert had admitted to him being the strangler of eleven women (as opposed to the thirteen he allegedly told Mezer he'd killed) and that his knowledge was worth a great deal of money—ten thousand dollars per victim. Setterlund further stated that Albert had told him that he had cased the residences of his female victims and then entered them with the intent of committing robbery and rape. If the women screamed or fought, he strangled them. He cleaned up after himself, leaving no physical evidence behind, and would purposely refrain from taking all the money and valuables from the apartment so that police would believe the victim had been murdered by a sex maniac and not by a robber.

Setterlund testified that Albert had told him that he didn't want to spend the rest of his life rotting in prison, that he wanted to be sent to a mental hospital and be cured of his condition—and that *Life* magazine had offered him ninety thousand dollars for his life story, the *Saturday Evening Post* forty thousand.

Setterlund also told the court that he had first met Albert in the company of George Nassar, and that his— Setterlund's—own attorney had once been F. Lee Bailey.

John A. Keriakos, deputy master of the Billerica House of Correction, testified that Albert's behavior during his 1961 incarceration there had been perfectly normal; Adam Kozlowski, a senior officer at the Middlesex County House of Correction, deemed the defendant a model prisoner. Thereafter the Commonwealth called to the stand several of Albert's previous employers, all of whom told essentially the same story: that the defendant was a hard worker, courteous, congenial, and entirely normal in his speech, behavior, and dress. He had put in an eight-and-a-half-hour day for the Highland Contracting Company on June 8, 1964, the day of the assault on Virginia Thorner, and an eight-hour day for the same company on October 27, 1964, the day of the assault on Suzanne Macht.

A Malden man, Harold Orent, testified that he had known Albert from April of 1963 to November of 1964 and never noticed anything out of the ordinary about his actions or demeanor. Albert had in fact been in the Orent home on over a hundred occasions to do remodeling work. Anna Orent, Harold Orent's wife, said that she and her children had been alone in the house with Albert on a number of occasions and that his behavior had always been impeccable.

The Commonwealth's final witnesses were three psychiatrists: The state called back Samual Allen and called in Ames Robey and Samuel Tartakoff, both of whom had figured in Albert's various competency hearings in the spring of 1965 and the spring and early summer of 1966.

Ames Robey was the first to take the stand. He testified that Albert had told him also of faking his hallucinations, something Albert had admitted anyway at his February 1965 hearing. Robey further described the defendant as a con artist and a manipulator who could clearly distinguish between right and wrong. His present diagnosis of Albert was that the man suffered from a sociopathic personality disorder with schizoid features. Robey concluded that Albert had not been driven by an irresistible impulse to commit his Green Man offenses.

As far as Robey was concerned, the only uncontrollable urge Albert suffered from was the desire to be branded the Strangler.

Doctors Allen and Tartakoff substantially agreed with Robey that Albert knew right from wrong and that no inner demon had goaded him into his actions.

Tartakoff added that he had taken no history from
Albert of any "brain sensations" or "little fires" (as
Tartakoff called them) occurring in the defendant's
head, as defense witness Brussel claimed he had. Albert's sociopathy was treatable, but the prognosis for
him was not good.

Before he left the stand, Tartakoff mentioned that
Albert had once described himself to the psychiatrist
as having a fast mouth and the ability to talk his way
into anything.

The jury heard no further testimony.

The press coverage of the trial was, as might be
expected, phenomenal. Although Albert himself was
under heavy guard—clearly the authorities feared
not just an escape attempt but that someone might
try to kill him—it was his attorney whose life appeared to be in danger. In a typeface only slightly
smaller than that generally used for a declaration of
war, the *Record American* ran this headline on Thursday, January 12: BAILEY'S LIFE THREATENED. The paper went on to report that additional court officers
and fifteen cops were "rushed" to the trial because
two gunmen were believed to be on their way from
Boston to assassinate not only Bailey but his "attractive blonde wife" Wicki.

The threat had apparently been phoned in to
the Middlesex County District Attorney's Office.
When word of it was passed to Assistant District
Attorney Conn, Judge Moynihan declared a recess.
Wicki Bailey was hustled from the courtroom and,
according to the *Record,* Bailey, Conn, and Moynihan adjourned for "a mysterious, hour-long, lobby
conference." Bailey emerged from it looking grim.
When reporters asked him what the problem was,
he replied, "I can't tell you." As to the whereabouts

of the abruptly vanished Wicki, Bailey would only say, "I've got her locked up."

Happily, no assassins appeared at the Middlesex County Courthouse that day, nor for the duration of the trial. The *Record* reported that the threat had *not* been in retaliation for his defense of the Strangler (Bailey says it was), although how this could be established with any precision is unclear since no trace of the gunmen who could provide the explanation for their motive was ever found. Wicki was released from purdah and the trial resumed.

On Friday, January 13, the *Record* bore another banner headline: DESALVO IS THE STRANGLER, with the subheading "Bailey Bares 13 Murders in 18 Months as Acts of an Insane Man." Framing the headlines were close-up mug-style shots of Albert arriving at Superior Court, looking grim in the full-face shot and somewhat bemused in the profile. According to the *Boston Herald*, Bailey had in court that day described his client as "a completely uncontrollable vegetable," in need, the *Herald* writer dryly suggested, of a suitable bin.

Also in its Friday the thirteenth issue the *Record* announced that it would begin running excerpts from Gerold Frank's *The Boston Strangler*. And directly underneath that announcement, on page four, ran a notice that the *Advertiser*, the Sunday edition of the *Record*, would run in its *Pictorial Living Coloroto Magazine* an article by resident gossipist Harold Banks called "At Home With the F. Lee Baileys"—a piece promised to be "*as bright and informal* as the Baileys really are. The cover shows the family relaxing before a blazing fireplace."

A small article at the bottom of the same page informed anyone who might be interested that the death toll of U.S. servicemen in Vietnam that week had dropped to sixty-seven.

For the fashion-conscious reader, the *Record* also

thoughtfully provided a commentary on Wicki's court-room couture.*

Ames Robey edged Bailey and Albert from the *Record* headline sweepstakes on January 17: MD SHAKES STRANGLER STORY. On January 18, it was John Bottomly's turn to be tabloid man of the hour: CALL STRANGLER PROBER TO TELL CONFESSIONS. The former assistant attorney general didn't rate the all-caps treatment Bailey, Albert, and Robey had.

(Not only was Bottomly relegated to the lower case, he never even mounted the stand. Judge Moynihan tartly refused to allow his testimony, on the grounds that Albert wasn't being tried for the Strangler murders, which in any case they'd already heard far too much about from Dr. Mezer. Bottomly's exclusion was a defeat for Bailey.)

Given its magnitude, Albert's trial was a short one. On January 19, the *Record* informed its readers that JURY HOLDS STRANGLER'S FATE. Not the Green Man's fate. The *Strangler's* fate.

The jury had not, incidentally, been sequestered, nor had it been prohibited from reading press accounts of the trial. That was also true of the prosecution and defense witnesses.

On the morning of January 18, Bailey and Conn made their closing arguments. Bailey asked the jury to find his client not guilty by reason of insanity: "It is up to you to determine whether he is sick. I suggest that he is, based on the testimony of witnesses. I did

---

* Singer Connie Francis, appearing at Blinstrub's in Boston, took time out from her rehearsal schedule to attend one day of the trial. Albert was reported to have thought that very nice of her. Ironically, Francis herself would in later years fall victim to a rapist more savage than any of Albert's Green Man victims claimed him to be.

not cross-examine some witnesses for reasons of decency. Their own stories about Albert indicate that he did not act like a normal human being. He was then, as he is now, very sick."

Bailey then went on to ask the jury to heed the testimony of doctors Brussel, Mezer, and Tartakoff, but to disregard that of Robey. The lawyer then accused Robey of changing his diagnosis of Albert to suit the circumstances. "You can expect at least consistent testimony and proof," Bailey declaimed. "If, as Shakespeare said, 'let's kill off the lawyers,' I say, well, let's kill off the psychiatrists, too."

Donald Conn, who had snickered audibly—and quite deliberately—at Bailey throughout his summation, had his turn at bat: "This is a man [DeSalvo] who wants you to believe he is a vegetable, overwrought and overwhelmed by irresistible impulses," the assistant district attorney charged. "Don't be dissuaded [sic] by his cuteness and cunning. You're going to have to live with your conscience when you get out of here just as I am with mine. Are you going to sit there and let this man get in a hospital and get out in a few years? Stamp his conduct for what it is—vicious, wrong, cruel, criminal conduct. Don't allow him to fake, feign, and con you right out of your shoes like he conned a couple of doctors."

Judge Moynihan instructed the jurors that there were three possible verdicts in this case: guilty, not guilty, and not guilty by reason of insanity.

The jury went out at 12:37 P.M. on January 18.

Three hours and forty-five minutes later, the foreman sent word that a verdict had been reached. The jurors filed back into the courtroom.

"All rise," the bailiff ordered. Those present shuffled to their feet. Albert, wearing a neat dark suit, white shirt, and tie, stood quietly awaiting his fate.

"How do you find the defendant?" Judge Moynihan asked.

The answer was unhesitating: guilty on all counts.

Judge Moynihan pronounced sentence: imprisonment for life. It was a statutorily imposed sentence, he explained, that would not ordinarily have been handed down but for the very clear indication that Albert was the Strangler.

Bailey's strategy had backfired; his insistence on identifying Albert as the murderer of thirteen women had resulted in exactly what attorney and client had striven to avoid. The jury of twelve men, all of whom had mothers if not also daughters, wives, sisters, granddaughters, and nieces, were not about to run the risk that this "twisted, driven vegetable" ever again be permitted to walk the streets. Nor was Cornelius Moynihan.

Nonetheless, Bailey today has no regrets about how he handled Albert's defense, maintaining still that he saved his client from the electric chair.

Francis C. Newton, Jr., smiles slightly at this claim: "If Bailey hadn't done what he'd done, Albert would be alive and free today."

PART THREE

13

A Great Escape, a Musical Interlude, and More Wheeling and Dealing

The same day he was sentenced to spend the rest of his life behind bars,* Albert was committed to the custody of the superintendent of Bridgewater State Hospital. That night he was back at the institution he so despised to await shipment to the state's toughest maximum security prison, MCI-Walpole.

Bailey moved immediately for a stay of execution of the sentence to Walpole, which Moynihan granted. On January 20, Asgeirsson and Bailey filed on behalf of their client a motion for a new trial, claiming errors of law regarding the standard of criminal responsibility

---

* On the armed robbery charge; the indecent assault convictions earned him a ten-year sentence.

applied to Albert. One week later, the attorneys amended that motion with further grounds: The guilty verdict in the case was against the weight of the evidence.

Moynihan denied the request for a new trial on February 1. On February 21, Bailey and Asgeirsson filed a claim of appeal to the Supreme Judicial Court of Massachusetts.

At 11:00 A.M. on the same day, Herbert DeSimone, the attorney general of Rhode Island, had a meeting with Massachusetts State Police Detective Lieutenant Joseph Simons, Detective Phillip DiNatale of the Boston Police Department and the Strangler Bureau, Charles Burnim, a lawyer from Bailey's office, and Ira Schreber, a lawyer who would serve as DeSalvo's Rhode Island counsel. The meeting was held to discuss the assault and robbery of a Central Falls, Rhode Island, woman that had taken place on July 3, 1964. Albert had allegedly volunteered the information that he'd committed this crime. But another man, Roland Petit, had been charged with and convicted of the offense and was now serving time for it. The victim had apparently identified Petit as her assailant.

This, like all the other out-of-state charges against Albert, would eventually be put on a permanent hold.

On Friday, February 24, at 12:20 A.M., Albert and two of his fellow inmates, George Harrison and Frederick Erickson, escaped from Bridgewater.

That the three had vanished from their adjoining cells in the I Wing went unnoticed until 6:15 on Friday morning. One hour earlier, and again a half-hour after that, a guard had looked into each cell through a peephole and seen what he would swear were human forms in each bed. In fact, those forms were blankets plumped and twisted to resemble sleeping bodies.

The breakout, which Albert, Erickson, and Harrison

had apparently been planning for several days at least, was childishly simple to accomplish. One of them had obtained a key to unlock their cells. The three then walked down a third-floor corridor to where an elevator was being installed. They removed the plywood covering the shaft, climbed down the scaffolding inside it, and stepped out onto the hospital grounds. They scaled a twenty-foot inner wall, a second thirty-foot outer one, and dropped down to freedom on the other side, landing in a bed of new-fallen snow.

Albert was supposedly armed with a gun, Erickson and Harrison with a half a pair of scissors each.

At 2:20 A.M., the stolen car in which they were driving ran out of fuel, so they coasted into a gas station on Route 28 in North Easton. Albert tried to charge three dollars' worth of gas. The teenage attendant wouldn't let him, so they asked the young man to call them a taxi. Instead, he called the police—not because he was aware that he had three escaped felons on his hands, but to report a vehicle breakdown. Albert, Erickson, and Harrison had disappeared into a nearby woods by the time a cruiser appeared.

Either Albert and the others somehow retrieved their car and got it going or stole another one. Police and press reports are confused and conflicting about this particular part of the escape. What is definite is that the trio managed to reach Everett, where Albert's brother Joseph lived, before running out of gas again. Albert called Joe; Harrison and Erickson made phone calls of their own.

A few minutes later Joseph picked up the three and drove them to Richard DeSalvo's house in Chelsea. Richard gave Albert money and fresh clothing. All five then drove to Sullivan Square in Charlestown, where Harrison and Erickson wanted to be dropped. Albert gave them ten dollars apiece.

By this time, the escape had been discovered and reported. Hundreds of state troopers and municipal police joined in the manhunt for the fugitives. Armed guards were posted around the homes of the witnesses, judge, and prosecutor in Albert's trial.

Joseph and Albert took Richard to work in Chelsea. From there, Joseph drove Albert to Lynn, where they parted company in front of a drugstore on Western Avenue.*

Albert, thinking that he had been spotted, broke into an apartment to hide for a few minutes. When it seemed safe, he left the apartment and broke into the cellar of a house on Western Avenue. He put together a makeshift bed and turned on his transistor radio to listen to the news of his escape.

By 10:23 P.M., Harrison and Erickson, who had spent their first and only day of freedom drinking—and in Harrison's case, ingesting drugs—at the Melody Lounge in Waltham, were back in custody. They had surrendered voluntarily to the authorities, who bought the pair hamburgers to blot up some of the alcohol they'd consumed before returning them to Bridgewater.

Albert went for a walk around the Lynn General Electric plant until 2:00 A.M. Cold and hungry, he went back to his cellar refuge. There he broke into a locked bin and discovered two sea bags, one of which held a navy uniform. Albert dressed in that, leaving his dis-

---

* Richard and Joseph would be indicted but never tried or convicted for aiding and abetting the escape. The next day, Richard would also be arrested by the FBI and charged with illegal possession of a weapon and transporting it over state lines. Richard's defense was that his employer, a New Hampshire trucker, required his drivers to keep a handgun in their vehicles. The FBI, which stated that Richard's arrest had nothing to do with Albert's escape, did not pursue the charge. Richard's lawyer was Jon Asgeirsson.

carded clothing—and an automatic pistol wrapped in a white T-shirt—on a bench.

Around 2:30 in the afternoon, he walked into the Simon Uniform Store on Western Avenue and asked to use their phone to call his lawyer. He feared the authorities were closing in on him, and he didn't want to be shot by an overzealous cop.

Five minutes later he was arrested by a Lynn patrol officer and taken to the police station and then to court. The judge ordered him to MCI-Walpole immediately. He arrived there at 7:15 P.M.

To quote from the police report: "DeSalvo entered the Walpole State Prison and was thoroughly searched by Supervisor John J. Mahoney and Senior Officer Edward J. Cronin. After DeSalvo was stripped naked and searched, he was placed in his cell for his long-term sentence."

Albert had gone from bad to worse.

He had also been reunited with George Nassar.

At the news of Albert's escape, the press went wild. The *Record* promptly offered a five-thousand-dollar reward for his capture. It furnished a list of protection do's and don'ts alongside an article entitled WOMEN BEWARE! HE'S A SMOOTHIE. It warned that the female population was in grave danger not only from Albert but from Erickson and Harrison.

The public reaction was predictable. "I'm scared out of my mind," a Beacon Hill secretary told Jonathan Klarfeld of the *Globe*. Klarfeld also reported that a resident of the town of Bridgewater was keeping a shotgun by her side as she did her housework. A local sportswriter, a twelve-year-old at the time, today recalls that his mother made him stay indoors for two whole days. Nor were any of his friends permitted to play outside while Albert was on the loose.

In Harvard Square, however, where sangfroid

reigned supreme, women shrugged off the danger. The same was true in the affluent suburbs, just as it had been during the Strangler scare of 1962–64. According to one Andover woman, Albert's escape was "sort of a distant joke, really. We knew he wouldn't be coming here."

If Albert's destination wasn't Andover, what was it? Media speculation abounded. Ames Robey thought he might try to lose himself in the population of a big city, wrote the *Globe*'s Sara Davidson. Mexico might be his goal, another source felt. And Samuel Allen thought Albert might head for Germany, where Irmgard, Judy, and Michael were now living near Bremen. Allen supposedly characterized Albert's putative need to see his wife and children as a "keen, twisted desire."

Erickson and Harrison later told authorities they'd overheard him discuss with Richard and Joseph the possibility of taking a plane somewhere, of "flying out."

While all this was going on, F. Lee Bailey was in Charleston, South Carolina, defending Air Force Captain Jack Simon in court-martial proceedings. Simon had been charged with molesting four children at the base swimming pool. On the evening of February 24, the captain was acquitted. BAILEY DOES IT—AGAIN! the *Record* crowed the following day.

Bailey's first step on learning of Albert's escape was to offer a reward of his own—ten thousand dollars for the *safe* return of his client to custody. He feared that the five-thousand-dollar booty put up by the *Record* might encourage some trigger-happy citizen or cop to shoot Albert on sight. He also angrily denounced the Commonwealth for "double-crossing" his client by reneging on its promise to get him good psychiatric help.

Bailey added that he wasn't surprised Albert had

fled Bridgewater, because he had been extremely depressed and despairing after his conviction, resentful
that the Commonwealth had so ill repaid his cooperation with it. (Albert would later claim that he had
escaped in order to dramatize the hellish conditions
at Bridgewater.) Bailey also said that he didn't think
the self-admitted Strangler posed much danger to the
public at present, since his urge to kill had been
sated years ago with the murder of Mary Sullivan.

The fact that DeSalvo, Erickson, and Harrison had
been able to slip so easily out of Bridgewater was a
major concern and a major embarrassment to the
authorities. "I'm shocked and very upset," said Governor John Volpe, who ordered Public Safety Commissioner Leo Laughlin to look into the matter.* State
Representatives Robert Cawley and George Sacco
would ask a legislative committee to investigate. "It
could only happen in Massachusetts," the *Globe* edito-
rialized acidly, going on to remark that while most
states in the union had mass murderers, only the Commonwealth seemed incapable of keeping its mass murderers under lock and key.

The saga of Albert Henry DeSalvo, already bizarre,
sordid, and tragic, took on a dimension that was down-
right ludicrous the following month. Having transferred the literary and theatrical rights to his life story
to Gerold Frank, Albert had now gone into the music

---

* Superintendent Charles Gaughan, who had been pleading
  for years that the state upgrade security at its principal
  holding facility for the criminally insane, without result,
  may have been grimly amused by this sudden flurry of
  attention.

business. On March 15, C-C-M Productions of Cambridge announced the release of a recording based on a poem Albert had written while in Bridgewater.

It was entitled "Strangler in the Night."

All the profits from the record would go to the Foundation to Study the Cause and Treatment of Sexual Disorders—established by C-C-M.

C-C-M Executive Vice President Samuel A. Cammarata told the press that "this recording tells, in part, [Albert's] feelings during the period he was undergoing psychiatric tests at Bridgewater State Hospital . . . DeSalvo would not receive a penny from the sale." C-C-M legal counsel Joseph Balliro said that the foundation expected to realize ten thousand dollars from sales.

"Strangler in the Night" did not make the Top Forty, although it did become a very minor kitsch classic.

On March 20, Bernard Schultz, manager of the main Lynn post office, reported to the police that he had a package addressed to Mr. A. DeSalvo of 785 Western Avenue. The package was a bundle of books from the Doubleday Book Club. Some anonymous practical joker had made a note of Albert's hideout address as published in the press and used it to enroll him in the club.

It was the kind of stunt Albert himself might have pulled.

While Albert was busy fashioning a new career as the Frank Sinatra of Walpole State Prison, Donald Conn was settling into his new position as assistant attorney general of the Commonwealth, to which he had been appointed very shortly after the Green Man trial.

He was hired by Elliot Richardson, who had succeeded Edward Brooke as attorney general.

Richardson and Conn, along with Herbert Travers, head of the Criminal Division, were taking a serious look at the possibility of trying Albert for the stranglings.

And the Boston Bar Association was taking a serious look at F. Lee Bailey's role as Albert's defense attorney.

Nineteen-sixty-seven saw a number of setbacks for F. Lee Bailey. One was the April trial of Carl Coppolino in Florida. It ended that same month with Coppolino being convicted of second-degree murder in the death of his wife Carmela. And in August, George Nassar would be reconvicted of the murder of Irwin Hilton. This time, the jury recommended that Nassar be sentenced to life imprisonment rather than execution. Judge Donald Macauley followed its recommendation.

There were other difficulties for Bailey. In *The Defense Never Rests*, he writes that his tribulations with the Boston Bar Association began in June, after he applied to the Supreme Judicial Court of Massachusetts for a certificate of good standing in order to represent Coppolino at his Florida appeal.* Bailey expected the application to be routinely approved. He was instead informed that it would be held up because the Bar Association had some "matters of concern" regarding Bailey that they wanted to discuss with him first.

These "matters of concern," according to Bailey, were "a report that [he] intended to play [him]self in a movie about the Sam Sheppard case," "a contract [he] had signed with David Susskind's Talent Associates for an ABC-TV series that fall," "[his] appearance

---

* A lawyer must obtain one of these from his home state to be eligible to conduct legal business in another state.

on CBS radio in Boston to discuss [an aspect of the Plymouth mail robbery case] with a local interviewer named Paul Benzaquin [one of George Nassar's supporters]," "[his] appearances on the Joey Bishop and Johnny Carson TV shows after Carl Coppolino's conviction, during which [he] attacked the verdict," and "the fact that [he] had contracted to write [*The Defense Never Rests*], and engaged a literary agent [Sterling Lord]."*

Bailey asked another lawyer to assist him in addressing the questions the Bar Association's grievance committee had raised about his conduct. That lawyer was Joseph Balliro, counsel for the Cambridge corporation producing "Strangler in the Night."

Bailey and Balliro met with the grievance committee, and, Bailey writes, it accepted his explanation of "the matters of concern." He received his certificate of good standing.

But documents on file in the Massachusetts State Record Office clearly suggest that the Boston Bar Association had in mind issues somewhat weightier than book contracts and guest shots on late-night talk shows.

On March 15, Hiller Zobel, then an attorney with the firm of Bingham, Dana and Gould and now a superior court justice, had the following letter hand-delivered to Attorney General Elliot Richardson:

> The Boston Bar Association has appointed me special counsel to investigate certain aspects of the professional conduct of a member of the Bar of the Commonwealth. I write to you now at the suggestion of Theodore Chase, Esq., Chairman of the Committee.
>
> Our investigation has just disclosed information of the most disturbing and sensitive nature, per-

---

* Bailey, p. 235.

taining directly to a series of matters now before the courts. The occasion is, in my opinion, urgent, and I request an opportunity to lay the issue before you personally as soon as possible. I stand ready to cancel any other professional appointment in order to serve your convenience.

At the bottom of the page is this handwritten note: "I talked with Zobel on 3/15/67. He is particularly interested in the actions of Sandra Irizarry and Lt. Tuney [former Strangler Bureau members], who went to work for Bailey. HFT [Herbert F. Travers, Jr.]."

On April 24, Zobel requested access to the attorney general's files on the strangling murders, in particular a long memo dated February 2, 1967, and written to Travers, head of the Criminal Division of the attorney general's office, by Tuney, Irizarry, and Phillip DiNatale. This document furnished a history of the Task Force and an account of how Gerold Frank had been permitted access to the volumes of material it had gathered on the homicides. It also mentioned that the Task Force personnel had objected vehemently to Frank's constant presence in the Bureau offices while he was doing the research for the book that would become *The Boston Strangler,* which they felt inhibited their discussions on how to proceed with their investigations of the murders. In late April of 1964 Bottomly had, however, ordered them to cooperate fully with Frank and permit him to read and make notes on even the most top secret police files.

Travers passed Zobel's request for a copy of this memo on to Richardson, who replied:

What is Zobel's interest in this material? I ask partly because it would seem to me better, somehow, if instead of opening our files—or any part of them—to him we simply answered any relevant questions he may ask (where there is no reason why we shouldn't), referring, where necessary, to our own files for purposes of refreshing recollections, etc. What do you think?

The reason Richardson was loath to surrender the Strangler files to an outsider was simply that while the Bar was investigating Bailey, Donald Conn was investigating the possibility of prosecuting Albert for at least some of the stranglings.

To this end, sometime around May 8, a new subdepartment was created in the Office of the Attorney General. It was called the Trial Section of the Criminal Division; in reality, it was simply the old Strangler Bureau under a new name. It would be headed by Conn and staffed by Detective Lieutenant John Butler and Corporal Paul O'Brien of the Massachusetts State Police and Phillip DiNatale, the lone holdover from the original Task Force.

The new bureau was formed just after Richardson and Conn met with Bailey—a meeting at which Bailey said that he'd be willing to have DeSalvo questioned about his role in the Strangler murders provided certain conditions were met. These were that Albert be examined by two qualified psychiatrists about his competence to make a voluntary confession; that he be given a lie detector test; and that the investigation and prosecution of any case against him be controlled by the attorney general's office.

Richardson and Conn agreed.

Conn, as chief of the new Strangler Bureau, had the chore of gaining the consent of the district attorneys of Middlesex, Essex, and Suffolk counties to Bailey's demand that the prosecution of any case against Albert be overseen by Richardson. Almost immediately he ran into some serious obstacles. Conn and Richardson met on May 11 with Conn's former boss, Middlesex County District Attorney John Droney, to discuss the possibility of proceeding against Albert in the Beverly Samans murder. They explained to Droney the conditions Bailey had laid down as a part of the deal. Droney was not, to say the least, enthusiastic. As Conn would later write, "Mr. Droney was not receptive to the idea of homicide prosecutions and the control of the Attorney General's Office in a consolidated prosecution." Droney also felt that such a move might disrupt Albert's pending appeal of his Green Man conviction. And Droney also objected on the grounds that "Mr. Bailey's motives were purely financial and that $110,000.00 of reward money [for the Strangler murders]* was still uncollected" and that "Mr. Bailey's motives, if not financial, were purely for publicity and that [the] Attorney General's and the District Attorneys' Offices of the respective counties involved could be greatly criticized for becoming a party for an attorney 'throwing his client to the wolves.' "

When, on May 17, Conn and Richardson met with Suffolk County District Attorney Garrett Byrne to confer with him about indicting Albert, they got a similar response. Any murder cases that had taken place in his jurisdiction, Byrne said, *he* and not the attorney general would prosecute. Byrne also conveyed, to use Conn's own words, "a distrust for Bailey."

The next day, Conn got together with Essex County District Attorney John Burke. Again Conn proposed what he'd proposed to Droney and Byrne. And again, he got the same answer. Burke was no more taken with the idea of a consolidated prosecution of DeSalvo under Richardson's aegis than had been Droney and Byrne.

Like Droney, Burke claimed not to want to do anything that might boomerang on Albert's Green Man appeal. He also suggested that DeSalvo's attorney was

---

* Droney, like DeSalvo, misunderstood the amount. It was $10,000.

motivated by a desire for money and publicity. And he concluded by stating that Albert wasn't the Strangler anyway, although he did have a good idea who was.

Burke's favored suspect was George Nassar.

That same day, Conn met with Hiller Zobel, who was still attempting to wrest from the attorney general's office the documentation he needed to pursue his investigation of Bailey. Conn wrote an account of this meeting two weeks later:

> Mr. Zobel indicated to the writer and Lt. Butler that there were currently pending five (5) charges or violations of the cannons [sic] of ethics of the bar association against F. Lee Bailey, Esquire, of Boston. He further indicated that there was a distinct possibility that information would be filed with the Supreme Judicial Court requesting Mr. Bailey's disbarment. One of the areas of inquiry of the Boston Bar has been Mr. Bailey's representation of the alleged or self-styled strangler, Albert H. DeSalvo. In some of the statements attributed to Mr. Bailey about the DeSalvo case are part of the charges and allegations against the said Bailey. Det. Lt. Butler and the writer indicated in a general way to Mr. Zobel that we were currently engaged in very delicate negotiations with Mr. Bailey as an attorney of record for DeSalvo and that we were not too happy with the prospect of the bar association getting into a current criminal investigation. It was further indicated [to] Mr. Zobel that since you cannot seperate [sic] Bailey and De-Salvo, that we would appreciate it if the bar association, for the moment, consider holding those proceedings in abeyance until the DeSalvo picture is clarified.

The Bar Association complied with the request. Bailey may never have known how close he came to getting his request for a certificate of approval rejected as well as losing his privilege of practicing law.

Having persuaded the Bar Association to call off its grievance committee dogs—at least temporarily— Conn had surmounted one of the roadblocks in the path toward indicting Albert for some if not all of the stranglings. The next day he interviewed a polygraph operator from Chicago who appeared to have the proper credentials for administering a lie detector test. The expert wanted the new Strangler Bureau to turn over virtually all its data on the murders to him before he questioned Albert. Although Conn was fairly impressed by the man and his qualifications, the assistant attorney general nonetheless felt that the polygraph operator would have to be "controlled" so that whatever case there was against Albert would not be jeopardized.

On June 2, Conn, Richardson, and Butler had a meeting in the attorney general's office with Garrett Byrne, John Droney, and John Burke. After a lengthy wrangle, they hammered out a tentative agreement, and it is obvious from reading Conn's record of the session that concessions on both sides were made only very grudgingly.

No one had a problem with the suggestion that Albert be moved from MCI-Walpole to MCI-Norfolk (a medium security prison a short distance from Walpole) before any interrogation of him took place. Everyone was amenable to the idea that Albert submit to lie detector tests. They all even eventually agreed to a consolidated prosecution, and that any indictments against DeSalvo not be sought until after his Green Man appeal had been heard and decided.

The real struggle took place over the issues of who would question Albert and when any psychiatric evaluation of him would be conducted. Burke, Droney, and

Byrne insisted that their own representatives be allowed to interrogate Albert about the murders committed in their jurisdictions. Conn was violently opposed to anyone other than the attorney general's designate handling any part of the questioning. To keep the political peace, Richardson decreed that a compromise between the two positions be worked out at some future date.

Conn, the irresistible force, wanted Albert checked out by the psychiatrists before he confessed. Burke, Byrne, and Droney, the immovable objects, wanted the examination to take place *after* Albert had said his piece. Again Richardson interceded with the suggestion that the psychiatric testing be done midway through the interrogation.

Droney again made it plain that he didn't believe Albert had killed Beverly Samans. Burke, who was also still maintaining that Albert wasn't the murderer of Helen Blake, Joann Graff, Mary Brown, or Evelyn Corbin, didn't want to make any kind of legal move until George Nassar's second trial had concluded. Burke's assistant John Jennings—who would three months later prosecute Nassar—furthermore expressed grave doubt that it was even worthwhile to question Albert at this point. Or, as Conn phrased the comment, "Jennings raised the legal issue of whether or not Bottomley's [sic] abortion so confused the legal rights of DeSalvo as to make it impossible for anyone ever to procure a valid confession from the said DeSalvo." Whether Conn in using the word *abortion* was referring to his own or to Jennings's estimate of Bottomly's interrogation of Albert two years previously is impossible to say.

The atmosphere at this meeting must have been thick with hostility. The district attorneys, Conn wrote, "repeatedly made reference to the old strangler bureau and the lack of trust they have for the Attorney General of Massachusetts. They repeatedly talked about money motives of Bailey and DeSalvo. Particularly stressing movies and releases. They particularly were concerned about reward money feeling that Nassa [Nassar] would make a move to collect the reward money if DeSalvo was indicted. Their hatred for Bailey seems to be matched by their hatred for the Brooke Administration and the strangling bureau. The only point of importance which revolved [sic] from this continual discussion of past events was that they were assured by the writer and the Attorney General that both Bailey and DeSalvo would be interrogated on a public record about a financial involvement in movies and other rights pertaining to the story of the Boston Strangler.

"Repeated reference was made to the fact that many people apparently are in possession of records of the strangling bureau including John S. Bottomly and [they] asked the Attorney General when he was going to make some definitive moves to get those records back. As a good faith position [I] suggest it would appear wise that the Attorney General should make a serious attempt to get those records back."

Conn had one of his assistants research various legal issues relating to the possible prosecution of Albert. One question that might arise was whether Albert could claim that Bailey had been incompetent as a defender in allowing him to make his initial confession. Another gray area was whether separate indictments—in the case of the stranglings, one for each killing—could be prosecuted jointly. And would a joint prosecution deprive Albert of his constitutional rights?

The points were all ultimately moot. The drive to prosecute Albert for the strangling murders lost momentum over the summer and on into the next year, slowing, sputtering, and finally grinding to a halt. The matter never went to a grand jury. No indictments were ever handed down in any of the murders.

* * *

Did Donald Conn believe that Albert was the Strangler? Bailey today says yes. Ames Robey today says no. Conn died suddenly in 1986 at the age of fifty. Whatever his private beliefs may have been, they were buried with him.

George Nassar's retrial was a fiasco for Bailey. The prosecution produced eighteen witnesses, the defense three, far fewer than it had the first time around. One of the prosecution's witnesses came as a surprise to Bailey: a woman who claimed to have seen Nassar in Andover shortly before the murder of Irvin Hilton. Nassar took the stand—and admitted that in 1964 he had lied to his parole officer about being employed at the time. He also told the court that he had forged pay slips in order to foster this deception.

The jury took less than three hours to find him guilty. He was back in Walpole that night.

Bailey vowed to seek a third trial for his client. He also asked that the court appoint him as the now-indigent Nassar's attorney so that he could be fully compensated by the state for his efforts on his client's behalf. Judge Donald Macauley denied his request because Bailey hadn't been a member of the Bar for a minimum of ten years, which one had to be in order to qualify as a court-appointed attorney.

John Bottomly, the target of so much derision* on the part of his colleagues in the criminal justice system, had long since returned to the private practice of law in Boston. One of his clients was a woman named Sonya Marie Anderson Nichols. In a previous life, she had been known as Irmgard Beck DeSalvo. In August, Bottomly would negotiate with Twentieth Century-Fox

---

* Richardson says today, "I never had warm feelings for Bottomly."

an agreement whereby Sonya (she had married one Earl Nichols and was now returned from Germany and living in Denver) authorized the use of the names Irmgard, Judy, and Michael DeSalvo to be used in the movie to be made of Gerold Frank's *The Boston Strangler.*

The payment she received in return for this consideration was twenty-five thousand dollars.

As for agent Bottomly, he went to work for Twentieth Century-Fox himself, as a consultant to the Strangler movie. For the use of his name, and his services as a technical adviser, he was paid a reported one hundred thousand dollars.

The Bottomly character, played by Henry Fonda, would be the hero of the film version of the story.

14

Hooray for Hollywood

On January 4, 1968, Albert DeSalvo's appeal to the Supreme Judicial Court of Massachusetts for a new trial was denied. The justices found no basis for Bailey's and Asgeirsson's claim of "errors of law" in the standard of criminal responsibility to which Albert had been held. Neither did they agree that the guilty verdict reached by the jury in any way contradicted the psychiatric testimony presented at the 1967 trial. "Criminal acts have been committed," the justices wrote, "and the evidence not being conclusive, a determination was required whether the perpetrator was responsible or irresponsible under the law. No better way appears to determine that than by leaving to the twelve citizens of the jury the application of a reasonable and understandable rule after a fair trial and under fair and full instructions. That is what happened in this case."

On July 7, 1968, DeSalvo's appeal for a review of his sentence received this response: "The Appellate Division has ordered that no action be taken on this appeal for the reason that it was not filed in compliance with the provisions of the General Laws, Chapter 278, Section 28B, and, therefore, the Appellate Division is without authority to act." A copy of this notice was sent to F. Lee Bailey.

Meanwhile, the Robert Fryer production of the movie version of Gerold Frank's *The Boston Strangler* had gotten under way. It would be filmed on location in Boston and Cambridge, providing the occasion for a great deal of media ballyhoo. Along with Henry Fonda as John Bottomly, actor Tony Curtis would portray Albert and actress Carolyn Conwell would play Irmgard. Sally Kellerman would have a small but crucial role as the only survivor of a Strangler attack. The director was Richard Fleischer, the screenwriter Edward Anhalt.

In January 1968, Phillip DiNatale, who had spent the last four years on special assignment to the old and new Strangler Bureaus, resigned from the Boston Police Department to work as a technical adviser on the movie. The department gave him a choice—us or them, according to former BPD Detective Sergeant James McDonald—and DiNatale chose the latter. McDonald adds that John Bottomly—who apparently was not merely acting as a consultant to Twentieth Century-Fox but trying to recruit other consultants for it as well—went to each member of the Boston homicide squad (including McDonald) to ask if he'd be interested in emulating DiNatale. He got no takers.

For his services, DiNatale was paid a reported sixty thousand dollars. Actor Mike Kellin played him in the film. Later DiNatale would go on *The Tonight Show* to discuss his show business experiences with Johnny Carson.

Bottomly and DiNatale were virtually the only law enforcement (or ex-law enforcement) personnel in the state who would cooperate with the movie company. The Boston Police Department, which clearly hated the whole project, provided at best only one or two officers to divert traffic when scenes were being filmed at the city locations. Elliot Richardson flatly turned down a request from Fox for the assistance of the attorney general's office, citing his displeasure that the movie would actually name Albert as the Boston Strangler and expressing concern that the film might jeopardize any future trial in the case. Edward Brooke rejected first a five-figure and then a six-figure offer to portray himself. He too disliked the first script he was shown, for the same reasons as had Richardson. And neither the past nor the present attorney general was happy with what each perceived as the tremendous number of factual distortions in Edward Anhalt's screenplay. Nor did Brooke care much for the way his role had been written. He dropped a few broad hints that he might consider legal action if the part wasn't changed to reflect reality.

Brooke wasn't the only one to make such a threat. Edmund McNamara declared that he'd sue Twentieth Century-Fox if the shooting script so much as mentioned his existence. Detective Lieutenant Edward Sherry also declined to grant the moviemakers permission to use his name. The studio was going to get around this impasse by rebaptizing Sherry "Lieutenant Brandy," but a wiser head at Fox fortunately prevailed. In the end, Sherry was incarnated as Detective Lieutenant Joe Corsi, a name not on the rosters of the BPD, and the role was filled by actor George Kennedy.

Casting director Marty Richard had problems of his own finding suitable extras to play crowd and incidental scenes. Some of the hundreds of aspiring bit players did not take kindly to rejection. One such woman, denied her chance at five seconds' worth of screen immortality, chased after the hapless Richard and bludgeoned him with her handbag. This made the headlines of the following day's *Record American;* the front-page story was illustrated with a cartoon rendition of the fracas.

Richard was also having difficulties finding women

to enact the corpses of the Strangler's elderly prey. He issued a plangent appeal to reporter Marjorie Adams: "Do you know a lady with seventy-year-old feet? We are looking for one whose legs and feet will be right to portray a victim of the Strangler. Her face and body won't be shown."

Film costumer Billy Travilla, favorite designer of Marilyn Monroe, lamented the dreary state of Boston fashion. But he was nonetheless game to do a great deal of taxing on-site research. "I've just come from the gutters of Cambridge," he confided to *Herald-Traveler** writer Romola Metzner. "I've been living in a big parka, ski sweater, heavy underwear, and boots." The designer envisioned "the atmosphere of Albert De-Salvo in low-tone green get-ups."

It was breathlessly reported that Tony Curtis would definitely *not* undergo a nose job in order to resemble more closely the character he was playing.

The subject of *The Boston Strangler* may have been high tragedy; the circumstances of its filming were indubitably low farce.

As Brooke and Richardson had assumed, the movie version of *The Boston Strangler,* which had its U.S. premiere in the fall of 1968, bore little resemblance to the truth. It didn't even stay close to the book on which it was based. In the film, the murders are out of sequence and in the wrong cities—two, for example, take place in Cambridge. The Strangler Task Force is formed well before the death of Sophie

---

* The *Boston Herald* had recently merged with the *Traveler*. Several years later, the *Herald-Traveler* would merge with the *Record American*, becoming the *Herald-American*. In 1982, under the ownership of Rupert Murdoch, it would become, again, the *Boston Herald*.

Clark.* The character played by Sally Kellerman is beaten into a coma by Curtis-DeSalvo. Albert is finally arrested in Boston after being chased by a man who spots him trying to break into an apartment. He is then committed to Boston City Hospital, not Bridgewater, where a psychiatrist diagnoses him as a multiple personality. He is shown attempting to strangle Irmgard when she and the children visit him in the hospital.

Interestingly, no mention of F. Lee Bailey is made in the film. Albert's lawyer is instead identified throughout as Jon Asgeirsson. Harold Banks reported in the *Record American* that Bailey had been dropped from the movie because he didn't care for the script, nor for the payment he was offered for the use of his name.

The meatiest and most sympathetic role in the film goes to Fonda-Bottomly. He is initially reluctant to take on the responsibility of Strangler Bureau chief, but is talked into it by the Brooke character, who tells him he is "uniquely qualified" for the post because he has one of the finest minds the attorney general knows. Bowing to this pressure—and flattery—Fonda-Bottomly throws himself wholeheartedly into the undertaking, going so far as to prowl the mean streets of Boston at night in search of the killer. He spends sleepless nights brooding in his book-lined study. He even directs the interrogation of a suspect at Boston police headquarters, and when the man being questioned becomes violent, he lunges across a desk and punches him into submission, thus rescuing the armed cops in the room.

---

* Here called Lisa Gordon. All the victims were given pseudonyms.

"If you ever met Bottomly," says a retired Boston police detective, "that scene would make you cry laughing. Bottomly had to get permission from his mom to swat a fly."

The movie ends with Fonda-Bottomly taking Curtis-DeSalvo's confession to the murders. The Task Force chief urges the Strangler to unburden himself because if he does he'll "feel better." And the Strangler complies in a series of stream-of-consciousness revelations punctuated by catatonic fits.

A former Cambridge police officer gives a succinct two-thumbs-down to the production: "It was a crock of shit."

Later that year, it would also become a bone of contention.

George Nassar's appeal for a third trial in the Irvin Hilton slaying was rejected by the Supreme Judicial Court of Massachusetts on May 6, 1968. Bailey had contended that at Nassar's 1967 retrial, the defense had not been given sufficient opportunity to question potential jurors; that Nassar's constitutional rights had been violated by excluding as jurors people opposed to capital punishment; and that the judge had erred in not instructing the jury that eyewitness identifications were often unreliable. Bailey lodged eight other complaints; the Supreme Judicial Court justices found no basis in the record for any of them. They did, however, authorize the Superior Court to compensate Bailey for his efforts on Nassar's behalf.

Nassar moved immediately to get himself a new lawyer: William Homans of Boston. Homans would take the case to the United States Supreme Court in October of 1968.

That summer Albert, perhaps following Nassar's lead, would also fire Bailey. To represent him he retained Thomas C. Troy.

Bailey says today that he and DeSalvo remained firm friends until the latter's death. Events subsequent to the summer of 1968 seem to indicate otherwise.

15

From Jet Plane Lawyer to Helicopter Lawyer

Today, at age sixty-five, Tom Troy is no longer the "two-fisted drinker" he describes himself as once having been. Heart surgery and diabetes have drastically altered his habits; the only bars he frequents now are the ones in the gym he had installed in his home. Six-feet-two-inches tall and trimmer than he was a decade ago, he can still fill a large room by himself. And he has lost not a whit of the color that has made him a Boston legend.

Born in 1930, Troy was the son of a Boston detective killed in the line of duty. After a stint in the Marines, Tom followed his father's career footsteps, first into the Wilmington, Massachusetts, police department and thereafter into the Metropolitan District Commission police. What might have been a lifetime in law enforcement was ended when he suffered a work-related injury. He retired with a pension from the force and enrolled in law school, from which he graduated in 1967. His specialty: defending the kind of people he'd once arrested.

When Troy passed the Massachusetts bar in 1967, he celebrated—and announced—the occasion by renting a helicopter to fly him over Boston. He had the pilot land on the front lawn of the District Court in Dorchester. The gesture accomplished exactly what Troy intended it would—it served notice that a major presence on the legal scene had arrived, one who had quite literally descended from the heavens.

Although Troy's extravagant personal style would grate on some of his more conservative brethren, it won him a great deal of amused admiration from others—and considerable publicity. In 1983, *Boston Magazine* would designate him one of "The Toughest S.O.B.s in Town." Troy accepted the accolade graciously.

All this attention brought him a steady stream of clients. He rapidly developed a reputation as the defender of the indefensible. By March of 1984, when Troy received a court appointment to represent William Douglas, the Tufts University Medical School professor charged with bludgeoning to death the object of his sexual obsession, prostitute Robin Benedict, the lawyer had already tried about fifty-five murder cases. He had lost none of them.

As it is for all successful litigators, the courtroom is Troy's theater. The drawled sardonic remark or question is his most potent rhetorical weapon. Representing the accused in a notorious rape case, he demolished a prosecution witness with substance abuse problems by asking her if she chased the pills she took with the alcohol she guzzled. In his closing arguments, he traditionally includes a poem of his own composition.

His philosophy as a defender has been honed by time and experience: "If somebody throws down the gauntlet, pick it up and beat the shit out of them."

* * *

Albert retained Troy as his attorney on September 4, 1968. The first meeting of client and lawyer took place under epic circumstances. Since Albert obviously couldn't leave Walpole to visit Troy at his office, the mountain went to Mohammed—by helicopter. As the craft settled to the ground inside the prison wall, it was approached by machine-gun-toting guards unhappy, to say the least, with this intrusion. Troy emerged from the helicopter and pushed past the official greeters, barking, "Get the hell out of my way. I'm a lawyer."*

They let him through.

Albert was thrilled with the bravura performance of his new attorney. In F. Lee Bailey he'd had a jet-plane lawyer. In Troy, he exulted, he now had a "helicopter lawyer."

Troy's first legal move on behalf of his new client was to try to obtain a preliminary injunction preventing the local premiere of the movie *The Boston Strangler.* His primary argument was that a public screening of the film would make it impossible for Albert ever to receive a fair trial should he be indicted for any out-of-state criminal offenses or indeed for the Strangler murders. But the attorney's real purpose, as he remarks today, was to demand an accounting from F. Lee Bailey. "Albert was due a reasonably substantial amount of money [from the sale of the rights to his life story]," Troy says. "And where was it?"

The lawyer proposed to find out.

Another crucial issue for Troy was whether Albert was competent to sign the various releases and contracts he had in 1966. Troy maintained that he was

---

* A story widely current in legal, media, and show business circles has it that the prison escape scene in the Charles Bronson movie *Breakout* was inspired by this incident.

not, and that any agreements Albert had made then were invalid.

The matter of *Albert H. DeSalvo versus Twentieth Century-Fox Film Corporation and the Walter Reade Organization* (the movie's distributor) came before Judge W. Arthur Garrity in the United States District Court in Boston on October 10, 1968. Attorney James P. Lynch appeared for Fox and Attorney Jerome P. Facher for Walter Reade. The first witness to take the stand was the plaintiff himself. Troy came right to the point by asking Albert if he was the notorious Boston Strangler. Albert replied that he really didn't know who he was. Troy requested a clarification of this statement. Albert gave one:

> Well, the best way I can explain it is that I have been locked up now in a room, and everywhere I go, a guard is with me. I am not allowed to talk with anybody. My food is brought to me by an inmate. I can't talk to anybody. Anywhere I go, I have to go with a guard with me. I am not allowed to talk. I am constantly being threatened that I will be locked up if I talk to an inmate or something. If I go out [of solitary] on weekends, which I have just recently been allowed to go out on Saturday or Sunday, I go to the movies, I look like Jacqueline Kennedy with all these guards around me. I am escorted to the movies [within the prison] and escorted back. I just don't know what I can do or what I can't do. I don't know who to trust. I am constantly threatened that if I talk to this or that person, I am going to be locked back in my room again. I am allowed to vegetate. I mean I am allowed to work in the [prison] hospital there where I am isolated in a little area but unallowed to talk with people.

Troy then asked Albert if he'd ever discussed with Bailey the publication of the book *The Boston Strangler.*

Albert admitted that he had, sometimes. Troy asked him to describe these conversations:

> Mr. Asgeirsson and Mr. Bailey were my counsel. Mr. Asgeirsson would tell me, "Don't listen to Mr. Bailey and don't trust him," and Mr. Bailey would tell me, "Well, we will get rid of him," so I informed Mr. Asgeirsson about three or four times through Mr. Bailey telling me this here, because it happened I told Mr. Asgeirsson that Mr. Bailey wanted me to sign certain things and I told him I don't understand what they are, and when it did come about that certain things were to be signed, Mr. Bailey, in front of George McGrath and Charlie Burnim,* came to Bridgewater and Mr. Bailey got me first alone and says, "I want you to sign," he said, "Don't worry about what it is. I am going to get you into Johns Hopkins Hospital." He said, "You will be able to buy two hospitals." And I said, "What do you mean?" He says, "Look—I've got some papers I want you to sign. Sign them, and I will explain them to you later."

Albert demurred on the grounds that he'd promised his brothers he wouldn't sign anything. Bailey insisted. Albert still refused to put his signature to the papers. Then Bailey delivered an ultimatum: If Albert didn't do as he was told, Bailey wouldn't get him a civil commitment (to a mental institution rather than a prison) when he went to trial.

At this point, in the early summer of 1966, Albert was seemingly unaware that he *would* go on trial as the Green Man in January 1967. (Bailey says he and Edward Brooke had decided this in April 1966.) Shocked,

---

* Charles Burnim was the lawyer in Bailey's office who had argued Albert's appeal of his 1967 conviction before the Supreme Judicial Court.

he reminded Bailey that the lawyer had assured him
this would never happen. "Well, things are changing
now," Bailey had replied, according to Albert, which
if true is a cavalier way for an attorney to break such
news to a client.

Under this pressure, Albert told the court, he signed
the documents. Did he know what was in them? No—
Bailey had held them folded in such a way that their
contents were invisible. All he could see was the lowest
part of the page, where he was to append his signature
along with those of F. Lee Bailey and George McGrath.

> I said, "Why can't I read it?" And Mr. George
> McGrath was there and Charlie Burnim was there
> [at Bridgewater]. He [Bailey] said, "If any of the
> guards sees us or looks in the window, we are in
> trouble." I said, "Yes, but I don't understand what
> is going on." He said, "I am your attorney. Trust
> me. I will show it to you later." I was scared, I
> know I shouldn't sign it, but he said, "I will show
> it to you later," and he was my attorney and I
> signed my name again, but he stressed to me after
> George McGrath left and Charlie Burnim, he
> grabbed me aside and said, "Look—promise me
> never to tell John [sic] Asgeirsson or your brothers
> or anybody that you signed these papers, or we
> are in big trouble." I said, "But why?" He says,
> "Don't worry about it. I am your attorney. Trust
> me."*

---

* DeSalvo's comments would find a haunting parallel in
remarks made long after his death by Patricia Campbell
Hearst in her 1982 memoir of her kidnapping, *Every Secret
Thing* (with Alvin Moscow, Pinnacle Books, 1982). Hearst's
father had hired Bailey and his associate J. Albert Johnson
to represent his daughter at her 1976 bank robbery trial.
Part of Bailey's fee would be the right for Bailey to write
a book about the case: "Al [Johnson] had said he would

* * *

A year or so afterward, Albert told the court, he asked Bailey if he (Albert) had ever signed a power of attorney over to Bailey. Bailey told him he hadn't, but Albert, apparently disbelieving, persisted in asking the question. He wrote letters to Bailey that, according to Albert, went unanswered. When Charles Burnim visited Albert at the prison, Albert would put the same queries to him. Burnim told his client he had no answers: "As you probably know, Mr. Bailey is sending me up here just to pacify you."

Albert said that he finally had to threaten to discharge Bailey in order to get the lawyer to meet with him at Walpole. "What happened was, Mr. Bailey did come in and I did confront him, and he said, 'Well, yes, you did sign a power of attorney, but it was limited.' " Albert then asked to see any and all documents he might have put his signature to. Bailey promised to provide copies, Albert claimed, but he never did.

Albert asked Charles Burnim if there was any way to prevent people from writing about him (such as *Parade* magazine author Lloyd Shearer and *Record American* gossip columnist Harold Banks), a question he'd also posed to Bailey, and Burnim offered a reply similar to Bailey's: Albert's story was in the public domain and whoever wanted to print some version of it couldn't

---

be giving me a paper to sign later on. Meanwhile, he said, I had to learn to trust my attorneys . . . About three days after my conviction, Al came to me with a letter. "Remember the paper I told you I was bringing you to sign one day? Well, here it is." The letter was to a publisher. It stated that I agreed to F. Lee Bailey writing a book about me and the trial and pledged I would cooperate with him and not compete with a book of my own for at least eighteen months after his was published. I couldn't argue. I signed it for him, confused as to the necessity for it." (p. 449)

be stopped. Albert inquired about the possibility of suing such authors. Burnim answered that such a course of action would be disastrous because "everything would be exposed then."

Albert noted that Jon Asgeirsson, when informed of these developments, told his client, "You're being taken right down the drain."

Albert had read Gerold Frank's book, and was shocked and angered that, among other things, his most intimate family correspondence had been reproduced in it. He asked Bailey how this could have happened. Albert was particularly upset that a letter he'd given Bailey to deliver personally to Irmgard had been printed in the book. Bailey told him that the attorney general's office must have handed over all those materials to Frank.

Troy asked Albert if Bailey had made clear to him what payment he'd receive for Frank's use of his life story.

> It was just so much he would explain. He mentioned [again?] something about I will be able to buy two hospitals, and then he said something about money being hidden in the name of McKay, money he has secretly hidden, that if the public knows about it, that suits would be brought against it. I said, "Well, what do you mean?" He said, "Don't worry about it. I'll take care of everything," and it is placed under the name McKay or something, money, but he would never explain, and that is why I have always asked Charlie Burnim to please explain, and he says, "I can't. I wish to hell I never got into this mess."

Albert did recall endorsing a check for fifteen thousand dollars made out to Robert McKay and presented to him by Bailey for that purpose.

Troy asked his client what his mental state had been in the summer of 1966.

ALBERT: Scared, pressured, under complete pressure. I didn't know what to do, but I had to rely on my counsel, and I did everything he told me.*

TROY: Were you aware of everything that was going on around you?

ALBERT: No, sir, I was not aware, because my counsel wouldn't tell me anything. He kept everything to himself, and Mr. Burnim said that "Mr. Bailey is neglecting you and his other clients."

THE COURT: Excuse me. The question is, how did you feel, and you have stated you felt scared and under complete pressure and not aware of what was going on. If you have anything further to state in response to that question, don't go off on some other subject.

TROY: At some time while you were at Bridgewater, Mr. DeSalvo, were you subject to hypnotism?

ALBERT: Yes, sir.

TROY: Were you subject to multiple psychiatric interviews?

ALBERT: Yes, sir. I was put under hypnosis many times, and I was subjected to all kinds of doctors and everything.

TROY: Sure. And were there people coming and going all the time to talk with you, either with or without your attorney?

ALBERT: Yes, sir.

TROY: People from the Attorney General's Office?

---

* Except for occasional interpolations in brackets for the purpose of clarification, the transcript is reproduced exactly. No attempt has been made to regularize spelling or punctuation.

ALBERT: Yes, sir.

TROY: Various doctors?

ALBERT: Yes, sir.

TROY: Outside consultants?

ALBERT: Yes, sir.

TROY: And hypnotists?

ALBERT: Yes, sir.

TROY: Were you a little confused?

ALBERT: Yes, sir.

Troy then brought up the issue of whether Albert might be indicted or tried for offenses he'd allegedly committed in Rhode Island and Connecticut. The lawyer was questioning Albert on his knowledge of any out-of-state warrants pending against him when James Lynch, the attorney for Twentieth Century-Fox, asked permission to approach the bench. Lynch told Judge Garrity that F. Lee Bailey, who was present in the courtroom, had just informed him that he (Bailey) had to leave to make an afternoon appointment. In view of this emergency, Lynch wondered if it would be possible to postpone Albert's cross-examination so that Bailey, who had been scheduled to testify later in the proceedings, might take the stand now. Garrity ruled that Albert's cross-examination be suspended to accommodate Bailey, unless of course Counselor Troy had an objection. Troy did, on the grounds that Bailey hadn't been sequestered but allowed to listen to Albert's entire testimony.

THE COURT: Excuse me. I don't get your point. You object to Mr. Bailey testifying at this time?

TROY: No, no.

THE COURT: That is all I am ruling on.

TROY: I do.

THE COURT: You say you do object.

TROY: I do.

THE COURT: On what grounds?

TROY: I think cross-examination of DeSalvo should
come first.

THE COURT: Why?

TROY: Not that Mr. Bailey would tailor his testimony,
he would insert his testimony for the benefit of the
respondent, but it might just happen that way.

Garrity was not swayed by Troy's objection. Bailey
mounted the stand and took the oath to tell the truth,
the whole truth, and nothing but the truth.

Questioned by Troy, Bailey said that he'd first met
Albert at Bridgewater in late February of 1965 and that
three different parties (he didn't say which ones) had
requested him to make this visit. He thought that it
had been reported to him that Albert had escaped
from incarceration in February of 1967.

Bailey identified a copy of the June 17, 1966, release
given to Gerold Frank and verified his own, Albert's
and George McGrath's signatures at the bottom of it.
He said that a lawyer for New American Library,
Frank's publisher, had drawn up the document. Bailey
didn't know the lawyer's name.

Troy asked Bailey if he'd explained the meaning of
the release to Albert and Bailey testified that he had,
"in painful detail."

TROY: Was one of these painful occasions the date
of the signing?

BAILEY: The occasion wasn't painful, the detail was,
and that was one of the occasions.

TROY: And did you explain to Mr. DeSalvo what the
word "perpetuity" means?

BAILEY: Yes, in somewhat more simple terms.

TROY: I see. And did you explain the word "biographical" to him?

BAILEY: Yes.

TROY: You took all these words that you felt might

not be familiar to Mr. DeSalvo and you explained them in detail, didn't you, Mr. Bailey?

BAILEY: You mean word by word?

TROY: Yes.

BAILEY: No, I did not.

Troy kept hammering at the same point.

TROY: Did you give [Albert] a capsule explanation of the document?

BAILEY: I explained it to him in simple lay terms, as I would to any client, yes.

TROY: I see. And, of course, your testimony will be that he understood, is that correct?

THE COURT: Well, now, don't ask the witness what his testimony will be. Ask him questions, please.

TROY: Do you think he understood you?

BAILEY: He said that he understood.

TROY: You didn't answer my question, Mr. Bailey. Do you think he understood?

BAILEY: I thoroughly believed that he understood, yes.

TROY: Did George McGrath hear this explanation?

BAILEY: My recollection is that he was sitting three or four feet from me at the time I gave it, so I would have to say that he probably did. I cannot say what his aural stage was at the time.

TROY: He probably did.

BAILEY: I would assume that he did, yes. I think he commented on it at one time.

TROY: Do you know if Mr. McGrath saw Albert peruse it?

BAILEY: I don't know what Mr. McGrath saw.

At this point, the exchange between Troy and Bailey began to take on the quality of an Abbott and Costello routine.

TROY: Was Mr. Burnim there?

BAILEY: I think that was the first occasion Mr. Burnim met Mr. DeSalvo, but I am not sure.

TROY: And did he witness this signing?

BAILEY: If he was there he witnessed it, yes.

TROY: If you know.

BAILEY: You mean did he sign as a witness or did he observe what went on?

TROY: Did he observe it?

BAILEY: He was in a room so small facing toward DeSalvo that I would say he must have observed it if that was the occasion of his first visit, I am not sure.

TROY: Well, do you know if he saw Albert peruse it?

BAILEY: I don't know what he saw. I would assume he saw what I saw.

TROY: Do you know whether or not he heard you explain the content of the document?

BAILEY: No, I don't. I know he was within earshot.

TROY: What is earshot, Mr. Bailey, how many feet in distance?

BAILEY: I don't think I need decide that. I would say three feet is definitely within earshot, and what the outer limits are I cannot calculate.

TROY: How far away was Mr. Burnim?

BAILEY: Oh, three feet.

TROY: Three feet?

BAILEY: It was a very small room.

Bailey didn't recall discussing the Bridgewater guards with Albert on the occasion of the signing of the release. He also said that the document hadn't been folded when Albert had put his name to it and that he had fully explained to Albert what compensation he could expect to receive from Frank under the terms of the agreement. Some $18,443.52 had been paid out so far. Troy asked where that money had gone. Bailey said that fifteen thousand dollars had gone to George McGrath "for the benefit of De-Salvo" and the rest had gone to Albert's brother Richard.

"Mr. Bailey," said Troy, "who is Robert McKay?"

BAILEY: Robert McKay is a fictitious name. In this case.

TROY: Sort of a straw?

BAILEY: What's that?

TROY: Sort of a straw.

BAILEY: Well, I don't know that he is a straw. The name is fictitious.*

Troy inquired again as to the whereabouts of the fifteen thousand dollars. Bailey replied that "it was deposited in [his] account and used in part for expenses relating to DeSalvo; in part it was given to his brother Richard."

Bailey was actually keeping ten thousand dollars in reserve in case he ended up having to pay the reward he'd offered for the safe capture of Albert after the latter had fled Bridgewater in 1967. Two clerks in the uniform store in Lynn where Albert had surrendered to the local police had claimed the bounty. Bailey had understandably refused to pay, and the shop attendants sued him. Happily, the suit came to nothing, thus relieving Albert of the necessity of footing the bill for his own arrest.

Troy then produced a copy of a letter purportedly written by Albert on April 21, 1968. It read:

---

* Troy says today that Bailey told him outside the courtroom that Robert McKay was in fact F. Lee Bailey. Bailey says today that Robert McKay was Albert DeSalvo.

Dear Mr. Bailey:

Why do you give me the runaround when I asked you to show me all the papers you had me sign? I am asking you for the last time, I want to see and have a copy of all what [sic] I have signed by this coming weekend. PS: Wrote last week. My letters are not being answered.

Bailey didn't know if he'd ever received an original of that letter, nor did he recall Albert ever asking "in those terms" to furnish him with any copies of contracts. He believed he recognized Albert's signature on the paper Troy showed him. He couldn't say that the actual handwriting of the letter was familiar to him.

Returning to the subject of the release, Troy asked if Gerold Frank had been in the Bridgewater vicinity at its signing. Bailey thought that Frank was in the Boston area at the time, because the lawyer had flown the author up from New York himself. He did recall that Frank certainly hadn't been admitted as a visitor to Bridgewater that day to witness the signing. He couldn't remember if the writer had been waiting in a car outside the institution for Bailey to return with the document.

Again, Troy pressed Bailey on the circumstances of the signing of the release.

TROY: Was Burnim looking out the window for the guards?

BAILEY: Not that I recall.

TROY: Did you make a statement "sign it quick, before the guard comes?"

BAILEY: Did who ever make such a statement?

TROY: You.

BAILEY: To whom?

TROY: Albert H. DeSalvo.

BAILEY: Not that I recall, no.

TROY: Never?

BAILEY: No.

Troy, who had been circling his prey, suddenly pounced: "Do you know if it is a violation to have an inmate sign a document while they are inmates at Bridgewater?" Said Bailey, "Yes, I know whether or not it is a violation in my judgment to have an inmate sign a document for his lawyer."

That was not precisely the question Troy had asked. He let it pass for the moment.*

The proceedings continued, with Troy quizzing Bailey on Albert's 1967 trial and the publicity generated thereby; Albert's hypnosis at Bridgewater, which had taken place at Bailey's instigation in order to elicit from Albert more details of the stranglings; Albert's interrogation by John Bottomly; and Bailey's putative interest in the Strangler movie—Bailey denied that he had ever been offered money by the filmmakers for the use of his name. Then Judge Garrity announced that he had been advised that members of the media, toting camera equipment, were gathering in the corridor outside the courtroom. He reminded those present that it was illegal for any photographs to be taken or recordings to be made of the present proceedings.

Under cross-examination by James Lynch, Bailey ex-

---

* Bailey's repetition of the phrase "I don't recall" during this court proceeding resonates again in the memoir of Patricia Campbell Hearst. Hearst, who writes that her attorney instructed her to give brief answers to all questions asked her at her trial, comments also that he coached her in the use of certain key expressions. "For some reason I could not fathom, Bailey added that I should never say on the witness stand, 'I can't remember.' If I could not remember something, I should reply, 'I don't recall.' " (Hearst, p. 426.)

panded on his previous testimony: that Albert was aware of and agreeable to the deal with Frank as well as fully comprehending of its terms, and, further, that Albert had endorsed the plan to have the money he received from Frank entrusted to "Robert McKay." Bailey didn't think Albert had ever objected to the publication of the Frank book, although he had wanted one anecdote in it deleted because he viewed Frank's version of the incident as inaccurate and insulting.

Bailey did say that late in 1967 or early 1968, Albert had asked him to see about halting production of the Strangler movie, and inquired whether it would be possible to void the contract with Frank.

> I said no, I think that it [the release] is perfectly good, and that a lawsuit would not win you, and he said, "Well, I have been told that if I were to claim that I had a bad memory or I didn't understand it, that I might have it put aside and then they couldn't put out the movie." I asked him who told him that, and he said an attorney. I said, "Who was it?"

Judge Garrity interrupted: "Well, we don't need any names, I don't suppose. He had counsel. I don't think the identity of the attorney is important. He said he had been told. What else?"

Bailey continued: "I said, 'Albert, the only way that could be done is if Mr. McGrath would get up and tell a false story about the circumstances surrounding this document. Would you expect us to do that?' He said, 'No, I wouldn't.' That was most of what was said about the breaking of the release during that conversation."

"Sometime thereafter," asked Troy, "did you cease to be Mr. DeSalvo's attorney?"

"Yes," answered Bailey. "This summer."

"When, sir?"

"This summer."

It was in fact in July that Albert had discharged Bailey.

Questioned by Jerome Facher, Bailey told the court that he'd informed Albert that he'd read the script for the Strangler movie, and that while it wasn't particularly accurate, it was fairly sympathetic to Albert—perhaps even more so than the book. He also testified that Albert had many times between 1966 and 1968 inquired about the progress of the publication of the book and the filming of the movie and what monetary returns he could expect from both.

On redirect examination, Troy picked up this question of finances. Bailey revealed that in addition to the ten thousand dollars he was holding in reserve in case he had to pay the reward, he had charged an additional ten thousand dollars to Albert's account. George McGrath had submitted a bill in that amount to Bailey for *his* services on Albert's behalf. Bailey had the request for reimbursement in his files.

"Sure," said Troy. "Now, was Mr. McGrath court-appointed?"

"Yes," said Bailey.

"Did you feel that the money should come out of DeSalvo, right?"

Bailey didn't respond.

"Yes or no," Troy persisted.

"What was the question?" Bailey asked.

"You feel the money that McGrath should have earned should come out of DeSalvo, is that correct?" Troy repeated.

"That is not my judgment to make," Bailey said.

"Well, I am asking you, sir," said Troy. "Do you feel the money should come out of DeSalvo? Yes or no?"

"Out of his estate, yes."

"Before or after you get your fee?"

"It doesn't look like I am going to get my fee," Bailey replied. "So I haven't had to reach that decision."

"Well, are you not worried about it?"

"I am not happy about it, but I am not all broken up—"

"But you are not happy about it," Troy nudged.

Troy's question about McGrath's fee was a pertinent one. McGrath had received a court appointment to serve as Albert's guardian, which meant that he would be paid by the Commonwealth, not by his client. But after McGrath had been removed as Albert's guardian—at Bailey's urging—he continued to serve (or so Bailey told the court) as Albert's informal business adviser. Perhaps part of the bill for ten thousand dollars McGrath sent Bailey reflected this consulting work.

When Bailey had concluded his testimony, Albert returned to the stand for cross-examination by Lynch, who was endeavoring to show that Albert had not only heartily approved of the filming of the Strangler movie but had even enjoyed friendly relationships with some of its principals, including director Richard Fleischer. Albert was evasive and defensive under Lynch's questioning, and did not acquit himself particularly well, taking refuge in rambling circumlocutions rather than delivering the kind of straightforward answers he had to Troy. It is possible he feared a trap. Indeed, Ames Robey, who had been summoned to testify by Troy from Michigan, where Robey was currently the director of the Center for Forensic Psychiatry in Ann Arbor, felt that Albert was now presenting some of the classic symptoms of paranoia. Then again, Robey also considered Albert to be "a bullshit artist *par excellence*" as well as a chronic manipulator. Perhaps the truth of Albert's condition lay somewhere in the middle.

Lynch asked Albert if he'd made a leather wallet as a gift for Richard Fleischer. Albert said he hadn't. Lynch produced a copy of a letter to Albert from Fleischer thanking him for the wallet.

Following the afternoon recess, Judge Garrity announced that Detroit was leading, three to nothing, in the World Series. Lynch continued chipping away at

Albert's credibility. He entered as an exhibit a friendly letter Albert had apparently written to Phillip DiNatale, in which Albert seemed to assure DiNatale that he'd get him two free tickets to the Strangler movie when it opened. Albert claimed the tickets in question were ones to a basketball game.

In trying to conceal his contacts with Fleischer and DiNatale, Albert irretrievably damaged his believability as a witness. And the irony is, he would have been far better off admitting sending the wallet to Fleischer. He was a man who was easily led and easily swayed, and he was dazzled by powerful and glamorous people. To be on a first-name basis with a Hollywood figure like the director would have enthralled him—and it was a fact that could have been used to illustrate how easily Albert could be influenced and even programmed to do whatever a stronger personality wanted him to do.

Albert, the con man, was as simple as a baby to con.

The final bit of legal business for the day was the private screening of a print of *The Boston Strangler* for the judge and the attorneys, to be held at a location away from the courthouse. Troy asked that Albert be permitted to view the movie. Garrity said no. Troy asked that Ames Robey be permitted to view it. Garrity said no.

Albert was led by a marshal back to the holding cell in the courthouse where he would spend the night. Garrity adjourned the session until the following morning. Then he and the lawyers piled into the three cabs that had been waiting to drive them to the screening room.

The first day of high-wire acts in the Burnim and Bailey circus had drawn to a close.

16

The Burnim and Bailey Circus, I

One of the witnesses who had been due to testify at the October 1968 hearing was John Bottomly. He never did; urgent business called him to London a few days before the hearing started. (He returned to the United states the day it ended.) He did, however, provide an affidavit stating that he had obtained for Twentieth Century-Fox a release of privacy granted by the former Irmgard DeSalvo on behalf of her and her children. ("One could suspect there might have been a conflict of interest here," Tony observes dryly of Bottomly's role in this negotiation.) Bottomly also stated that to his knowledge Albert had never been declared incompetent to handle his own business affairs.

"Well, that's just not true," Tony says today.

And of course it wasn't. That Bottomly could make such a claim in view of the fact that he himself was party to the arrangement whereby George McGrath was made Albert's guardian precisely because Albert was deemed incompetent to handle business transactions is simply staggering.

The affidavit, which was notarized by James Lynch, was entered as an exhibit at the 1968 federal court hearing.

On Friday, October 11, Jerome Facher resumed the cross-examination of Albert. If anything, Albert's performance was even worse than it had been the previous day. He claimed to be unable to understand Facher's purpose in asking him about any agreements he might have struck with Gerold Frank. He was vague about dates. He denied discussing money with Bailey.

He fared much better on redirect examination by Troy. This is hardly an uncommon phenomenon in courtroom proceedings. A prosecution witness, for example, will very often appear confident and fairly relaxed and thus eminently believable under questioning by the state's attorney, whom he perceives as an ally. That same witness, interrogated by a defense attorney, whom he on some level views as an enemy, may withdraw and turn defensive or even hostile, to the detriment of his credibility.

Troy asked Albert if he could tell the court why he had dismissed Bailey as his counsel.

"Yes, sir," said Albert.

Because from the moment from the day of my escape, and I went out and wrote a letter before escaping why I was escaping, to expose the conditions of Bridgewater, and when I came back in, I was placed in confinement, maximum security. Now, all that time I was there I wrote many letters to Mr. Bailey to come and see me, and I finally come to the point that I threatened to fire him if he didn't come in, and he sent me that telegram saying, "Don't do anything till I come up," and he sent Charlie Burnim up to pacify me. Charlie Burnim did say, "There is nothing I can do for you, Al. Mr. Bailey sent me up, like I explained, to pacify you." But I said, "Look—all these things that is going on, I am unable to communicate with other people. He [Bailey] said I've got to rely on my attorney." [Burnim] said, "I can't help you." Finally it came to be, after nine, ten, eleven months being locked up in one room, John [sic] Asgeirsson, my first attorney, came up and I was allowed to see him. He said, "Look, Al, I told you, you are being conditioned by your attorney, Mr. Bailey. You have been placed her to be conditioned. You watched Mr. Bailey in a month or two sign [you] in for thirteen murders." He said, "You are being conditioned. Mark my words. I told you before, Bailey promised you he would give you a civil commitment on this trial you are going to get, and I told you he is using this as a financial gain and there is no way possible he can give you or promise you a civil commitment . . . So around January or February, you watch. He will come in and he will have you sign a piece of paper and say 'I'll see you later, Albert.' You'll be the first guinea to slide in."

What gives this speech of Albert's weight and credibility is that it echoes sentiments Asgeirsson is recorded as having expressed to the attorney general's office in 1965.

Albert continued:

So what happened, on a Sunday morning Mr. Bailey came in, and that is when I cut my arms on a Monday.* I saw Mr. Bailey, and he told me in private that "We got a lot of money stashed

---

* In Walpole, Albert had slashed his wrists, although not badly enough to do him any permanent damage. No doubt his despair was real enough, but the gesture was probably more histrionic than it was a genuine suicide attempt.

away. Remember, I told you I tried to give George McGrath some money and he wouldn't accept it." All these things here [Bailey] told me, "that he wouldn't touch the money because it's too hot right now, but after you confess to these things, then we can get the money out of where it is." But he wouldn't explain. I said, "Where is those contracts?" That is the reason why I asked for those contracts, if there was any, and he said there was none, and when he refused again to give me any papers or anything, I said why, if I didn't sign anything? I asked Charlie Burnim, "Did I ever sign for a movie?" He says, "Look—don't ask me. I should have got out and sold insurance, the way things are going. I'm getting out of the office anyhow."

Troy then asked Albert why, if he'd been so displeased by Gerold Frank's book, he hadn't written to the author to complain. Albert answered that Bailey had told him there was nothing to be done. "I believed him to be God. And I did everything he told me."

That Albert did have a profound, almost worshipful, regard and trust for Bailey is evident from a letter he wrote to his brother Joseph from Bridgewater on March 18, 1965.

Joe you are the only one I can trust. and my Attorney Mr. F. Lee Bailey. Don't ever do anything before first calling or seeing F. Lee Bailey. No other person or me. He is in charge of everything.

The next witness to take the stand was Charles Burnim, who was no longer in the employ of F. Lee Bailey. It seems clear from the transcript that Burnim was uncomfortable at having to testify. He told the court that he had first met Albert in June of 1966, in a meeting room in the visiting area of Bridgewater. Burnim had been in the company of Bailey and McGrath on this occasion.

Troy showed Burnim a copy of the release and asked him if he'd ever seen it before.

Burnim said he hadn't. He also testified that he couldn't recall Albert reading any papers in his presence. Nor signing them.

Burnim did have some memory of Bailey explaining to Albert the nature of an agreement with Gerald Frank. Then Troy slipped into his attack-attorney mode, pressing Burnim for a description of just how comprehensive Bailey's explanation of the release had been. "Did you hear [Bailey] mention or explain away the word 'perpetuity'? Yes or no."

BURNIM: I don't recall that.

TROY: "Biographical?"

BURNIM: I don't recall that, no.

TROY: "Dissemination?"

BURNIM: No, I don't recall that.

TROY: Did you hear him explain at all that Albert would be waiving any of his constitutional rights he had?

BURNIM: [No response]

TROY: Mr. Witness?

BURNIM: I am thinking.

THE COURT: He is endeavoring to recall.

TROY: Well, I am not as close to him as your Honor and I can't see that he is.

THE COURT: Well, I am not even looking at him and I can tell that he is.

TROY: I see.

BURNIM: At this moment, I do not recall discussion concerning constitutional rights.

TROY: Did you hear Albert DeSalvo testify today?

BURNIM: Yes, I heard him.

TROY: Is it true that you went to Walpole State Prison on several occasions?

BURNIM: It is.

TROY: Did you go there to pacify him?

BURNIM: It depends on how you look at it. I didn't consider it as such.

TROY: Did you ever tell him you went there to pacify him?

BURNIM: I do not recall telling him that.

TROY: Did Albert ever have a conversation with you where he said Bailey was giving him the run-around?

BURNIM: There were times when Mr. DeSalvo was suspicious.

TROY: Did you agree with him or disagree?

BURNIM: Did I agree with him?

TROY: Or disagree with him.

LYNCH: Well, I don't understand that question.

THE COURT: Do you object?

LYNCH: I object.

THE COURT: I sustain that objection.

TROY: Did Albert DeSalvo ever tell you he couldn't talk to Bailey?

BURNIM: He told me at times he had difficulty speaking with Mr. Bailey.

TROY: Did he tell you he couldn't understand him?

BURNIM: He also said at times he had difficulty understanding him, yes.

TROY: Did he say he couldn't understand why Bailey wouldn't let him see these papers that he had him sign, that he never read them?

BURNIM: I don't recall him saying that.

TROY: Well, did he say words to that effect?

BURNIM: I don't recall. He discussed the papers with

me. I don't recall whether he said anything to the effect that he couldn't understand why Mr. Bailey wouldn't show him the papers.

TROY: Well, isn't it fair to say that he constantly talked to you about getting copies of papers that he signed that he didn't know the contents of?

BURNIM: On more than one occasion he asked me for copies or to obtain copies.

TROY: So at some time in June you were down at Bridgewater and George McGrath was there, Lee Bailey was there, and there was signing of some papers.

BURNIM: No, I—No, that is not so. I don't recall the signing of any papers. Sometime in June I was there with Mr. Bailey and Mr. McGrath.

TROY: All right. I show you Exhibit Number 4, sir. [This was the designation of fiduciary making McGrath Albert's business agent.]

BURNIM: Yes, I have looked at it.

TROY: That document prepared by your office, Mr. Bailey's office, at that time?

BURNIM: I don't know.

TROY: Do you know who Mr. McKay is?

BURNIM: Mr. McKay?

TROY: Yes.

BURNIM: I understand he is a fictitious person, fictitious name.

TROY: And you also understand that checks were drawn and made out in McKay's name?

BURNIM: I understand that was done. I do not know.

TROY: Did you ever say to Mr. DeSalvo when he complained to you, "Why don't you tell Mr. Bailey these things?"

BURNIM: Yes. Well, I made such a statement to him, yes.

TROY: Did Albert say to you, "He don't listen to me.

I can't understand him. When he comes in here I
freeze up. He's like God.'"?

BURNIM: He has made such a remark, yes.

TROY: Did you ever say, sir, "Well, I used to think
he was God, too"?

BURNIM: I don't recall saying that."*

Garrity refused to let Ames Robey testify, saying that
the doctor's views concerning Albert's competence and
any adverse psychological impact the Strangler movie
might have on him would be better aired at a trial than
at a hearing such as this. Troy was not happy with the
ruling, not the least because he'd brought Robey back
to Boston at his own expense. All he could do was object.
Garrity noted the objection—and overruled it.

George McGrath, who was scheduled to testify next,
hadn't appeared in the courtroom yet. That being the
case, Troy asked for a short recess so he could take
his ulcer medicine. Garrity granted the request, one
of the few of Troy's he *did* grant.

Under questioning by Troy, George McGrath told
the court that he had visited Albert many times at
Bridgewater, with and without Bailey and Burnim, and
couldn't recall† if Gerold Frank had ever accompanied
them. He didn't remember any exact dates, although
he did recollect "being at Bridgewater when Albert
DeSalvo signed a paper or two."

Troy showed him the release. McGrath said he'd
seen it, although whether for the first time when Albert
signed it he couldn't say. He hadn't helped to draft

---

* In three and a half pages of testimony, Burnim used this
  expression nine times. Even Garrity latched on to it.
† It must have been contagious.

the document—that had been done by Bailey and the attorney for the New American Library.

Bailey, of course, had earlier testified that he had nothing to do with the drawing up of the release.

McGrath said he'd never seen Albert read the papers. He also had "no specific memory" of hearing Bailey explain the document to Albert, a statement that undermined Bailey's previous comment that McGrath and Burnim must have heard him giving this explanation since they were sitting only three feet away at the time.

McGrath went on to say, "We wrestled very seriously—that is, I did—with the question—the ethical question, I being [Albert's] guardian, of whether a man who had assumedly committed very serious crimes, should profit personally as a result of [their] exploitation . . . and I came to the conclusion . . . that it would be possible for this to happen under very controlled conditions, and those would involve the exclusion of any material benefit to Albert by the proceeds."

He reiterated that insofar as the release to Gerold Frank was concerned, he had "no recollection of Albert having—reading this or having it read to him or having the details of it explained to him in my presence."

During cross-examination by Lynch, McGrath told the court that he had found Albert in any general discussion of the waiver of his right to privacy for material gain to be perfectly rational and capable of grasping the principles entailed in such a waiver.

McGrath was careful to note that he had never discussed the release itself or any of its contents with Albert.

He also said that he had read the document but had not made any "study" of it, and that he didn't "know the provisions of it in detail." But as Albert's business adviser, he had nonetheless had no seeming problem with putting his own signature to that agreement.

* * *

McGrath was the final witness. Garrity took closing arguments. In his, Facher suggested that Albert, who was not in Facher's opinion at all credible, was trying to wriggle out of a deal he'd entered into of his own free will and with a full understanding of its implications, by claiming now that he'd been deceived as to its meaning. His legal action against Fox and Reade was furthermore simply an effort to gouge from them, in the form of damages, the huge amount of money he'd anticipated getting from Gerold Frank.

Facher had implied that Albert was a liar. When it was Troy's turn to speak, he implied the same of Bailey: "I say you take into consideration the credibility of Attorney F. Lee Bailey. Although a member of the Bar, and I find it hard and painfully so to question his veracity, I say it is a fit subject to be questioned."

Garrity denied the plaintiff's request for a preliminary injunction. He expressed his intention to assign the case for trial, and as speedy a one as possible.

Troy requested an early November date—although he would have been happy to have it be the next day.

Garrity wanted to give Facher and Lynn adequate time to prepare. Both seemed agreeable to a November trial date.

Civil Action Number 68-832-G did not, however, open until five days before Christmas.

Robey went home to Michigan. He would return to Boston at Troy's behest in December.

17

The Burnim and Bailey Circus, II

Ames Robey, sixty-six, the son of a prominent Boston family, received his undergraduate degree from Harvard and his medical degree from Boston University. Certified by the American Board of Psychiatry and Neurology, he was a Special Fellow in Psychiatry and the Law at the Law-Medicine Institute of Boston University. He has taught at Harvard, Tufts, and the University of Michigan. As a forensic psychiatrist, his job has been to probe the ugliest and most convoluted recesses of the criminal mind. He has come face-to-face with the worst demons spawned in the cesspool of the id—serial killers, mass murderers, and homicidal rapists.

He is a tall man with a dry wit and an ironic perspective on the criminal justice system of which he was so long a part: "I used to think when I first got into this business that the courtroom was a place where there was a search for truth, and that it was honest and people told the truth and were sworn to do so. It took me a couple of years to have that fiction bashed

out of me and to begin to learn that it's a battle between two knights on their chargers, with lances, in
full armor, the referee to make sure they don't commit
a foul. Charging down the lists, hoping to be awarded
the victory, which might be somebody's head. If it happens to be the head of the poor defendant, why, that's
really of little significance."

Robey was the first witness to take the stand on De-
cember 20, 1968, when the matter of *Albert DeSalvo
versus Twentieth Century-Fox Film Corporation and the Wal-
ter Reade Organization* came to trial in the U.S. District
Court. Judge Garrity again presided. Appearing for
Fox was Robert W. Meserve, temporarily filling in for
James Lynch. Jerome Facher was still representing
Reade.

At stake was the two million dollars for which the
plaintiff was suing the defendants.

One of Troy's first questions to Robey was whether
the doctor thought that Albert, while at Bridgewater,
had possessed "sufficient mental capacity" to engage
in business dealings. Robey replied that in his opinion
Albert at that time hadn't the ability to handle any
transaction more sophisticated than the purchase of a
candy bar or batteries for his transistor radio. In any
event, the point was moot because Bridgewater regulations prohibited the inmates from entering into any
kind of financial negotiation involving more than small
change. "No one is allowed to have money," Robey
declared flatly. Nor, he continued, was any patient at
the hospital allowed "to make any public statements,
to sign any papers, to make any recordings, or to do
any of this sort of thing without having it cleared
through the institution. The guards, the superintendent, the Medical Director, myself at the time [of Albert's incarceration from 1964 to 1966], are, I suppose
it is really more ex officio, but we are their guardians,
and all this material must be cleared through us. Indeed, if the guards notice anything of this sort, they

are under orders to immediately stop the process and bring the whole situation et cetera to me or to Mr. Gaughan, the Superintendent."

"Is it fair to say," Troy inquired, "that nothing was ever presented for your perusal as far as a contract is concerned with Albert DeSalvo and Gerold Frank?"

"That is correct," Robey replied. "Nothing was presented."

"And if it was signed there at Bridgewater during the period of time that Albert was there," continued Troy, "then it would be a violation of the regulations of the institution, is that correct?"

"Yes, sir," Robey said. "It would be."

Meserve and Facher objected and were overruled.

Asked Troy: "Did Attorney F. Lee Bailey ever discuss the possibility of Albert signing a contract with you, or was it ever brought to your attention?"

No, Robey said, not before the fact of the signing.

Troy then showed Robey a copy of the release and asked him if he'd ever seen it. Robey said he had.

"In your opinion," asked Troy, "was Albert DeSalvo able to understand the nature and quality of the transaction or grasp its significance or have the capacity to execute such an instrument?"

"Well, Mr. Troy," Robey replied, "I will have to give you really two answers to this. In October of this year, I went to the Walpole State Prison, where he is presently held, having seen the contract at that time for the first time myself, and went over in detail with him not only words in it but context, so the two-fold answer would be that, first, just in terms of his educational background, disregarding for the moment, any evidence of mental illness, it was my opinion and certainly was my opinion, based on my previous knowledge when I was at Bridgewater, that his educational background alone would not have allowed him to understand even the wording and the consequences of this, but further, the degree of mental illness would totally abort his ability to appreciate its significance."

"When you say the degree of mental illness," Troy pressed, "will you explain to the Court which portion of the mental illness you are talking about?"

"Yes, sir," Robey said. "Mr. DeSalvo shows in his [personality] structure and as part of this whole schizoid or schizophrenic—chronic undifferentiated schizophrenic pattern, he has shown consistently a tremendous insecurity and a need to identify himself to the world as a notorious character, as though if he could not be well known for being good at something, then he would be notorious for being bad at something, and this overwhelming, compulsive confessor aspect would so distort his ability that there would be no appreciation of any consequences, because the identification of himself to the world as important would override all other considerations."

But suppose the wording of the release had been explained to Albert, Troy countered. "Assume that great pains, quite painfully time was taken to explain to him in detail to him by more than one person both before its signing and both after its signing. Would he be able to comprehend and understand the contract and the nature of its consequences?"

Robey still didn't think so. "With careful explanation, even his diminished educational background would allow him to perhaps understand the wording, if he listened, and the hypothetical question you ask that this was explained, you would also have to add the hypothesis that his mental illness would allow him to even listen except solely to the issue that he would be famous, and it is my opinion, based on my experience with him and my training, that he could not by reason of his mental illness listen to anything except that he would be famous, he would be known, he would be a watchword on everybody's lips."

Troy's next effort was to determine if Albert was still suffering from a mental defect.

"Since you came to Boston the first time for the last hearing," he asked Robey, "did you have an opportunity to see Albert DeSalvo?"

"Yes, sir," said Robey.

"Conduct a psychiatric interview with him?"

"Yes, sir, on three separate occasions."

"And make certain evaluations?"

"Yes, sir."

"Form an opinion?"

"Well, an opinion as to what?" Robey asked.

"As to his present mental status."

"Yes, sir."

"And would he now be a person competent to engage in a contract?"

No, Robey replied, he wouldn't be.

Troy had a final question. "Doctor, at the time Albert DeSalvo is alleged to have signed this contract, sometime in June, on or about the 17th of June, would his illness have prevented him from knowing or caring whether or not he signed away any of his rights civilly or constitutionally?"

"Yes, sir, his illness would have prevented this," Robey said. "They would have been of no concern, because the overriding concern above all else, perhaps fed by counsel to a degree, would have been—he would be world-renowned, and his rights at this time would be of no concern to him; not even that, their being of no concern—he would not even think of them. I am quite sure you could even say, 'Albert, you are signing away your rights,' and Albert would be thinking to himself, 'Yes, but I will be world-renowned. Everyone will know of me.' "

In addition to this insatiable thirst for celebrity, Robey said, Albert had another striking characteristic: a phenomenal memory. "He has absolute, complete, one hundred percent total photographic recall," the doctor told the court. "I have only seen this in perhaps incredibly brilliant people, although they are often suspect of being a little psychotic."

Robey's cross-examination by Meserve and Facher degenerated into a prolix wrangle over when Albert had been adjudged incompetent, by whom, for what reasons, and by whose standards. On several occasions the parties on both sides lost track of the questions they were, respectively, either posing or answering. Garrity had to intercede to request clarification. The dates of Albert's various hearings and the names of the presiding judges were a particular source of confusion.

At one point, Facher asked Robey if it were true that he'd once offered to work for F. Lee Bailey. The doctor, startled out of his professional demeanor, uttered a horrified, "Good Lord, no."

Robey's testimony had taken the entire day. At the end Garrity thanked him. Robey was eager to be gone; he had a plane to catch back to Ann Arbor.

"You may fly away, Doctor." Troy beamed.

Court was adjourned until Christmas Eve.

On December 24, Albert took the stand. And, like Robey before him, he remained there the entire day.

Troy asked Albert if he'd ever discussed the release with Bailey. Albert said he had, but only after he'd signed the document. "I told him that I didn't know what it was, and I had asked him to disregard that and stop it, I didn't want it, and he never paid no attention because he has never given me or told me that it has been stopped."

How, Troy wondered, had Albert's life been affected since the publication of Frank's book and the release of the movie?

"Well, every day, like I will be called, 'Hey, Strangler,' or people who I used to have as friends, they don't associate because I am supposed to be the alleged Strangler or the Strangler as they see it now," Albert said. "And my relatives, nobody who I used to know before don't write to me any more. My own brothers except for one now [Richard] and my own relatives because of the wide publicity and everything else that they just don't write to me any more, I just don't get any more mail, and every time I walk down, I am pointed out by the officers by visitors coming in at certain places and to, like take the ward or the place where visitors come, and they say, 'There is the Strangler,' and they point it out, and it is very embarrassing, everywhere you go you are pointed out."

"Are you called any other names besides 'the Strangler'?" Troy asked.

"They call you 'Silky' or 'Choker.' "

"Do you have any children?"

"I have a daughter and a son."

"Do you hear from them?"

"No, sir."

"Do you hear from all of your family?"

"One or two only."

"Any of your former friends write you?"

"None."

Troy turned the questioning in a slightly different direction. "Mr. DeSalvo, Mr. Bailey testified that you called him down [to Bridgewater in March of 1965] to find out if the story of your life was saleable. Is there any truth to that?"

Albert seemed puzzled, or confused. "Mr. Bailey— repeat that again, please?"

"Mr. Bailey testified that you called him to Bridgewater to find out if the story of your life was saleable."

"That is not true."

"Did you ever ask him at any time if he could sell your life story?"

"No, sir."

"Did you ever ask anybody to do it for you?"

"No, sir."

Albert's cross-examination was initiated by James Lynch, who wanted to establish exactly when Albert's friends and relatives had stopped communicating with him. He also wanted Albert's recollection of the date he'd read Gerold Frank's book. The exchange was brief and sharp.

Facher quizzed Albert about his divorce. He tried to get Albert to admit that the purpose behind selling his story was to get money for the support of his wife and children. Albert replied that as far as he knew he hadn't yet sold his life story, although doing so might not be a bad idea.

Facher's last questions to Albert concerned the gift he'd allegedly made and sent to Richard Fleischer. Albert denied having done anything of the sort. "Phil DiNatale made it or gave it to him," he stated.

"All right," Facher said, no doubt exasperated by Albert's recalcitrance.

"I made no wallet," Albert insisted.

They were the last words he would ever speak in a court of law.

"Is there further evidence?" asked Judge Garrity.

"No, Your Honor," replied Troy.

"That is the plaintiff's case?" Garrity inquired.

Said Troy, "It is."

Lynch had a further witness to call, and asked for a continuance.

Garrity adjourned the proceedings until 2:00 P.M on December 30.

The following Monday Lynch called to the stand Robert Ross Mezer, Bailey's psychiatric consultant who had last testified at Albert's Green Man trial. Mezer recited his credentials: a medical degree from Tufts; residences at various hospitals; certification by the American Board of Psychiatry and Neurology; and teaching appointments at Harvard, the Massachusetts General Hospital School of Nursing, and BU Law School.

Mezer told the court that he had seen Albert at Bridgewater on February 11, 1966, between 2:00 and 3:30 in the afternoon. The purpose of the visit was to establish whether Albert was capable of getting along without a guardian. He seemed, in Mezer's opinion, quite able to oversee his own financial affairs, to the extent of cashing the thirty-eight-dollar check he received each month from the Veterans Administration, sending money to his family, and inquiring through his attorney Jon Asgeirsson as to the whereabouts of some missing or delayed Social Security checks.

"I then asked him if he knew what was involved in a guardianship of the person, and he gave me an excellent answer, which I will quote here: Guardian of the person concerns the ability to sign contracts, make confessions, hire people, to get married or divorced, apply for admission to the hospital, to apply for a driver's license, to make a will, to change counsel, to deal with insurance benefits and beneficiaries, to decide on his own future, and to decide on his visitors. A guardian of the estate, on the other hand, by contrast, he told me, concerns only the ability to handle money."

"He told you those things you have just testified about, Doctor?" asked Lynch.

"That is directly—a direct quote," replied Mezer.

It was also a remarkably polished one from a man whose grasp of English grammar was, to say the least, a bit loose.

Garrity interrupted: "Was he reading from something?"

"No, sir," replied Mezer. "I copied it right down while he was telling me these things."

"And are you reading from notes you made contemporaneously?" Lynch asked.

"Right here," said Mezer. "Just as he was talking I was writing."

"Now," said Lynch. "Did you reach some opinion, Doctor, as a result of that interview and anything else as to whether or not Mr. DeSalvo at that time was competent to handle his business affairs without a guardian?"

"Yes, sir."

"What opinion did you reach?"

"I thought he was quite competent to handle his own business affairs without a guardian."

"Now," said Lynch. "When did you next see Mr. DeSalvo?"

"I next saw Mr. DeSalvo on June 27, 1966."

"Where, sir?"

"This was also at the Bridgewater State Hospital."

"Doctor, based on your observations and conversations with Mr. DeSalvo, do you have an opinion as to whether or not on June 17, 1966, Mr. DeSalvo was competent to sign business instruments provided the contents thereof were explained to him by his attorney?"

"Yes, I have an opinion, sir," said Mezer.

"What is your opinion?"

"That he was competent to do so."

"What is the basis of your opinion, Doctor?"

"The basis of my examination of him, on the various dates that I have just talked about."

"Did Mr. DeSalvo suffer from some mental illness during this period of time that you have talked about?"

"Yes, sir."

Mezer had diagnosed Albert as a chronic undifferentiated schizophrenic, just as Robey had.

But there was a difference.

Mezer pronounced himself completely satisfied that Albert's condition, which the doctor himself described as "a serious, major mental illness in which the individual's ability to get along in society is seriously impaired . . . characterized by the presence of

hallucinations, delusions, [and] violent behavior,"
would in no way impede his ability to enter into a
complicated business transaction if his attorney explained it to him.

On cross-examination, Troy asked Mezer to review
his knowledge of Albert's financial transactions at
Bridgewater.

Mezer, whom Troy had just subjected to a lengthy
inquisition on the exact nature of schizophrenia, was
a little weary. Nevertheless, he repeated his earlier remarks about Albert cashing VA checks and making purchases in the Bridgewater canteen.

"You don't mean that he handled this himself at all,
do you?" Troy asked.

"Mr. Troy—" Mezer began.

"No, Doctor, will you answer my question?" the lawyer thundered.

"Yes, but your yelling at me won't get me to
change."

"I am raising my voice so everyone can hear," explained Troy, "because I am a very meek individual in
nature."

"What I said was that he signed his own checks and
that he used the money to buy things for himself at
the hospital and he sent money to his family, and that
he handled these aspects of it himself."

"Don't they handle all the funds of an inmate at
Bridgewater for him?" Troy asked.

"I have no idea," Mezer replied.

"You have no idea," Troy said. "And you want to
leave your testimony that Albert handled these checks
himself and the money himself, right?"

"That is just precisely the way I would like to leave
it," said Mezer.

"Okay," said Troy. "You gave great weight, did you
not, to the statement of Albert DeSalvo when he said
'to engage in contracts, to make wills, to get a driver's
license, to get married,' you gave great weight in your

consideration of competency to that statement he made, did you not?"

"I gave it weight to the point that it showed that he knew what was involved in the various guardianships, yes, sir."

Troy moved in for the kill. "And every time you spoke with Albert DeSalvo, why, he spouted long phrases like that to you, didn't he?"

Lynch objected. Garrity overruled him.

"Doctor?" Troy prodded.

"No, sir," Mezer said.

"In fact," Troy went on relentlessly, "he never did it before, did he?"

"What is that again?" Mezer asked.

"He never gave you a statement like that containing such depth about anything, did he?"

"I think he did at other times," Mezer said.

"When?" Troy inquired. "Check your notes if you want to."

"At times we discussed different criminal charges," Mezer said, "and he had a very excellent knowledge of criminal charges and the penalties that were involved."

Troy struck with his broadsword. "Almost like they were memorized?"

"Yes, sir," said Mezer.

In January the matter of *Albert DeSalvo versus Twentieth Century-Fox and the Walter Reade Organization* was decided.

Judge Garrity found for the defendants Fox and Reade.

Troy requested an appeal.

His request was denied.

18

Endgame

Meanwhile, Bailey was having problems of his own with the judicial system of New Jersey. He had undertaken the defense of a publishing executive named Harold Matzner, who was accused of murdering Judith Kavanaugh, the wife of one of his employees, and Gabriel DeFranco, a minor underworld figure. Bailey felt that Matzner was being railroaded by the prosecution, whom he accused of bribing and threatening witnesses.

On April 28, 1968, Bailey wrote a letter to New Jersey Governor Richard Hughes outlining his complaints, with copies to United States Attorney General Ramsey Clark, New Jersey Attorney General Arthur Sills, the president of the New Jersey Bar Association, and the state's United States senators and congressmen. Because of a misunderstanding on his secretary's part, Bailey says in *The Defense Never Rests,* copies also went to every one of New Jersey's state legislators.*

Two days later it was also printed in the newspapers. As a result of this publicity, the New Jersey Supreme

---

* Bailey, p. 242

Court gave notice that it intended to remove Bailey from the Matzner case unless he could furnish it sufficient reason not to.

Bailey claimed before Judge Gordon Brown that he had nothing to do with the letter being given to the press; Judge Brown found nonetheless that Bailey had overstepped the boundaries of his professional sphere and in fact had demonstrated a "shocking contempt" for the code to which New Jersey lawyers were supposed to adhere—that of not attempting to try a case anywhere but in the courtroom.

Bailey was indeed removed as counsel to Harold Matzner. Ultimately, he was suspended from the practice of law in New Jersey for one year.

In 1969, Tom Troy dropped Albert as his client. Relations between them had grown strained after the failed lawsuit against Twentieth Century-Fox and Walter Reade; Troy had begun to find Albert's nonstop demands wearisome and irritating. "He was constantly asking me for money, and I told him I wasn't a banker," Troy says today. "I was a lawyer and if he didn't like it, he could place his lips upon my posterior."

Bailey says that the trouble he ran into in New Jersey inspired the Boston Bar Association to take a fresh look at his conduct in Massachusetts. In September 1969 it filed a complaint against him with the Supreme Judicial Court of the Commonwealth. Two of the charges against him were the same as those that had been leveled in 1967—his appearance on *The Tonight Show* to talk about the Coppolino case and the radio interview he'd done with Paul Benzaquin on the Plymouth mail robbery. The Boston Bar Association was also disturbed by the letter he'd written to the governor of New Jersey, Bailey says.

Perhaps unbeknownst to Bailey, a second party was gearing up to launch a formal complaint against him. That party was his former client Albert DeSalvo.

On Christmas Eve, 1969, Albert sent a letter (clearly written by someone else) to the Grievance Committee of the State Bar Association. In it he claimed that "since 1965—the beginning of my representation by Mr. Bailey—I have been unethically served by Mr. Bailey to such an extent that I have been seriously disadvantaged . . . In substance my charges are that Mr. Bailey knowingly involved me in contracts and litigations which essentially served his own interests and completely distorted or abandoned my own."

Five days later, Albert followed this with a four-page document in which he enumerated in detail his charges against Bailey. They were very much similar to the claims he'd made in U.S. District Court the previous year: that Bailey had refused to let him read the release to Gerold Frank, that the lawyer had not given Jon Asgeirsson or Albert's brother Joseph the chance to look it over, and that Bailey had misled him as to the contents and duration of the release. In addition, wrote Albert, "Bailey never established a guardianship for me that would have put competent people in charge of my personal, legal and medical affairs, when he knew perfectly well that I was not competent to handle my own affairs when they involved such complex issues." And, "Bailey made promises which he knew he couldn't or wouldn't keep and cited a legal fact or procedure what was not true." Albert said that Bailey had assured him that if a movie were to be made of Frank's book, a separate contract between Albert and the filmmaker would be forthcoming. "The truth was that the Frank 'release' empowered Frank to do this himself in spite of what I may wish."

Albert was entirely correct in believing that he had

already signed away his movie rights. On file in the
U.S. District Court in Boston is a document dated
September 2, 1967, in which Gerold Frank notified
Twentieth Century-Fox that he was granting to it the
permission he obtained from Albert DeSalvo for his
name and biography to be used in the film version of
Frank's book. Fox had optioned *The Boston Strangler*
for $15,000 and bought the property for an additional
$185,000. That option money was then turned over to
"Robert McKay" by the William Morris Agency, Frank's
representatives.

In the letter to the Bar Association Albert stated that
Bailey had promised him a civil commitment if the
verdict in the Green Man trial went against him. "He
lost the case and the question of civil committment
[*sic*] is a dream." And Albert bitterly accused Bailey of
appealing his case to the Supreme Judicial Court of
Massachusetts purely for form's sake, and with no expectation of winning a reversal of the conviction.

Frederick Norton, the secretary of the Boston Bar
Association, suggested that Albert be more specific in
describing his complaint against Bailey. On January 11,
1970, Albert replied to Norton—clearly with literary
help from his friend, George Nassar—providing this
account of the circumstances of the signing of the release:

> I told [Bailey] I wanted my brother present to
> look everything over and I asked him why my
> brother wasn't here. He said that he would ex-
> plain the release to my brother and I later. When
> I asked why I couldn't read them now he said that
> he didn't want anyone to know about the signing
> at this time because it was illegal; he said we could
> get into trouble. Even the guard outside the door
> couldn't know what I was signing or that I was
> signing anything. And Lee told me I shouldn't say
> anything specific to McGrath when he came into

the room to witness the signing. Lee said he would definitely show my brother the release next week and that I would have time to see it with him and Lee. But now I had to sign right away because Gerald [sic] Frank was waiting outside in a car and was impatient. Lee told me he had a hard time convincing Frank to go along with the release. Lee explained that Frank had already written his book and he could publish it without me. Therefore when Frank agreed to have me sign a release for fifteen per cent of the profits "He's doing you a favor."

Lee reminded me that the *Parade* magazine article about me being the Boston strangler had shown that I was now public domain. Therefore if I didn't take this opportunity with Frank now I would lose out completely.

I told him I wanted to be sure of what Frank was putting into the book about me. Lee said that nothing would be put into the book that would be detrimental to me. He promised he would get the book and show it to me and my brothers and that if we didn't want something in it he would have it taken out, that definitely the book wouldn't be published until it was shown to me and my brothers. "Trust me," Lee said. "I'm your attorney."

He explained how hard he had worked to get the release. He said he had to go out of his way to fly to New York to bring Frank here, that Frank was so uninterested Lee had to run after him. When I said that I wanted to look the papers over until next week Lee said that if I didn't sign them now Frank might go ahead without us: "You wait until next week and you may not get anything."

I told Lee I wanted time to think about it, to read the papers, to confer with my brothers and to get other people's opinions. Lee insisted that

time was important, that I couldn't now tell anyone what was happening, that I mustn't ever tell
my other attorney, Jon Asgeirsson, about the release.

Besides, Lee said, the release was only to last
for two years and they would have to get my signature again to continue to publish the book. Lee
also said that if the book were popular and the
movie companies wanted to make a picture of it
they would have to get my signature for a contract.

Lee explained that the book would do me good.
Frank was going to write about my needing hospitalization; the book could help me get into a
hospital.

Lee told me to call George McGrath into the
room. When McGrath came in Lee sat opposite
me across a small desk and McGrath sat beside
Lee. Lee told me to lean over close to him, with
my back to the door, and he leaned over close to
me and took out his pen and gave it to me. He
told McGrath to keep his eyes on the small window in the door for the guard. Lee took out the
folded papers from his breast pocket and lifted
one end of them so I could sign on the line above
my typed name. As I signed one page after another I tried to see the writing above my name
but Lee told me to hurry. Finally I got impatient
and unfolded the papers and saw the line about
the fifteen per cent. But I was so nervous I
couldn't read anything else; it was all just a series
of words. Lee made me hurry and when I finished
signing he told me to turn and watch the window
in the door while McGrath signed. Bailey said,
"I'll sign later."

When McGrath was through signing Lee said
that he had to leave immediately because Frank
wanted to get back to New York. He promised me

again he would show me and my brother the release, next week, which he never did.

On February 10, 1970, the Massachusetts Bar Association's action against Bailey was heard in the Suffolk
County Courthouse in Boston. Hiller Zobel, who had
been one of the principals in the 1967 investigation of
Bailey's conduct, was one of the prosecutors in this
matter. The presiding justice was Paul Kirk.

In *The Defense Never Rests* Bailey writes that Chief
Prosecutor Calvin Bartlett subjected him to rigorous
questioning about his literary activities, his television
show (canceled in midseason), his 1964 radio interview
on the Plymouth mail robbery, and his conduct in New
Jersey.

The hearing concluded on February 12. Bailey submitted briefs contesting the proceedings. Judge Kirk
arrived at his verdict and handed it down: censure.
Kirk's ruling seemed to indicate that he had considered disbarring Bailey.

Bailey wanted at first to appeal; on reflection, he
decided not to for fear of making matters worse.

That spring, the Bar Association asked one of its
members, Francis C. Newton, Jr., to look into Albert's
complaint against Bailey.

Newton, today seventy, is a tall, genial man with a
relaxed and unassuming manner. A World War II veteran, he is an avid Civil War buff whose office near
North Station in Boston is overflowing with books
about and memorabilia of the War Between the States.
He can discourse as fluently about Antietam as he can
on a point of criminal law.

Newton has many vivid memories of his famous client. One of these is of the very close relationship that
had developed between Albert and George Nassar.

"George had a rather strange hold over Albert," the lawyer says. "When you talked to Albert in George's presence, George would inject himself into the conversation." Nassar would also answer questions put to Albert before the latter could open his mouth to reply. Never was the one unaccompanied by the other.

Newton's experience in this respect was almost identical to that of Tom Troy. "On most occasions when I visited DeSalvo, I visited him in the presence of George Nassar," comments Troy. "He said Nassar was his adviser." And Nassar seems to have indeed acted as such. Newton has no doubt that Nassar helped Albert write the letters of complaint to the Bar Association, since the language and grammar of the documents was of a far more sophisticated level than Albert could attain on his own—although it was not at all beyond the grasp of the literate and articulate Nassar.

The sway Nassar held over Albert made Newton uneasy; the lawyer regarded his client's closest associate as "a very dangerous and twisted man." And he was concerned about the direction Nassar's influence over the easily led Albert might take: "George was a schemer."

His distaste for Albert's choice of advisers notwithstanding, Newton agreed to take the case. For even if the language of Albert's complaint against Bailey was Nassar's, the sentiments expressed therein were Albert's own, and to Newton they had merit. At base was a simple—and single—issue. "What it came down to was, Bailey had a lot of Albert's money, and where the hell was it?"

Again, Newton's reaction mirrored that of Troy, whose primary purpose in bringing suit against Twentieth Century-Fox and Walter Reade had been to get these funds disbursed.

Albert, who had once deified Bailey, had come to loathe him. And he was vocal about it to Newton. "All the time I knew Albert," says the lawyer, "he never had anything good to say about Bailey."

The trust Albert had once reposed in Bailey he now transferred to Newton. That much is evident in a letter he sent to the lawyer on July 27, 1970. This letter, which was probably worded by Nassar, also gives considerable insight into just how deeply dependent Albert was on any strong personality who offered him help or friendship. And it illuminates the intensity of his bond with Nassar.

F. Lee Bailey, who has been through the prison a couple of times recently to see a client, told me as he passed me in the corridor today, "I'm going to be down to see you shortly."

Needless to say I haven't been having any conversations with Mr. Bailey; in fact I practically ignored his greeting the last time he passed through here. So his comment today surprised me. And I thought that it is necessary that I write and tell you of this incident.

What should I do if he comes in to see me? Your associate told me that you would be down in about three weeks, and it is about that time now. Does his greeting indicate that he is coming down with you? And when can I expect to see you or hear from you? . . . If Mr. Bailey has me called out for an interview, I will insist, unless I hear otherwise from you, that at least George Nassar be present. When you come to see me, please sign in to see George Nassar also.

On August 16, 1970, in the very early hours of the morning, Albert and seventeen of his fellow inmates were rousted out of bed and shepherded into Walpole's Block Ten, the prison segregation unit. There they were kept "locket up," to use Albert's phrase, and denied any visitors other than their attorneys for thirty days. Walpole authorities had ordered this move as part of the investigation of a drug ring that was suspected of flourishing within the prison. Albert heatedly repudiated any involvement and prevailed on Newton to extricate him from the "hellhole." The lawyer went to work on it.

Over the summer, Newton and one of his assistants had been checking the matter of Albert's finances. Having conferred with Bailey, Newton was able to inform his client that "a reasonably substantial" sum of money appeared to be due him. Albert was pleased by that news, but very shortly another event occurred that took some of the edge off his satisfaction. He learned that Donald Conn, who was now running for attorney general of the Commonwealth, was using the fact that he had won a conviction against the "Boston Strangler" as the biggest plank in his campaign platform. Albert was furious at being thus identified, and wrote so in no uncertain terms to the incumbent Massachusetts attorney general, Robert H. Quinn: "What gives Donald D. Conn the right! To further prejudice any cases pending against Albert H. DeSalvo? . . . Mr. Conn here shows his true self, his stability, when he had to stoop so low as to use the name of a mentally-ill person who has never been 'indicted,' much less 'convicted,' of being the Boston Strangler.' To gain votes! . . . I plead to you, not only for myself, but for my family who much suffer every time my name is used by a person such as Mr. Conn." On a lighter note, Albert added that Conn ought to be sued for polluting the air of Massachusetts: "running his mouth throughout the commonwealth, 'unregistered and creating illegal exhaust!' P.S. When one loses their sense of humor. He loses his sense of being."

It is clear that Albert composed this letter without any assistance from George Nassar.

Then Albert complained to Newton that he hadn't yet heard from the Bar Association about the grievance he'd filed against Bailey. It is fortunate that Newton, who was currently engaged in trying to get money out of Bailey as well as getting Albert out of Block Ten, where he was still confined, was a patient man.

In November, Albert had a visitor other than his attorney or his brother and sister-in-law, Richard and Rosalie, the only relatives other than his mother who still maintained a connection with him. That visitor was Stephen Delaney, late of the Strangler Bureau. Delaney had left his investigative post with Bailey. He too had gotten in trouble in New Jersey during the Matzner case; he'd been accused of trying to tamper with the grand jury. Bailey says this was because Delaney had made the mistake of consulting a chiropractor who happened to be related to one of the grand jurors.*

Delaney was now in the employ of a Boston lawyer representing Roy Smith, the handyman convicted of raping and strangling Bessie Goldberg in Belmont in March of 1963. Smith had always maintained his innocence. Delaney had come to Walpole to question Albert about any possible involvement *he* might have in the crime. "In short, from what I gathered listening to him," Albert noted dryly to Newton, "he had high hopes it was I who did the Bessie Goldberg murder."

The following February Albert erupted in a fresh rage against Bailey. His reason? Bailey, along with defense attorneys Melvin Belli and Percy Foreman, had appeared on *The Merv Griffin Show* to discuss their most famous cases. During the broadcast Bailey, according to Albert, had stated that he had evidence to prove his former client was the Boston Strangler and that, furthermore, Albert shouldn't be confined to a mental institution because he would only escape from it. Albert demanded that Newton immediately launch a civil

---

* Bailey, p. 237.

suit (to the tune of five million dollars) against Bailey, and a further suit against the television network that had carried the show. He also wanted to get an injunction preventing Bailey from making any further public pronouncements on his case. He added that he would really prefer it if Bailey were disbarred, but this wasn't necessary.

He wrote a letter (with Nassar's apparent help) to Paul Reardon, a justice of the Supreme Judicial Court of Massachusetts, detailing this fresh complaint against Bailey. Then he shot off another irate missive to Frederick Norton, the Bar Association secretary, accusing the Association of doing "a wonderful job of covering up for [Bailey] so far as my case is concerned." And he wrote to the Massachusetts chapter of the American Civil Liberties Union asking for its help.

Newton took all this drama in stride—and kept on methodically pressing Bailey to disburse the funds due Albert.

That spring Albert became the victim of a practical joke. Representative Tom Moore sponsored before the Texas legislature a resolution commending Albert as one "officially recognized by the state of Massachusetts for his noted activities and unconventional techniques involving population control and applied psychology." The resolution further stated that "this compassionate gentleman's dedication to his work has enabled the weak and lonely, throughout the nation, to achieve and maintain a new degree of concern for their future."

The Texas House, to whose members the name Albert DeSalvo apparently meant nothing, passed the resolution without comment.

They did so on April Fool's Day.

While Newton was disentangling the financial skeins that still bound Albert to Bailey, Albert was by 1972 consulting another attorney, P.J. Piscitelli of Brockton, on different matters. He had decided—or perhaps someone had persuaded him—to go public with his story, or some version of it. To this end, he had made an agreement with reporter Steve Dunleavy to sit for a series of tape-recorded interviews that would form the basis of a book Dunleavy would write. Piscitelli drew up the requisite release forms for the various parties to sign. This time, at least, Albert seems to have been slightly more aware of what he was getting himself into. And he clearly believed that this project would yield him a considerable monetary return, which is probably the major reason he embarked on it.

The prospect of making some money on his terms may have lent some brightness to a life that was otherwise unremittingly bleak. Albert had had no contact whatsoever with his children since 1965. Irmgard, long since remarried, was lost to him forever. Richard and Rosalie continued their weekly visits, and he still heard from his mother. Otherwise he had been abandoned by the outside world, or by that part of it he most wanted to see.* And Walpole, which has been described as "the world's largest private nightclub" because of the relative ease with which its inhabitants can obtain drugs, liquor, and sex in one form or another, was to Albert the blackest of holes. In a letter to Piscitelli, he offered an evocative description of what hap-

---

* Women were still, however, attracted to him. But they were probably reacting more to his sinister glamour as a celebrity felon than to the man himself. He had contact with a woman in Maine; he had also developed a long-distance relationship (of which very little is known) with a woman in the South to whom he occasionally sent money. And he was visited fairly frequently by another woman, married with several children, whom Richard DeSalvo suspected of running drugs into the prison.

pened in the prison after two inmates were discovered missing:

Then the pigs came into our cells, one at a time, four pigs to a cell, they took every thing out of our cells, throwing them over the tier below smashing them and laughing, after they had us strip naked, skin shake!!! Leaving only a bed, chair, table, locker, pictures of loved ones were torn apart, and the frames broken as well as the glass, as they threw it over the rail below . . . The so-called food they are bringing around to us, pigs wouldn't eat it!! I throw it right back at them, so do the others. At least, at Franklin Zoo, they throw in a nice chunk of meat, could you get me a transfer there? I'm at least losing weight, they took every bit of food anyone had in there cells, name it they threw it out over the tier below. Tension is building up unbelievable!!! No one has any smokes, they closed the canteen, is only a matter of time, before. Its sad to think just the other day, another convict, so young, hung it up. Like so many other weak convicts will . . . I feel because of the type of So-called Supt. here. He is turning this place into a house of horror, and he is the one who is the man who will be responsible for all the many more deaths that are to follow!!! . . . Instead, he is building a H Bomb here!!!

Nassar, whom Albert had identified to Tom Troy as his adviser, now became, for all practical purposes, Albert's literary agent. On June 24, 1973, he wrote a letter to Piscitelli informing the lawyer that he would be handling any book offers that came Albert's way (as well as the arrangement with Steve Dunleavy) and would shortly be retaining a New York lawyer who specialized in publication contracts. Any inquiries along these lines that might be made to Piscitelli should be directed to Nassar himself.

Just how thorough Nassar's domination of Albert had become is made clear by the fact that Nassar was now even instructing Piscitelli on how Albert's criminal business should be conducted. "I think the time is approaching when you should begin preparing for the special trial," Nassar wrote. "In particular you should, as we see it, give us a general idea, and even point-by-point run-down, on the major factors of bringing the case to trial and the trial itself."

Piscitelli (who died in 1990) was apparently exploring the possibility of having Albert indicted for at least one of the strangling murders. Francis Newton, who was operating under the assumption that he was Albert's principal counsel, knew nothing of this plan and was astonished to learn of it twenty years later. It is impossible today to say whose idea this originally was.

Nassar wrote also to Richard and Rosalie DeSalvo to inform them that he had dismissed Piscitelli as Albert's attorney for publishing affairs. "If Pat is going to take offense at being pushed out of the literary business he'll insist on talking to you and Al personally about his status," he told them. "I know I don't have to caution you to be polite but firm with him. Pat can be very useful to us."

Nassar thought *Penthouse* as well as six or seven publishing houses was interested in buying Dunleavy's book. "I feel very good about the way things are going," he wrote to Richard and Rosalie. "We've got it more and more together, laying a good foundation for taking on publishers and New York attorneys and concluding a good deal. Between all of us we'll come out on top yet."

Nassar had more in mind than simply making money. "Maybe," he concluded in his letter to Richard and Rosalie, "[we'll] even buy Bailey's jet, since he won't be able to use it in jail."

That was in July of 1973.

By the autumn, the deal with Dunleavy had collapsed.

And Nassar and Albert were no longer best friends.

Richard DeSalvo, a muscular man of medium height with blue eyes and chestnut hair, bears a strong resemblance to Albert. Rosalie is shorter than her husband by several inches; she has dark curly hair threaded with gray and a round, youthful face. They have five children and several grandchildren and live quietly on a small farm northwest of Boston. Richard, who is legally blind—a vision problem he inherited from his mother—works the farm with the occasional help of one of his sons. Rosalie is employed at a local chain retail store.

Neither Richard nor Rosalie will ever forget the fall of 1973.

"Things were happening in the prison," Richard says today. "We had the feeling something was wrong. Al mentioned several times that he was fed up and sick and tired." Richard pauses. "We were in fear for him. He was acknowledging this."

Rosalie and Richard's weekly visits to Walpole had always been one of the great high spots in Albert's life, and they were certainly no chore for Richard and Rosalie. "We brought him cakes and pepperonis," Rosalie says. Albert, who worked in the prison shop as well as in the prison hospital as an orderly, made in return gifts for them—jewelry and handcrafted wooden items, for which he had a particular talent.*

What too some of the pleasure out of these hours with Albert for Rosalie and Richard was the constant

---

* Being the comedian that he was, he specialized in choker necklaces, which were sold to the public.

presence of George Nassar. "A freezer" is how Richard describes the latter. The intrusion made Richard suspicious as well as ill at ease. "It was like Nassar was there to make sure Al didn't say or do anything he wasn't supposed to." Rosalie was similarly edgy in Nassar's company.

Then, in the fall of 1973, Albert and Nassar had some sort of falling-out. Albert indicated to Richard that they'd disagreed over Albert's plans for his future.

The beginning of November was the last time Rosalie and Richard ever saw Albert. On that occasion, Albert did something he'd never done before. "He put his arms around me and gave me a big hug," says Richard. Then Albert said to his brother and sister-in-law, whose company he cherished, "I want you not to come visit me for a while." He couldn't—or wouldn't—explain why in any kind of concrete terms.

Richard and Rosalie left Walpole, confused and more than a little alarmed.

On Sunday evening, November 25, Albert telephoned Richard and Rosalie. He seemed in fairly good humor to them, laughing and joking about the Thanksgiving gifts he'd received.

He made another telephone call to someone else that same night. This time his tone was frightened; his message was urgent. There were no jokes about Turkey Day.

The next morning, Albert Henry DeSalvo, forty-two years old, was found dead in his bed. He had been stabbed multiple times in the heart and left lung. Any one of the wounds would have been sufficient to kill him.

Walpole went into lockdown. A prison authority remarked that Albert's murder had been carried out like a professional execution.

* * *

A week or so later Richard and Rosalie went down to the prison to retrieve Albert's personal effects.

Conspicuously absent from them was a manuscript Albert had been writing. He had been deliberately vague when discussing its contents with Richard and Rosalie; he hinted to them that it told, finally, the truth about his life.

Leaving the prison with the remnants of Albert's existence, Richard and Rosalie bumped into George Nassar. He asked them if they'd like a copy of Albert's autopsy report. Without waiting for an answer, he produced the document and gave it to Richard. Richard, barely sensible with grief, numbly accepted it.

Then Nassar turned to Rosalie and, smiling, embraced her.

"Now you can be *my* family," he said.

PART FOUR

19

Grave Doubts

"There isn't a cop in Cambridge who ever believed DeSalvo was the Strangler," says Captain William R. Burke, Jr., a patrol officer during the Strangler investigation.

"I don't know who the Boston Strangler was," says Tom Troy. "I just know it wasn't Albert DeSalvo."

"When I saw Albert," says Francis Newton, "I thought, this is not the guy who committed those stranglings."

"I don't think Albert DeSalvo strangled any one of those women," says retired Salem Police Lieutenant John Moran.

"Albert DeSalvo did none of the Boston stranglings," says former Boston Police Detective Sergeant James McDonald. "Nor any of the others."

His former boss, Commissioner Edmund McNamara, agrees. "I knew there was more than one killer."

"From what I know of Albert DeSalvo, he didn't kill anybody," says Cambridge Detective Sergeant Fidele Centrella. "If this guy had been involved in any homicide, believe me, he would have been charged."

And indeed Albert never was, except in that most high and merciless of all courts, that of public opinion.

* * *

Other than his own confession and the assertions of his attorney F. Lee Bailey, there is absolutely nothing to substantiate Albert's claim to be the murderer of Anna Slesers, Nina Nichols, Helen Blake, Ida Irga, Jane Sullivan, Sophie Clark, Patricia Bissette, Beverly Samans, Evelyn Corbin, Joann Graff, Mary Sullivan, and Mary Brown. Not a shred of physical evidence (including fingerprints) exists to connect him to any of the crimes. Nor was any eyewitness able to place him at the murder scenes or even in their vicinity.

At around 3:30 in the afternoon of November 23, 1963, the day of Joann Graff's murder, a man had knocked on the door of one of her neighbors at 54 Essex Street in Lawrence, Kenneth Rowe, an engineering student at Northeastern University. The stranger asked for "Joan" Graff. Rowe told him he had the wrong apartment and directed him to the proper one.

This individual later became a prime suspect in Joann's rape and strangling.

When shown a photograph of Albert, Rowe could not identify it.

Jules Vens, proprietor of Martin's Tavern in Lawrence, a short distance from 54 Essex Street, reported to police that at 2:00 P.M. and again at 4:30 P.M. on November 23, 1963, a man—not a regular customer—had come into the bar. During his second visit he was visibly nervous and agitated, seemingly apprehensive about being followed. He used the men's room and left without ordering a beer as he had on his first visit.

He was dressed similarly to the man who had spoken with Kenneth Rowe. At the time of his second visit to the tavern, his clothing was wrinkled.

When shown a photograph of Albert, Vens could not identify it.

A little before 3:30 P.M. on January 4, 1964, the day Mary Sullivan was murdered, schoolteacher Eileen

O'Neil happened to glance out a window of her apartment, which looked onto the rear of Mary's building. In one of the windows she saw the profile of a man whom she assumed to be standing in a hallway. (It was later determined that whoever this person was, he was in fact in the bathroom gazing at himself in the mirror.) The man appeared to O'Neil to be tall and to have reddish-brown hair.

When Eileen O'Neil was shown a photograph of Albert, she could not identify it.

Three fresh Salem cigarette butts were found in an ashtray near Mary Sullivan's bed. Neither Mary nor her roommates Pamela Parker and Patricia Delmore smoked this brand.

A Salem cigarette butt was found floating in the toilet of Apartment 4-C at 315 Huntington Avenue in Boston the day Sophie Clark died there. Salems were one of the brands that Sophie and her roommates Audri Adams and Gloria Todd preferred. The butt in the toilet may have been left there by Sophie's killer.

Albert DeSalvo did not smoke.

Marcella Lulka, a resident of 315 Huntington Avenue, told police that at 2:30 in the afternoon of December 5, 1962, a man calling himself Thompson had come to her apartment stating he was there to paint it. He then began making complimentary—and suggestive—remarks about Mrs. Lulka's figure. She got rid of him by telling him that her husband was home asleep in the bedroom. She described the stranger to police as approximately twenty-five years old, about five feet nine inches tall, with pale honey-colored hair combed straight back and an oval face. At first she thought he might be a light-skinned black male; later she claimed he could be white.

At 5:00 P.M. on December 5, 1962—a half-hour before Sophie's body was discovered—William Ronalder of 315 Huntington described this person as a light-skinned black man, around twenty-five years of age, with long hair, possibly dark, combed back. He wore a dark waist-length jacket, just as the man who'd come to Mrs. Lulka's door had. Ronalder didn't think he'd recognize the man if he saw him again.

Eartis Riley, wife of Anthony Riley, the nurse who'd attempted to resuscitate Sophie, told police that at about 4:30 on the day of the murder "a light-skinned colored man whom she new as 'Al' came to her door and asked for a book he claimed Anthony had promised to lend him. Mrs. Riley knew nothing about any book. She noticed that Al "was perspiring heavily and also appeared to be very excited."

The description she gave the investigators was that of a black man about six feet tall, 160 pounds, twenty-six years old, with light brown skin and sandy hair waved backward. He was clad in a dark waist-length cloth jacket.

None of these descriptions in any way resembled that of Albert DeSalvo.

Mrs. Lulka later sketched for police a portrait of "Thompson." It shows a delicately featured young man with a long, narrow face, a very thin nose, a pointed chin, and large, almond-shaped eyes. It looks nothing like Albert DeSalvo.

The same can be said of any composite drawing made of any suspect in the Strangler case.

In March of 1965, after Albert had begun confessing to the stranglings, Mrs. Lulka was taken by authorities to Bridgewater. There she viewed Albert in person. She had never seen him before in her life.

Accompanying Mrs. Lulka was a woman named Erika Wilsing, formerly of 26 Melrose Street in Boston, thought by some police officials to be the sole survivor of a Strangler attack. On February 18, 1963, Wilsing, a native of Germany, had been assaulted in her apartment by a man who told her that if she didn't fight him, he'd let her go. Despite this warning, Wilsing struggled furiously with her assailant; he grabbed her around the throat and she bit him on the right hand.

The man fled without raping or seriously injuring Miss Wilsing.

Albert had allegedly confessed to this assault. He claimed he'd had a knife. Wilsing couldn't really recall if the man who'd attacked her had been so armed.

Albert also reportedly described Miss Wilsing's apartment perfectly, even noting details of its appointments she herself had forgotten after she moved out of it. (A kitchen chair she thought was brown was in fact blue, as Albert had said it was.)

Gilbert Chinn, a handyman working at 28 Melrose Street the day Wilsing was attacked, told investigators that at about 12:30 P.M. he saw a man enter Wilsing's apartment building "as if he lived there." Five or ten minutes later, Chinn heard a woman scream. Shortly after that, the man he'd seen earlier emerged from the building, yanking on a blue raincoat.

Chinn was unable to identify a photograph of Albert.

Erika Wilsing, brought into Albert's presence at Bridgewater, did not recognize him either.

Another inmate did, however, catch the eye not only of Wilsing but of Marcella Lulka. Both women told police that they found him very familiar-looking. In fact, Mrs. Lulka claimed that but for the fact that this man's hair was dark, he could have been the double of the "Thompson" who'd shown up at her front door that cold gray day in December of 1962.

The man Wilsing and Lulka found so familiar-looking was George Nassar.*

---

* According to F. Lee Bailey, Albert said that *he* recognized Erika Wilsing and Marcella Lulka. (Lulka's photograph had been in the newspapers.) Of the tentative identification of George Nassar, Bailey states in *The Defense Never Rests* (p. 164) that it was rigged by someone at Bridgewater who wanted to deflect suspicion away from

* * *

The Cambridge Police Department has had plenty of experience with sadistic murderers, violent sex offenders, and serial killers. And it is this experience that, apart from anything else, leads its officers to the conviction that Albert DeSalvo was none of the above. He simply didn't fit the type.

Retired Detective James Roscoe was one of those who investigated the so-called "Hitchhike Murders" that plagued the greater Boston area in the early 1970s. Several of the victims had been known to thumb rides regularly to and from work or school, hence the nickname.

One of the first to die horribly was nineteen-year-old Ellen Reich, an Emerson College student whose body was found in an abandoned apartment on Seaver Street in the Roxbury section of Boston. It had been concealed in a closet, the door of which had been nailed shut. Forensic evidence proved that Ellen had been raped, or had engaged in sexual intercourse with her killer, just before her death. She had been strangled and shot in the chest and stomach.

The last day anyone saw twenty-two-year-old Damaris Synge Gillespie alive was November 29, 1972. Her body was found twenty miles away in Billerica on February 3, 1973. The Cambridge resident and university student had been strangled to death on the day she vanished.

The perpetrator was one Anthony Jackson, a man distinguished by a phenomenally high I.Q. and a terrifying and seemingly insatiable appetite for cruelty. A pimp who lived with (and off of) three women in Roxbury, he was arrested in Cambridge on the night of December 26, 1973, when Officer John Conroy spotted

Albert and onto George Nassar.

him driving down a city street gesturing at a young woman on the sidewalk. Jackson was apparently trying to pick up the girl. When he noticed the police presence, Jackson sped off in his Cadillac. A chase ensued and Jackson shot at Officer Joseph McSweeney, who returned the fire and downed Jackson.

Anthony Jackson is today serving a life sentence, without the possibility of parole, at Walpole State Prison. He has been linked to as many as twenty-seven murders of young women. Some authorities believe that the corpse of one of his victims lies beneath the foundation of a high-rise office building in Cambridge. Jackson had apparently quite deliberately placed the body in the excavation just before the concrete was to be poured.

James Roscoe, who knew Anthony Jackson, and knew Albert DeSalvo, sees no resemblance between the two. Roscoe had several long conversations with the latter after Albert was brought into the Cambridge police headquarters on the charge of assaulting Suzanne Macht.

"I sat and talked to him," Roscoe says today. "But I did not think he had the brutality to strangle women."

Albert's personality, Roscoe adds, was altogether different from that of a proven serial killer such as Jackson.

Former Cambridge Detective Michael Giacoppo concurs with Roscoe's assessment. "A gentle guy" was the phrase one of albert's sexual assault victims used to describe him to Giacoppo. She added, to Giacoppo's complete astonishment, that she wouldn't have minded if Albert had paid her a return visit.

Such comments raise the question of whether Albert was even a serial rapist, much less a serial killer. There is no doubt that he suffered from an ungovernable sex drive. He told one Cambridge detective that at one point he had masturbated so vigorously and so frequently that he passed blood when he urinated. And there is Irmgard DeSalvo's testimony that she simply couldn't meet his desires.

Certainly in his Measuring Man days he was never violent. And if women resisted his advances, he left them alone and unharmed. "He didn't fight back," says an ex-Cambridge detective. "He took off."

How often Albert had to leave his sexual appetite unsatisfied after he entered a woman's home is a good question. The Cambridge detective quoted above describes how Albert charmed his way into the home of a local university professor, whose wife offered to put on a leotard and dance for him. Later, while Albert and the woman were having intercourse on the living room floor, her husband called from work. She chatted with him in an offhand fashion while Albert continued making love to her. The woman later filed a complaint with the Cambridge police but refused to identify Albert, although she apparently recognized him. She also indicated that the sex act had been consensual.

Albert's specialty, it seems, was oral sex.

"He was a superb seducer," says Ames Robey.

And one with a keen and appreciative eye for good-looking women. A former Cambridge detective, reminiscing about the day a number of Albert's local assault victims were summoned to police headquarters to give their stories, says, "It looked like they were holding the Miss Universe Pageant at the front desk."

Says another cop, "He had some of the prettiest girls you ever did see. Beauty queens."

The youth and physical appeal of the women who succumbed to Albert's sunny smile (and other distinctive corporeal attributes—he clearly was possessed of a silver tongue in more ways than one) and boyish con routine made it hard for the Cambridge police to believe he would abruptly turn to assaulting elderly women such as Nina Nichols, Helen Blake, Ida Irga, and Jane Sullivan.

"We never could figure out why a guy who had champagne and caviar every day suddenly went to beans and hot dogs," says one detective.

In any case, "Al never had to kill anybody," states another Cambridge cop. "He was a very gentle guy."

The word *gentle* comes up often when those who knew Albert DeSalvo speak of him.

Albert had allegedly begun hinting that he was the Strangler in January of 1965, and confessing to being the Strangler in very early March of that year.

Months later, nobody was taking him seriously except for F. Lee Bailey, Jon Asgeirsson, and Lieutenants John Donovan and Edward Sherry of the Boston Police Department. Donovan and Sherry had been providing Bailey with extensive and hitherto (it was claimed) unpublished information about the murders so the lawyer could verify DeSalvo's statements.

On May 4, 1965, John Bottomly wrote to Edward Brooke, "As you know the DeSalvo story does not stand up well when compared with the relatively little objective evidence and witnesses now available to investigators. However, in view of the proclivities of one of his counsels it appears that more will be necessary to either eliminate DeSalvo as a suspect or charge him with one or more of the murders."

Part of Bottomly's skepticism may have been engendered by an investigation being conducted by Task Force member Stephen Delaney. At 2:45 P.M. on March 18, 1965, a fifty-two-year-old chambermaid named Effie MacDonald had been found strangled to death in Room 318 of the Boston House in Bangor, Maine. Her supine body, clad in a white uniform, had been found on the floor very near to and facing the room entrance. Her shoes and stockings had been removed, her dress was ripped open all the way down the front. Her eyeglasses lay next to her right foot; a towel cov-

ered the lower part of her body. Her legs were apart,
her left shoe between them before her crotch.

The tight ligature around her neck consisted of two
stockings. There was a large swollen bruise over her
left cheek. Her body was still warm when she was
found.

On April 5, 1965, Delaney wrote Bottomly a long
memo detailing the similarities between the murder of
Effie MacDonald and those of Anna Slesers, Helen
Blake, Nina Nichols, Ida Irga, and Jane Sullivan. "The
victim, like our earlier victims, was divorced, lived a
quiet life with just a few friends, no boyfriends, did not
drink or smoke, was 55 [sic] years of age, about 130
lbs, which was the average weight of the Boston victims . . . The manner in which she was assaulted and
the MO of the assault especially the trickery of getting
this woman into the room are all characteristic to the
methods employed in the Boston crimes. The element
of surprise and trust was also utilized in this case and
I cannot attribute these to the average rapist."

Delaney concluded his memo with the comment
that "obviously it is my feeling that this woman is very
possibly the latest victim of the multiple 'Strangler.' "

Delaney, who would quit the police and go to work
for F. Lee Bailey the following year, would later considerably modify his belief that as of the late spring of
1965 the Boston Strangler was still on the loose and
not incarcerated in Bridgewater State Hospital trying
to convince someone other than F. Lee Bailey of his
guilt.

20

Origins of a Hoax

If Albert DeSalvo was not the Boston Strangler, where did he get the information about the killings that enabled him to persuade F. Lee Bailey, Jon Asgeirsson, Gerold Frank, Edward Sherry, John Donovan, Phillip DiNatale, Andrew Tuney, and some members of the media that he was the savage murderer of thirteen women?

The answer is that there was a minimum of six excellent sources for the necessary data readily available to him.

Even so, how did Albert manage to absorb, assimilate, and retain so much varied and detailed information?

The answer to that question lies in a piece of testimony given by Ames Robey at the 1968 court proceeding launched by DeSalvo against the maker and distributor of the Strangler movie. Robey had commented of his former patient that the latter had "absolute, complete, one hundred per cent total photographic recall."

Robey was not the only person to note—and remark on—this talent.

"He [DeSalvo] had a very retentive memory," says one Cambridge detective.

"Albert had a phenomenal memory," says Jon Asgeirsson.

"It was remarkable," says Tom Troy.

Robey cites an example of how he tested Albert's ability to make instantaneous mental carbon copies of people, places, and things: "We had a staff meeting [at Bridgewater] with about eight people. Albert was walked in and walked out. The next day we had him brought back in. Everyone had on different clothes, was sitting in different positions. I said, 'Albert, you remember coming in yesterday. Describe it.' "

Albert did, perfectly.

The first source of information about the killings available to Albert was the press itself. Newspaper accounts of the stranglings had been extraordinarily detailed. With respect to the murder of Anna Slesers, the *Globe,* on June 15, 1962, reported that she had been found naked but for her housecoat, which had been ripped open, its cord tightly knotted around her neck, and that she had been beaten before being choked. On the same date the *Traveler* informed its readership that Anna's body bore bruises and that she had been dead for about three hours before she was found by her son. The *Traveler* article included the further detail that there was blood from the victim's right ear on the kitchen floor. The *Herald* repeated this latter finding, noting too that Anna lay on her back on the kitchen floor. On July 4, the *Globe* reported that the killer first tried to strangle her with a man's leather belt, but it broke: "Police said he would have to be a man of unnatural strength to do that."

Even the sexual assaults on the women were graphically described. Whoever glanced at the *Globe*'s account of Nina Nichols's death could conclude that she had been not only strangled but abused with a wine bottle. That Evelyn Corbin's killer may have forced or coerced

her to perform oral sex on him was also a published
fact.

As frank as the *Globe,* the *Traveler,* and even the *Herald* may have been, they were left in the shade by the
Record American daily and its *Sunday Advertiser.* On January 9, 1963, the tabloid launched a series on the murders written by ace reporters Jean Cole and Loretta
McLaughlin. The lead article the *Record* entitled TWO
GIRL REPORTERS ANALYZE STRANGLER.*

On January 14, McLaughlin and Cole gave an exceptionally detailed account of the murder of Helen
Blake. Included in it was not only an exact description
of the layout of the victim's apartment, but a step-by-step rendition of how the killer had rummaged though
Helen's belongings:

> Some drawers are pulled out of a desk and a
> bureau. Others are removed completely and set
> on the floor. The drawers have been examined.
>
> A large black trunk has been taken from the
> bedroom closet and placed on a chair. The lock
> has been released with a broken knife, and the tip
> of the blade, broken in the process, is still in the
> lock hinge. The handle of the knife and the rest
> of its blade rests [*sic*] against Helen's moccasin-slipper on the floor under her bed.
>
> Helen's watches have all been examined and
> placed on the bureau. Her jewelry boxes have
> been opened and are on the floor. Her pocket-books have been gone through. Even the sugar
> bowl and teapot have been looked into.

McLaughlin and Cole's January 15 article gave even
further details of the crime and the crime scene. ("Her

---

* The "girls" were in their early thirties, married, and
  mothers.

coffee cup still clean was set out on a small table in the living room") and the murderer's actions ("He opened a footlocker, storing bed lines and towels").

It was brilliant investigative journalism. It was also practically all the information anyone needed in order to make a plausible-sounding confession to the murder.

On January 23, McLaughlin and Cole examined the death of Ida Irga. Again, the detail included in the story was astonishing: that a hand mirror lay on a table in Ida's living room; that the toilet seat was raised (here, as in the case of Sophie Clark, a cigarette butt was found floating in the bowl); that Ida's suitcase rested on the studio couch in the living room.

Toward the end of the piece was this paragraph:

> When he rendered Ida unconscious, her assailant dragged her to the living room where he assaulted her, this time locking the feet of the victim in the slats of two chairs.

On January 23, under full-face photographs of Anna Slesers, Helen Blake, Ida Irga, Jane Sullivan, Sophie Clark, and Patricia Bisette, the *Record* printed THE FACTS: ON REPORTERS' STRANGLE WORKSHEET. Rather than an article, this was a chart that listed the names of the victims, their ages, the times of their deaths, the times their bodies were found, the causes of their deaths, the probability of sexual assault, where the bodies had been found, where the victims had been killed, what they had been wearing, and whether their apartments had been ransacked. There were also detailed notes on the victims' hobbies and personal interests, on their employment, and on their affiliations—if any—with area hospitals.

That DeSalvo had memorized this chart is apparent because in his confession to John Bottomly, he regurgitated not only the correct data on it but the few pieces of misinformation it contained as well.

A second source of information about the crimes was law enforcement. "The case had leaks all over it," says Edmund McNamara, his disgust with this state of affairs obvious even today.

One of the major leaks was Suffolk County Medical Examiner Richard Ford, who according to McNamara held frequent unauthorized press conferences at which he liberally distributed information about the autopsy findings on the victims. Ford was at odds with—and in direct competition with—his colleague Dr. Michael Luongo. In terms of personality, the two men were polar opposites. Luongo was a reserved, methodical, thoughtful man who, as procedure dictated, submitted his findings directly to the district attorney's office and gave minimal information to the press. Ford, in contrast, was handing out copies of the autopsy protocols to reporters. Understandably, they loved him for his largesse.

Former Boston Police Department Detective Sergeant James McDonald says today that the Strangler Bureau itself was appallingly lax in its handling of the confidential files on the murders. Rather than being kept under lock and key, McDonald states, the files, or casebooks, were left strewn around the State House headquarters of the Bureau, readily available to be leafed through by any visitor who wished to do so. One of McDonald's colleagues on the Boston Homicide Squad, having business to discuss with the Strangler Task Force, entered the Bureau offices one afternoon and bumped into a group of State House pages goggling over the crime scene photos and trading them back and forth like baseball cards.

The Strangler Bureau's failure to exercise tight control over the material it had accumulated concerning the murders is confirmed by the Task Force members themselves. In the February 1967 memo to Herbert Travers written by Sandra Irizarry, Andrew Tuney, and Phillip DiNatale, they described how in April of 1964 they had been ordered by Bottomly to throw open the murder files to Gerold Frank, an order to which they objected vehemently, but to no avail; The trio also stated:

> During the monumental task of xeroxing the casebook files to be distributed to the Boston Police Department, the Department of Public Safety, and the Cambridge Police Department, several different Eminent Domain Division office boys were pressed into service. They had, therefore, the opportunity to read over certain material. In addition, it must be remembered that until the files were organized and sent to the other police departments involved, the lack of space available at the time required that much of this material was spread out over every available desk and table. They were subject to the *casual perusal* [emphasis added] of the regular staff members of the Eminent Domain Division. *Also, all outside telephone calls and conversations between staff members took place within probable hearing distance of both eminent domain staff members and casual visitors to the department* [emphasis added].

The end result of the Strangler Bureau's carelessness was that any leaked or purloined so-called secret information about the murders that wasn't published in the newspapers ended up public property anyway. That Mary Sullivan had been found dead with the handle of a broom inserted three inches into her vagina had never been printed or broadcast. The general population was nonetheless quite aware of this ghastly fact.

Even Gerold Frank reports that "it was common knowledge on the streets."

Where, presumably, anybody, including Albert De-
Salvo, could have picked it up.

A third source of information on the murders was
the "research" Albert had done himself. After DeSalvo
was convicted on the Green Man charges, Robey asked
him how he'd obtained the familiarity he'd shown with
the layouts of the Strangler's victims' apartments. That
was child's play for him, Albert maintained. So fascinated had he been by press accounts of the murders
that he'd taken the trouble to visit—and tour—each
crime scene. He'd had no trouble slipping in and out
of each dwelling.

He was, after all, a past master of the art of housebreaking.

What data Albert didn't procure through the street
grapevine, from the newspapers, or through his own
investigations, may have been fed to him before and
after he began confessing—inadvertently in some cases
and quite deliberately in others.

On March 20 and 21, 1965, Bailey had brought
hypnoanalyst William Joseph Bryan III to Bridgewater
for the purpose of putting Albert into a trance in
order to elicit from him further details of the murders that might be buried in his subconscious mind.
In their respective books, Gerold Frank and Bailey
offer partial transcripts of these sessions. According
to both, Bryan urged Albert to think of the strangling
victims as substitutes for his wife, Irmgard, and his
daughter, Judy—the true targets of Albert's homicidal rage, Bryan opined. As Frank himself wrote,
"those who witnessed the hypnoanalysis wondered
how much DeSalvo had been led or influenced by Dr.

Bryan, so forceful and domineering." And indeed, Bryan's questions seem to have been highly suggestive: "Each time you strangled, it was because you were killing Judy, wasn't it? You were killing Judy . . ."*

Bryan drew a further connection between the kind of massage Albert had been taught to perform on Judy as therapy for her hip disease, which entailed placing painful pressure with the thumbs on the child's thighs, and the sexual molestation of the murder victims.

Who can say to what extent, too, the resolve of Albert (who had been injected with sodium pentothal as well as hypnotized) to be known as the Strangler might have been strengthened by Bryan's words?†

It may be possible, too, that F. Lee Bailey, when conducting his initial interrogations of Albert, accidentally let slip some of the confidential information Donovan and Sherry had given him.

Beyond that, what kind of questions did Bailey pose? How did he phrase them? How difficult were they to answer?

In a book entitled *Confessions of the Boston Strangler,* published in February 1967 by Pyramid Books, author George Rae wrote that "[John] Donovan primed Bailey with half-questions and key words such as *'What was Nina's last name?'* . . . *'What happened on June 30, 1962?'* *'What kind of foreign objects figured in the stranglings'* . . . *'How were these foreign objects used?'* . . . *'What was the color of this chair?'* . . . *'Miss Clark's first name'* . . . and so on."‡

If Rae is accurate, then Bailey was asking questions that could have been answered by any reasonably alert

---

* Frank, p. 274.
† Dr. Bryan had acquired his hypnoanalytic skills from his parents, a pair of vaudevillians whose stage act included inducing members of the audience to emulate chickens.
‡ The ellipsis and italicizations in the above passage are Rae's (p. 13).

newspaper reader—even one not blessed with a photographic memory.

Two people are suspected by local law enforcement authorities of having deliberately provided Albert with information about the stranglings so as to make his confession to them the more substantive and therefore believable. One of these individuals was a Boston police detective, now deceased, who resigned from the force when Edmund McNamara relieved him of his investigative duties and returned him to uniformed patrol. When this person left the department, he took with him handwritten copies of sensitive and privileged information (in enormous quantity) about the murders. He was known, prior to April 1965, to be in regular contact with Albert at Bridgewater. Some of this man's ex-colleagues believe he may have been motivated by revenge against the Boston Police Department to feed data on the stranglings to Albert. Others think he did so in order to solve the case and claim the reward money.

The second person investigators speculate might have coached Albert for his role as a serial killer was George Nassar.

There is, however, a third party, who beyond the shadow of a doubt, *did* knowingly and quite intentionally provide Albert with information about the murders—while he was taking the latter's confession to them.

That was John Bottomly, during August and September of 1965.

As a tutor, Bottomly was persistent but ultimately inept. Lengthy as the confession was that he extracted from Albert, it is remarkably thin in incriminating detail, which explains why the only versions of it ever made public were abbreviated and heavily doctored.

The full version virtually exonerates DeSalvo.

21

The Confessions of
Albert DeSalvo, I

When Bottomly quit the attorney general's office in 1966, he took the original tape recordings of DeSalvo's confession—some fifty-four hours' worth—with him. It was clear he didn't want the contents made public. Elliot Richardson, who succeeded Edward Brooke as chief law enforcement official of the Commonwealth, suspected that Bottomly had removed the recordings, but he wasn't sure of it until *Globe* reporter Ronald Wysocki confirmed the fact on February 14, 1968.

Interviewed by Wysocki, Bottomly agreed that the tapes were the state's property. He also told the reporter that he'd asked Richardson, Donald Conn, and Herbert Travers (the head of the attorney general's office's criminal division) what they wanted him to do with the tapes, but none of the men bothered to respond to the question.

"Does anybody want them now?" Bottomly blandly inquired of Wysocki.

Richardson apparently did. And he emphatically denied that Bottomly had ever said anything to him about the disposition of the recordings.

In the story he wrote for the *Globe,* Wysocki compared his effort to get Bottomly to reveal the location of the tapes to "playing '20 Questions.'"

"Do you know where they are?" Wysocki asked.

"Yes," Bottomly replied.

"Where?"

"In a bank vault," Bottomly said.

"Who got the vault?" Wysocki asked.

"I did."

"Who has the key?"

"I have."

"Are there any other keys?" Wysocki wanted to know.

"Not to my knowledge," Bottomly said.

"Then you have the tapes," Wysocki deduced.

"No," Bottomly said. "The bank has them."

"But you have the only key?" the reporter asked.

"To the best of my knowledge," Bottomly replied. Then he said, "Why don't you ask the really important question? Why hasn't the Attorney General come and gotten the tapes—because they're not going to try the guy anyhow."

That much was true.

Shortly after Albert's murder in 1973, there were calls from the press that the tapes be made public. And in fact some news organizations did eventually acquire recordings of one sort or another of Albert describing some of the murders. At least one of these tapes seems to have been made in 1967, well after Gerold Frank's book had been published—and well after the purported Strangler had read it.

Bottomly's own transcript of the 1965 interrogations still exists. It includes a list of the questions Bottomly would put to Albert, and some notes to himself that the Task Force chief had scribbled.

"Start by learning all you can about Albert," one of these notes reads. "Learn all you can."

Having made what preparations he felt were necessary, Bottomly went down to Bridgewater in early August of 1965 to begin interrogating the man who so badly wanted to be known as the Strangler.

Albert was eager to talk, which Bottomly encouraged by adopting a jocular yet sympathetic manner toward him. (In this respect, at least, Bottomly showed some ability as an interviewer.) Albert boasted of his sexual exploits. Bottomly responded with the appropriate exclamations ("Fantastic!") of awe and admiration. Albert, warmed by the flattery of this important man, began to regard the Task Force chief as his buddy—precisely as Bottomly had intended he should.

The con man had fallen for yet another con.

Albert spoke at length of his embittered love for Irmgard: "I gave her everything. I gave her every dime I ever had. Never kept a dime in my pocket. I didn't drink. Didn't go out anywhere. Didn't go out nights for two years."

"She gave nothing in return," Bottomly observed.

"Nothing," Albert said. "Ah, you might say I tried to buy her. That's one way of looking at it. But I loved her so much that I would give her anything. See?"

He grimly predicted that Irmgard might change her name, might remarry, might flee to the ends of the earth. But she would never escape his memory.

Bottomly told Albert that a detective had interviewed Irmgard at her new home out west.

"How did she talk about me?" Albert asked eagerly. "What kind of attitude did she say?"

"Oh terrific," Bottomly assured him. "She was—couldn't praise you enough."

"She still cares for me in many ways," Albert said.

"Oh, yes," Bottomly said. "Yes."

The Task Force chief explained to Albert how Edward Brooke had charged him with the responsibility of solving the strangling murders.

"In other words," Albert commented, "he gave you something you couldn't handle?"

"I don't know," Bottomly replied. "Here we are. Maybe we could handle it."

Albert then remarked that in the six months that had elapsed since he'd begun confessing to the murders, the Task Force hadn't been able to find a trace of evidence to connect him to the crimes. All they had was one man's (interestingly, Albert here referred to himself in the third person) statement of guilt.

"That's right," Bottomly said. "I couldn't do it without your admission."

"Right," Albert said. "But I—I—"

"And even more than that," Bottomly continued, "I have to convince myself that your admissions aren't self-serving. I've explained this to you."

"Yuh, you—"

"You—you've got motives that, uh, could explain why you're confessing—I'm not saying they are—but they could explain why you're confessing though you may not have done [all the murders]. You might have done some and you tie them all in. You might have done one, and you might not have even done any."

"That's right," Albert said.

He spoke scornfully of Jon Asgeirsson, telling Bottomly that the information he'd given the attorney in January of 1965 (when he'd told Asgeirsson he was the Strangler and furnished details about a few of the murders to bolster his claim) had been a complete fabrication. He also told Bottomly that it was Asgeirsson who'd advised him in early 1965 to feign hallucinations so he'd be transferred out of the East Cambridge jail and into a mental institution while awaiting further legal action on the Green Man charges.

Bottomly asked Albert if Ames Robey had been a party to this fakery.

"Nah," Albert said dismissively. "He has no brains to have any conspiracy, to be honest witcha."

* * *

Albert did not confess to the murders in their chronological order—probably because, despite his much-vaunted memory, he not only had terrible trouble recalling *when* some of them occurred but even *that* some of them had occurred. But if Albert couldn't come up with a date, Bottomly would oblige with it—along with any other relevant details Albert might require to flesh out his rambling fantasy of rape and murder.

That Albert was not only receptive to these cues but was also desperately trying to anticipate the kind of response Bottomly wanted, and to gauge from Bottomly's reaction whether he was answering the Task Force chief's questions "correctly," is obvious in the following exchange about the murder of Anna Slesers. Bottomly had asked Albert to describe the victim's clothing.

> ALBERT: . . . The type of blue robe she had on was like a cloth, you know what I mean?
>
> BOTTOMLY:: Flannel?
>
> ALBERT: Ya, oh well ah, flannel if you want it cotton.
>
> BOTTOMLY: Cotton.
>
> ALBERT: Ya but ah—
>
> BOTTOMLY: Thick or—
>
> ALBERT: Ah, it was a kind I don't like. It bothered me. Very funny thing to it.
>
> BOTTOMLY: Ya.
>
> ALBERT: But it was nothing funny about it. It was just dark. It was a navy, a light navy blue you might call it—light.
>
> BOTTOMLY: Ya.

"And there was that on that there on her," Albert concluded, in what must have been a near-babble.

Despite Albert's apparent desire to get off the subject of the housecoat, Bottomly kept pressing the point, asking what color the robe's lining had been.

ALBERT: The lining—

BOTTOMLY: Yuh? The inside—

ALBERT: There was no lining.

BOTTOMLY: Well, the inside, on the inside, do you remember?

ALBERT: As far as I can remember, blue.

BOTTOMLY: Yuh. You don't remember any different color?

ALBERT: Not—no.

BOTTOMLY: OK. Now do you wanna, do you wanna go on to some other cases or do you work with—

ALBERT: I'll do anything you want but—

He had certainly tried. And failed. The proper answer to the question about the lining of the housecoat would have been "red." The garment was thus described in the autopsy report. That and the police report taken at the crime scene stated that the outer part of Anna's robe was blue cloth.

The "Strangle Worksheet" chart published in the *Record* had described the housecoat as "blue quilted taffeta" with no reference to any kind of lining. One wonders if this was where Albert got *his* description of the robe, and whether his impression that there was something "very funny" about it referred to the quilting he'd read of in this paper.

Bottomly had further questions about the crime scene that Albert couldn't answer.

BOTTOMLY: Do you remember a wastebasket in her kitchen? Do you see a wastebasket? Do you see a table?

ALBERT: Ah, there is ah, (whisper) I can picture this, um, wastebasket? On her? I don't recall, but I do remember what her bedroom set looked like.

There was in fact a wastebasket in Anna's kitchen, and bits and pieces of its contents were strewn about the floor near it. Anna's killer may have rifled the basket, for whatever bizarre reason.

This fact had not been printed in the newspapers, and Albert was clearly unaware of it.

Albert was on a little surer ground when Bottomly questioned him about Anna's personal interests.

BOTTOMLY: Was [the record player] playing?

ALBERT: I think it was playing and ah, I shut it off. I'm not sure. It's possible—

BOTTOMLY: Well, if it was playing do you remember the music, the kind of music?

ALBERT: It was like um, I call it long-hair music. Everybody has there [sic] own name. It's ah—

BOTTOMLY: Anything you recognize.

ALBERT: Oh, no. It would be um, like symphonies and stuff like that.

The "Strangle Worksheet" had described Anna as enjoying "symphonic music." The radio component of her stereo system had been turned off, although the record player itself was still on when her body was discovered. This fact was also publicized in the press.

Albert's problem with dates was given a slapstick exposition when he and Bottomly tried to establish exactly when he was supposed to have killed Nina Nichols.

ALBERT: It was just before the first part of the next month. I don't know if it was the 31st or the 30th—I do recall it was on a—

BOTTOMLY: What month was it?

ALBERT: It was—uh—in June.

BOTTOMLY: O.K. Well how many days in June?

ALBERT: I don't know.

BOTTOMLY: Don't you remember the old song— "thirty days hath September—April, June and November"?

ALBERT: No, I don't—

BOTTOMLY: Well, there are thirty days in June—

ALBERT: Must have been the last one.

BOTTOMLY: So you think it was June 30th?

ALBERT: I'd say June 30th—if it's on a Saturday.

BOTTOMLY: If it's on a Saturday? You're positive it was done on a Saturday.

ALBERT: I know.

BOTTOMLY: All right. O.K. then—what's—that's one, two, three. Now what's—No. 4.—

ALBERT: I want to do—this is where I'm getting mixed up in.

BOTTOMLY: Yes?

ALBERT: I'm getting mixed up in years—

BOTTOMLY: Well, that's—I'll help you there—that's 196-

ALBERT: No, I—let me do it.

BOTTOMLY: All right.

ALBERT: This is what's messing me up. Now these were done in '62.

BOTTOMLY: Yes.

ALBERT: Uh, there was three [murders] in June?

BOTTOMLY: Yes.

ALBERT: Now, there's nothing in July whatsoever.

BOTTOMLY: Any particular reason you remember that?

ALBERT: No.

BOTTOMLY: Just didn't do anything?

ALBERT: There's nothing in July.

Albert also had trouble remembering where Nina lived.

BOTTOMLY: What her apartment number?

ALBERT: Either 34 or 43.

BOTTOMLY: You've got the numbers mixed up in your mind, huh? Those two numbers, three and four, in order or the other.

There was some confusion about the first and second floors in Nina's building.

BOTTOMLY: The ground floor is—

ALBERT: Still doesn't go—

BOTTOMLY: You call the ground floor the first floor—

ALBERT: That's what messing me up.

BOTTOMLY: The first floor you call the second floor.

ALBERT: Yah.

BOTTOMLY: And the second floor up from the ground floor, you call the third floor.

ALBERT: The way I can see it now—if it's all right with you—

BOTTOMLY: Sure.

ALBERT: The way I can see it—the elevator shaft— it's a nice one—the elevator went all the way up— and I think—to my knowledge—that these two old ladies—was not the next one up the second like I said—but the next one—and—

BOTTOMLY: That would be the third floor.

ALBERT: Well maybe—to you it's—not the third floor—to me it's only—the second.

BOTTOMLY: To you—we'll use your system.

ALBERT: No, I'm reverting back to yours, now. I'm forgetting the bottom, and I'm sayin, that one here, which would be the first to you, and the second one, which would be the third like I always said it was, right?

BOTTOMLY: But it's the second—it's the second floor above the ground floor.

ALBERT: Yah. So therefore I would say that I was going one more and forget that and then go another one and say that she was on the fourth floor.

BOTTOMLY: Right—okay.

ALBERT: Becuz I was so high up—in Nina Nichols' apartment—and I would say she was on the fourth floor.

BOTTOMLY: Right.

Albert then described Nina.

ALBERT: All right. Now. Also, on her—she did have glasses. And—

BOTTOMLY: You've said that before.

ALBERT: But I know now—she had that—her hair wasn't bad at all—nice-tight-like—but it wuz gray.

BOTTOMLY: Uh huh.

ALBERT: This is to me, seeing her now as she is—understand me? Her hair is gray—and she was a very frail woman between five five and a half and five-six, no more. Y'know there's sumthin funny about what she had on her feet—y' know that?

BOTTOMLY: This is still Nichols?

ALBERT: This is Nina Nichols. She has sumpin on her feet—that was different. Y'know that? it wuz—ah—like—like tennis shoes or—

BOTTOMLY: Uh huh.

ALBERT: I could be wrong—

BOTTOMLY: Sneakers?

ALBERT: Sneakers, like—Rubber, they were rubber.

BOTTOMLY: Uh huh.

All these details of Nina's appearance were given in the "Strangler Worksheet," even to the sneakers. Albert knew he had committed a murder in Lynn, but couldn't remember the victim's name. The Task Force chief refreshed him.

BOTTOMLY: You mean Blake.

ALBERT: That's it. Blake, Helen Blake.

BOTTOMLY: Yes.

ALBERT: Ah, on her she had that pj they call em, pajama top and bottom too. I'd swear I left her she was the only one I left on her stomach.

BOTTOMLY: You did leave her on her stomach.

ALBERT: Did leave her on her stomach. I remember I did. I left her right on her stomach. When I first picked her up.

BOTTOMLY: Well, would you say you had, you described that before that she was facing the bed and then . . .

ALBERT: And then I picked her up. No when I, I remember this here, let's see like this over here and she went under my left arm and I picked her up.

BOTTOMLY: Uhuh. She passed right out?

ALBERT: And then.

BOTTOMLY: She pretty heavy Albert?

ALBERT: She's heavy. She must been about 140 or 150 lbs. and ah I laid her facing me at first.

BOTTOMLY: Right.

ALBERT: And I do remember playing with her busts, she had a very large bust and I did have intercourse with her.

BOTTOMLY: While she was facing you.

ALBERT: Ya. And I did remember, I remember putting a nylon stocking around her neck too and then there was a bra. It was on the dresser, ah, there was a bra there, a white bra and I remember taking the bra and also putting it and tying it around her neck too. And, ah, she was all blue in the face. I remember this. And I turned her over, I remember, before leaving. I turned her over on her stomach with her feet straight down.

BOTTOMLY: Do you remember any reason why you did it or you just did it? Were you thinking of anything when you did it?

ALBERT: No, but it's so clear, I thought of it last night. It all came to me last night. I went all the way back to the first day. You were asking me about dates.

BOTTOMLY: Right.

That Helen's body had been left prone on the bed, that she had been wearing pajamas, and that stockings and a bra had been intertwined about her neck were details of her killing that had repeatedly been published in the *Record.* The "Strangle Worksheet" said that a sexual assault on her had been "evident."

Albert had claimed he'd had intercourse with Helen.

According to the autopsy report, there were no spermatozoa present in either her vagina or her rectum.

22

The Confessions of
Albert DeSalvo, II

Albert claimed to have been in a "fog" when he murdered Ida Irga, which is one reason why the account of the killing he gave to Bottomly on August 24 is so riveting.

BOTTOMLY: What happened in August?

ALBERT: There wuz two in August.

BOTTOMLY: How do you remember?

ALBERT: I remember because the first one was this—on Grove Street.

BOTTOMLY: Who was that?

ALBERT: Ida Orger—Ida Orger—uh—

BOTTOMLY: How do you—

ALBERT: Right back the Massachusetts General Hospital.

BOTTOMLY: Mmmm-hmmm.

ALBERT: There was a street, the main drag, going that way and then there was uh—on Grove there—I don't know how many floors were there, three or four floors or five floors, but to me, to me anyhow it was on the top floor.

BOTTOMLY: Uh-huh?

ALBERT: And this was uh—

BOTTOMLY: You went all the way to the top on this one?

ALBERT: All to the top, yuh. There wuz a front door, right. As you walk up there's a bunch of stairs maybe, uh, maybe six stairs, right, and on the left was some bells and then, uh, this had a buzzer type door—

BOTTOMLY: Buzzer door?

ALBERT: Buzzer type—well there was a—uh.

BOTTOMLY: Street door and then an inside door?

ALBERT: No, uh, it was a double door meaning, uh, she hadda ring the bell for the buzzer, right.

BOTTOMLY: I see. Right.

ALBERT: And then the stairway would be right there. And you hadda pass quite a few apartments going up.

BOTTOMLY: Could she talk to you when you rang the bell? Was there a telephone—speaker?

ALBERT: Uhhh—I don't think so. No, becuz when I gut ta—when I gut all the way up the stairs, right?

BOTTOMLY: Yes?

ALBERT: She was already on top of the landing.

BOTTOMLY: She was waiting for you?

ALBERT: Oh, yes. She was already on the landing, on the stairs.

BOTTOMLY: Did you meet anybody going up?

ALBERT: Uhhh—Jeez, I think one door on the way up wuz maybe that much open, and about four or five inches where you can look in or more than that. It was open, but I went right back, right by it—

BOTTOMLY: You didn't see anybody in there?

ALBERT: No, and I went all the—she was on top of—on top of the landing—

BOTTOMLY: On the top floor?

ALBERT: On the top floor rather looking over the railing.

BOTTOMLY: Right.

ALBERT: And, uh, as I was coming up and make that little curve that goes to the apartments was the—on the left of the stairs on the top and I—I'm not sure if there was another place, another apartment, but I know that there was another set of stairs going up. I don't think it was an apartment but there was another set of stairs there, uhhh—

BOTTOMLY: Going to the roof?

ALBERT: Possibly, but there was a set of stairs there— she was to the left.

BOTTOMLY: Well did this other set of stairs look like the stairs you'd come up, the same kind of stairs?

ALBERT: Somethin' like them, yes, same thing, about the same. But—uh—she was right there, she talked to me and uh—

BOTTOMLY: What line did you use there?

ALBERT: I told her I was gonna do some work in the apartment and she says she didn't hear nothin' about it, but I says, "Well, look if you don't wanna be bothered by me going in, then I won't bother you." She says, "Well I don't know who you are." And uh, we had—kept talking and I says to her, "Well, look, forget it. If you don't want it, then I'll just tell them that you told me you don't want it done." And I started to walk down. She says, "Well, never mind, come on." And I went in, and I went in and first it was to your left was like a parlor and then to the right I went through a living room with the, uh, square type dark chairs they were, and there was a—uh—

BOTTOMLY: Is that on the left, did you say, or the right?

ALBERT: To the left was the parlor going in.

BOTTOMLY: I see.

ALBERT: And going through I went through a living room.

BOTTOMLY: Through the parlor?

ALBERT: No, I'm wrong then, I'm calling the wrong one—What do you call it, a dining room? Where there's a table in there—

BOTTOMLY: Chairs?

ALBERT: Chairs: Right.

ALBERT: And these chairs I believe had the—uh—cloth in the center.

BOTTOMLY: Yuh—straight-back chairs?

ALBERT: Yes, they were straight-back chairs.

BOTTOMLY: That's the dining room. Which way is that?

ALBERT: Uh—come in the door—

BOTTOMLY: Yuh?

ALBERT: Take a right turn.

BOTTOMLY: That's the dining room?

ALBERT: Well, I took a right turn—

BOTTOMLY: Yes?

ALBERT: And I kept walking down the hallway and, right there, and you could look from the, where I was, it could have been the kitchen because there was the dining room right here and straight ahead I could look and I could see the bed, it was a dark-type bed and there wuz—uh—sheets—I could see the sheets and the pillow becuz I did take the pillowcase offa that—

BOTTOMLY: Right.

ALBERT: I did take the pillowcase offa that.

BOTTOMLY: What did you do with it?

ALBERT: Put it around her neck, but not before I saw the blood, uh

BOTTOMLY: What did you do with the pillow?

ALBERT: Uh, the pillow? I put it around her neck.

BOTTOMLY: Not the pillow—

ALBERT: Oh, the pillow?

BOTTOMLY: The pillow, the pillow itself—?

ALBERT: I think I took that out and put it underneath her.

BOTTOMLY: Mmmmm-hmmmm.

ALBERT: And then two chairs—

BOTTOMLY: How did—how did—yuh—

ALBERT: These two chairs, I remember taking them and laying them down on their backs and I put her legs up there.

BOTTOMLY: Where'd you get the chairs? From the dining room?

ALBERT: From the dining room—that's why I saw that—the bedroom was right there—there was a door—'member the door, a door frame—I could see the bed.

BOTTOMLY: This was on the other side of the dining room? You had to walk through the dining room to the bedroom?

ALBERT: You see, to me right now it's very easy. I can see this whole, I can see this whole thing the way it—the way it is.

BOTTOMLY: Would it help you to draw?

ALBERT: Uhhh, yuh, I can do it for you—it would be very easy.

BOTTOMLY: I'll get you a pen.

ALBERT: All right.

BOTTOMLY: Do you want to use yours?

ALBERT: Right.

BOTTOMLY: You like your pens better.

ALBERT: No, uh—(Long pause while sketching) This could have been a, about a four-inch board on the bed there on the bottom like—probably a sideboard—?

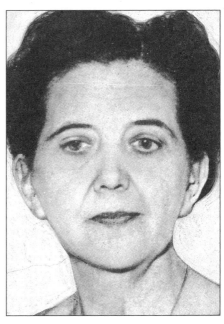

Anna Slesers, 56, the first victim.
(Photo courtesy the Boston Herald*)*

Site of Slesers's murder on Gainsborough Street, Boston.

Helen Blake, 65,
the third victim.
*(Photo courtesy
the Boston Herald)*

Ida Irga, 75,
the fourth victim.
*(Photo courtesy
the Boston Herald)*

Site of Irga's murder on
Grove Street, Boston.

Sophie Clark, 20,
the sixth victim.
*(Photo courtesy
the Boston Herald)*

Sketch of a suspect drawn by
Clark's neighbor, Marcella
Lulka. *(Courtesy James McDonald)*

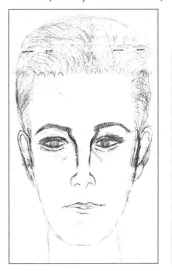

Site of Clark's murder on
Huntington Avenue, Boston.

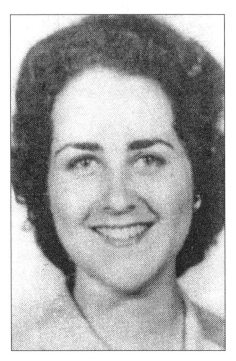

Patricia Bissette, 23,
the seventh victim.
*(Photo courtesy
the* Boston Herald)

Site of Bissette's murder
on Park Drive, Boston.

Beverly Samans, 26, the eighth victim. *(Photo courtesy the* Boston Herald)

Site of Samans's murder on University Road, Cambridge.

Lafayette Street, Salem, where ninth victim, Evelyn Corbin, 58, was murdered.

Corbin's killer left evidence of his entry on the fire escape outside her window.

Essex Street, Lawrence, where tenth victim, Joann Graff, 23, was murdered.

Mary Sullivan, 19,
the final victim.
*(Photo courtesy
the Boston Herald)*

Site of Sullivan's
murder on Charles
Street, Boston.

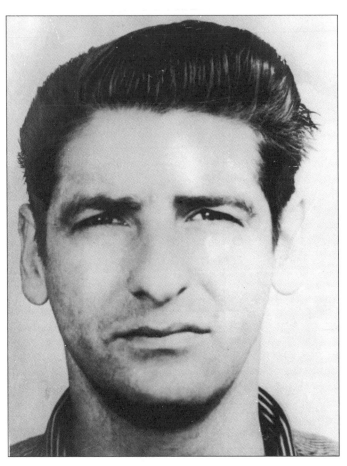

Albert Henry DeSalvo, 33.
(Photo courtesy Cambridge Police Department)

DeSalvo *(left)* as a
young man.
*(Photo courtesy Richard
and Rosalie DeSalvo)*

DeSalvo served in the
army from September
1948 to February
1956. *(Photo courtesy
Richard and Rosalie
DeSalvo)*

DeSalvo's nine-day trial was headline news.
(Photo courtesy the Boston Herald*)*

DE SALVO
IS THE
STRANGLER

Bailey Bares 13 Murders In 18 Months As Acts of an Insane Man

Charge of Albert DeSalvo . . .   STORIES ON PAGE THREE   . . Arriving in Middlesex Court

Record American investigative reporters Loretta McLaughlin and Jean Cole at site of Irga's murder. *(Photo courtesy the* Boston Herald*)*

Dr. Ames Robey in 1995.

Strangler Task Force
Coordinator John S.
Bottomly in August 1959.
(Photo courtesy the Boston Herald)

Boston Police Commissioner
Edmund McNamara in April
1962. *(Photo courtesy
the Boston Herald)*

Massachusetts Attorney
General Edward Brooke.
(Photo courtesy the Boston Herald)

Retired Salem Police
Department Lieutenant
John Moran.

Captain William R. Burke, Jr.

Former Cambridge Police
Officer Michael Giacoppo.

Defense Attorney Jon
Asgeirsson in 1968.
(Photo courtesy the Boston Herald)

(From left to right) Dr. Robert Ross Mezer,
Defense Attorney F. Lee Bailey,
and Boston Police Lieutenant John Donovan
at DeSalvo's Green Man trial, January 13, 1967.
(Photo courtesy the Boston Herald)

Attorney Thomas Troy in
1968, the year he began
representing Albert DeSalvo.
(Photo courtesy the Boston Herald)

Francis C. Newton, Jr.,
DeSalvo's last attorney.
*(Photo courtesy
Francis C. Newton, Jr.)*

George Nassar, 32, at his arraignment for the September 1964 murder of Irvin Hilton, 43.
(Photo courtesy the Boston Herald)

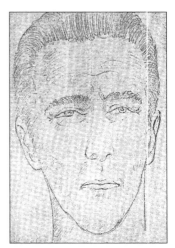

Composite sketch of Hilton's killer drawn by Andover Police Officer William Tammany.
(Courtesy Massachusetts Attorney General's Archives)

The Andover service station where Hilton was murdered.

Lawrence Police Department sketch of the suspect in the 1948 murder of Dominic Kirmil.
(Courtesy Massachusetts Attorney General's Archives)

DeSalvo showing off his handcrafted jewelry at Walpole State Prison.
(Photo courtesy the Boston Herald)

DeSalvo dancing with an unidentified older woman during a senior citizen's outing to Walpole State Prison.
(Photo courtesy the Boston Herald)

Timothy and Richard DeSalvo at the October 26, 2001, exhumation of Albert DeSalvo.

DeSalvo's casket is raised.

(From left to right) Traci Starrs, James Starrs, and Timothy DeSalvo watch as Mitchell Calhoun videotapes DeSalvo's exhumation.

BOTTOMLY: Yes.

ALBERT: Anyhow from the door from where she was right here, left right here, she was left here, not too far from this thing here—legs up on a chair—

BOTTOMLY: What room did you leave her in?

ALBERT: All I can tell you is that the bed was here and she wasn't no more than, uh, no more than, uh, between five and ten feet from where the—the frame of the door.

BOTTOMLY: I see.

ALBERT: Over there—

BOTTOMLY: Next room to the bedroom?

ALBERT: Yes. The dining room chairs were in the other room.

BOTTOMLY: I see.

ALBERT: And they were dark, I remember that, straight-backs—

BOTTOMLY: The room you left her in wasn't the bedroom, wasn't the dining room and it wasn't the kitchen, so what was the kind of furniture in that room, do you recall, where you left her? (Pause) You don't recall? You're shaking your head no?

ALBERT: Shut that off so we won't waste it, so we won't waste so much tape.

BOTTOMLY: Oh, no, that's all right, it can be used again. O.K. now you recollect seeing something else before you left her. You could look into the bedroom and what could you see?

ALBERT: Mmmm—In the bedroom, uh, coming from out of the bedroom from where she was in this room here—there was a—uh—a dark walnut, or—dresser draws and, uh, I'm almost positive they were empty. There was little if anything if anything in 'em very little if anything maybe handkerchiefs or somethin'.

BOTTOMLY: Yuh?

ALBERT: Let me see. Uh, if I think a little clearer, I'll tell you what was in the top draw.

BOTTOMLY: O.K.

ALBERT: The top draw, uh, was very little of anything, if anything there was handkerchiefs in it, but that was all, very little—There was something there! There was something in there.

BOTTOMLY: The top draw?

ALBERT: The top draw there was little, but there was nothing to speak of, but it was there, you know what I mean? Nothing of any value. Uh, the top draws were empty, the draws were empty, just about all of them. There was little bit of anything in those draws. I'm tryin' to figure out where the room was—

BOTTOMLY: Well was she moving or something.

ALBERT: No, she was uh, this woman,

BOTTOMLY: She just moved in?

ALBERT: This woman here, to me, weighed about 160.

BOTTOMLY: Yuh? Pretty heavy-set?

ALBERT: Very heavy set. And she had a white hair with black, very dark, to me it looked like black stringy hair,

BOTTOMLY: Uh-huh?

ALBERT: And, uh—she

BOTTOMLY: With white in it?

ALBERT: Yes.

BOTTOMLY: White and black?

ALBERT: Yes, yes, but stringy, meaningly the black was going through it and from what I can see on her—she had like a—uh—a housecoat on, think it was black and something, black and white with some kind of marking on it and the—uh—like a print or squares or somethin'.

BOTTOMLY: Yuh?

ALBERT: And, uh—

BOTTOMLY: Was it cotton, wool?

ALBERT: It was cotton.

BOTTOMLY: Yuh. Did she have any shoes on?

ALBERT: I don't know but I see socks or somethin'.

BOTTOMLY: Uh-huh—somethin' on her feet—

ALBERT: Socks.

BOTTOMLY: What color, do you recall?

ALBERT: Dark, I don't know if they were black, dark and the, uh—this is very important, uh, uh, there was first blood came outa her ear.

BOTTOMLY: Blood came out of her ear, you say?

ALBERT: Yuh, wait, this is a—

BOTTOMLY: How did you get her now? How did you maneuver her?

ALBERT: The same way, uh, this way here. She went down—

BOTTOMLY: You threw your right arm around her throat from behind.

ALBERT: Right. I would say that—

BOTTOMLY: Did she go down fast like Blake?

ALBERT: She went right on top of me.

BOTTOMLY: Was she out? Was she out?

ALBERT: Naturally, she passed out.

BOTTOMLY: Uh-huh?

ALBERT: Uh-huh—but something about her, the blood that I saw was real, purplish dark.

BOTTOMLY: And that came from where? Her ear, you say?

ALBERT: Ear.

BOTTOMLY: Which ear, do you remember?

ALBERT: I'll tell you in a second.

BOTTOMLY: O.K.

ALBERT: I'm tryin' to see, the uh—

BOTTOMLY: Take your time. Don't press yourself.

ALBERT: Blood came out of her ear I know.

BOTTOMLY: O.K. You're standing behind her and you fall over backwards?

ALBERT: Right.

BOTTOMLY: Did this blood fall on you?

ALBERT: No, it—as a matter of fact, it stopped.

BOTTOMLY: Did you see it come out at the time it came out?

ALBERT: The blood came out the right ear.

BOTTOMLY: Her right ear?

ALBERT: Right ear.

BOTTOMLY: And you saw it when it started coming out?

ALBERT: Yes.

BOTTOMLY: What'd you do, did you try to scramble out of the way of it?

ALBERT: It didn't come out like you're trying to say.

BOTTOMLY: Just sort of oozed out?

ALBERT: It came out a little bit, enough for me to see it.

BOTTOMLY: Yuh—like Blake's nose?

ALBERT: Yuh, that was the same way as hers. Hers came out on the right side I would think and, uh, I saw it more clearly when I put the pillowcase around her neck.

BOTTOMLY: Saw the blood more clearly.

ALBERT: Yuh, that's—

BOTTOMLY: That's when you got out from under her, though?

ALBERT: I was—I was already out from under her.

BOTTOMLY: So you got out from under her and then what did you—

ALBERT: Came outa her right ear.

BOTTOMLY: All right. You got out from under her and what did you do then?

ALBERT: Took the—uh—took the pillow from the bed—

BOTTOMLY: Yuh?

ALBERT: From the bed, she had black-white house-coat, housedress on, took the pillow. I think she—I'm almost positive she had underwear on, took it off and, uh, I ripped—there's something about it—

BOTTOMLY: You ripped something?

ALBERT: I'm almost positive I ripped it open—

BOTTOMLY: Ripped open the dress?

ALBERT: The clothes, yuh, she was nude, I remember this here.

BOTTOMLY: You tore her dress?

ALBERT: Tore it open.

BOTTOMLY: And she was nude underneath?

ALBERT: No, I think she had pants on; I may have ripped them off her.

BOTTOMLY: Uh-huh? But no bra?

ALBERT: Uhhh—yes, she had a bra.

BOTTOMLY: Uh-huh.

ALBERT: But—uh—I did it—I don't know if I left that pillow under her, her bottom.

BOTTOMLY: Uh-huh?

ALBERT: With her legs on these two chairs—

BOTTOMLY: Yuh?

ALBERT: Opened.

BOTTOMLY: Yuh? Do you remember, do you remember, were you thinking of anything when you did this?

ALBERT: No.

BOTTOMLY: Just did it. What kind of a sex act did you perform with her, any?

ALBERT: No, nothing on her.

BOTTOMLY: Nothing at all.

ALBERT: I—I had intercourse with her but when you say, you said to me "sex act" right, I know what you're trying to have me—

BOTTOMLY: No, no. No, I'm not—any kind—normal or abnormal—?

ALBERT: Yuh, I had a—I think I had intercourse with her.

BOTTOMLY: Well what do you mean by intercourse? We've talked about this before. Does that mean you ejaculated in some manner?

ALBERT: Inside her—

BOTTOMLY: Was it inside her outside or what?

ALBERT: This is the most baffling thing. This is what bothers me.

BOTTOMLY: Do you specifically remember having intercourse with her or do you just want to remember it now?

ALBERT: I know how, how I set her up. I remember taking her clothes apart, ripping them right?

BOTTOMLY: Yes.

ALBERT: And, uh—

BOTTOMLY: Oh you set her up after you strangled her with the pillowcase?

ALBERT: Yes, after I strangled her with the pillowcase.

BOTTOMLY: Did you strangle her with your hands or with the pillowcase?

ALBERT: First, I put my arm around backwards, right?

BOTTOMLY: Right.

ALBERT: And then I put the pillowcase around her neck.

BOTTOMLY: Uh, did you, real tight?

ALBERT: I think so.

BOTTOMLY: Do you remember tying any knots in it?

ALBERT: Yes, I did, I did.

BOTTOMLY: How many?

ALBERT: Uhhh—

BOTTOMLY: Can you see that?

ALBERT: I can't see it, but uh—I'm almost positive, well, ya, I think I only made it one tight and then one more.

BOTTOMLY: Right.

ALBERT: Makes it two.

BOTTOMLY: Right. Were you standing over her while you did this?

ALBERT: Uhhh—this was tied uh—

BOTTOMLY: Where was the knot, in front or back?

ALBERT: No, it was tied in front. The knot should have been anywhere on the side or the front of her.

BOTTOMLY: So you're standing right over her?

ALBERT: Uh—

BOTTOMLY: Or beside her?

ALBERT: Yes, over her.

BOTTOMLY: Well, then you fixed her legs? You didn't have time to, you didn't do any sex act with her, did you? Can you specifically remember having intercourse with her? You're shaking your head which means no?

ALBERT: I—I'm trying to be sure about everything I say.

BOTTOMLY: Right.

ALBERT: Uhhh—

BOTTOMLY: Well you can remember so much here—

ALBERT: I—I would say yes, I have inserted my penis inside her and ejaculated I would say.

BOTTOMLY: But you don't sound very positive to me.

ALBERT: It's—to me, it's sickening even to talk about this.

BOTTOMLY: Yuh.

ALBERT: It's so damn real—I can see that blood coming outa her ear.

BOTTOMLY: Yuh, you can see that very clearly but you're not as positive when you're talking about the sex act. Are you saying you had intercourse with her because you think you did or because you remember you did?

ALBERT: I know I did.

BOTTOMLY: You positively remember it now?

ALBERT: Yes.

BOTTOMLY: Are you positive you ejaculated inside her?

ALBERT: Coulda pulled out.

BOTTOMLY: You could have pulled out? Do you remember what time of the day this was now?

ALBERT: (Long pause) This happened to be around uh—around two something.

BOTTOMLY: Well when you pulled out, you ejaculated, you fixed her legs up, you propped her legs up. Did you then go through the apartment again to make it look as if it was messed up or did you just get out?

ALBERT: I just went out.

BOTTOMLY: You swung out. O.K. Downstairs? Did you meet anybody?

ALBERT: No sir.

BOTTOMLY: In a hurry? Took your time?

ALBERT: Walked out.

Perhaps nowhere in the entire confession is Albert's need to please Bottomly by giving him the "right" answers more urgently expressed than in this account of Ida Irga's murder. And Bottomly's maneuverings to elicit those appropriate responses from Albert are equally blatant, particularly in the passage dealing with the purported rape of the victim.

In fact, Ida had not been raped—at least, there were

no spermatozoa found in either her vagina or rectum, which is why Bottomly had to attack Albert's initial confident assertion that he'd had full intercourse with the victim. No one had, although the slight injury to her external genitalia discovered during the autopsy indicated that she might have been assaulted with an object. Albert was insistent that he had committed no such brutal perversion.

Albert was entirely correct in claiming that Ida had been strangled by a pillowcase tied tightly around her neck; that the pillow itself had been placed beneath her body; that she had salt and pepper hair (it was actually brown and gray rather than black and white as he said); that she was found supine with her feet propped up on two chairs; and that her bedroom furniture was made of dark wood.

All those details had been printed—more than once—in the *Record*.

So had the fact that there was blood on Ida's head.

So had the fact that she had been assaulted in the bedroom.

Albert said twice that Ida had been wearing a black and white housecoat with "squares" on it.

The "Strangle Worksheet" claimed she wore a "polka dot duster."

The police report, written by the first officer to arrive at the crime scene, stated that Ida's body was clad in a torn light brown nightgown.

Albert said he had placed the chairs on which he propped the victim's feet on their backs.

The crime scene photo shows them standing upright.

But Albert made his worst mistake when—after a long hesitation—he told Bottomly that he'd assaulted the victim around 2:00 P.M.

If Albert was in Ida Irga's apartment at that time, he was there by himself. She was in the Public Garden with a friend—until shortly before six o'clock.

23

The Confessions of Albert DeSalvo, III

It was August 19, 1965, and George McGrath, Albert's legal guardian, had joined Bottomly in the small room at Bridgewater.

"Okay," Bottomly said. "Now—so when you grabbed her, you probably fell back into the kitchen, into the kitchen area, I mean—"

"In the kitchen area," Albert repeated.

"Boy, there must have been a thud when the two of you hit the ground," Bottomly commented.

"Oh, yeah," Albert agreed.

"And she gave you a good struggle, huh?"

"No struggle," Albert said. "She just didn't move, but I mean she couldn't do nothin' about it."

"But it took a long time to knock her out, though?"

"No, I wouldn't say too long. It was just another—" Albert paused.

They were talking about the murder of sixty-seven-year-old Jane Sullivan, who, like fifty-six-year-old Anna Sleser, sixty-five-year-old Helen Blake, sixty-eight-year-old Nina Nichols, and seventy-five-year-old Ida Irga, had died in the summer of 1962.

Jane's body was not found until nine days after her death, and its state of decomposition was well along, making the medical examiner's task a more difficult one. He was, however, able to establish that she had been strangled with a ligature of two stockings. There was no evidence of trauma to her vagina or anus.

When her body was found, it was facedown in a kneeling position in the bathtub. A housecoat covered the upper torso; the underpants were pulled down on the legs. Jane's bra was on the bathroom floor.

There were bloodstains on the kitchen floor, in the hall, and in the bathroom. The apartment did not appear to have been ransacked.

The "Strangle Worksheet" reported accurately the date and manner of Jane's death as well as the position in which the killer had left the corpse. It also reported that the victim was wearing a duster, a slip, and a girdle, and that her underpants were around her ankles.

Albert's confession to this murder was not specific in its details, and Bottomly had to work particularly hard to wrest answers from him that weren't either evasive or contradictory.

BOTTOMLY: Did you have regular, normal sex relations with her? Did you ejaculate before—?

ALBERT: Uhhh—no—I don't know about her. This is somethin' different now, you see? This is gonna be a weird one. This is a weird one.

BOTTOMLY: This one is a weird one?

ALBERT: Yes, uh, because the urine made me disgusted—

BOTTOMLY: Yuh?

ALBERT: Right, uh.

BOTTOMLY: Oh, yuh, when she—Did she get on you? Did she urinate on you?

ALBERT: No.

BOTTOMLY: Or had you gotten out from under her?

ALBERT: Maybe it's possible she did or did not, I don't know.

BOTTOMLY: Well anyhow she urinated?

ALBERT: Yuh—and uh—I do not believe—its possible I did a movement on her, you know what I mean, it's possible because afterward I put her in the tub, you see, but I'm trying to see if I can remember if I had intercourse with her—I do remember biting her bust, possibly other parts of her body, too, her stomach maybe, too.

(The medical examiner's report shows no indication that during the autopsy any teeth marks were found on the body.)

ALBERT: Uh, what I'm trying to do is see if I had intercourse with her. It is possible.

BOTTOMLY: It isn't fresh in your mind right now?

ALBERT: No, maybe at this moment it isn't. But I—I just like I'm trying to remember as to what I even put on her, you know what I mean?

BOTTOMLY: Right.

ALBERT: I do know that I—I know I didn't strip her naked.

BOTTOMLY: What did you do—just push her dress up out of the way or something?

ALBERT: Yuh—

BOTTOMLY: And then you pulled off her bra?

ALBERT: Yuh—This here thing she had on her, I think it was still on her becuz I ripped open her bra and ripped it off.

BOTTOMLY: Yuh?

ALBERT: Or pulled it up or somethin'—either I either pulled it up—

BOTTOMLY: Or pulled it off?

ALBERT: Or off, and I don't know if she had the heavy-type girdle on or what, heavy-type bra thing, I'm not sure but she had that heavy-type—

BOTTOMLY: She must have—well she was an older woman?

ALBERT: Oh, yeah, she was around 55, 60. I think she had on one of those wider ones, ever see the wide ones? Well the wider type.

BOTTOMLY: But anyhow you pulled it off?

ALBERT: It went off, right?

BOTTOMLY: Yuh.

(The tape transcript is riddled with incidents like these in which Albert asks Bottomly to confirm a detail of a crime scene, and Bottomly does.)

ALBERT: And, uh, I remember putting the nylon stockings—I don't know if on her I used those white nylons. I'm not positive on her.

BOTTOMLY: (Word distorted)

ALBERT: White nylons, possibly.

BOTTOMLY: Yuh?

ALBERT: On her.

BOTTOMLY: How many did you use, do you recall?

ALBERT: Two, I think.

BOTTOMLY: Uh-huh.

ALBERT: And I think maybe, you know what I—

BOTTOMLY: The sex part of this one isn't too clear in your mind, huh, I mean it doesn't seem to be as big a part as some of the others?

ALBERT: No, that's why I say this here part of the sex to my opinion was a way of revenge.

BOTTOMLY: It's an incidental thing, really?

ALBERT: Yuh.

BOTTOMLY: So why did you pick her up? Have you

ever thought about that? Why did you put her in the tub?

ALBERT: You know something, the tub was filled, so full.

BOTTOMLY: Yuh? Do you think she was getting ready to take a bath?

ALBERT: Same way with Nich—uh, Anna, Anna Slesers.

BOTTOMLY: Yuh?

ALBERT: She was getting ready to take a bath, right? All she had on was the blue robe, stripped naked underneath, right.

BOTTOMLY: Right.

ALBERT: There was nothing about her that would interest any man. You follow me? And that's why I'm trying to figure this one out here, too.

BOTTOMLY: That's why you think sex didn't have too much to do with it?

ALBERT: Yes, I'm very sincere about this here. I don't feel sex had somethin' to do with this here. As the green man, yes I—I feel sex had something but this is a different thing but still I'm trying to keep on one subject now.

BOTTOMLY: Right.

ALBERT: I can't understand why I didn't put Anna Slesers [sic] in the tub when she was taking a bath and why did I put Mrs. Sullivan in the tub and she was taking a bath. Just like why did I leave a broom and a bottle?

BOTTOMLY: Yuh?

ALBERT: Everything was done differently.

BOTTOMLY: Yuh.

ALBERT: You see, but it was done and, uh, the tub—much different—

BOTTOMLY: Well, was this, is this in the morning then? Or is it the end of the day?

ALBERT: No, this to me would be around the middle of the day, around two o'clock—

BOTTOMLY: About two o'clock.

ALBERT: Uh, this time element there I don't know.

BOTTOMLY: Uh-huh. Well is it after lunch? Can you place your lunch that day?

ALBERT: No. I don't know the exact time of day.

BOTTOMLY: What day was it, do you remember?

ALBERT: No I don't. You see—

BOTTOMLY: Where were you working then, do you remember?

ALBERT: On Jane Sullivan, it was in, uh, let me see— Jane Sullivan. If I knew what year it was, I can tell you where it was and then maybe I can place where I was working, but uh—

BOTTOMLY: I'll give you the year—it was 1962.

Albert had a great deal of difficulty recalling the murder of Evelyn Corbin, whom he kept calling "Ellen Corbett" or "Evelyn Corbett" despite Bottomly's constant corrections. He also did not know when the crime had been committed.

"Is there any chance of me knowing what year it was?" he asked Bottomly. "You tell me," Bottomly replied, and Albert chuckled.

BOTTOMLY: You hate to talk about Corbin?

ALBERT: Corbett, Corbett the name is.

BOTTOMLY: Corbett? C-O-R-B-I-N.

ALBERT: Uh, Corbin, uh—

BOTTOMLY: You don't like to talk about her?

ALBERT: Well, uh, there was no intercourse with her.

BOTTOMLY: Yuh? What did you do with her?

ALBERT: Well she did it for me.

BOTTOMLY: Yuh? What'd she do? (Pause) What'd she do? Come on.

ALBERT: They—use a professional name for it. Also—

BOTTOMLY: What's the professional name for it?

ALBERT: Also the pillow was involved on her.

BOTTOMLY: Oh.

Reluctantly, almost coyly, Albert admitted that he'd gotten Evelyn to perform oral sex on him. She couldn't have regular intercourse, he said, because of a medical problem.

Bottomly then tried to pin him down on when the murder had occurred. Albert said he thought it was either in the wintertime or the summertime.

Evelyn had been slain on September 8, 1963.

Albert was correct when he told Bottomly that the victim had died on a Sunday, that she had been getting ready to go to church, that she was going to have Sunday dinner with a man friend, and that another woman in the building had a key to her apartment.

All these facts had been widely publicized.

Albert thought the weather had been "nice" that day; in fact, it had been foggy in Salem the morning Evelyn died.

Albert must have been sweating bullets throughout this interrogation. At one point he said to Bottomly, "I can't get no breaks." Said Bottomly, "You're getting plenty of breaks."

When Bottomly asked Albert how old he thought Evelyn had been, Albert replied, "She looked, uh, to be about fifty-two or fifty-three and she had, uh, brownish hair like. She was, uh—"

Press accounts of the murder had in fact variously given Evelyn's age as fifty, fifty-one, and fifty-three. But everyone who knew her agreed that her appearance was startlingly youthful; she was often mistaken for a woman in her thirties.

Albert said that Evelyn had been wearing only a "negligee" and a housecoat. In fact she had been clad in a short robe, a nightgown, and white socks. Her killer had left her supine on her bed, two stockings tied around her neck and a third around her left ankle. She lay with her right hand and forearm tucked beneath her. To Salem Police Inspector John Moran, one of the first investigators on the scene, it looked as if someone had tied her feet together and then cut the bond.

Albert had told Bottomly that he'd tied Evelyn's hands behind her back. Bottomly kept pushing him on this detail.

BOTTOMLY: You say you tied her on the bed. You mean hand and foot?
ALBERT: No. Just her hands.
BOTTOMLY: What did you do about her feet? Anything?
ALBERT: It, it's possible that I did.

All he would admit to was binding the victim's hands. There was no indication at the scene that that had been done; at any rate, the stocking Albert said he'd used to do so was missing and he didn't say he'd taken it with him.

Albert told Bottomly that after Evelyn had finished fellating him, he'd ejaculated into a tissue. Bottomly asked him if he thought the victim had caught any of his semen in her mouth. He wasn't sure.

That she had was confirmed by the autopsy. The really interesting detail here is that Albert was clearly aware that crumpled semen-stained tissues, as well as lipstick-stained underpants, were found on the bedroom floor. His knowledge of this would seem to indicate that he had a firsthand knowledge of the crime.

But it could just as easily have been gleaned from the close-up photos of the scene—which Bottomly had shown Albert for identification purposes *prior* to the confession.

Albert was on somewhat surer footing with the Sophie Clark murder, perhaps because unlike that of Evelyn Corbin, this case had been diagrammed on the "Strangle Worksheet" as well as highly publicized elsewhere.

Albert recounted what had happened after he knocked on Sophie's apartment door.

ALBERT: The door swung open to my left.

BOTTOMLY: All right.

ALBERT: And she presented herself to me.

BOTTOMLY: What did she look like?

ALBERT: A Negro girl, light complexion, black hair—

BOTTOMLY: Long, short—?

ALBERT: No, she had very long hair, beautiful, her eyes were—dark br—I don't know, dark brown— she looked like a Hawaiian girl—her eyes were—

BOTTOMLY: Outstanding eyes?

ALBERT: Yes, it was a very beautiful girl—I'd almost say the—that her eyes were brown—but that her features were so—so—*so tall*—she wuz a very tall girl.

BOTTOMLY: As tall as you are?

ALBERT: About five ten—she could be as tall as me or more—she wuz at least 140, 150 pounds. She wuz built solid—

BOTTOMLY: No fat.

Sophie's height and weight had been given on the "Strangle Worksheet," as had her coloring.

ALBERT: Oh, no, she wuz really—really built beautiful—she had on a—when she opened the door she had a uh—a white type—white type uh—throw on there, right? And she had a half slip, a bra— her—she musta been going somewhere—or she wuz dressed when she came in becuz—she had black high heels on I remember—ah—it wuz very appealing the way she wuz dressed.

BOTTOMLY: Mm-mm.

ALBERT: She also had on black stockings—with a garter belt—

BOTTOMLY: Uh-huh.

ALBERT: Uh—very attractive.

BOTTOMLY: What color was her outer garment, what did you call it, a negligee, Al?

ALBERT: It wuz—ah—like two or t'ree together, what do you call those there ah—

BOTTOMLY: You mean different linings?

ALBERT: Yeah, that's it, yeah—

BOTTOMLY: What colors do you remember? Was it a filmy kind of thing?

ALBERT: Yeah, yeah. It wuz—ah—she wuz tall.

BOTTOMLY: But you couldn't see through it—

ALBERT: N—no, no I couldn't see through it.

BOTTOMLY: Kind of sexy-looking, with all of this?

ALBERT: Yes—yes, very appealing. But ah—on that there—

BOTTOMLY: You remember any colors? If you don't all right.

ALBERT: I really don't.

BOTTOMLY: Okay.

ALBERT: To me, right? It looked—white.

BOTTOMLY: Uh huh.

ALBERT: It looked white to me, but—

BOTTOMLY: Were there other colors, too?

ALBERT: Possible—but I remember—I remember the half slip.

BOTTOMLY: She was wearing a half slip?

Albert's Frederick's of Hollywood fantasy was only partially accurate. Sophie's hair wasn't very long at all—it was done in a medium-length bouffant flip, the style Jacqueline Kennedy as First Lady had made so popular. That Sophie had been wearing a blue floral housecoat (not white, as Albert had said), a bra, a garter belt, a half-slip, black stockings, and black shoes was noted on the "Strangle Worksheet," and tallies with the description of her attire given in the autopsy report. Albert seems to have taken this description and embellished it, turning the plain baggy robe (or so it appears in the crime scene photo) into a diaphanous negligee and the flat, corrugated-sole tie shoes on Sophie's feet into sexy spikes.

The power the image of Sophie as seductress had over Albert is clear from the fact that he described her thus even after Bottomly had shown him the police photos of the crime scene, which are graphic close-ups of Sophie sprawled on her back, legs apart, the half-slip she had been wearing wrapped around her neck.

It also explains how he knew she had been menstruating, and was wearing a sanitary napkin and the harness to hold it in place. Albert said he had ripped the pad from Sophie and thrown it behind a chair.

Albert also told Bottomly that he had used his Measuring Man con on Sophie, telling her that with her superb figure and statuesque bearing (although not in those words), she would make a perfect model. He said that he'd grabbed her around the neck with his right arm and that she'd lost consciousness almost immediately.

BOTTOMLY: Were you surprised she went out so fast? Did you expect a struggle?
ALBERT: I didn't expect anything.

There was some debate about when the crime had been committed. "Now, this is a work day, Al, this isn't like your usual routine, y'know that?" Bottomly said. "I'll tell ya, December fifth."

ALBERT: December 5th.

BOTTOMLY: —was a Wednesday.

ALBERT: December the fifth.

BOTTOMLY: Did you work at all that day?

ALBERT: Ah—December fifth—anniversary—ah—lemme see, lemme find out where I wuz workin' first—December the fifth, I wuz workin'—I wuz workin' for Munroe Shipyard up until September of sixty-two—'n September of sixty-two until September of sixty-three I worked for Russell Blumett [Blomerth]—now on December the fifth—right? It wuz on a Wednesday, right?

BOTTOMLY: Right.

ALBERT: Ah—now—this is very important, now, remember this—ah—Russell Blumett—had taken a job—a contract—for work in Belmont—he worked all winter long on that contract in Belmont building a studio for a couple over there?

BOTTOMLY: Right.

ALBERT: And this has a lot to do with me taking it—like ah there'd be nuthin' doin' that day, right?

BOTTOMLY: Uh huh.

ALBERT: Or this week, and I'd take—I'd say, okay, I'll take it off, I gut work to do myself—and I'd take the day off, y'see? Now on December the fifth—wuz a work day, right?

BOTTOMLY: Right.

ALBERT: I think that I might have been—working on—on my—yes—ah—I musta taken a day off—that could easy be checked—

BOTTOMLY: Did you go to work at all?

ALBERT: No, I—probably checked in—

Albert had in fact worked three hours that day, although just when was not clear. The weather had been quite stormy; Albert didn't recall this fact. The anniversary he spoke of on December 5th was that of his and Irmgard's wedding.

Albert recounted for Bottomly how he'd wandered around Sophie's building seeking an appropriate target. (The layout of 315 Huntington Avenue, with its distinctive divided staircase, had been minutely described in the *Record American* series by Loretta McLaughlin and Jean Cole.)

BOTTOMLY: You knocked on the door—you were looking for a woman.

ALBERT: Yah.

BOTTOMLY: And a man answered, so you brushed him off as fast as you could. Right?

ALBERT: Yeah—but I did talk to him for a minute.

BOTTOMLY: Is that before you—first you said that you went—

ALBERT: Before.

BOTTOMLY: Yuh. You first went up the right hand side [of the staircase]—right?

ALBERT: Right in—right inside.

BOTTOMLY: The first door you knocked on—there was—

ALBERT: He hadda be on the right side, too.

BOTTOMLY: All right then—was he the first one you knocked? Or the second?

ALBERT: The second.

BOTTOMLY: Who was the first?

ALBERT: I think it wuz Tobin.

BOTTOMLY: How did you—

ALBERT: Told—I had told her—ah—

BOTTOMLY: Did you use the measuring on her?

ALBERT: No—I did tell her she looked—I tol' her she looked very pretty or sumpin'—she said a hus— somethin about a husband—

BOTTOMLY: Oh.

ALBERT: Sumpin about a husband—wuz next door or sumpin—wuz comin' right back or sumpin—and she wuz a little nervous—told her she looked very pretty or sumpin—I don't know, whether I used da model or nurse or not, but I explained to her that I wuz doin some paintin' and uh—told her my name was Thompson—and I—moved out very fast with her.

BOTTOMLY: When you heard about the husband, you got outta there.

ALBERT: No, not necessarily becuz—well, maybe—you could if you wanna say that.

The fact that a man named "Thompson" had come to Marcella Lulka's door claiming that he had to paint her apartment had of course been extensively written up in the newspapers. So had the fact that "Thompson" had made advances to Lulka. Similarly, her ruse—telling the intruder that her husband was asleep in the next room—to get rid of the man had been well publicized.

The "honey-haired" man who identified himself to Lulka as Thompson had worn, according to the eyewitness descriptions of three different people, completely different attire than Albert claimed he had the day of Sophie's murder: a light gray hooded cloth jacket and green pants for Albert as opposed to "Thompson's" dark leather jacket and black pants. And one of the witnesses was actually acquainted with the man who posed as the apartment painter—a man who despite the bizarre coincidence that he was nicknamed "Al" clearly wasn't Al DeSalvo, since the former was black and the latter was white.

Bottomly brought up an interesting point during this interrogation: that discussing the murders of the older women didn't seem to bother Albert nearly as much as discussing the murders of the younger ones such as twenty-year-old Sophie. "I can't see hurting no girls, nobody," Albert said. "What a hell of a feeling to know you really hurt somebody."*

It was as if he were speaking of the actions of another person. "It kills me, boy," Albert added.

> BOTTOMLY: Uhuh . . . Sophie, ah, you didn't have any sex relations with her either did you? She like Ida Irga?
> ALBERT: Ah, on Sophie?
> BOTTOMLY: You pulled the napkin off were you just too shocked? What did you do?
> ALBERT: I don't know what it was, but . . .
> BOTTOMLY: Do you remember having sex relations with her specifically?
> ALBERT: No, she was lying on the floor. Her legs were facing towards the, towards the coffee table. It was a light coffee table, very light.

Whoever had killed Sophie had apparently masturbated just afterward, because the forensic investigator found a seminal stain on the rug near her body. Albert seemed not to know that this had happened. In any case, he told Bottomly that he had left the apartment quickly but discreetly.

> BOTTOMLY: You always kept a cool head, though, you never run out.
> ALBERT: I never ran.
> BOTTOMLY: Never brought attention to yourself.

Eyewitnesses told police that the man they'd seen had been agitated and perspiring heavily.

---

* An interesting echo of the horrified remark he'd made to a Cambridge police detective in 1964: "I wouldn't hurt no broads. I *love* broads."

Albert said he'd passed a few people on the stairs to whom he'd nodded "very politely."

BOTTOMLY: But you always, ah, ducked your face.
ALBERT: So they couldn't see my face.
BOTTOMLY: Ya.

Albert then said he hadn't encountered anyone while leaving the building.

He talked about the length of time it had taken him to enter Sophie's apartment, kill her, and depart.

ALBERT: As to how fast it was done, I would say it didn't take no more than, in that apartment, no more than five or ten minutes.
BOTTOMLY: Oh, I see.
ALBERT: That's how fast . . .
BOTTOMLY: You talk about . . .
ALBERT: This is what I feel, anyhow.
BOTTOMLY: Ya. Course that's what it seemed like to you.
ALBERT: That's what I mean, that's right.
BOTTOMLY: It coulda been a half an hour.
ALBERT: That's right see? And that's what ah . . .
BOTTOMLY: You just don't remember, Albert.

This last comment was one of Bottomly's most revealing.

24

The Confessions of
Albert DeSalvo, IV

Albert was no more eager to confess to the slayings
of Patricia Bissette, Beverly Samans, Joann Graff, and
Mary Sullivan than he was to that of Sophie Clark—or,
indeed, to any of the others, despite his initial stated
desire to unburden himself and despite his disclaimer
that the details of the older women hadn't affected
him the way those of the younger women had.

He couldn't explain why he had moved nineteen-
year-old Mary Sullivan's body from one bed to another
in the room she'd shared with Pamela Parker and Patricia Delmore at 44A Charles Street in Boston. He also
blanked on other significant details of that murder.
And there was physical evidence left at that crime
scene that could not be connected with him.*

On September 9, 1965, Albert and Bottomly discussed at length the fact that one of Albert's Bridgewater acquaintances was a young man incarcerated

---

* To be discussed fully in chapter 33.

there for killing his wife. This man had known Mary Sullivan on Cape Cod—had in fact dated her—and, according to Albert, had referred to Mary with considerable contempt as "a skinny little bitch." The wife-murderer's opinion of women in general was low; they were all, he confided to Albert, "no God damn good."

Albert also told Bottomly that after this young man had found out that Albert had admitted to Mary's murder, he remarked, "Well, I don't have to. I don't have to play a game with you."

Bottomly asked Albert to place when he had killed twenty-three-year-old Patricia Bissette. Albert thought it was after the death of Sophie Clark, which was true, and after the attack on Erika Wilsing, which wasn't.

ALBERT: And then, uh, this was Patricia Bissette hadda come next and you know what, how I figger this? This hadda be done Sunday morning.

BOTTOMLY: Yuh?

ALBERT: And the date to my knowledge would be around the, uh, twenty-eight or twenty-ninth.

BOTTOMLY: Whatever that Sunday was, the last Sunday in December?

ALBERT: Yeh, becuz, uh, you know something'? we had coffee there. I know that I had my cup with me becuz she drank hers and I don't like coffee, not that much.

That Pat had offered her killer (or someone) this hospitality had been widely reported in the press, the *Globe* even stating that "the coffee in one cup had been served black and the other mixed with cream." It was also noted that one unwashed cup had been found in the living room, the other in the kitchen.

Albert said Patricia had a Christmas tree in her living room and a record player with a broken cover. Again, he had previously viewed the crime scene photos.

Albert's confession to the murder of twenty-three-year-old Joann Graff of Lawrence was not particularly convincing. Because it had taken place the weekend after the death of John F. Kennedy, it received somewhat less press coverage than it ordinarily might have.

BOTTOMLY: Can you think back now to the Graff place? Did you see a telephone?

ALBERT: No, I didn't.

BOTTOMLY: You didn't notice the telephone?

ALBERT: No.

BOTTOMLY: Did you take anything from the Graff place?

ALBERT: No.

BOTTOMLY: You didn't take a wallet?

ALBERT: Possible. It's possible.

BOTTOMLY: What would you have done with it if you did?

ALBERT: Threw it away.

BOTTOMLY: See what was in it and throw it away?

ALBERT: It's possible.

BOTTOMLY: Do you specifically remember anything?

ALBERT: What's that, in the wallet? Or taking it?

BOTTOMLY: Do you even remember taking it?

ALBERT: It's possible I took it and threw it somewhere.

BOTTOMLY: Mmm. But you're not positive either way.

ALBERT: No.

Even aided by these extremely leading questions, the Task Force chief was unable to draw the correct responses from Albert. Joann did in fact have a telephone. And her brown leather clutch wallet was missing from the apartment, presumably taken by her killer.

Bottomly persisted. "Now, remember the Anna Slesers case, you got a lot of blood on you which caused you some problems."

ALBERT: Yes.

BOTTOMLY: Was there any blood in the Graff case.

ALBERT: None, none.

BOTTOMLY: None that you recall?

ALBERT: Graff? None.

According to the Lawrence police report by the officer who had discovered Joann's body, there was blood on the bedspread and on the victim's bra, which had been ripped open.

Bottomly asked Albert what had happened when the latter had walked around Joann's building—as Albert claimed he had, and as had been reported in news accounts—looking for the victim's apartment.

BOTTOMLY: Okay. Now, ah, you mention that you ah saw this guy up on the, up one floor up and asked where Graff lived.

ALBERT: I recall going into this apartment. Going up and going to the farthest to the left and talking with this man. [This was Kenneth Rowe, who could not later identify Albert.]

BOTTOMLY: Right, and—

ALBERT: I remember talking to him.

BOTTOMLY: I thought you said leter [sic] or maybe earlier you couldn't remember exactly which you talked to a woman.

ALBERT: Yes.

BOTTOMLY: An older woman and you described her?

ALBERT: The opposite side of her apartment up in the left corner.

BOTTOMLY: Now, how did you represent yourself to that old woman, do you remember?

ALBERT: No, I don't.

BOTTOMLY: What lines you used with her?

ALBERT: No, I think I may have just talked to her

occasionally that's all. As to what I said to her I don't recollect.

The Task Force chief was not about to concede defeat so easily.

BOTTOMLY: Did you represent yourself as being in for maintenance or—

ALBERT: I don't recall.

BOTTOMLY: What if I used the word detective does that help you at all?

ALBERT: No. Never used that word.

BOTTOMLY: You never represented yourself as a detective?

ALBERT: Never used myself as a detective.

It wasn't the answer the Task Force chief wanted.
Despite repeated requests from Bottomly, Albert didn't wish to discuss the murder of twenty-six-year-old Beverly Samans in Cambridge. He also made clear the reasons for his reluctance.

ALBERT: I don't want to talk about her.

BOTTOMLY: Oh, why not?

ALBERT: Not her.

BOTTOMLY: Why not?

ALBERT: I was told not to.

BOTTOMLY: Why?

ALBERT: You know, just on this basis until things are clearer.

BOTTOMLY: You mean on account of Droney? On account of the D.A., there? [John Droney, district attorney of Middlesex County, who did not believe Albert had murdered Beverly Samans] Well, I mean—it's gonna—the deal we had is you're supposed to tell about everything you know.

ALBERT: Yeh, but I also was told by Mr. McGrath in front of you and Mr. Bailey until he comes back and he talks to you—Mr. Bailey's gonna talk to you, he says, when he comes back and Mr. Bottomly is present with him we will discuss that together. He says until you hear from me further, don't talk about it. He says when Mr. Bottomly and I will get together. He says, unless he says—

BOTTOMLY: Well that's gonna hold everything up.

ALBERT: Huh?

BOTTOMLY: That's gonna hold everything up.

ALBERT: No. Well he told me not to discuss that until that will be the last one he says til he talks to you privately. I gotta do what he tells me cuz you know yourself I'm going all the way. There's your fourth one right there, the question mark? There's no question at all there.

BOTTOMLY: The question mark meaning you can't talk.

Later that same day, August 24, 1965, Albert told Bottomly that he was "blocking out" Beverly's killing.

BOTTOMLY: You're doing that on orders, and I think it's messing some other things up, so I think we ought to—

ALBERT: Till we find out.

BOTTOMLY: Till we get cleared on Samans—to talk.

ALBERT: Ah—possibly you can bring Mr. McGrath—or—

BOTTOMLY: I'll get in touch with him tomorrow—I'll tell him the point that we've reached—

ALBERT: Uh huh.

Albert was ready to confess to the slaying fully on September 9, 1965. Whatever consultations or arrangements with F. Lee Bailey that needed to be made had clearly had been taken care of in one fashion or another.

ALBERT: Tryin' to think where I wuz that morning, why I wuz there. She let me in. I'm tryin' to think what I said to her. Uhhh—Jesus Christ—I remember it too clear—on her—(Long pause) (Heavy sighs)

BOTTOMLY: Well you tell it your way.

ALBERT: Do you want to—first sketch out the bath— the uh the apartment—

BOTTOMLY: Just as it comes to you in the story, then sketch it.

ALBERT: All right, uh—the uh—the way she opened the door. Gee I think she had a zipper—she had a zipper on in front of her.

BOTTOMLY: A housecoat on?

ALBERT: I think it was a housecoat or somethin'. I could be wrong on the zipper becuza that's what I don't see—I gotta talk about it whether I like it or not.

BOTTOMLY: I see.

ALBERT: She uh—I opened it up—and she went into the bathroom and I went with her and I had—I had gutten a knife from—that's it—this ties it up now. (Bang) You know somethin'—I wuz in there doing this job on the side. That's what happened. I wuz doin' a home in Belmont. That's how I gut to be over there in East Cambridge. [Beverly actually lived west of Harvard Square, about two miles from East Cambridge.]

BOTTOMLY: I see.

ALBERT: See—I wuz a—working in a home in Belmont for a woman on the side doin' extra work.

Albert told the Task Force chief that while he was working in the Belmont house, he went down to the cellar, where he opened some drawers and looked into them.

ALBERT: And this knife wuz in there. There wuz a knife in there. And I took it.

BOTTOMLY: What kind of knife?

ALBERT: It wuz a push button knife.

BOTTOMLY: Switch-blade?

ALBERT: 'Bout that long—yeah—switch-blade. Very sharp, pointed—never see 'em around here. I never seen one before.

BOTTOMLY: Curved, was it?

ALBERT: This wuz a—an Armenian family, that wuz livin there—an uh—it wuz a—you just pushed the button—p'tew—

BOTTOMLY: Did it come out this way, or up straight?

ALBERT: Think it wuz straight.

BOTTOMLY: Uh huh.

ALBERT: Came straight—you just push the thing, right?

BOTTOMLY: Yuh.

ALBERT: She shot right out.

BOTTOMLY: Shot right out of the handle, huh?

ALBERT: Yuh—pretty sure it shot right out. And uh—that there wuz in there an I put it in my pocket and I had carried it one or two days wit me—

BOTTOMLY: Uh-huh.

ALBERT: Could be three days—and I think—I'm almost positive—on my way from—home—that I shot over that way.

BOTTOMLY: To Cambridge.

Albert claimed that this stolen switchblade was the weapon he had used on Beverly, and that after leaving her apartment he'd driven to Malden (a small city just north of Boston) and thrown the knife in a swamp. This wetland had been filled in with gravel and houses built atop it, Albert said.

The point that the switchblade obviously couldn't be recovered now was moot; it wasn't the murder weapon anyway. Beverly had been stabbed to death with one of her own paring knives, which the killer had washed and put on the drainboard along with an assortment of other knives, forks, and spoons in an attempt to mislead the Cambridge police. The cleaning job was as inadequate as was the effort to conceal; the knife was still bloodstained.

On September 29, Bottomly asked Albert how he had killed Beverly. In the earlier session, Albert had volunteered that he'd stabbed her 'three or four times. Maybe five." Now he was prepared to elaborate. "I stabbed her twice right underneath the right bust," he said.

BOTTOMLY: Right underneath it?

ALBERT: Uhmm.

BOTTOMLY: Did you lift it up?

ALBERT: Yes.

BOTTOMLY: Did she still talk?

ALBERT: I don't know.

BOTTOMLY: Then what did you do?

ALBERT: I kept stabbing her right in the throat.

BOTTOMLY: In her throat. Did blood spurt out? (Long pause) How many times do you think you stabbed her? (Long pause)

George McGrath, who was present at this session, jumped in to break the silence. "Where was the knife, Albert? You said you got it at a painting job in Belmont?"

BOTTOMLY: He explained that in detail already, previously.

MCGRATH: Oh did he, ya.

ALBERT: About 5 or 6 times, 7.

BOTTOMLY: What made you stop?

ALBERT: I don't know.

BOTTOMLY: Thought she was dead?

ALBERT: I don't know.

According to the medical examiner's report, Beverly had been stabbed *seventeen* times above, below, in, and on either side of the *left* breast.* Her neck also bore four horizontal incised wounds, two on either side.

Albert kept changing the details in his story, perhaps in response to pressure from Bottomly.

BOTTOMLY: Her hands were tied?

ALBERT: I—yes, I think so—yes—yes—yes

BOTTOMLY: This is a hard one for you, isn't it? Do you remember what you tied her hands with?

ALBERT: I think this wuz with—my kerchiefs. I'm not sure.

BOTTOMLY: Kerchief.

ALBERT: Possibly kerchiefs.

Later during that same session, he said, "I coulda used a nylon stockin' to tie her hands—that's possible."

Bottomly was still pressing the issue on September 29. "What did you tie her hands with, do you recall?"

ALBERT: It must have been a pair of those, ah, it musta been a nylon stocking.

BOTTOMLY: You tied her hands, you think, with a nylon stocking?

And later still:

BOTTOMLY: What did you tie her hands with?

ALBERT: Wha, what I remember was one nylon stocking. Yes, one nylon stocking tied behind her.

Actually, Beverly's hands had been bound behind her back with one of her own multicolored scarves. One newspaper account of the murder, however, mistakenly reported that the ligature had been formed of

---

* Newspaper accounts gave varying numbers.

handkerchiefs, which may have provided the inspiration for Albert's initial statement.

On September 9, Bottomly asked Albert if he'd put anything around Beverly's neck. Albert said yes, but he didn't know what. A little time passed and he amended this response: "I don't know if I put a nylon stockin' around her, I don't think so, I don't think so—coulda—" By September 29, however, he'd revised his memory yet again.

> BOTTOMLY: After you stabbed her did you tie anything around her neck?
>
> ALBERT: No, no.

The autopsy report indicated that Beverly's killer had put two nylon stockings and a white scarf around her neck—in an obvious though poor imitation of the Strangler, police said.

Albert seemed familiar with the layout of Beverly's apartment, but then, as he told Bottomly, he'd cruised the whole complex in years past during one of his Measuring Man escapades.

> BOTTOMLY: Did you score in that building before?
>
> ALBERT: Many times.
>
> BOTTOMLY: Do you remember any of the people in there?
>
> ALBERT: On the whole block, ya. Well, see, this side, two girls before her, all the way around. That whole building. I was in most every apartment.

Albert did know a great deal about Beverly—that she was an aspiring opera singer (he described her as built like one); that she was hard of hearing; that she was a student; and that she was writing a master's thesis. He also knew that there was a typewriter and a piano in the living room-bedroom of her two-room apartment. He knew that when her body was found she lay faceup on a studio couch, with a cloth rag in her mouth. He knew that she'd worn a housecoat before her killer stripped her or forced her to strip. He knew that she had not been strangled or raped in the traditional sense. He knew that the shades in her apartment had been pulled down to the window-sills.

All these details had been printed—more than once—in the newspapers.

Albert told Bottomly that Beverly had said to him that she understood the kind of problems he had: "She seemed to know a lot about abnormal sex acts."

The *Record American* had carefully noted that Beverly's thesis concerned "abnormal sexual behavior."

What Albert didn't seem to know was that a television set on a broken-wheeled cart stood at the foot of Beverly's studio bed. This fact apparently was not mentioned in any of the papers. The Cambridge police found a handprint, probably a man's by its size, in the center of the screen. It was not that of Albert DeSalvo.

That Albert did have a highly developed facility for absorbing and retaining information he'd picked up from the newspapers he demonstrated to Bottomly during one of their August 24 discussions. Albert said he'd been working in Belmont on a contracting job when Bessie Goldberg had been killed there.* Mrs. Goldberg, Albert said, had "living in a brick house with white trim. I remember those things."

---

* Albert had always maintained his innocence of this murder. There would have been little point in him faking a confession; Roy Smith had already been convicted of killing Mrs. Goldberg on the basis of very good evidence.

"Yuh?" said Bottomly. "How do you remember? Did you go over when it happened?'

No, Albert said, he hadn't. "But I remember seeing the picture in the paper."

"I see," Bottomly said.

"It was like a two—a single family home, the shades were all down, white shades," Albert recited. "It was a brick, a red brick house and it had the drain pipes on the right side, square type?"

"Uh-huh," Bottomly said.

"No," Albert said. "But I read this in the papers."

His description of the Goldberg house, recalled after three and a half years, was accurate.

Bottomly then asked him how he'd remembered the identities of all his alleged victims. "You must've read it in the paper."

"I did," Albert said. He then hastily assured Bottomly that he'd *first* learned the victims' names when he'd seen them above the doorbells of their apartments—which doesn't explain why he kept calling Evelyn Corbin "Ellen Corbett."

"And that's how you remember the names," Bottomly said.

"Yes," Albert replied.

"Oh," said Bottomly. "I thought you just picked it up from the paper afterwards when you read about it."

The long interrogation came to an end on September 29, 1965. Whether Bottomly believed any of what he'd just spent the last two months hearing is impossible to say. He told Albert he didn't think a grand jury would put too much stock in his story. And there were other troubling factors.

"Like Mr. McGrath said, Albert, you were a very smooth operator," the Task Force chief commented, "and a lot of people who saw you [at the crime scenes] don't even know they saw you and, on the other hand, this is such a notorious thing we're talking about and it has so many implications beyond the crimes themselves that a Grand Jury—"

"What do you mean by implications?" Albert asked quickly.

"Well," Bottomly began, "the—"

Albert interrupted. "Somebody trying to make something out of it."

"Well," said Bottomly, "the monetary aspects of it alone—"

"What do you mean by mone—?"

George McGrath, sitting in at this last session, interceded. "The money involved."

"Money," Bottomly added. "The money-making aspects of it."*

Some people would end up profiting handsomely indeed from their roles in the Strangler saga. But before that could happen, something else would have to take place. "Well," Bottomly told Albert, "we have to corroborate what you're saying in every way that we can."

"Yuh," Albert said.

George McGrath—whom Bottomly had just incorrectly informed Albert was no longer his legal guardian† apparently shared the Task Force chief's anxiety about verifying the confession. "See, this is the big thing, Albert," he said. "There's got to be some things here that are provable."

"Yuh," Albert repeated.

---

* Bottomly and McGrath were doubtless referring not to the reward money offered for the solution to the killings (which DeSalvo couldn't collect if he were the killer) but to potential book and movie sales.

† Whether Bottomly was lying or simply mistaken is unknown. And, if McGrath *wasn't* Albert's legal guardian, why was he present at the latter's interrogations?

"Because if we get to the point where all we know is what you've told us," McGrath concluded, "we're gonna be in trouble."

PART FIVE

25

The Murders of Anna Slesers, Nina Nichols, Helen Blake, Margaret Davis, and Jane Sullivan

If Albert DeSalvo didn't kill Anna Slesers, Nina Nichols, Helen Blake, Ida Irga, Jane Sullivan, Sophie Clark, Patricia Bissette, Mary Brown, Beverly Samans, Evelyn Corbin, Joann Graff, and Mary Sullivan, who did?

There was certainly more than one murderer and—according to a number of law enforcement authorities—perhaps as many as twelve.

Far better cases can be made against these individuals than can be made against Albert DeSalvo. In at least one of the homicides, authorities were ready to go to the grand jury to seek an indictment against a particular suspect. And despite the basic similarity among the crimes—strangulation by a ligature consisting of articles of the victim's clothing—the disparities were equally numerous.

* * *

If a single killer was responsible for more than one of the murders, it would most likely be for the group that occurred in Boston between mid-June and late August of 1962: those of Anna, Nina, Ida, and Jane. Helen, although she lived somewhat far afield of the others in Lynn, might also be one of this number.

The Strangler Bureau itself recognized this fact. Attorney General Brooke's report, written in the summer of 1964, noted that "the homes of the [older] victims were quite similar in many respects. Though they are multiple dwelling structures they are not apartment houses in the modern sense or flats of the type found in, for example, the Dorchester and Roxbury area. They are comfortable, stone and brick structures with 3 to 6 stories and 3 to 5 room apartment units. They are similar to the 19th century row houses and some are converted town-houses. Presently they are somewhat run down. However, they have sturdy walls and construction of the type which puts them among the most isolated and sound-proof dwellings in which the inhabitants may have almost complete privacy.

"Of these four victims the youngest was 55 [Anna, who was fifty-six] and the oldest was 75 with three others in their 60's. Each of the women lived relatively isolated lives with many acquaintances and few friends. Their living pattern at the time of their death was one of rigid respectability. All were pleasant, very neat and well-groomed with a much younger physical appearance than usual at their ages. All were apparently of north European stock. It appears they all had a liking for music. As patients or members of the profession they had a fairly constant association with the medical world and were generally not interested in others."

Although there were some inaccuracies and too-sweeping generalizations in this description of the victims—the "rigid respectability" of their present lifestyles contrasted with their sometimes less conventional pasts—it was basically correct. An intriguing commonality of three of the women was that they were either immigrants (Jane Sullivan from Ireland) or refugees (Anna Slesers and Ida Irga from Eastern Europe). And there were professional connections: Anna and Ida were seamstresses, Jane was a nurse's aide, Helen was a practical nurse, and Nina was a physiotherapist. This latter "medical parallel" among the victims (Anna had been an outpatient at New England Hospital and Ida an outpatient at Massachusetts General Hospital as well as a sometime visitor to Massachusettes Memorial Hospital, where Nina had been employed) particularly interested some authorities, giving rise to the theory that all five women had been killed by a deranged doctor, orderly, or other sort of health care worker. An alternate theory was that the murderer was a psychotic patient who harbored an irrational hatred of late-middle-aged and elderly women associated somehow with a hospital setting.

Some investigators also found it significant that Anna, Nina, Helen, and Ida shared a love of classical music—although it must be said that in the early 1960s it would have been difficult to find a reasonably cultivated older white women whose tastes ran to rock or rhythm and blues. Could the killer therefore have been a man with similar "longhair" (as Albert DeSalvo would have said) preferences? Or even a musician? Or someone whose work brought him into regular contact with the music world?

Anna and Jane were recent tenants of the apartments they occupied when they died, which led to speculation that their murderer or murderers had first met them during the process of moving their households and settling into new residences. And it was posited too that all five women might have been victimized by a delivery man or a door-to-door salesman, the elderly being particularly easy prey for solicitors.

* * *

One suspect who came under intense police scrutiny in the spring of 1963 was a twenty-eight-year-old man named Bradley (Barry) Waring Schereschewsky, the son of the controller of one of New England's most prestigious preparatory schools. A college graduate with a checkered employment history, Schereschewsky had been in and out of mental hospitals since September 1959. In April 1962 he was living in a rooming house on Harvard Street in Cambridge and hanging out regularly at the King's Tavern in Central Square.

Subsidized by his father, Schereschewsky worked sporadically at various jobs. At the beginning of July 1962 he was a gravedigger at the Mount Auburn Cemetery in Cambridge. From July 27 to August 27 that year he was a counselor at the Duxbury Stockade, a camp for eight-to-fourteen-year-old boys in East Pembroke. He helped coach the track and swim teams, receiving in return a salary of $125 and his room and board. On August 20 he interviewed for a teaching position at a private secondary school in Connecticut. He took a bus from Boston to Hartford and returned from his appointment, again by bus, at nine-thirty that night. The police would later go to great pains to verify this event.

Schereschewsky didn't get the teaching post. In mid-September he went to work as a salesman at a retail store in Lexington. This lasted only a month; Schereschewsky was recommitted to Danvers State Hospital on October 23, 1962. The intention this time was to make the commitment permanent.

Schereschewsky's first incarceration in Danvers began on September 22, 1959. The reason for his institutionalization was an unusually horrifying one: the twenty-four-old had attempted to rape his own mother. When the elder Schereschewsky came to his wife's rescue, the young man turned on his father and beat him savagely. "Mr. Schereschewsky labors under the impression that it is perfectly all right for him to sleep with his mother and [that he] should be allowed to have intercourse with [her]," the police report noted with dry understatement.

What brought Schereschewsky to the attention of the authorities investigating the stranglings was not simply his pathological sexual drive but the fact that each of the murders of the elderly women occurred when he was on extended release from whatever institution had been holding him.

Anna Slesers was killed on June 14.

Schereschewsky was on the loose.

Nina Nichols and Helen Blake had died on June 30.

Schereschewsky was on the loose.

Margaret Davis, the alcoholic vagrant strangled in a fleabag hotel, died on July 11.*

Schereschewsky was on the loose.

Ida Irga died on August 19.

Schereschewsky was on the loose.

Jane Sullivan had died two days later. Schereschewsky was on the loose.

There were other disturbing coincidences.

On June 30, Schereschewsky was a guest of his aunt in Lynn. She lived on the street adjacent to Newhall Street—where Helen Blake had lived.

During the late spring and early summer of 1962, Anna Slesers was a frequent visitor to Duxbury, right by the summer camp where Schereschewsky worked from late July to late August. He had visited the camp several times in May and June. Since he had no car, he had to hitchhike back and forth from Boston.

Anna, who traveled to Duxbury by car, was known to pick up hitchhikers—a practice less hazardous than

---

* Margaret Davis's murderer was believed, probably correctly, by most police to be the drifter with whom she'd checked into the hotel and spent the night.

it is today but nonetheless suggesting she was somewhat less cautious and straitlaced than the attorney general's report had indicated.*

Schereschewsky frequently visited his sister in Boston. She had been living in an apartment at 102 Gainsborough Street since mid-March of 1962—a block down from Anna.

Schereschewsky had a close female friend whom he visited at her home on Beacon Hill, near where Ida Irga had lived.

On January 23, 1965, Schereschewsky escaped from the violent ward at Danvers. The state police were put on alert by Andrew Tuney, who also notified the Cambridge police at 2:45 that afternoon that Schereschewsky was out and might be heading their way. Tuney also got in touch with Bottomly, who in his turn notified the Boston police through John Donovan. Bottomly then called Schereschewsky's father and urgently requested that the elder Schereschewsky make contact with him at once if the escapee turned up at his parents' Andover house. Bottomly gave the father the numbers of his private telephone lines at the State House and at home.

At this point—about six weeks before Albert began his confession to F. Lee Bailey—the Strangler Bureau not only considered Schereschewsky a menace to the public welfare but a prime candidate for the murder of at least five women.

Fortunately, Schereschewsky was captured and recommitted before he could do anyone else any harm.

By a bizarre twist of fate, Schereschewsky was friends with yet another suspect in the stranglings of the older women. His name was William Axel Lindahl, and his father was a Boston cop who had been recruited for

---

* Jane Sullivan had an illegitimate daughter, again an indication that her past life was slightly less than conventional.

the job as a strikebreaker during the Boston police strike of 1919, when then-Massachusetts Governor Calvin Coolidge had called in the militia to restore order.

Lindahl's mother died in his infancy, and his father subsequently remarried, more than once. The boy did not get on well with any of his stepmothers, nor did he have a particularly close relationship with his father, a stern and rather cold man. He attended the Boston Latin School, where he was a good enough student to be offered several college scholarships. He went to Harvard, from which he graduated in 1955.

Lindahl's innate tendency toward homicidal violence first unleashed itself after he joined the naval ROTC; he tried to strangle a drill instructor. The ROTC promptly dismissed him. The next person he attempted to strangle was his girlfriend—when he found her in bed with another woman. Later he married and had a child, and obtained a teaching job at Lake Forest Academy in Illinois. According to one police report, Lindahl knew fourteen languages.

The marriage did not last. After the breakup, Lindahl's wife and child went to Texas. Lindahl was warned never to set foot in the state, so it seems evident that he was considered a threat to at least the peace of mind if not the actual physical safety of his former wife. Lindahl returned to the East and eventually got a job teaching Greek and Latin at a private school. In later years he would work for a while as a tree surgeon; he told an acquaintance that he enjoyed hacking and sawing and chopping the job entailed.

In the summer of 1962 he was living in Cambridge and frequenting the King's Tavern with Schereschewsky and another counselor at the camp that had briefly employed the latter.

Those who knew Lindahl say that he hated women—a hatred he did not bother to conceal but rather spoke of openly and often. He had very powerful hands.

During the period Anna, Nina, Helen, Ida, and Jane were strangled, Lindahl was working at Symphony Hall as an organist. Symphony Hall was a two-minute walk from Anna's door. She also had a subscription to the symphony. Nina and Ida were known to attend concerts there. These facts were of considerable interest to the police.

The wife of one of Lindahl's Harvard friends—the two men had belonged to the Fox Club—was convinced that Lindahl was the Strangler. She found his consuming rage against women terrifying in its force and scope. This woman would die in 1970. Her husband would be charged with her murder, tried, and convicted of manslaughter.

Lindahl attended his twenty-fifth Harvard reunion in 1980. The occasion plunged him into an acute depression, which he may have tried to alleviate with heavy drinking. He died a few months later, and was buried in a Lutheran cemetery in Worcester next to the mother he never really knew.

Peter Howard Burton, another former Harvard student and Cambridge resident, was as vociferous and vocal as Lindahl in his hatred of women. A young man with a genius-level I.Q. and, according to Ames Robey, "the eyes of a real paranoid," Burton was finally sent to Bridgewater in early 1964, where Robey interviewed him extensively. The doctor's diagnosis: "a genuine, certifiable nut."

A psychiatrist whose findings agreed with those of Robey was William Shelton, director of the Cambridge Court Clinic. In early December 1963, Shelton observed Burton and wrote the following report: "This young man was seen in the Detention Center of the East Cambridge Jail. He appeared grossly disturbed, walking back and forth. He acted odd and peculiar with a glased [sic] look in his eyes. He showd [sic] many of the characteristics of an acute hebephrenic schizophrenic with a silly laugh and answering inappropriately. For instance when I asked him his age he stated 'the last time I measured it, it was twenty-two.' " Shelton advised immediate hospitalization.

Burton, the son of a doctor and a nurse, was born in Brooklyn on April 5, 1941, the oldest of four children. The family moved to Troy, New York, and there he was educated at local schools, graduating from high school in 1958. Burton claimed to have won a congressional appointment to West Point; he attended the military academy for sixteen months before being dismissed in October 1959 for being a "nonconformist." Thereafter he matriculated at Harvard. He also maintained that he had studied for six months at the Woods Hole Oceanographic Institute and the Scripps Institute of Oceanography. While he was at Woods Hole, he told police, he had set up a drug manufacturing business. The enterprise was abruptly curtailed when the makeshift pharmaceutical lab blew up.

He was first arrested a little before three in the morning on April 19, 1961, in Newton, Massachusetts, along with four other Harvard students. The charge was possession of high explosives. (Burton apparently had an affinity for things that went boom in the night.) Burton had built a bomb out of gunpowder taken from seven high-velocity twelve-gauge shotgun shells, a flashlight bulb, a cast-iron pipe, a battery, and some wires. The five pranksters had planned to detonate the gadget somewhere along Route 128 but were balked by a mechanical failure.

That June, Burton either voluntarily withdrew from or was asked to leave Harvard for a year. He later boasted that he had been "thrown out" of the college because of the bomb episode. He spent that summer and fall in Los Angeles, returning to Cambridge and renting an apartment on Irving Street in early December. In February and March of 1962 he traveled in Europe. In early April he was back home in Troy, working for the Rand Joint Company. And he would travel on weekends to Cambridge to visit his girlfriend Carolyn, a nurse's aide.

Burton's sexual preferences were unsettled; two of his closest friends at Harvard were certain that he had had homosexual experiences (perhaps the reason for his dismissal from West Point). At any rate, they claimed Burton had spoken to them of making love to men. The proclivity was clearly one that frightened and angered Burton; once while cruising around the East Side of New York, he viciously attacked a gay man. The victim had apparently done nothing to provoke the assault. Burton later boasted of having "beaten up a faggot."

He was a heavy user of drugs, particularly mescaline and LSD—which in the early 1960s were substances unknown to the general public. He told people that he made the drugs himself and sold them to students in the Harvard Square area. He ingested the LSD and mescaline in triple doses.

He resumed his studies at the college for the 1962–63 academic year. Thereafter he took another leave of absence. This time it was forever.

Burton was next arrested in Cambridge on December 5, 1963—the first anniversary of the murder of Sophie Clark. The charge this time was disturbing the peace.

A little after five o'clock that morning, two residents of Reservoir Street called the police to complain that someone was wandering through their backyards, running about and singing loudly. It was Burton, and his antics managed to rouse the entire neighborhood. When the police arrived to take him into custody, he explained that he was looking for the home of a friend. Unfortunately, he not only didn't know where the friend lived but what the friend's name was. He was trying to locate the house by peering into cellar windows. If he saw a motorcycle stored in a basement, then he'd know he'd found the right place.

Another thing he couldn't remember was where he himself was staying in Cambridge.

At his arraignment that day he demonstrated his song-and-dance routine (apparently he performed country and western numbers) in the courtroom. The judge, finding these capers less entertaining than demented, ordered Burton to be examined by Cambridge Court Clinic Psychiatrist William Shelton and, on Shelton's recommendation, ordered the troubadour to Westborough State Hospital for observation.

Burton was returned to court on December 28. The hospital had diagnosed him as suffering from "Personality Trait Disturbance" and an "Emotionally Unstable Personality," which description seemed a trifle understated given his manic courtroom shenanigans.

On January 4, 1964, Burton was in Troy getting married. The Presbyterian ceremony took place in his parents' home. The bride wasn't his former girlfriend Carolyn but a young Californian named Penelope Dowler whom he had met in July 1963. Up until November 27, when they returned to Cambridge, they had lived on a farm in New Hampshire. Penelope was eight months pregnant at the time of the marriage; there was some confusion about the expected child's paternity. At one point Burton claimed that the best man at the wedding was the father. At another point he told a friend, "God, how neat it will be when I've got my own kid."

From its inception the marriage was a disaster. Penelope later told authorities that her new husband physically abused her; the black eye she had when she made the complaint gave her statement an undeniable substance. And he abused her emotionally as well, accusing her of sleeping with other men, including the supposed father of the child—with whom Burton nonetheless carried on an amicable relationship. (The accusations of promiscuity were "a complete lie," one of Burton's friends would later tell police.) Tenants at the rooming house on Harvard Street where the couple lived off and on during December and January said that they were continually being woken up at two, three, or four o'clock in the morning by the couple's loud and protracted fights.

On January 8, Burton went back to court on the charge of disturbing the peace that had been filed against him in early December. The judge dismissed the case. He felt that Burton had been sufficiently punished for his misdeeds by the stay in Westborough.

A little over two weeks later, Burton was taken into police custody again, this time in Harvard Square. Officer James Roscoe wrote the following report:

> In regard to Peter H. Burton, the subject was arrested by me noontime on 1-22-64. I was driving down Mass. Avenue and noticed the defendant pulling a girl (later identified as his wife) towards a vehicle; she was yelling and trying to pull loose. I approached the defendant and told him to take his hands off the girl; he then yelled that she was his wife and would go with him when he wanted her. His eyes were dilated and he had a wild appearance about him. He opened his coat and I saw a hunting knife stuck inside his pants belt. I pushed him away with my left hand and drew my service revolver, ordering him up against the wall. At this time a crowd gathered and he started to dance and yell that he was going to Hollywood with a dance group. His wife Penelope later stated that she was afraid of him and that he was acting strange for quite a while. Judge Viola ordered a dangerous weapon complaint and assault and battery on [Burton's] wife; I had arrested him for a disturbance charge.

Taken to Cambridge police headquarters, Burton was handed over to Sergeant Leo Davenport for questioning. Davenport and Burton had been acquainted for two years. The sergeant wrote an account of this most recent meeting to Captain John Grainger:

Subject Burton was brought into the Detective Bureau and seated in the vicinity of my desk. I glanced at Burton and recognizing him, I said: "Peter, what the hell is the matter with you?" He asked why. I said: "You give a perfect resemblance to Othello." . . . He gave a broad smile and said: "That's right, I'm living the part of Othello." I said: "That's fine, except for one thing, Peter. I notice you have the curly hair and you have your beard grown and clipped with the scissors so that it is a short beard, and I notice that your right ear is pierced with an earring in it. Of course, you are wearing the sandals. You fit the picture of Othello with the exception of one thing—" He said: "I know. I don't use much Man-Tan on my face to resemble [the] Moor."

I asked him why he was going around dressed in this manner. He told me that at the present time he had a dancing and singing troupe of his own which performed in Wellesley on different occasions, and he was getting ready to take his troupe to Hollywood. They were going to put on a film about why people should like policemen. I said: "Peter, you don't have to go to Hollywood, you better go to a psychiatrist." He said: "I just did. I was arrested last month and I went away to Westboro [sic] and they said I was sane."

I asked him why he had the knife in his possession, stuck in such a manner in his belt so as to be concealed. He stated that it was actually a stage prop which he carried with him at all times so that when he gave a display of his talents, he would have a prop.

I then asked him why he was involved in an altercation with his wife in Harvard Square. He stated that he had just purchased some champagne and cheese and had rented a car from Avis Rental Service and that he wanted to take his wife on a picnic. I stated it was rather cold to have a picnic on the outside and he said: "It's never too cold to have fun. But my wife didn't want to come, and I was trying to get her to go in the car."

Burton was arraigned the day he was arrested. His courtroom behavior was as peculiar on this occasion as it had been the previous December. He laughed uproariously for reasons known only to him, and burst into song. He was openly hostile to his wife. Spotting a young black man also awaiting arraignment, Burton asked the court to give him custody of the teenager. The youth could join his dance company and get a good headstart on a career, Burton said.

Judge Edward Viola vetoed this generous offer. Instead, he ordered Burton to be sent to Bridgewater for observation. He was at the institution by nightfall. Three days later Penelope moved out of the rooming house on Harvard Street, paid the rent in full, and went back to California.

Burton's enormous hatred of women was revealed in his conversations with Ames Robey at Bridgewater. Women couldn't be trusted, Burton told Robey. He particularly resented what he saw as a female usurpation of male prerogatives. "They are receiving the justice of my anger because they wear the pants and they shouldn't wear them."

Burton told Robey that he was going to create an invention of some sort and sell it. With the profit he'd buy an island off the coast of Australia and fence it with barbed wire. No women would be allowed to set foot on this private preserve.

Listening to this venomous diatribe, Robey began to wonder.

What had Burton meant when he spoke of women receiving the "justice" of his anger?

The implications were frightening.

Back in Cambridge, Leo Davenport was beginning to wonder, too—about the possible meaning of Burton's identification with Othello. Shakespeare's Moor had killed his wife because he believed her guilty of infidelity. Burton had been obsessed by *his* belief in Penelope's faithlessness. Davenport outlined his thoughts in a memo to Captain Grainger.

Back at Bridgewater, Robey began, very carefully, to question Burton. He elicited the information that the young man had been in the Boston area on June 14, June 30, August 19, and August 21. Those were the deaths of Anna, Nina, Helen, Ida, and Jane.

Two of those women had been in nursing; a third had been a physiotherapist. The remaining two were regular hospital patients and visitors.

Burton, a doctor's son, had a consuming hatred for nurses, which not only his mother but his girlfriend Carolyn had been. And his relationship with the latter had been far from idyllic. Some weekends—and on those of the deaths of the older women—he'd travel all the way from Troy to Cambridge to see Carolyn and she'd have nothing to do with him. Overwhelmed by fury and frustration, Burton told Robey, he'd roam the streets of Boston and Cambridge in search of a woman, any woman.

What did he have in mind for this woman once he'd found her? Robey asked.

Oh, Burton, replied, he was looking for one "to destroy."

Robey notified the attorney general's office and the Cambridge police of his suspicions. He also men-

tioned them to Donald Kenefick, the head of the
Medical-Psychiatric Committee that had profiled the
Strangler for the Task Force. Kenefick interviewed
Burton himself to confirm Robey's findings. In the
course of the session Kenefick asked the patient to
demonstrate for him what kind of a knot he'd tie if
he were going to strangle someone. Burton, sensing
where further questions would lead, refused to do
so—and demanded a lawyer.

Leo Davenport spoke to some of Burton's close
friends, who gave vivid testimonial to his burgeoning
mental illness. Said one, on February 11, 1964:

He came up once [to the friend's rooms in one
of the Harvard houses], apparently within a very
short time when he was arrested. And at this time
he was in a very strange way. He came at night
first and talked to us. I don't really know what he
was talking about because he seemed to be a little
bit out of his head at the time. And he came back
the next morning. I was getting ready to do something and I walked out of the corridor and saw
him then. And he was looking quite ferocious, and
he went through a very strange interchange—. I
will relate this—. There was a ring on the bell
because our rooms are partitioned off and you
have to ring the outside bell to get in the rooms
where we live, and I went to the door and opened
it and Peter was there at the time and he looked
very thin to me and sort of sickly. He had a beard
and his eyes were almost of one color. You really
couldn't distinguish the pupil from the whites of
the eyes. And I asked him to come in, or something of that nature, and I asked him how he was,
and he stared sort of defiantly and he did not
answer. I asked him again: "Peter, how are you?"
And he said: "John, HOW ARE YOU," like that.
I said that I was okay, so he responded immedi-

ately: "You are not okay, you are not all right!" I decided to leave it at that because I really didn't know what to do. And after that he didn't speak much. I think the night before he came into our room, and he was just wandering around hitting himself on the head and pacing the floor, obviously thinking ill of himself. You couldn't really talk to him or anything.

The friend described to Davenport Burton's problems growing up:

I remember my roommate told me that Peter had a very strange childhood. And my roommate said to me that one of the things that Peter remembers was his father coming home when he was around three. [The absence of the elder Burton may have been due to military service during World War II.] And since then there have been a whole lot of indications possibly that Peter's father had been a little harsh with him and mistreated him, and it was told that he used to beat him around a little, things like that . . . I was thinking how Peter's father in Peter's mind may have rejected him.

Burton felt rejected by a lot of people, the friend continued.

And he complained bitterly that people had not come to see him when he was in the mental home that first time, and even when it had been explained to him that there were no visiting hours, he would still harp on the fact that people wouldn't come and see him. And if he wanted to build up his own ego, which he was doing—how good he was, how much of a genius he was, it was to compensate for the fact that deep down he had been totally left alone. Maybe he felt that he had been turned down by his father. I know he doesn't like his father an awful lot, or doesn't seem to. And if he tries to build himself up enough, maybe it's just an indication that he is realizing deep down that nobody gives a damn about him, nobody loves him, including his wife—

Burton remained incarcerated in Bridgewater for the spring, summer, and fall of 1964. He was given to periodic outbursts of violence that could be contained only by massive doses of tranquilizers. Robey was angry that Westborough had so badly misdiagnosed the young man in its judgment that he was suffering from a mere "personality disturbance." That he had behaved sufficiently calmly to be released from Westborough was the result of Thorazine rather than therapy. The drug had simply masked his worst symptoms.

In October of 1964, Burton's lawyer requested that he be transferred from Bridgewater to the Massachusetts Mental Health Center, where he might receive more specialized treatment. The attorney wrote Robey that he had "been in receipt of numerous telephone communications from responsible persons at Harvard University who are concerned about Mr. Burton." He had also gotten a similarly anxious letter from the young man's father.

Robey wrote to Judge Viola that he would have no objection to Burton's transfer out of Bridgewater to an institution where he might be accorded more individual care. But Robey emphasized to the judge that security at Massachusetts Mental Health was less stringent than that at Bridgewater and that Burton in his opinion still "represent[ed] a very severe danger to the community." His drug-dealing had been investigated by the Secret Service and his psychosis, far from being cured, could not even be controlled. "It would fill me with a great deal of unhappiness," Robey wrote, "if he were to be released, to then hear of more stranglings, either in this part of the country or in New York or California, the other two places to which he would be likely to go."

Ultimately Burton did not go to Massachusetts Mental Health. His constitutional right to a trial prevailed and he was returned to East Cambridge jail to await a hearing before Judge Viola on December 14, 1964. Robey was not especially happy with this decision, but there was nothing he could do to circumvent it. He later heard that Burton had gone back to New York State and enrolled in a small college near Albany.

Burton's stay at Bridgewater had overlapped with that of Albert DeSalvo by five weeks. And, in an ironic turn of events, Burton had been represented by Paul Smith, the attorney for George Nassar before F. Lee Bailey had taken over Nassar's case. Smith would also counsel Bailey when Edward Brooke enjoined the latter from visiting Nassar or Albert DeSalvo at Bridgewater in March 1965.

In late June 1967, Robey became director of the Center for Forensic Psychiatry for the state of Michigan. Throughout the summer he commuted back and forth between Ann Arbor and Wellesley, Massachusetts, where he and his wife and daughters made their home. Shortly after Robey's arrival in Michigan, young women in the Ann Arbor and Ypsilanti area began dying in various hideous ways. Over a period of two years seven of them, aged thirteen to twenty-three, would be sexually mutilated and shot, beaten, or strangled to death. One of the victims would have the branch of a tree shoved eight inches into her vagina; police fervently hoped that she had been dead, or at least unconscious, when this atrocity had been inflicted on her.

Robey's family had joined him in Michigan in October 1967. The murders of young local women continued. One day in early April 1969, shortly after the discovery of yet another violated female corpse, Robey picked up a copy of the *Ann Arbor News*. In it he saw a story about a rent strike being led by a University of Michigan student who happened to be named Peter Burton. "It was indeed the same Peter Burton," Robey says. "Of all the screwy luck and circumstances to suddenly land up going out to the University of Michigan, where I was also working. So I reported to the Ann Arbor police detectives that I had no idea, that it might only be utter coincidence, but that Peter Burton was the one who at one time had been at least suspected, but then had had his charges dismissed and had vanished, for the first four or five of the Boston stranglings. The police—I thought it was very interesting—asked 'By the way, when did *you* start out here?' I said, 'In June.' They said, 'That's when the murders started.' [It was actually early July.] Fortunately for me, all the murders had been committed on weekends [when the Boston murders of the older women had been] and I was going out to Ann Arbor on a Monday morning and coming back to Massachusetts on a Thursday night plane. And I had a practice here, which I was winding down, jammed into Friday, Saturday, and Sunday."

Robey continues: "Nothing came of this. Peter immediately vanished [right after he spotted Robey walking across the university campus]. He was next noted to be out in Los Angeles just at the time the Hillside Stranglings started. Interestingly enough, they subsequently got somebody on one of the Ann Arbor killings. And while I don't think this guy confessed to the rest, it was sort of assumed because the modus operandi was so similar that he had committed the rest of them. And as you know they got two people out in L.A. for the Hillside Stranglings. But one wonders."****

Burton was reported to have bragged to university acquaintances that he had been a suspect in the Boston stranglings. And even before Robey had gone to the Ann Arbor detectives, he had come under police scrutiny. His drug activities and involvement with the local underground had brought him to their attention.

What has stayed with Robey all these years is the name of a street that ran through the county in which the Michigan murders were committed.

It was called Burton Road.

Another truly terrifying principal suspect in the deaths of Anna Slesers, Nina Nichols, Helen Blake, Ida Irga, and Jane Sullivan was a jug-eared, mentally defective grotesque by the name of Arthur W. Barrows (sometimes spelled Barrow), who once tried to kill his mother by throwing her down a flight of stairs. Barrows's mother survived the fall but did ultimately die in the hospital of a heart attack induced by suffocation. This occurred immediately after her son had paid her a visit. To quote from the police report, "she was found semi-conscious on the floor. At this time she was being fed and medicated intravenously. The hospital had taken normal precautions of putting sides on her bed to prevent her falling out. She was never able to tell the circumstances which caused her to fall because she died shortly thereafter. Some of the hospital personnel believe that her son threw her from the bed just before he left." With calculated brutality, the intravenous equipment had been yanked from Mrs. Barrows and left to dangle uselessly.

This was in April of 1961. Convicted once before for assaulting his mother, whom he regularly punched and kicked, Barrows had two other convictions on the same charge. In these instances, the victims were his sisters.

Barrows had once been employed as a door-to-door Bible salesman.

He was a large, shambling creature who, despite his gangly frame and awkward gait, was possessed of great physical strength. When the occasion demanded, he could move quickly and quietly in the sneakers he constantly wore. He was probably not nearly as stupid as his I.Q. tests indicated. He was profoundly psychotic.

To look at mug shots of Barrows taken during one of his various incarcerations in mental institutions (Boston State Hospital in Mattapan; Bridgewater) is to look at a face that in some subtle way seems almost extraterrestrial. None of the features quite appear to fit the attenuated bony face and Dumbo ears. The eyes are unevenly set, the Cupid's bow mouth far too small for the enormous chin it surmounts and the long gaunt cheeks that frame it. He is less human than humanoid, as if hastily assembled from a kit by a child in another galaxy.

While wandering around New York City one time he had been picked up by the police and sent to Bellevue for a brief period of observation and treatment. His family finally committed him to Boston State Hospital, where he was a patient in 1962.

He was not kept locked up at Boston State, nor were his movements rigorously supervised. Ground privileges had been accorded him, which enabled Barrows to leave the hospital premises whenever he chose. He would disappear for days at a time, often breaking into the basements of apartment buildings at night to sleep behind furnaces or coal bins. On other occasions he'd take refuge in alleyways. Filthy and disheveled, he was a memorable sight on the streets—except when he chose to conceal himself. A police report comments that Barrows "was very adept at appearing and disappearing with great speed and stealth."*

---

* In *The Boston Strangler* Gerold Frank writes that Barrows (whom Frank calls Arnold Wallace) had been brought to the attention of police by a psychic who had uncannily accurate visions of Barrows at his homicidal activities (pp. 68–81). It was later established that these visions had their basis in an acquaintance the psychic had formed with Barrows at Boston State Hospital.

While AWOL from Boston State, Barrows would haunt various churches looking for food. Clergymen would give him meal tickets he could cash at coffeeshops and other inexpensive restaurants. He was a regular customer at some of these establishments, although, given his horrific appearance, probably not an especially welcome one.

A little before 10:00 P.M. on April 9, 1963, a young modeling student, returning from a church service, was walking down Gainsborough Street. She passed the apartment where Anna Slesers had lived. Seeking a shortcut back to her dormitory, she entered an alley that led to Hemenway Street. And a nightmare vision rose up from the pavement before her.

The tall, cadaverous figure who had sprung so quickly out of the darkness grabbed the scarf the young woman was wearing and began to twist it, choking her. She kicked out at him twice and managed to scream despite the fact that her throat was closing. A young man, a student at one of the local colleges, heard her cries. He arrived at the scene to find the young woman lying unconscious in the alley. His approach frightened her attacker, who fled. Police took the victim to Massachusetts General Hospital, where she was treated for bruises on her neck and throat.

On nearby Edgerly Road another young woman, a former patient at Boston State, was attacked. A grubby tall man confronted her, saying "You're the cause of all my trouble." He grabbed her by the throat. She screamed and fought him, apparently hard enough to discourage him, for he released her and ran off down the street.

Both young women positively identified Barrows as their attacker.

Barrows was missing from Boston State on June 14, June 30, July 11, August 19, and August 21—the days Anna Slesers, Nina Nichols, Helen Blake, Margaret Davis, Ida Irga, and Jane Sullivan had been strangled to death. All these women were old enough to be the twenty-seven-year-old Barrows's mother, for whom he had borne an untrammeled hatred. It was noted that some of the elder strangling victims possessed a distinct facial resemblance to Mrs. Barrows. (Jane Sullivan and Ida Irga looked enough alike so that Ida's son Joseph nearly mistook a photo of one for the other.)

Barrows had worked in various menial jobs in local medical schools and hospitals—which put him in an environment that Anna, Nina, Helen, Ida, Jane, and Margaret also frequented.

The church on Gainsborough Street just a few doors down from Anna's apartment was one that Barrows visited frequently in his quest for meal tickets—up until June 14, 1962.

In December 1961 Barrows was briefly employed as a dishwasher in one of the dining halls of the Boston College campus. He was fired for making suggestive remarks to the female students. This dining hall was half a mile from Nina's apartment. The weekend of her death, a witness observed a man whose description greatly resembled Barrows furtively entering her building.

A number of the cellars in which Barrows spent his nights were in Ida Irga's neighborhood. A witness saw him in the area near the time of the murder—and many times prior to it.

One of the reasons Jane Sullivan had moved to Columbia Road in Dorchester was that she thought it would be safe. She had previously lived on a dark street, and had feared being attacked.

Barrows had once lived near Jane's building. And, on his forays from Boston State, he returned to the neighborhood quite often, seeking financial handouts at a church just two blocks from the murder scene.

He was a constant presence in the South End, where the only survivor of a Strangler attack, Erika Wilsing, had lived, and where he himself squatted in basements.

In 1962, Barrows's sister Claire was a resident of the House of the Good Shepherd on South Huntington Avenue in Jamaica Plain. Barrows would come to the home at night and repeatedly ring the doorbell. The person who answered it, Margaret Davis, would be murdered that July.

Barrows also reportedly told Claire that he was the Boston Strangler. His other sister later denied to investigators that he had said any such thing.

In September of 1962, Frank Parodi, a psychiatrist at Boston State, became suspicious enough of Barrows to speak to the police about him. Parodi felt there was a "strong possibility" that his patient was indeed the Strangler.

Parodi had had a strange encounter of his own with Barrows. One evening, while the doctor was in an area of the hospital off-limits to patients, he found Barrows roaming aimlessly.

"I want to talk to you," Barrows said.

"What about?" Parodi asked.

"The stranglings," Barrows replied.

Parodi was about to inject Barrows with sodium pentothal—and question him—when the phone rang. It was an emergency call that Parodi had to take. The questioning never took place.

Parodi, who would soon take another job out of state, advised the police to keep a close eye on Barrows.

Eventually the authorities decided that Boston State Hospital, with its easygoing attitude toward inpatient mobility, was not the most secure facility in which to keep someone of Barrows's tendencies. In February of 1964, he was transferred to Bridgewater.

He was still there when Albert DeSalvo arrived that November.

Peter Burton enjoyed boasting about his criminal exploits as much as he did broadcasting his hatred of women. Arthur Barrows freely shared his fantasies of "screwing" women and choking them.

Did they find a receptive listener to their tales in their fellow inmate Albert? Did he mentally file away the stories they told for future reference?

26

The Murder of Sophie Clark

At the age of twenty, Sophie Clark was beautiful, intelligent, and popular, although some of her friends considered her a bit reserved and perhaps overly cautious. As it turned out, she may not have been cautious enough.

She had been a student of medical technology at the Carnegie Institute on Beacon Hill. The day of her death, December 5, 1962, she left school after midday and returned to the apartment she shared with two other Carnegie students, Gloria Todd and Audri Adams. She shed the white lab coat she customarily wore to class—the rest of her school uniform consisted of black stockings and flat-heeled tie shoes with corrugated soles—and slipped into a housecoat. She may have puttered around the apartment for a while or simply relaxed after the morning of classes. She did start to write a letter to her steady boyfriend, Charles Drisdom, who, like Sophie's parents, lived in Englewood, New Jersey. It was close to 2:30 when she began the letter; she mentions the time in the course of it.

She tells "dearest Chuck" that she's going to do some homework later and then start preparing dinner for herself, Gloria, and Audri. (That evening's menu would feature liver and onions, mashed potatoes, gravy, and a vegetable.) The letter is full of solicitude: Sophie asks Chuck if his cold is better. Would he like to have chicken when he visits next weekend, or is he tired of that dish? What does he suggest? She might be able to make a pizza this coming weekend.

The letter is unfinished. It was the last one Sophie would ever write. At 5:30 that afternoon she would be found dead on the living room floor, a nylon stocking knotted tightly around her neck and a white half-slip loosely tied over the primary ligature. She lay on her back, legs apart, the housecoat open to expose her body, still clad in menstrual harness, garter belt, stockings, and shoes. Her bra, now torn, her pink flowered underpants, and a stained sanitary napkin lay on the floor near her. She had been gagged with a white handkerchief.

Who could commit such an act?

A number of people, as it turned out.

For eighteen months prior to Sophie's murder, several of her classmates had been the unhappy targets of threatening messages. The siege had begun in June of 1961. A previous roommate of Audri Adams received a sequence of obscene letters in which the writer promised to rape her. So terrified was the young woman that she moved out of the apartment and back to her family's home in suburban Weston. She refused to venture outside except to go to class.

That September yet another Carnegie student began getting anonymous phone calls at her Roxbury home. The caller, like the letter-writer, threatened rape. In January and February of 1962, a third Carnegie student was victimized by menacing phone calls and letters stuffed into the mailbox of her Beacon Hill apartment. Throughout all ran the same theme of sexual violence.

Around this time Audri Adams and Gloria Todd, then sharing an apartment on Spruce Street in Beacon Hill, began receiving similar telephoned threats. Someone slit the convertible roof of Audri's car; Gloria's was pushed off the street and onto the sidewalk and vandalized.

And someone painted the initials "KKK" on their front door, clearly someone who didn't like the fact that a black woman (Gloria) and a white woman (Audri) were rooming together.

Justifiably frightened by these incidents, Gloria and Audri moved to 315 Huntington Avenue that spring. Sophie joined them there that September, when school resumed. The disgusting phone calls continued unabated. The caller, speaking in an obviously disguised voice, vowed he would come to the apartment and assault Gloria and Audri. Interestingly, none of these threats were directed at Sophie—who of the three roommates was the one who ended up sexually violated and dead. Was she the victim of a deranged bigot who saw in a woman who was half-black and half-white the perfect symbol of his rage at the spectacle of representatives of the two races living, studying, and socializing together? Someone who, to express his total contempt for his victim, didn't bother to rape her but ejaculated on the carpet near her body instead?

This was one theory, and it remains a plausible one. Most authorities, however, tend to the belief that Sophie was killed by someone she knew and felt comfortable admitting to the apartment. Her death may have been the result of what Edmund McNamara calls "a rape gone wrong"—in which her assailant was so revolted by the evidence of her menses that he wouldn't complete the sexual attack he'd intended and so garroted his victim in a rage of frustration.

Despite her modesty, reserve, and caution, Sophie came in regular contact with a number of unsavory characters—some of whom had long-standing criminal records for sexual offenses. Many of them were associated with the Carnegie Institute.

Far from occupying a rung in the upper echelons of academe, or even its middle, Carnegie had no scholarly accreditation whatsoever. It was indeed on the verge of being closed down by order of the court—an injunction against it had been sought by the Massachusetts attorney general's office. Countless complaints about the place were on file with the Boston Better Business Bureau. The Approving Authority for Schools of Medical Technology in Massachusetts had awarded Carnegie its seal of disapproval. The American Medical Association found the school's training requirements substandard to its own.

Carnegie was one of a chain of schools owned and operated by a lawyer named E. L. Koenemann of Cleveland, Ohio. In addition, Koenemann ran a lending service to which the students at his schools could apply for tuition loans. (The tuition at the Boston branch of the school was twelve hundred dollars, steep for the early 1960s. A decade later, an institution such as Boston College would still be charging only a little over two thousand dollars.) Koenemann was also the founder and director of an accrediting agency. Its purpose was to award accreditation to his own schools, since nobody else would.

Lawsuits were pending against the various Carnegie schools not only in Boston but in Washington, D.C., and Cleveland.

Carnegie purported to graduate expert X-ray technicians, laboratory technicians, and dieticians. Yet its curriculum offered courses in poise, wardrobe, and elocution—hardly essential skills, one would think, for a career amid test tubes and slides. Carnegie also gave a course in the maintenance of "a live [presumably a misprint for "lithe"] well-proportioned body," again not a credential a health care worker might be expected to list at the top of her résumé.

Carnegie did not require its entering students to have good scholastic records. It apparently didn't even require grade transcripts. Its campus recruiters were salesmen who received a $125 commission for each student who enrolled and paid the tuition. The commission itself came out of a $150 application fee tendered by the student.

Among the Carnegie faculty was a radiation therapist who had been dismissed from a Pennsylvania college for running a phony cancer cure business on the side. Another was an alcoholic sexual pervert who had once operated his own "School of X-Ray Technology" under the Carnegie aegis. Yet another was a narcotics-addicted doctor whom Carnegie actually fired for being unfit, which says a lot given the caliber of the employees the school retained.

The shadiest member of this retinue of undesirables, however, was its dean, an habitué of Boston's sex-for-sale Combat Zone who had managed to rack up an impressive series of arrests for open and gross lewdness, unnatural acts, and suspicion of grand larceny of an automobile. His name was William Russell Keany. Those who knew him described him as a very intelligent and highly cynical opportunist with a mean streak that never stayed very well hidden. One acquaintance said of him: "He is like the man Oscar Wilde described—one who knows the price of everything and the value of nothing."

On the day of her death, Sophie left Carnegie at 12:30 P.M. She and her classmates had been scheduled that afternoon to have their pictures taken for the house organ of a laundry company. The photographer wasn't able to make it to the school to do the shoot, however, because his truck wouldn't start. At 1:00 P.M.,

Keany announced to the students that the picture session had been canceled.

He had apparently informed Sophie (and her alone) of the cancellation at least a half-hour earlier. That was why she had gone home. The normal ending time for day classes at Carnegie was 2:00 P.M.

Keany's rancid reputation, coupled with his knowledge of Sophie's whereabouts the afternoon of her murder, drew the attention of some investigators. Competing for their interest, however, were two other outstanding suspects. One was the young "honey-haired" man who, giving his name as Thompson, had come to the door of Sophie's neighbor Marcella Lulka and made suggestive remarks to her. Over two years later Mrs. Lulka would tell police that George Nassar was identical to "Thompson" but for his hair color.

The other suspect was the twenty-two-year-old son of a Cambridge minister. His name was Albert Williams.

At 4:30 P.M. on December 5, Eartis Riley, the wife of Anthony Riley, the nurse who'd attempted to resuscitate Sophie, heard a knock on the door of the apartment she shared with her husband at 315 Huntington Avenue. It was Al Williams. He said he was there to collect a book Tony Riley had promised to lend him. Eartis noticed immediately that Al was sweating profusely and seemed extremely agitated. He explained that he'd just come up five flights of stairs, and furthermore that it was hot in the building. It wasn't. Eartis got rid of him.

Just before 6:00 that evening, Al visited another acquaintance, Antoinette Grace, who lived nearby on Symphony Road. She let him into her apartment; he asked her if he could sleep there that night.

Antoinette had been listening to the radio when Williams showed up on her doorstep. A few minutes after she admitted him to the apartment, a news bulletin interrupted the regularly scheduled program. It was announced that a young woman had been found murdered at 315 Huntington Avenue.

"I'm going over," Antoinette said.

"I'm not going near that place," Williams replied. Then he left the apartment.

Antoinette described Williams to the police as being an "oddball." She also told them that he had been "sort of forcing his attentions on her."

Where Williams spent the night is unclear. He couldn't go to his parents' home in Cambridge—his father had kicked him out of it six months previously and hadn't seen him since. He *did* pay a brief visit to his grandparents at their Boston home on West Canton Street, where he wasn't particularly welcome either. When police interviewed the grandparents later that evening they claimed to have no idea where Williams was now. Nor were they especially cooperative with the authorities.

Williams was the possessor of a medical discharge from the army as well as a long criminal record. The police had been looking for him anyway in connection with breaking and entering and larceny and assault charges.

He had also once worked as a laboratory technician, which of course was what Sophie had been studying to be.

The killer did not ransack the apartment, but he did search it, rifling through photographs, examining the contents of bureau drawers, and scattering several packages of cigarettes on the floor. He left behind virtually no physical evidence of his presence*—not even wet footprints on the carpet, despite the fact that it had been raining heavily that afternoon.

It emerged that Williams had not only known Sophie but had dated her at least once—about three and a

---

* Apart from the semen stain.

half weeks before her murder, he'd taken her to the movies. Audri and Gloria said that he'd visited the apartment on two or three other occasions.

Those who knew Williams often used the word "neurotic" when referring to him. He sometimes suffered blackouts, the result of a head injury sustained in adolescence. He had always been a braggart and a troublemaker.

Williams was a bisexual who had been kept by men as well as women, necessary because he was unable to hold even menial jobs. He was also a sadist; he enjoyed inflicting pain and punishment on his female sexual partners.

The police finally tracked him down and questioned him. They had to release him; there was no physical evidence left at the crime scene sufficient to press charges against him. After that he vanished again—and wasn't found again until May of 1964. At that time, he was staying in a hotel in Harlem.

He agreed to take a lie detector test, and one was given him in New York. The polygraph operator asked the key question: Had Williams been in Sophie's apartment the afternoon of her death? He answered no.

According to the test results, he was lying.

The polygraph was readministered. The operator asked the same questions. Again, the machine indicated that Williams was lying.

This was still not enough to charge Williams with homicide. He was free to go. Police could only hope that given Williams's tendency to boast of his sexual exploits, he might one day slip and incriminate himself to a friend or acquaintance, who might then turn state's witness.

Unfortunately he never slipped—or if he did, no one bothered to inform the authorities.

27

The Murder of Patricia Bissette, I

If the wintertime murder of Sophie Clark—young, attractive, black, and sharing an apartment with two friends—was a deviation from the pattern set in the summer of 1962, in which all of the strangling victims had been white, late middle-aged to elderly, and living alone, the slaying of Patricia Bissette just before the end of that year fell into neither category. It borrowed from both: The victim was young, she was white, and she was the sole occupant of her apartment on Park Drive. And there was a new dimension. Patricia's killer had not degraded her corpse. He had instead left her tucked in bed, almost as a mother would her child. Or a lover his mistress.

Patricia Bissette, twenty-three at the time of her death, was raised in Middlebury, Vermont, by her adoptive mother, Hazel, and her aunt, Ruby Rogers, who ran a gift shop on Main Street. She attended local schools and sang in the choir of the Middlebury Meth-

odist Church. At the high school she was an editor of
the student newspaper and of the senior class yearbook. She served as a delegate to the model United
Nations assembly held one year at Plymouth State
Teachers College in New Hampshire. She was a member of the school chorus and the glee club, and played
basketball after school. She was said to be gifted in
math, science, and physics, and to have a flair for foreign languages.

After graduation from high school, she attended the
University of Vermont for one year, but dropped out
in search of wider horizons. She followed her star to
airline school in Missouri, and thereafter to New York
to work in communications for American Airlines at
Idlewild (now Kennedy) Airport.

Her stay in New York was not altogether pleasant.
She became engaged to a man who worked as a meteorologist at the airport. The engagement was a short
one, and ended at Patricia's behest. She nevertheless
continued to date the meteorologist even after their
breakup; she felt sorry for him even though he was "a
pest," or so she confided to a friend. In late April of
1961 she was involved in an automobile accident in
Queens that required brief hospital treatment. It was
perhaps this last incident that sealed Patricia's disen-
chantment with New York. At any rate, she packed up
and moved to Boston, a much smaller and ostensibly
more manageable city.

In the late fall of 1961 she took a job as secretary
and receptionist with an engineering firm on Commonwealth Avenue. For a while she shared an apartment on Newbury Street with another young woman.
The July before her death, she moved into 515 Park
Drive. The rent for her three-room first-floor apartment was normally $130; Patricia was allowed to pay
only $75 in exchange for letting the building's owner,
Ada Kotock, and maintenance man Harry Martin use
it to conduct rental business.

"Very pleasant and punctual," her coworkers described her. "A very friendly, very happy girl," high school friends would recall, "a very thoughtful and intelligent girl." "Very kind," Harry Martin said. On January 18, 1963, Hazel Bissette, understandably pained and angered by other, less generous assessments of Patricia's character, would write to Boston Police Detective Lieutenant Edward Sherry: "It is hard for you to believe that she was—Sweet, trusting, gullible, high morals, never would hurt anyone, give her last penny to someone with a hard luck story."

Dorothy Rancourt, who had worked with Patricia in New York, called her "a sucker for a sob story."

Patricia was all of those things, and more. It was the *more* that killed her.

At 10:00 on Saturday morning, December 29, Patricia went to work for a while at Engineering Systems, Incorporated. Her boss, company vice-president Jules Rothman, lent her his car so she could do some shopping. At 1:30 that afternoon, he went to Patricia's apartment to retrieve the station wagon. He joined his secretary for a cup of coffee.

Sometime between 3:00 and 5:00 P.M., Patricia left her apartment with a sack of dirty clothes. She ran into Christian Van Olst, the janitor for her building and 509 Park Drive. He asked her where she was going. She told him she was going to do her laundry, and inquired whether all the machines in the basement of 509 were busy. Van Olst watched her walk down the alley between the two buildings and enter the basement of 509.

At about 5:30 or 5:45, Patricia was back in her own apartment. Two of her neighbors, Linda Ladinsky and Charlene Adelman, spoke with her briefly when they returned a toaster Linda had borrowed.

From that point on, Patricia's movements became a little more difficult to trace.

On Sunday morning, December 30, between 10:00

and 11:00, Harry Martin knocked on the door of Patricia's apartment. When he got no response, he unlocked the door. The apartment was dark, so he switched on the light in the entry hall. He used the telephone to call Ada Kotock and discuss with her some business concerning another apartment building in Allston. They talked for perhaps five minutes. Then Martin went into the kitchen, again turning on the light, to see if Patricia had left any mail there for him or Mrs. Kotock. He noticed that the bedroom door was open, and also that one of the beds was piled with boxes. He later claimed not to have seen any sign of Patricia herself.

That day a woman who lived at 500 Park Drive thought she heard screaming sometime between 3:00 and 4:00 P.M. She thought nothing of it until the following day when she learned that Patricia had been found murdered at 515 Park Drive.

A waitress at the lunch counter of a local drugstore claimed that she'd seen Patricia having a snack at 4:30 on Sunday afternoon. She was accompanied by a dark-skinned man who spoke heavily accented English and whose manner toward the young woman was extremely possessive.

At about 7:30 A.M. on Monday, December 31, Jules Rothman arrived at 515 Park Drive to pick up Patricia and drive her to work. He knocked at her door; she didn't answer. After a few moments, he left. When he got to his office, he called Patricia. Her telephone went unanswered. An hour or so passed with no word from the secretary who was usually so reliable. Rothman, now very worried, returned to the apartment. With the help of Christian Van Olst, he climbed a stepladder to a front window, removed a screen, raised the unlocked window, and entered Patricia's living room, knocking over the Christmas tree in the process. He found the young woman dead in her bed and called the police.

The autopsy, performed by Michael Luongo, resulted in these findings:

> The body of the deceased lay flat in bed covered by bedding. About the neck was a ligature composed of several garments . . . The bedroom atmosphere was very cold. There was full rigor mortis. The body was clothed only in a blue and red print housecoat which was pushed up above the breasts together with an imitation leather [leopard?] skin pajama top which was also pushed up about the breasts. The right hand and wrist lay compressed under the right buttock . . . In the mouth is a moderate amount of blood-tinged mucus and froth. Similar material is present in the nose . . . In the anterior surface of the right leg over the shin is a linear area of brownish-black soiling without injury, measuring six inches in length . . . There is no injury of the external genitalia. There is a moderate amount of mucoid secretion within the vagina. Several smears of this material [were] made and found to be loaded with spermatozoa . . . The ligature, which tightly encircles the neck, is composed of four articles . . . 1) white blouse, knotted 3x anteriorly, 2) single stocking, 3) 2 nylon stockings.

Although there was no injury to Patricia's vagina, there was a slight one to her rectum. She was at least one month pregnant.

One thing that became clear almost immediately on the last day of 1962 was that fifty-three-year-old Jules Rothman, married and the father of two grown sons, and twenty-three-year-old Patricia Bissette had been something considerably more intimate than employer and employee. The Boston cop who interrogated Rothman got right to the point:

Q: How long have you been seeing her socially?
A: Probably about, we were good friends, let's see, for about March, since January she was my secretary.
Q: How long has she been employed?
A: A year and four months.
Q: How long have you been lovers?
A: We weren't lovers, exactly, we were, let's see, I would say January or February of this year.
Q: Almost from the beginning?
A: Yes.
A: Have you stayed overnight at Newbury Street or on Park Drive with her?
A: No.
Q: You visited many times at her apartment?
A: Just when she asked me to come over. She trusts people.
Q: Do you know of any other man having intercourse with her?
A: No.
Q: How often did you go to her apartment?
A: Maybe once a week or so.
Q: Do you personally know any other fellows that were going with her or having intercourse with her?
A: We never discussed it but there was a John, he is from Vermont but he is away for the weekend. I met him at the party. We were invited to a Christmas party and she told me about him and she may have had others but we never talked about people.

The detective asked Rothman if Patricia had dated anyone else at Engineering Systems.

A: She is friendly with Sheldon Kurtzer. She tells me she was out with him but never overnight.

Once somebody took her home at 3 A.M., a sales-man, and once she was out with Jim.

Q: What is his last name?

A: I don't know his last name. This John is the one she has been going out with lately. She has been going out to Route One, in Dedham.

The detective asked about Patricia's attitude toward sex.

Q: Was she an easy girl to have intercourse with?

A: Yes, that is the trouble with her.

Q: Was she a pushover?

A: Yes, she was. She came from New York and she must have had some love affair. It wasn't till she went to this apartment. [Rothman presumably was referring here to the onset of his involvement with Patricia.]

Q: In other words, she didn't say no?

A: No, not to me.

The detective raised the issue of Patricia's preg-nancy.

Q: You knew there was something wrong with her?

A: She told me she missed her period.

Q: When did she tell you this?

A: About a month ago.

Q: And she told you you were responsible?

A: No, she didn't say that.

Q: What did you do about it?

A: I got in touch with a friend of mine.

Q: What is his name?

A: John Price, who had a similar situation once and I saw him Friday night.

Q: What Friday night?

A: This Friday night.

Q: That was December 28th?

A: Yes.

Q: What time did you see him Friday night?

A: I had an appointment at the Smith House with him.

Q: What is his name?

A: John Price.

Q: Where does he live?

A: Peabody.

Q: What is his address?

A: I got his card here.

Q: "John Price, Camden Associates, 8 Irving Street, Salem." What conversation did you have with him?

A: There were two phone calls and I didn't disclose Pat's name or anything. He had a problem about a year and a half ago and he sort of confided in me, somebody got in trouble and I said to John, "I know somebody who is in trouble like that." And I said, "John, I think you can help this party out." And he told me what he would do if he had to do it over again.

Rothman told the detective that Price had given him some information about a private hospital or convent in Buffalo, New York, that took in pregnant unmarried women, cared for them throughout the gestation period and delivery, and then arranged for the infant to be adopted.

Q: What did [Patricia] say [about this proposal]?

A: She would disappear to Buffalo and she would write a book.

Q: Did it bother you very much that Patricia had been made pregnant by you?

A: Yes, I don't know if it was by me.

Q: Did you tell your wife?

A: No.

Q: Did you tell your sons?

A: No.

Q: You must have told somebody, did you tell your [business] partner?

A: No.

John Price was the only person who was aware of the situation, Rothman claimed. Patricia had wanted it kept "confident."

Rothman told the detective that he had gone to Patricia's apartment that Friday evening and passed on the information Price had given him. He left there, he said, around 10:00.

The detective began to play hardball.

Q: [Price] had an abortion performed.

A: Yes.

Q: And you wanted the name of the abortionist.

A: No, I wanted advice, I wanted to help [Patricia] out.

Q: Did you discuss abortion with him, about his advice on having an abortion performed?

A: I asked him what he would do if he had a girl who was single, that was in that kind of trouble, I didn't say it was me because I wasn't sure. And he said if he had to do it again, he has a place out in Buffalo, New York, and they would take care of this girl and would adopt the child.

As Rothman grew more nervous, he grew more evasive and less coherent.

Q: Did you ask him if he knew where you could have an abortion performed on a girl?

A: I don't think I put it that way, maybe you can put it that way. I said, "A girl is in trouble, what would you do?" I didn't ask him about an abortion, if he knew a doctor.

Q: Did you ask him if he knew a doctor?

A: That's right, true, I would say that was the same thing. And he had told me that he knew a doctor but he told me that the problem that he was involved in and he had done in this way. And I said, "What is it?" And he had to go to his place of business and come back and he called up a place in Buffalo and talk [sic] to a sister and he wrote it down on a piece of paper.

Q: Where is that paper?

A: Patricia has it. I gave it to her Friday night.

Q: What I am getting at now is you asked him if he knew a doctor who would perform an abortion?

A: I asked him, I told him about the trouble, I didn't say it that way, I guess it meant the same thing. I didn't ask him that way, I asked him what he would do.

Q: Did you ask him if he knew a doctor?

A: I never asked him that question. He called up a place in Buffalo and he wrote it down on a piece of paper and if the girl went there for two months she would be incognito and the child would be adopted.

Rothman's story, already weak, would be contradicted by other, more credible witnesses.

28

The Murder of Patricia
Bissette, II

The "Jim" that Rothman had mentioned as one of
Patricia's dates was a very recent employee of Engineering Systems named James Michael Toomey. A
twenty-nine-year-old machinist, he was married to a
schoolteacher and had one daughter. He was unable
to hold a job for more than a brief period. He was
also a heavy drinker and a chronic philanderer. At least
three women at Engineering Systems told police that
they had been propositioned by him in the most crude
and aggressive terms. One of them said that Toomey
had asked her to spend a weekend with him in a hotel,
"where in forty-five minutes he would prove what a
man he was." (She declined the invitation.) Another
woman said that he had approached her and requested that she fellate him. (Toomey later claimed
that she had offered to do so.) He also admitted to
police that he had been after Patricia to go out with
him—which she did, once, for drinks at the Buckminster Hotel—and that he had badgered her to lend him
her apartment so he could bring his other women

there. This she apparently refused to do, but she did allow him to visit her at home.

After the date at Buckminster (Patricia probably had to pay the tab, since Toomey claimed he had only a dollar-fifty on him), the two had returned to her place around 9:00 and talked about sex, which in fact had been the topic of their discussion over drinks. Toomey said that Patricia had told him that Sheldon Kurtzer, Rothman's business partner, had commented to her that she could not be gotten. "I was therefore interested to prove him wrong and lay the ground work to get into her pants."

Toomey failed to achieve his goal that evening. Two young women friends appeared at Patricia's to collect the pet canary they had left in her care, which effectively curtailed the chat about sex. Toomey left about 10:00 that night.

With more than sufficient justification, the police considered Toomey to be a braggart and a degenerate, with a personality about as stable as nitroglycerine. But he appeared to be telling the truth about the extent and nature of his relationship with Patricia.

Toomey's behavior on December 31 was extremely peculiar. That morning, after the discovery of the body, Rothman had called one of his employees, Ann (Billy) MacKenzie, and asked her to meet him at 515 Park Drive. She took a cab over there. Toomey, for reasons that were never explained, accompanied her. (He had earlier suggested to Rothman that the reason Patricia had never shown up for work was that she "might be killed.") Billy and Toomey knocked on the apartment door. It was answered by a Boston police officer from the Back Bay's Division Sixteen. MacKenzie told a state police detective that

Jimmy [Toomey] asked him if Pat was dead and the policeman didn't answer and Jimmy said, "She was strangled, wasn't she," and the policeman just

looked at him and [Toomey] said, "She was strangled with a stocking wrapped around the throat,
wasn't she, is this a homicide?" and the policeman
said to him, "Who are you?"And he said, "Well,
I work for Jules Rothman," and [Toomey] says, "I
was just wondering about Pat."

Toomey also wanted to know if Patricia's body had
been nude.

Shortly after the murder, when Toomey learned that
everyone at Engineering Systems was to be questioned
by the police, he fled the premises. (He later claimed
he left because no work had been assigned him.) It
was reported that he had announced: "I will not take
a lie detector test," although no one had proposed
administering one to him. He visited several bars, including the Buckminster's. Drunk, he returned to Engineering Systems early in the afternoon. At around
six o'clock he telephoned Sheldon Kurtzer and then
went to the latter's house.

Toomey did end up taking a polygraph. The results
appeared to clear him of any involvement in Patricia's
death.

Patricia had told Billy MacKenzie that she planned
to be married (Hazel Bissette later claimed to know
nothing of this intent) and asked Billy if she would
come to the wedding. She hadn't yet set a date. She
did have a groom—the man named John whose presence at Patricia's Christmas-tree-trimming party Jules
Rothman had noted to police. Patricia had talked a
lot about John, Billy recalled.

Billy was unaware that Patricia had been pregnant
until the police informed her of the fact after the murder.

John was John Melin, a twenty-three-year-old native
of Barre, Vermont, who had moved to the Boston area

in 1961. Patricia had met one of his brothers, Daniel, sometime in 1962, while taking a bus back to Boston from a visit to Vermont. She had gone out a few times with Daniel, and he may have visited her at her apartment. John would later tell the police that Daniel had given him Patricia's phone number and her Newbury Street address. When John called there, Patricia's former roommate, Ruth Darling, told him that Patricia had moved, and offered to take a message. Pat returned John's call two days later.*

John told authorities that he didn't think Pat wanted to marry him; she knew he already had a wife and had no plans for a divorce. Nevertheless, he visited her at her apartment and they went out for drinks once or twice. When Detective Phillip DiNatale interviewed John, the young man emphasized that from his standpoint, the relationship had been casual.

DiNATALE: When was the first time you saw her?
JOHN: When I went to her apartment.
DiNATALE: Did you go out with her that night?
JOHN: I don't think so. We stayed in the apartment. I saw her a few times. It wasn't very often, somewhere between six and nine times.

On Thursday night, December 18, 1962, John took Patricia to the Boots and Saddles Club in Groton, Massachusetts, where they had drinks (stingers and Singapore Slings) and dinner.

DiNATALE: Did you know that Pat was becoming

---

* Ruth Darling reported to police that much to her disgust, John had asked *her* out when she told him that Patricia wasn't available. When she later met him, in Pat's company, her initial bad impression was confirmed: "He looked like a snake."

very fond of you, feeling affection for you? Did you ever kiss Pat?

JOHN: Yes.

DINATALE: Did it ever go beyond kissing?

JOHN: No.

DINATALE: Did you know that Pat had been making wedding plans?

JOHN: No.

DINATALE: Did you know that she was going around the office telling everyone that she was getting married to a man named John?

JOHN: No. I told her I was married. She knew this from the first time we met. Danny told her that "John was married." [Then why, one wonders, did he suggest that his brother date Patricia?] There was no doubt. I originally thought the police were just kidding. I never gave her any idea that I was getting a divorce.

DINATALE: Did you ever stay overnight at Pat's apartment?

JOHN: I never stayed overnight with Pat.

John claimed that the last time he saw or spoke to Patricia was that Thursday evening of the date at the Boots and Saddles. He drove her back home. "She went inside, she was falling apart," John stated. DiNatale asked him what he meant by that.

"I was supposed to be studying," John answered, not quite to the point. "My wife was working, and I just decided to pull out. That was all there was."

DiNatale still wanted to know how Patricia could have gotten the notion that John would marry her. "I really don't know," John said. "The first time she was going around the office she told a group of her friends I would be a good catch."

John intended to practice law in Vermont after he finished night school, which was where he was supposed to be on the evenings he was wining and dining Patricia or sitting in her living room discussing, no doubt, torts and civil procedure. His wife worked as a nurse on the late shift at a local hospital and didn't get home until 10:00 P.M.

John said that although he attended Patricia's tree-trimming party, he'd stayed for only a half-hour or forty-five minutes. The hostess had been a "social butterfly," paying him no particular attention. A great many photographs had been taken at the party. John, feeling bored and isolated, had left.

John's wife had told police that her husband had only been out for a half hour that evening. Yet the drive to Patricia's from his home in Brighton would have taken fifteen minutes, the return trip an equivalent amount of time. So someone was lying. It might have been the wife: She was reported to have instructed John to tell the police he had been home on the evenings he was with Patricia. He was obviously shrewd enough to disregard this advice.

DiNatale was still curious about the origin of Patricia's fantasy—if that is what it was—of marriage with John. "Maybe she wanted to get somebody at the office jealous," the young man offered by way of explanation.

He denied that he had ever argued with Patricia and grabbed her around the throat, which police had been informed he had done.

The good catch spent the weekend of Patricia's murder at home with his wife. On Sunday evening, December 30, he went out for a drink. DiNatale asked him if he'd passed Patricia's apartment en route to or from the bar. He repeatedly denied that he had. Then, at the end of the interrogation, he admitted that he had indeed taken a ride over there after leaving the bar. There were lights on in the apartment. He went home.

The results of polygraph examinations given on two different occasions appeared to clear John of any complicity in Patricia's death. A number of witnesses confirmed that she had had "a real crush" on him.

Engineering Systems had become a subsidiary of the Automatic Radio Company, at which Billy MacKenzie had been a forewoman for nineteen years. A tough-minded and straightforward person with excellent powers of recall, she was an invaluable source of credible information for the police. What she had to tell them about Jules Rothman sharpened their already highly developed suspicions about his involvement in Patricia's murder. She was interviewed by Detective Lieutenant Leo Martin of the state police.

One of Martin's first questions was about the relationship between Patricia and Rothman.

MARTIN: Did you know that Jules Rothman was intimate with Pat?

BILLY: Yes.

MARTIN: How do you know that?

BILLY: Well, I had to go get a blueprint from his office one day and I knocked on the door and no one answered, so I opened the door to go in and they were on the couch.

MARTIN: They were on the studio couch?

BILLY: Yes.

MARTIN: I see, and what were they doing? Were they involved in the sex act?

BILLY: Yes.

MARTIN: They were, you're sure of that?

BILLY: I'm positive.

MARTIN: And then you turned around and walked out?

BILLY: I just backed out and went out and closed the door.

MARTIN: Oh, I see, you closed the door. Did Jules

Rothman or Patricia Bissette ever mention this to you?

BILLY: No, I don't think they even knew I was there.

Martin asked Billy to describe Mrs. Rothman.

"She was a very dowdy-type person and a sloppy dresser," Billy said. "And you didn't expect her to be married to Jules Rothman."

Rothman, described by one witness as "a Continental type," was indeed that in a literal sense. Born in Vienna, he was educated there at the Real Schule before coming to the United States. A graduate of Columbia University, he was an electronics and communications expert with training and experience also in mechanical engineering. He had worked on such projects as the development of rocket engines and of the Norden bombsight.

Martin asked Billy to describe the events that took place on December 31.

BILLY: When I went into work Monday, just Jules was there and Pat hadn't come into work yet. And when I went in he asked me what I [meaning Rothman] should do about Pat because she hadn't shown up for work yet.

MARTIN: Did he appear nervous and concerned?

BILLY: Very.

MARTIN: What did he do?

BILLY: He kept asking me what I thought he should do. And I said, "Why don't you just wait and see," because it was snowing pretty bad that day. And he came in and sat at my desk and read the paper and he kept saying, "Gee, I'm worried about Pat. She hasn't shown up for work and she never does this, she's always on time." And he told me he had stopped at her house to pick her up.

MARTIN: What time, Billy, did he stop at her house?

BILLY: It must have been around 7:30 A.M.

MARTIN: 7:30, this is on Monday?

BILLY: Yes, this was on Monday.

MARTIN: This was on the second?

BILLY: No, this wasn't the second because January 1 was on a Tuesday.

MARTIN: Very good.

BILLY: So this was the last day of December. So anyway, he kept asking me, oh, for an hour, what I thought he should do and that she never did anything like this and I said to him, "Well, if I was that worried about her, I would go down to her house and find out." You know, knock on the door and if nobody answers, go down and get the janitor and see what was the matter. So finally he did go. And he was gone about 10 or 15 minutes and a call came for me and I didn't even recognize him. So he said, "Hello, Billy," and I said, "Yes, and he said, "Something terrible has happened." And I said, "What?" And he said, "Pat is dead." And I said, "What do you mean, she's dead?" And he said, "Well, I came over here and we had to come through the window and Pat is in her bed and she's got stockings wrapped around her throat and her eyes are bulging out of her head and her tongue is all swollen." And he said, "She's dead. She's been strangled." So I said, "Are you sure?" and he said, "Yes, I saw the stockings wrapped around her throat." And I said, "Well, did you call the police?" And he said, "Yes, and I have to go now because the police are at the door." And that was all.

MARTIN: Now, Billy, getting back to Monday again, what further conversation did you have with Jules Rothman?

BILLY: Well, when he was talking to me about Pat not coming into work I said, "Maybe she went home to Vermont, maybe she went home to visit her mother over New Year's." And he said, "Oh, no, because she already knows I planned for the New Year's party" . . . and I said, "Did you see her Saturday? Did you pick up your car?" And he said that he did.

MARTIN: He didn't say the time, did he?

BILLY: Yes, he said that he was there about 1:30 and that he picked up his car and that he went in and had a cup of coffee with her and that he picked up his car and went home.

MARTIN: Did he say that he had a cup of coffee in her apartment, is that it?

BILLY: He said that he went into her apartment and had a cup of coffee with her and then he left.

Two cups of stale coffee were found in Patricia's apartment after her murder.

Rothman's description to Billy of Patricia's appearance was grossly exaggerated. The dead woman's eyes were closed, as was her mouth, and she appeared to be asleep. The blankets on the bed were pulled to her chin.

"Now, Billy," Martin said. "Will you please tell me in your own words what further conversation you had with Jules Rothman after the homicide?"

Billy told Martin that Rothman had expressed to her just how much Patricia had meant to him. "Well, at first he started telling me that she was like a daughter to him, and then as he got more use to talking to me, he started telling me about them going out together and going different places and about the time they went up to her mother's." According to Rothman, his sons had treated Patricia like a sister, and she had often come to the family home for dinner.

Rothman had also given Patricia paintings to hang in her apartment, and he and Sheldon Kurtzer had given her a television set.

Billy told Martin that Rothman complained to her

of the aridity and isolation of his existence, and of the hole Patricia's death had made in his life.

> MARTIN: What further conversation after the homicide did you have with Jules Rothman in connection with her death and needing another woman?
> BILLY: Well, he told me that he led a very lonesome life and that his wife never went anywhere with him and that he used to take these long trips and that they were long lonely trips and that a lot of times Pat used to go with him.
> MARTIN: Out of state?
> BILLY: Out of state.

Martin asked Billy to elaborate on the theme of Rothman's loneliness.

"Well," Billy replied, "after Pat died he had some trips to take. One of them was up to New Hampshire, and he asked me if I wanted to go with him." Billy refused, on the grounds that her father was hospitalized with a serious illness. "Why don't you take your wife with you?" she asked, perhaps ingenuously.

"My wife never goes anywhere with me, and you know these trips are long lonesome trips and I don't like going by myself," Rothman had answered. "I thought maybe if you didn't have anything to do you could come with me."

Billy told Martin that "this went on all the time after Pat died," and that Rothman "had nothing to do with himself so he had to get someone to take Pat's place."

"Did he ever put his hands on you, Billy, in fondness?" Martin asked.

"Well, like holding my hands, he has," Billy replied. "And rubbing my shoulders and coming up behind me, you know. He didn't do anything fresh to me or anything."

"No?" Martin asked, possibly surprised by this un-characteristic restraint.

"I didn't even like the idea of him having his hands on me either," Billy said.

Martin wanted to know if Rothman had ever propositioned her. She said he hadn't, although she and he had certainly held a number of "crazy conversations."

A Boston homicide detective had asked Billy to furnish him with Patricia's personnel folder. When she went to look for it in the file, it was missing. She later found it in Rothman's desk, under a pile of papers. She also found there seven or eight black and white photographs of Patricia and Rothman.

Billy and Rothman were the only two people in the company who had access to the personnel files.

Martin wanted to know how Rothman had behaved after the homicide detectives had initially questioned Billy.

BILLY: Well, when the police came down to talk to me about it he stayed away from the room altogether. But when the police left, he came in and asked me all kinds of questions, about what did they say and who did they think did it; did they have any suspects; and did they think that he was the one who did it; and that he didn't want his family involved in it and then he told me that someone had told him that he had to bring his sons up to [the] homicide [bureau] and that he didn't want his sons involved in it, he didn't want to be involved in it himself, and that he was going away for a while. But he didn't go away, he stayed around.

MARTIN: Where did he stay?

BILLY: Where did he live?

MARTIN: I mean, where did he stay . . . He didn't stay at his own house after this occurred.

BILLY: No, he took a room. He took one room and himself and his wife and his two sons all stayed there in one room, because apparently he didn't want the police bothering him at his house and they must have been going there and asking him questions and calling or something because he moved out of his apartment and took a room.

Billy told Martin that the young woman who had replaced Patricia after the latter's death had been hired from another firm in the building. Prior to this, though, the woman and some of her male coworkers had joined Rothman and Patricia for after-hours parties in the Engineering Systems offices. "They had a refrigerator there with vodka and scotch and rye and all types of things." The young woman's mother did not want her working for Engineering Systems, Billy reported, and had finally sent her to Europe to get her out of the place. "I think she knows a lot more than she's telling anybody about," Billy concluded darkly.

Rothman had retained an attorney right after Patricia's murder because, he told Billy, he and one of his sons were suspects in the case. He had also refused to take any phone calls, business or personal, at the office. He had them transferred to his home number, and his wife would answer and take messages.

Martin asked Billy again about Rothman's invitations to her to accompany him on trips.

"He told me he wanted to take me up to New Hampshire," Billy replied. "To paint my picture under the trees, in a peasant outfit, and all those things. And he asked me if I'd go on a business trip with him, because he was lonesome on the road and he didn't like to be alone. And I said to him, so why don't you take your wife with you, and he said his wife didn't go anywhere with him . . . and he was always alone, by himself, and that he was lonely. And, he said, Pat used to take up a lot of his lonely hours."

Martin asked Billy why she had ultimately quit her

job at the engineering firm. Did it have anything to do with Rothman?

"I was afraid of him," she said.

"Thank you very much," Martin replied.

29

The Murder of Patricia Bissette, III

The exact time of Patricia's death was never accurately established, and the more information detectives gathered in the course of the two-and-a-half-year investigation, the more complicated the issue of time became. On April 28, 1965, Phillip DiNatale interviewed a close friend of Patricia, Jacqueline Johnson. The story Jackie told was a puzzling and disturbing one.

On Sunday, December 30, 1962, Jackie, an employee of the Massachusetts Eye and Ear Clinic, left work a little after three in the afternoon. Her destination was Patricia's apartment, and she arrived there around 4:00. She knocked at Patricia's door and got no answer, so she crossed the hall and knocked on the door of Apartment 1. In response to the question she asked through the closed door—did anyone know if Patricia was home?—the young woman who lived in 1 could only tell Jackie that Patricia lived in Apartment 2. Jackie returned to the other door. This time, she heard water running in the bathroom. She knew it was the bathroom because she was familiar with the layout of

Patricia's apartment from previous visits and was aware
that the bathroom was on the building hallway side of
the flat. She stood there for about ten minutes, listening to the water gush. She heard Patricia's telephone
ring and go unanswered. Five minutes later she left
the building, crossed the street to the Evans drugstore,
and called Patricia from the pay phone. She got no
response. She went back to the building and knocked
a few more times on the door of Apartment 2. No one
answered.

Jackie wrote two notes, one of which she slipped under the door and the other put on it. She hesitated a
few minutes. Then she went home.

There is no indication in the police report of
whether Patricia was expecting a visit from Jackie that
Sunday afternoon, although Jackie's actions seemed to
indicate that she hadn't simply dropped in casually.

Jackie also told DiNatale that she'd been a guest
at Patricia's tree-trimming party on Friday, December
19, and that Patricia had introduced her to John Melin and Jules Rothman. (Melin had told DiNatale that
the last time he'd spoken to Patricia had been December 18, although he did of course admit attending the party. This confusion about dates is
compounded by the fact that other people thought
that the tree-trimming party had been held on either
December 15 or 16. The date of December 19 that
Jackie cited seems most reasonable in view that December 19 was a Friday, a more appropriate time to
throw a party than midweek.)

Jackie, who like Patricia and John Melin was a Ver-
Melinr, knew that John was married. She told DiNatale,
however, that she didn't think that Patricia was aware
of this. She was also surprised to learn that Patricia
had been making wedding plans; she told DiNatale
that Patricia, whom she visited at least once a week,
had never mentioned them to her.

Jackie's story, which is extremely specific in its details, bumps up against that told by the waitress at the drugstore who claimed to have seen Patricia having a snack at the soda foundation, in the company of a dark-complexioned, foreign-accented man, at 4:30 Sunday afternoon.

The waitress's story is supported to some extent by Billy MacKenzie, who in her interview with Leo Martin said of Patricia that "she told me about meeting an Indian in the drug store across the street from her house, but she told me that she talked to him in the drug store and they were just friends. It wasn't anyone she went out with."

Patricia was also friendly with some Nigerian students, degree candidates at MIT, who lived in her building, and had gone to a party given by one of them. According to Billy, Rothman had not approved of Patricia socializing with nonwhites.

If, on late Sunday afternoon, Patricia had been having coffee or tea in the drugstore at the time the waitress gave, would not Jackie have seen her there? Or at least seen her leave her apartment and cross the street to the drugstore? By her own account Jackie had spent at least twenty-five to thirty minutes either knocking at Patricia's door, telephoning her from the drugstore, speaking to Patricia's neighbors, or standing around the first-floor hall of 515 Park Drive.

And who was in Patricia's bathroom running the water, if it wasn't Patricia?

And what significance does this have in connection with the testimony of the resident at 500 Park Drive who told police that she had heard screams between 3:00 and 4:00 P.M. on that Sunday afternoon?

The note Jackie left on Patricia's door was there when Jules Rothman arrived Monday morning.

And on Sunday evening, the lights had been on in the apartment, according to John Melin.

* * *

Christian Van Olst, the sixty-nine-year-old janitor at 509 and 515 Park Drive, told Leo Martin that as far as he knew Patricia was a quiet, friendly, clean-living girl who never threw wild parties or indeed caused any trouble during her tenancy. He saw no indication that she was promiscuous, although he did notice that one of her most frequent visitors was Rothman. Maintenance man Harry Martin told police that Ada Kotock, the owner of 515 Park Drive, had been a little upset by Rothman's constant presence, distressed by the spectacle of a married man carrying on a flagrant affair with a woman young enough to be his daughter.

Van Olst was sure that Patricia had rented the apartment herself. He had no idea whether Rothman was paying for or contributing to its upkeep, and he didn't think Mrs. Kotock would know either.

Leo Martin had asked Van Olst this last question for a good reason. In the late 1950s and early 1960s, Park Drive was informally known as "Mistresses Row." For whatever reason—perhaps its relative accessibility and air of slightly seedy gentility—it had become the neighborhood of choice for the extramarital love objects of well-off Boston business and professional men. If indeed Rothman had been keeping Patricia (when they first became sexually involved she was sharing an apartment with Ruth Darling on Newbury Street), this would have been the logical place for him to put her. And 515 Park Drive was only a five-minute walk from Engineering Systems, which made the arrangement convenient as well as in accord with local tradition.

More interesting than any speculation about Patricia's living arrangement that Van Olst could provide was his account of the events of the morning of December 31, when he had watched Jules Rothman climb through the open window of Patricia's apartment. (This unorthodox means of entry was necessitated by the fact that Van Olst didn't have a key to Patricia's apartment, nor to several others at 515 Park Drive.)

Van Olst said that he, not Rothman, had removed the window screen, and that Rothman had asked him to go into the apartment ahead of him. Van Olst refused, and added that Rothman, once inside, should open the front door. Rothman agreed.

Van Olst said that Rothman was inside the flat for a minute or two before he opened the door to admit the janitor. "It looks like something's wrong," Rothman said. "She's dead, I think. She's got a stocking around her throat."

Van Olst looked into the bedroom. He saw Patricia lying on her back, the sheets and blankets pulled up to her chin. He saw no stocking.

"And you didn't observe her tongue or anything hanging out of her mouth or she didn't look distorted in any way?" Martin asked.

"No, no, none whatsoever," Van Olst replied. "She looked to me like she was asleep on her back."

"I see," Martin said. "And from all outward appearances she'd look like that to anybody?"

"That's right, she would."

"Well," Martin persisted, "could you see any ligatures around her neck from where she—?"

"No, no, you couldn't," Van Olst said. "The sheets were right up to—now, he must have saw it and pushed them right back up again, because he told me that they [the ligatures] were there."

"Oh, yes," Martin said.

"When I looked you couldn't see it," Van Olst repeated.

The crime scene photos confirm Van Olst's statement: The bed covers are drawn up to Patricia's chin and no part of her throat is visible.

Rothman always insisted that he hadn't touched the bed covers. So if he didn't pull them down, as he said he hadn't, how did he know that there were stockings tied around Patricia's neck? And why did he say that her tongue was protruding from her mouth and her eyes were bulging when they obviously weren't?

In May of 1965, Phillip DiNatale showed Van Olst photographs of Albert DeSalvo and George Nassar. Van Olst said that he had never seen either man before.

At this point, a year after his interrogation by Leo Martin, Van Olst remembered another curious fact. On the morning of December 31, it was he and not Rothman who had made the call to the Boston police reporting the discovery of Patricia's body. As he was at the telephone he realized that he had only to turn his head slightly to see through the open door into the bedroom. Patricia's body lay in the direct line of his gaze.

Harry Martin, who said he had been standing in the exact same position sometime between 10:00 and 11:00 on Sunday morning, had looked into the bedroom and seen only a bed heaped with boxes.

Leo Martin interviewed John Price, whom Rothman had said he'd conferred with on the matter of Patricia's pregnancy because Price had once "gotten a girl in trouble" himself and knew how to deal with such situations. Price told a slightly different story: that Rothman, whom he barely knew and had had no contact with for several years, had telephoned him the week before the murder proposing that Price meet with him to discuss an exciting and potentially profitable business deal. Price said that he would indeed like to get together with Rothman sometime. They left matters there.

On Friday, December 28, 1962, Rothman called Price again and urgently requested a meeting that night. Price, who was tired, tried to stall Rothman, but the latter was insistent, and Price finally agreed to meet him at the Smith House in Cambridge for a drink.

That evening Rothman did indeed speak about business. Then he turned the conversation to other matters. According to Price, "Jules told me some friend of his knows a girl in trouble and he thought I could help him locate someone in the abortion field. After I heard Jules talk like that, I told him this was wrong lawfully and morally and would help him in another matter. I didn't like to talk about this, being a sticky matter. But, I told Jules that my wife knew of a convent located in Laconia [New Hampshire] that would care for any girl in the condition of pregnancy unmarried. I even called a priest named Father Baker and explained the situation to him and he referred me to sister superior at the convent. I don't remember the name now, but I wrote down the address and gave it to Jules."

Price never spoke to Rothman again after that evening. He thought of telephoning when he read in the newspaper of Patricia's murder and saw Rothman's name mentioned in the article.

Price's lawyer advised him not to have anything further to do with Rothman, and to dismiss the notion of getting involved in any business deal with the man.

On November 8, 1962, Patricia wrote a letter to her mother in which she requested that Hazel send her a photograph album. She had a drawerful of snapshots, clippings, and other such mementos, Patricia said, and she wanted something in which to put them. Hazel sent her the album.

After Patricia's murder, when Mrs. Bissette made the heartbreaking journey to Boston to sort through and pack up her daughter's effects, she found two things missing. One was a 1921 silver dollar Patricia had prized. The other was the photograph album. All that remained of Patricia's memorabilia was a single letter and one photograph.

Also absent from Patricia's handbag and wallet, which were otherwise intact, even to her last paycheck, were pictures of her friends. Mrs. Bissette had found this very strange. Patricia had carried such items around with her constantly.

Mrs. Bissette assumed that detectives had taken the photographs to use as evidence. But when she got in touch with the Boston police, they told her that all they'd found in the apartment were twelve letters.

Patricia could have lost—or even spent—the silver dollar herself, or given it to a friend as a special gift. Or a visitor to the apartment could have pocketed it. The absence of the photograph album was a little more difficult to explain. Would a mere thief have stolen it—but left Patricia's $125 watch on the dresser?

The only substantial collection of photographs that ever turned up were those of Patricia and Jules Rothman that Billy MacKenzie had found not very well hidden in Rothman's desk.

And it was odd that the police had found only twelve letters among Patricia's possessions. She was a pack rat where personal correspondence was concerned.

Had her killer taken the album and any other letters Patricia might have kept because his face or name appeared in them?

Engineering Systems, Inc., had been in serious financial trouble prior to its takeover by Automatic Radio. The one thing all the witnesses agree on is that Patricia was deeply embroiled in the situation. "She knew all the business secrets of ESI," said one of the principals.

Here is Billy MacKenzie's version of the story, as given to Leo Martin:

> Sheldon Kurtzer and Jules Rothman were partners and they developed some kind of talking book and Pat was the voice in the book, she was on a tape. She was the voice on the tape of Little Red Riding Hood and all those stories; they were making books for Christmas. And something went wrong, where Jules Rothman said the patent was

his and that he was the one who worked on it and
that it was his money and all kinds of things. And
there was a third partner and whatever happened
or went wrong, the third partner, his life was
threatened.

"Whose life?" Martin asked. Billy couldn't remember the man's name; she was sure that he, his wife,
and family had been subject to a frightening degree
of harassment. "I know that they were putting boxes
in dolls, too, to talk. Pat's voice was the voice on all
these tapes that were in the dolls and the books and
things."

"Who made that arrangement?" said Martin.

"Jules," Billy replied.

"Was she getting paid for this?" Martin asked.

"I don't know whether she was getting extra pay or
just her salary," Billy said. "But then the third partner
left and he wouldn't go back to work for them, so then
there was just Sheldon and Jules. And then Sheldon
left."

"Jules is still at Engineering?" Martin asked.

"Yes, as far as I know."

"And he has nothing more to do insofar as the ownership or partnership or anything to that effect, has
he?" inquired Martin.

"No," Billy said. "He's working for them at Radio
now."

At the end of August 1964, DiNatale interviewed Hazel Bissette. What follows is his report on that session.

"On Monday, March 4, 1963, Dottie [Dottie Chapman, a onetime employee of Engineering Systems]
called Mrs. Bissette. On one of the phone calls right after
Pat's death, she told Mrs. Bissette that after Pat had died,
she and Jules Rothman had a terrible fight, and she did
not want to tell Mrs. Bissette what the fight was about.
And that she had left the company to work for another
company. The other call was on March 24, 1963. Jules

called Mrs. Bissette about 7:30 P.M. after Mrs. Bissette had
returned from the second Boston trip. He said he wanted
to talk with her and said he would like to come to Vermont in May to talk with her and see Pat's grave. He
didn't make the trip.

"On March 27, 1963, Dottie Chapman called Mrs.
Bissette again and asked if Jules had called her. Mrs.
Bissette said that she seemed rather worried. She believed that while Dottie was talking to her that Jules
Rothman was in the same room and that he was listening to Dottie's phone conversation. Dottie kept asking Mrs. Bissette whether or not Pat had shown her
any stocks and bonds certificates or if Pat had showed
her any stocks and bonds recently while she was home,
and she wanted to know if Mrs. Bissette had the bonds.
While Dottie Chapman was talking to Mrs. Bissette, she
asked Mrs. Bissette if she didn't want to talk to her
about Pat's business with the company or what she
knew about the company. Dottie kept asking questions
about the company that Mrs. Bissette thought were
very funny at the time."

On September 24, 1964, DiNatale spoke with Ruth
Darling.

DINATALE: Did Pat ever talk about the company
where she worked?
RUTH: Yes, she talked about it a great deal. She
was very worried about that. Financial dealings
and . . . She was worried about the relationship
between her boss and the president, I believe.
DINATALE: And the vice president?
RUTH: And the vice president? I believe the other
man was president and Jules was either vice-president or treasurer or something next in line. And
when the company was finally on the verge of
bankruptcy, and Automatic Radio took them over,
and Jules was promoted to president of the company and the other man put under him.

DINATALE: Was there bitter feeling between these two people?

RUTH: I don't know how bitter the feeling was. I know there were disagreements and Pat felt the president had treated Jules very unfairly in a number of cases. There was a story I was going to tell you about the president of the company. Before they could be taken over by Automatic Radio, they had to get any stockholders to sell the stock back to them, I believe. And there was one man who held out and wouldn't and the president had planned to hire thugs, or I think had actually hired them, to intimidate this man, and finally the man agreed to sell, and nothing ever happened.

Ruth told DiNatale that Dottie Chapman and Patricia had been friendly. Other witnesses, including Kurtzer himself, confirmed this. Kurtzer said that Dottie's attitude toward the younger woman was that of a mother hen. Chapman, like everyone else in the company, was aware of the intimacy between Patricia and Rothman.

John Melin spoke about Jules Rothman: "There was something very secretive about the boss planning to dump Jules or vice-versa. It was not just a regular boss-secretary relationship [between Patricia and Rothman]. It was more than that. There were three silent partners in the company. It was something really hush-hush. [Patricia] was really upset about it. I guess Jules was planning his own maneuver."

Hazel Bissette told DiNatale that her daughter had written to her in the fall of 1962 "saying that she had a big problem and wanted some help." She could have been referring to her pregnancy. But Mrs. Bissette thought that Patricia was worried about her shares in Engineering Systems.

Arthur Marson, an ex-ESI employee, told DiNatale that Patricia had attended stockholder meetings to function as a "peacemaker." Marson also said that Rothman and Kurtzer had hired Mrs. Rothman and the two Rothman sons "to come to the factory and look busy" when company shareholders were present.

DiNatale also spoke to John Servetnick. Servetnick was an engineer who, while working for a Cambridge firm, had invented a certain type of tape recorder. A friend introduced him to Rothman and Kurtzer, who offered Servetnick a partnership in their company, a vice presidency, and a salary of eighteen thousand dollars. He in return would purchase two thousand dollars' worth of Engineering Systems stock per year until he owned one-third of the business. And he would also hand over to Rothman and Kurtzer his invention.

According to Servetnick, he never received one penny of his salary, just "a few dollars to pay [my] bills every now and then." He had, however, kept his end of the bargain and bought stock. Seeing no future for himself with Rothman and Kurtzer, he quit in the summer of 1962. Then, a few months later, he found out that Automatic Radio was interested in buying out the foundering ESI.

"In October or November I got a call from Sheldon," said Servetnick. "He wanted the stock. I had been to one or two stockholders meetings at which I was asked to return the stock. I refused to give the stock back until I got the original price back, which was one thousand dollars. I got the call about seven o'clock from Sheldon asking me to give the stock back. I refused. He said he would probably go to jail if I did not give the stock back, and if I did not give the stock back he would send a couple of guys after me and they would kill me and that he would not be connected with it. Jules was with Sheldon at the time of the threat. Jules visited my home the evening of the threat. Jules came over to the house to get the stock. I refused to give it to him. He admitted that he had heard Sheldon threaten me. He stated this in front of my wife and

his own son. When I asked him if he would be a witness
to this threat he denied hearing Sheldon threaten me.
At the time the company had run out of funds to meet
the payroll. Jules and Sheldon needed the money and
decided to sell stock to the employees. They then
spoke to Pat and apparently convinced her to buy
some stock (about four hundred dollars or five hundred dollars, I think). She was very elated at being
able to become part owner of the company and that
it was the first time she had ever purchased stock in
her life. She seemed very pleased."

The "Talking Doll" or "Talking Book" (Patricia had
applied to the government for a patent in Rothman's
name) incorporated the tape device invented by
Servetnick. He confirmed that Pat's voice had been
used in the recording to go into the doll. DiNatale
asked Servetnick if he knew what had happened to
that tape.

"No, I don't know where the tape is," Servetnick
said. "Jules and Sheldon had the right to borrow the
tape. They decided to borrow the tape and I turned
the tape recorder over to them. On this was the 'announce loop' with Pat's voice. They erased this 'announce loop' and it came back with Dottie Chapman's
voice." Servetnick added, "I recognized the voice as
Dottie's, and they admitted it was Dottie's voice."

Dottie, Servetnick recalled, had telephoned him
once to plead with him to give back the stock so that
she and the other remaining ESI employees could be
paid.

Two days after Patricia was killed, Rothman called
Servetnick to ask him if he could find a job for Dottie.
"He [Jules] said he had been down to police headquarters trying to find the murderer. Jules said he felt
terrible about it," Servetnick recollected. "He had
been down to police headquarters. He suspected Sheldon had done it. He wanted to tell the police but he
remembered Sheldon had threatened my life. He

asked if it was okay to tell the police. I said go ahead and he said that he already had."

Servetnick also informed DiNatale that any Engineering Systems certificates Patricia owned had to be phony, since the stock that she bought—or thought she was buying— already belonged to Automatic Radio.

"Either Jules or Sheldon were in such poor financial condition or debt," Servetnick commented, "that in my opinion either of them might have been driven to violence if the circumstances warranted."

DiNatale, remembering the story Rothman had told about paying for Patricia to go to a convent to have her baby, asked, "Do you think Jules was the kind of person to give Pat the money to go away?"

"No," said Servetnick. "I think he would rather go to Alaska. After I was threatened there was another meeting with Jules and his wife. I can't remember where we met. I think it was in front of their house. His wife was very upset that I did not give up the stocks. She intimated at this time that one of their mothers was in a rest home and that they were in charge of the trust fund and I got the idea that they had taken money from this trust fund and could not return it."

Ruth Darling reported to DiNatale that she considered Patricia and Rothman—whom she found distasteful—to be "awfully in love." DiNatale asked Ruth if she thought that Mrs. Rothman had been aware of the affair between her husband and Patricia. "I don't think she could help it," Ruth replied. "I think Pat was quite obvious, really."

On January 29, 1965, DiNatale and Sheldon Kurtzer had the following conversation.

KURTZER: Jules Rothman and I were not exactly close in many ways and Pat was a private secretary to Jules. She was very unconfidential, and Jules and I didn't get along very well.

DINATALE: Do you know the reasons why? Can you tell me about the company, why you and Jules never got along very well?

KURTZER: Right now I'm on pretty good terms again. He was the key man in the company for the most part and there was a series of things that caused the falling-out . . . They [Rothman and another ESI executive] tried to have me thrown out as president, and behind all of this, number one, I invented a tape recorder similar to John Servetnick's but about forty times better. Everything I made, the models and drawings, Jules Rothman copied and signed his names to the drawings and he also applied for a patent. I made a write-up called a talking book. We were using Pat's voice for these tapes. She did not have a good voice for this type of recording. Then I gave Pat the complete write-up and told her to keep it confidential and nobody was to see it. This was for her to type up and a copy was found on Jules Rothman's desk.

Ruth Darling had told DiNatale that Patricia had been taken out to dinner by Kurtzer and had gone out for drinks with him a number of times. He had driven her home on many occasions. He had complained to her about being unhappily married. One night he kissed her, a gesture she did not return.

DiNatale asked Kurtzer if he had been jealous of Rothman for his sexual involvement with Patricia.

"There was a little animosity on my part," Kurtzer said. "I didn't know how close they were. I was too involved with financial trouble to realize an affair between Pat and Jules."

Kurtzer talked about the business arrangement Patricia had made with ESI: "Pat was a stockholder. She had invested five hundred dollars in the company. When the company was sold her pay was brought up to date by Automatic Radio, which was two or three months' back pay. She got all her back pay."

Kurtzer admitted that he had argued with Servetnick over the latter's refusal to give back his stock in ESI for twenty cents on the dollar, an exchange that Kurtzer claimed all the other shareholders had approved. He also said he had threatened Servetnick—"I told him I would 'fix his wagon' for him"—but that the threat had been merely a ruse, nothing to be taken seriously.

Authorities collected the stock certificates issued to Patricia and purportedly signed by her, and sent them, along with an independent sample of her signature, to Carola Blume, the graphologist consulting to the Strangler Task Force. After a careful analysis, Blume concluded that the signature on the certificates had not been forged by Jules Rothman. She did think there was a strong possibility that it had been forged by Rothman's wife.

Just how close Patricia's relationship with Sheldon Kurtzer really was, or how close it might have become, is anyone's guess. She did write a letter to a very close friend in which she mentioned that if she succeeded in losing fourteen more pounds, "Shell" would buy her a dress.

Sheldon Kurtzer was given a polygraph examination. The test results appeared to clear him of any complicity in Patricia's murder.

The already *Rashomon*-like saga of the short life and violent death of Patricia Bissette had the following additional twists:

Very shortly before her murder, she had probably engaged in some form of rough anal sex as well as regular genital intercourse.

Jules Rothman told John Servetnick that his younger son, who was reputedly gay, was dating Patricia.

The younger son frequently lent Patricia his sports car, and spent some time in her apartment on Friday, December 28, 1962. This was before his father arrived there to give Patricia the information about the convent that would care for her during her pregnancy.

Just after the murder of Sophie Clark, Rothman announced to Patricia—in the hearing of Billy MacKenzie—that she shouldn't live alone because she might fall victim to the Strangler.

Leo Martin wrote this report on the case:

After the police interrogated Rothman, he changed his story about his being in [Patricia's] apartment for the last time on Saturday [December 29, 1962]. He said that he did come back Sunday morning and he further states that it had been a practice on Sunday morning for him to buy two newspapers at the drug store across the street [one for Pat], but on this Sunday he went to Pat's house and bought one newspaper, knocked at the door and receiving no answer, went home. Jules has an alibi—being with his two sons Saturday night to purchase a volt regulator in [Boston]. Sunday his wife and children alibi for him that he had gone out in the morning to purchase a newspaper and come directly back and watched television late that night. In conclusion and in my opinion, Jules was the only one that had been keeping steady company with the deceased, lieing [sic] about her personal habits by saying she was promiscuous because of her good nature. He changed his mind about not being at the apartment on Sunday and then stated he was. His family's alibis for Sunday were disproved due to Jules' own statements.

Mrs. Rothman and the two sons also changed their stories to accommodate Rothman's shifting accounts of his whereabouts the day of Patricia's death.

Hazel Bissette instructed the police to look carefully at Engineering Systems: "I think if you could concentrate a little on this company and its employees you will come up with some surprising stories."

Carola Blume analyzed Rothman's handwriting: "A man who is interested in money—dishonest. He is not abnormal in his sex habits, rather enjoys sensual pleasure, which would include everything . . . He is not a person to be trusted . . . unscrupulous . . . serves own best interest or advantage."

Jules Rothman was given polygraph examinations on several different occasions. The results did not clear him of knowledge of Patricia's death: "Reactions exhibited on his chart indicate that he is not telling the truth about his activities on Sunday, December 30, 1962."

There was a movement to bring the evidence in the case before a grand jury, with the intent to indict Jules Rothman for the murder of Patricia Bissette. Because of a turf squabble among the Boston Police Department, the attorney general's office, and the Suffolk County district attorney's office, in which the attorney general's office, in the person of John Bottomly, accused the district attorney's office of leaking word of the pending indictment to the press, the procedure was postponed.

Then Albert DeSalvo began confessing to the Boston stranglings.

30

The Murder of
Beverly Samans, I

As Tuesday morning, May 7, 1963, passed into Tuesday afternoon, and afternoon became evening, Minnie Samans grew increasingly worried. That day was Mrs. Samans's birthday, and she had received neither card nor gift from her daughter, Beverly. Nor had the young woman even telephoned. It was simply not like Beverly to forget an important occasion such as an anniversary or a birthday.

There was never a chance that Beverly would call her mother that Tuesday. Since very late the previous Sunday night or very early Monday morning the only child of Herman and Minnie Samans of Beckley, West Virginia, had lain dead in her apartment in Cambridge, Massachusetts.

Her killer had left her naked and supine on a disarrayed bed, legs apart, hands tied behind her with a multicolored scarf. Draped over her head and shoulders was a lace shawl or mantilla. Around her neck had been loosely knotted two nylon stockings and a white scarf. A cloth gag had been stuffed in her mouth,

which the person who had found the body had removed.

She had not been raped or sexually assaulted, despite the position of her body.

She had been stabbed and slashed twenty-one times
in the left breast and neck.

Twenty-six-year-old Beverly Samans, a superbly talented mezzo-soprano, had come to the Boston area in
the mid-1950s to study at the New England Conservatory of Music, from which she graduated in 1959. For
several years thereafter she worked at the Walter E.
Fernald School, a facility for retarded and emotionally
disturbed children and adolescents, as a music therapist. She left Fernald in the summer of 1962 to devote
more time to her studies; she had enrolled in a master's program in rehabilitation counseling at Boston
University. What she was learning she put into practice
two days a week working with patients at Medfield State
Hospital. She may have been unusually empathetic to
those with mental or emotional handicaps because she
herself suffered from a physical one: She was nearly
deaf and had to wear a hearing aid.

Despite this, music was the great love of her life and
she intended to make a career of it. Her highest ambition was to sing with the Metropolitan Opera Company. She kept a piano in her apartment and played
it constantly as an accompaniment to her singing. So
glorious was the music Beverly made that none of her
neighbors ever complained but rather simply listened—and appreciated. She was a member of several
local church and temple choirs—she also played the
organ at Sunday services—and of the Aeolian Singers,
a group who gave concerts in and around Boston, most
notably at the Isabella Stewart Gardner Museum. She
took voice lessons once a week from an instructor in
Braintree. On the last Sunday of her life she spent the

afternoon and evening rehearsing *Così fan tutte* with the other cast members at the producer's Brookline home.

Beverly, a small, attractive, dark-haired woman who dressed sufficiently stylishly for several people to comment on the fact to investigators and reporters after her death, had a wide circle of friends and acquaintances. Her neighbors found her friendly and pleasant, although some of them thought her a bit reserved. Her life seemed a full, active, and useful one.

It was not altogether a happy one.

Other than her killer, probably the last person to see Beverly alive was her best friend, Edith Scarcello. Known as Anya, Scarcello was the daughter of a Worcester physician. At about 8:30 Sunday night, May 5, Beverly had called Anya and suggested they get together for a light meal and some conversation. At 9:00, Anya and Beverly met at a restaurant in Brookline. Beverly was in good spirits; the rehearsal she'd just come from had gone extremely well. She and Anya talked for nearly two hours; a little before 11:00 Anya noticed the time and commented that it was getting late. A few moments later she and Beverly left the restaurant and walked to Beverly's car, which was parked in front of Anya's apartment on Saint Mary's Street. They talked for another ten minutes. Then Beverly drove home to Cambridge. She arrived there probably no later than 11:30.

On Wednesday, May 8, Beverly was scheduled for choir practice at the Second Unitarian Universalist Church in Boston. She also had an afternoon rehearsal of *Così fan tutte*. She missed both engagements. Mary Vivian Crowley, the church organist, became concerned. It was as out of character for Beverly to skip practice without very good reason as it was for her to allow her mother's birthday to pass unacknowledged by a card, a gift, or a phone call.

Mary left a note outlining her worries for thirty-three-year-old Oliver Chamberlain, the Aeolian conductor and a music teacher at local schools who had been good friends with Beverly and occasionally received mail at her apartment. The message had been left for Chamberlain at his rooms on Story Street in Cambridge. At 7:00 P.M., he went to Beverly's place on University Road to check up on her. He knocked on the door and got no answer. Using the key Beverly had given him, he entered the apartment.

Six minutes later he called the Cambridge police.

One of the first people Cambridge police Detective William Maher interviewed was a young woman named Leslie Loosli, a soprano soloist in the Second Unitarian Church choir that had also featured Beverly as a soloist. Leslie and Beverly had met in the latter half of September 1962 and had hit it off immediately. At first the friendship was a professional one. Then, as time went on, Beverly began to confide in Leslie.

Leslie had noticed that when Beverly came to choir practice, she was sometimes accompanied by Anya Scarcello and a young man named Gene Graff.* According to Leslie, the three had a very close relationship. "Gene and Anya and Beverly were like a triangle," Leslie told Maher and state police Lieutenant William Cronin, "and they would have supper together and go out together, as if they went many, many places together at the beginning of the year."

The last week of December 1962, Beverly went home to West Virginia for the Christmas holiday. During that

---

* No relation and no apparent connection to the Joann Graff who was to be raped and strangled in Lawrence in late November 1963.

vacation time she also visited Gene and his family at their home in upstate New York, and after that Beverly and the young man took a trip to the city.

On her return to Boston, Beverly told Leslie that Gene's family had been very hospitable and that she'd enjoyed her stay with them. She was a little saddened by the fact that Gene was leaving the Boston area to take a teaching job in his home state. Then she blurted out to Leslie, "You know, he's homosexual." Leslie replied that she had suspected that Gene was at least bisexual.

Beverly then remarked to Leslie that very shortly after she and Gene had begun dating, he had said to her, "I must tell you something very important." Beverly anticipated what she was about to hear and tried to make Gene's admission a little less difficult for him. He said, "I must tell you, you'll hate me for it and you won't want to go out with me any more, you won't want to see me any more, but I must tell you: I'm homosexual."

"I know," Beverly replied. "I've known almost ever since the first time we went out."

"But," Gene responded, "you don't mind? You'll still go out with me? You don't hate me because I'm homosexual?"

"No, I don't hate you," Beverly assured him. "Why should I hate you? It's a thing, it's a thing, that's all."

"I'm this kind of a person," Beverly told Leslie. "Therefore I could go out with him, although I felt as if I were a mothering type or I were not the so-called glamour girl or femme fatale, as far as he was concerned, still he could enjoy my company and I could enjoy his."

"At this point," Leslie commented to Maher and Cronin, "they were still very good friends and had a good relationship."

It didn't last.

A week after Gene moved back to his home state,

he wrote and telephoned Beverly. They spoke about how difficult it would be to maintain a long-distance relationship.

The following Sunday, as the Second Unitarian Church choir was beginning the anthem for the 11:00 service, Gene walked into the church. Leslie nudged Beverly and said, "Look who's here."

Beverly said, "What's *he* doing here?"

Leslie replied, "Well, he must be coming to see you."

Beverly was not only startled but very pleased to see Gene; her face shone. Leslie bit her lip and said nothing further. "It was not my business," she told the two detectives.

Several days later Beverly revealed to Leslie that Gene had in fact come to Boston that weekend to visit his male lover, although he had spent Sunday with her. The lover had telephoned Beverly, possibly to find out when Gene was arriving.

Beverly may have felt somewhat used by Gene.

"I tried to act rather coolly toward him," she told Leslie. "I must rid myself of this relationship because it bogs me down, Leslie, it drains me and I'm exhausted from it."

Gene continued to visit Beverly after that, but the bond between them had weakened. Beverly was taking steps to detach herself from it. "It was always this falling-off kind of thing where he would take her out to dinner and they would have, just have, a nice pleasant conversation and she would always let him know she was trying to go on to other men and was trying to start another life," Leslie told the police.

Beverly was not simply "emotionally and spiritually drained" by the failed affair with Gene but by her duties at Medfield State Hospital and the Fernald School. She had kept up contact with her patients at the latter. "Lots of these kids would come to the door sometimes and take her time," Leslie told the investigators. "You

know, come in and talk and then she would feed them
and just, you know, play big sister to them and try to
help them in any way that she could but on her own
home territory and in her own apartment."

Beverly was equally committed to her duties at Medfield State. "I'm very, very tired and I have so much
work to do and I'm following up these cases at Medfield and I'm very tired from it," she told Leslie. "I
try not to become involved, but it's very difficult because it's not easy to forget all these sad tales of woe
that you hear all day long."

Leslie gave a summation of Beverly's character to
the two detectives: She was a very intelligent girl and
I would say high-strung, and a very intensive girl.
Therefore, I would say she's the kind of person who
could be drained from a situation. She was not hard-
boiled, I don't think, in any sense of the word."

Fourteen months later, Carola Blume would analyze
Beverly's handwriting for the Strangler Task Force:
"Beverly Samens [sic] was sensitive, would have relationships with any type person, would go along, was
uninhibited. She was logical, had a high level of intel-
ligence, was egotistical, a high-strung individual. She
would help others, but for her own good. Other people
had to fill her own need. She was hungry for people.
Beverly was careless, untidy, *quick*, did not waste any
time." She had a great need for variety in her life and
"was aggressive and active, could be quite systematic
and at times could be brought out of her regular way
of life and conversely she was or rather could be completely out of order and completely mixed-up."

Despite the poor wording of the above quote, the
analysis it contained did seem to capture the essence
of Beverly's personality.

The two detectives interviewing Leslie Loosli at 2:00
in the morning of May 9, 1963, wanted to know if
there had been a particular reason for Beverly choos-

ing as the topic for her master's thesis "Some Factors Pertaining to the Etiology of Male Homosexuality."

Leslie asked if she could answer that question by providing some background on Beverly's life. On Easter Sunday, 1963, Mary Vivian Crowley had held a small postconcert party at her house. Among the guests were Beverly and Leslie. Beverly had a few drinks and began to relax after the pressure and excitement of that day's choral performance. She began talking with Leslie.

"You know," she said, "I was married once before."

"No, I didn't know that, Beverly," Leslie replied.

"Oh, yes," Beverly continued. "Even my parents will never know, because I'll never tell them. Yes, I was married when I was about seventeen, and it was just one of those things. I was getting out of high school and I married this fellow and we had a few weekends together in a hotel room or motel, wherever we were together. We were married, it was perfectly all right, but then we separated."

Beverly then implied that the marriage had been quickly and quietly annulled at the behest of the boy's parents (she was Jewish; he was Catholic). Leslie got the impression that the youth had been bisexual or gay and very much under the domination of his father and mother. "The longer we were together, married," Beverly said, "it was as if I was more of the leaning-post, sister kind of thing or the mother kind of thing. I really didn't feel as if I was losing that much by agreeing to have it annulled."

"Well, then," Leslie said, "that explains to me why you went out with Gene and why you're [studying] rehabilitation."*

---

* Beverly was a creature of her time, as was Leslie. In the late 1950s and early 1960s, many gay men sought—or were told to seek—counseling in the hope of finding a "cure" for their sexual orientation. The theory fashionable at the

"Well," Beverly said. "Yes, it all does tie in with this marriage I had several years previous, which never worked out."

She complained to Irene Fink, a friend from her hometown of Beckley, West Virginia, that the only kind of men she attracted were "weak" ones who wanted to unload their problems on her.

Shortly after the episode with Gene, Beverly went to Leslie and asked, "Where can I find a man who knows how to treat a woman like a woman and find a nice guy to go out with? I can't meet anyone where I am. I can't seem to find anyone whom I'm interested in."

That spring, she thought she had found two. One was a middle-aged professor at a local college, a good-looking man who seemed quite taken with her. The other was "a tall, dark, and handsome man"—a type Beverly, like countless other women, found irresistible—"at Boston University in one of her classes." Beverly met him at the end of February or the beginning of March, when he invited her for coffee at the student union. He had been interested in her for a while, he said, but reluctant to approach her because he'd thought she was seriously involved with Gene Graff.

Beverly had thought this beau ideal of her romantic imagination was shy. She found out differently on their first date. "I had to fight him off a little that night," she told Leslie. "But he's still very nice and you can't blame a guy for trying."

Leslie thought the young man's name was Ronnie.

Whatever dreams Beverly might have harbored about Ronnie dissolved quickly. He proposed to her a week after they'd met; she was basically too sensible a person to be swept off her feet by his apparent ardor. "I'm not going out with him anymore," she informed

---

time, according to gay men who underwent this therapy, was that they had been warped by their mothers.

Leslie. "He makes too many demands upon my femininity and I just don't know him that well."

Beverly may have been delicately hinting that she found Ronnie annoyingly, or maybe alarmingly, oversexed, and she resented the pressure he put on her to sleep with him. She was clearly suspicious of the motive behind his proposal. "He's in love with me and wants to marry me and I think he's out of his mind."

Leslie told the detectives that the last time she'd seen Beverly was at the conclusion of the services at the Second Unitarian Church at noon on Sunday, May 5. A half hour later, Beverly was at Anya Scarcello's apartment returning a medical textbook the latter had lent her.

Leslie added that she was never quite sure of what had happened between Beverly and the middle-aged professor. She knew only that Beverly had found him quite attractive and was extremely excited about his attentions. This man was somehow involved with television; he had asked Beverly if she knew of a "femme fatale" sort of woman who could appear in some production with which he was involved. Beverly suggested herself, jokingly. The professor said she wasn't the type he had in mind. Beverly swallowed this mild insult with good humor and told the professor he might want to speak with the tall, blond Leslie.

Leslie was positive this man was a bachelor. Another witness seemed equally sure he was married.

Toward the end of the interview, Leslie described to the two detectives the obscene phone calls that she, Beverly, and another woman had begun receiving after a group photograph featuring the three at a musical event had appeared in the newspapers. They had begun in March. That month Beverly mentioned them to another friend of hers, a fellow student at BU and a coworker at Medfield State. She had, according to this man, found these anonymous requests for sexual favors, couched in the most filthy language, quite up-setting.

Increasingly she felt the pressure of the circum-stances of her life: overwork, worry about career plans, and romantic difficulties. In the weeks before her death, Beverly, who dedicated her life to helping the emotionally disturbed back to mental health, sought psychiatric care for her own inner turmoil.

31

The Murder of
Beverly Samans, II

A Boston woman who knew Beverly for nine or ten years, although they were never close friends, would say this of her: "I think that she was, well, she was from a small town and I think perhaps she was a little casual about acquaintances coming and going perhaps in her apartment, more than she should have been in a city. She may have let people come and go that she wasn't too well acquainted with. Perhaps people she had just known very casually at any of the places she worked, the people she came in contact with when she was singing professionally. She was a friendly person to people she wasn't well acquainted with. I think that she may have been a little too free letting people come and go."

Irene Fink, who thought of herself as a "big sister" to Beverly, told investigators that the latter was a magnet for "kooks" whose problems she invariably undertook to solve. Not that she felt she had a choice; they were thrust on her.

No one who knew Beverly seemed in the least surprised that she welcomed into her apartment mental patients, some of whom were potentially quite dangerous people.

The Cambridge police found this fact of considerable interest, particularly when they arrested twenty-eight-year-old Daniel Pennacchio, a busboy at a local restaurant, on a charge of lewd and lascivious behavior.

Pennacchio, who had been a long-term in-and-out resident of the Fernald School, where Beverly had worked from 1959 to 1962, was released for good from that institution in June 1963, although he had not been confined to the premises before that. Almost immediately he embarked on a course of behavior that ranged from the annoying to the frightening. He would stand beside his parked car hungrily ogling the women who walked by him on the sidewalk. Every so often, he'd invite one of them to get into his vehicle. No one accepted the offer, although plenty complained to the authorities about having received it. Pennacchio was finally taken into custody in Cambridge when some nurses caught him trying to peer under the door of a women's restroom in Mount Auburn Hospital.

At the police station, just prior to being interrogated about his Peeping Tom activities, Pennacchio announced that he was ready to confess to the murder of Beverly Samans. Detective Paul Cloran questioned him and took his statement.

Pennacchio said that he had stabbed Beverly fifteen times with a kitchen knife, that he had put a gag in her mouth and a cloth over her head, and that he had gotten blood (as the killer must have) on his shirt and pants, which he later stuffed into a trash can behind the apartment complex.

The parts about the gag, the head cloth, and the kitchen knife were true. And fifteen was a much better approximation of the number of times Beverly had been stabbed than Albert DeSalvo was able to give.

Pennacchio also told Cloran that he had arrived at Beverly's apartment shortly before midnight on May 5—she was known to have been home at that point—and that she'd let him into the place. They had chatted together while Beverly worked on her thesis.

When the police went into Beverly's apartment on May 8, they found page 6 of her thesis in the carriage of her typewriter adjacent to her studio bed. It had been assumed that she had been working on the dissertation when her killer interrupted her.

Despite the astonishing accuracy of these elements of Pennacchio's confession, there were apparently some discrepancies in it—enough to dissuade Judge Edward Viola from issuing a murder warrant, although the Cambridge police had booked him on that charge.

The initial complaint of lewd and lascivious behavior still held.

Whether Pennacchio had invented his confession, or had some inside knowledge of the manner of Beverly's death, however obtained, was never determined. He died shortly after he gave his statement, in a swimming accident off South Boston's Pleasure Island. In an effort to impress his teenage female companions, he had executed a high dive from a bridge into shallow water and ended up with his head—and whatever additional secrets it may have contained—buried in the silt of the bay.

The mystery of Beverly's life continued to deepen. Irene Fink denied that Beverly had ever been married to anyone, let alone a high school classmate. Irene also knew the man who Beverly had claimed to Leslie Loosli had been her husband for a few weekends, and insisted that neither wedding nor annulment had ever taken place.

Oliver Chamberlain, who discovered Beverly's slashed corpse, had been described in some news reports as her fiancé. They were not engaged, and Beverly, according to her father, was not interested in marriage at the moment anyway. Chamberlain had been an old friend from Beverly's days at the New England Conservatory as well as being the conductor of the musical group to which she belonged.

At the time of her death, Beverly was seeing a young man named Gerald Shea—described in the newspapers as "tall and handsome"—but again, how close that relationship was is impossible to ascertain. Some news accounts identified Shea as her boyfriend. This may simply have been an exaggeration of the tabloid press, which then, as now, tended to label any casual male acquaintance of a female celebrity—or crime victim—her lover.

In *The Boston Strangler,* Gerold Frank commented that "the professor with whom Beverly was briefly involved—married, with a family—once suggested to her that they commit hara-kiri together, because he saw no future for their love." The eminently practical Beverly spurned this plea. Frank continues that "the professor was an odd man indeed: reports came to police that he would describe to listeners in detail the finer techniques of strangling, topping that off with a dissertation on the art of seduction."*

This was the same individual Leslie Loosli, Beverly's confidante, was certain had been a bachelor. And Leslie mentioned nothing in her initial interview with Detectives Maher and Cronin about any proposed suicide pacts, which seemed an odd omission.

On June 25, 1963, Sergeant James Sugrue of the Cambridge Police Department made out a report (called a Six-Fifty) to Captain Edward Tierney in which

---

* Frank, p. 209.

he gave an account of an incident brought to his attention by the wife of a Boston University professor. "She overheard the man who lives in the next apartment to them tell her husband that he was the man who killed the woman in Cambridge," Sugrue wrote. "The only description she gave of this man is that he always carries a briefcase."

The information was titillating, but not terribly helpful. Tens of thousands of men in the Boston-Cambridge area carried briefcases every day.

An eccentric and rather sinister man—one whose name would later crop up in connection with the murder of Joann Graff—was considered a fair suspect for Beverly's murder by the Strangler Bureau. This individual, a singer, had turned up at a September 1962 audition for the Second Unitarian Church choir; the normally easygoing Beverly had an argument with him. She later told Mary Vivian Crowley that he wasn't reliable.

No evidence connected this man with Beverly's death.

The investigation of Beverly's murder, when it was taken over by the Strangler Bureau, had a rather ludicrous sidebar. On April 10, 1965, John Bottomly wrote an irate letter to Middlesex County Medical Examiner Peter Delmonico in which he accused Delmonico (who had performed Beverly's autopsy) of giving a guided tour of the murder scene to a *Globe* reporter and a *Record American* reporter as well as handing over to them copies of Beverly's thesis. Five days later Delmonico fired back to Bottomly a reply that dripped with sarcasm: "Upon receipt of this note, may I respectfully request that you write a note for the record to the effect that there has been a very serious misunderstanding about my apparent lack of cooperation with reference to your investigation of the [Beverly

Samans] case. This may be a better representation of the truth of the matter and may also help to negate any strong innuendos or language that might not have been justified under the circumstances. Thanks very, very much for your kind and cooperative attention."

On April 22, Bottomly wrote a sheepish apology to the outraged Delmonico, deploring the "misunderstanding" and expressing his and Attorney General Brooke's gratitude for the doctor's help.*

In January of 1963, the water pipes in Beverly's building had frozen and burst. As a result, the ceiling in her apartment collapsed. Leslie Loosli advised her to move; Beverly shrugged and replied that she'd given the landlord hell about the situation. The men who came to repair the damage did most of their work in her apartment.

It was speculated that one of these workmen may have returned five months later and assaulted and killed Beverly.

None of them was Albert DeSalvo.

Most Cambridge police who investigated the Beverly Samans murder believe today that if she wasn't killed by Daniel Pennacchio, she was slain by someone very like him: one of the many seriously disturbed individuals she took under her wing and to whom she offered not only her compassion but her hospitality. Or less likely, she may have been murdered by one of the men she was interviewing for material for her thesis, who panicked at the realization that his sexual orientation might become semipublic knowledge.

---

* In an outlandish coincidence, the *Globe* reporter was a college friend of Strangler suspect William Lindahl, and would be accused in 1970 of murdering his own wife.

There is a third possible solution to Beverly's murder—one that lies in the very apartment building she had lived in for four years.

Today, the big red-brick pile that occupies a block on Mount Auburn Street and University Road has been rehabilitated and gentrified, a glossy, ultramodern office and residential condominium complex attached to it. In Beverly's time, however, and indeed throughout the remainder of the 1960s and 1970s, the place was occupied primarily by students and artists and was renowned not only for its Bohemian flavor but its general decrepitude and extremely lax security.

University Road—the building was named after its address—was situated just outside Harvard Square, then as now a Petri dish of the avant-garde culture.

"The Harvard Square scene in that period was what I think of as high-class low-class," says one woman. "Meaning that you could say the most outrageous and vulgar things, but get away with it if you said them in a prep school accent. And you could be as promiscuous as a bunny rabbit and never become declassé, as long as you had the proper pedigree and antecedents, and you had gone to the right schools, and you knew the right people. About the worst thing you could be was bourgeois. What a ghastly, unforgivable sin that was. It was a milieu that had its own rigid rules for behavior—it was the accepted convention of the unconventional to be shocking. This was how you demonstrated that you weren't, gasp, horror of horrors, middle-class. The whole way of thinking was very much the *nostalgic de la boue* attitude of the French aristocrats after the Revolution."*

---

* This atmosphere enabled Albert DeSalvo, in his Measuring Man phase, to move so freely around the Harvard Square area. He was in fact quite gleeful about the number of "high class ladies" he was able to seduce there. He claimed to have enjoyed a number of sexual successes with

Into this surreal world, in 1959, had wandered Beverly Samans, a bright, curious, adventurous, and somewhat naive twenty-two-year-old from a small town in West Virginia.

Just across the street from her apartment, a very young and not yet famous Joan Baez and an equally youthful and unknown Bob Dylan were playing to reverently hushed audiences at the Club 47. And a block away, on Brattle Street, in the shabby and subterranean Club Casablanca, poet Gregory Corso held court, along with that doomed hothouse flower of the American aristocracy and Andy Warhol queen Edith Sedgwick.

The Casablanca—or the Casa B, as it was known until it was urban-renewed out of existence several years ago—was the essence of the Square distilled in one grubby and cavernous room dominated by a funky jukebox filled with recordings by Marlene Dietrich and Edith Piaf and German drinking songs. Most of its waiters were Harvard upperclassmen. "It was a place where a lot of disparate people came together," says Joy Pratt, who served drinks there in the late 1950s and early 1960s. "People sowed their wild oats in the Casablanca and then went on to become stockbrokers."

Not all of them.

Head bartender Jack Reilly kept a close eye on his diverse—and often outré—clientele. "There was never any trouble," says Joy Pratt.

That was not always true in the early morning hours, after the Casa B had sounded its last call for drinks and the habitués went elsewhere to continue the party.

---

residents of apartments at University Road, which was probably why when he confessed to the murder of Beverly Samans, he was able to describe the layout (although not, interestingly, the furnishings and household effects) of her flat fairly convincingly.

Where they went, most often, was to University Road—the place a number of them called home.

Novelist Lee Grove, a Harvard graduate student in the early 1960s, describes this movable feast and its sponsors: "You would go to the Casa B to encounter people you suspected were wonderfully decadent, and then you would go across the street to University Road and discover real decadence."

People came and went there as they pleased; none of the entrances to the building were ever locked. Nor were the apartments themselves. A Casablanca bartender opened his door late one night to find on the threshold a nubile young woman, a stranger to him, who offered him her body as a gift. He accepted. The gift turned out to be the kind that keeps on giving: the bartender contracted a troublesome venereal disease.

Lee Grove found some of the sights and sounds of University Road ultimately more disturbing and repellent than exotic and seductive, and curtailed his visits to friends living there. "It was," he says flatly, "the perfect place for a murder."

The history of University Road proved him right.

Just eighteen months prior to Beverly Samans's death, a young woman occupant of the building had been pistol-whipped. She was never able to identify her attacker.

Violent fights took place at University Road in the aftermath of parties thrown by one especially notorious resident, who would get his underaged guests drunk, photograph them in compromising positions, and then use the pictures for blackmail. He was eventually murdered by one of the adolescents he picked up and seduced.

In January 1969, Jane Britton, a Harvard graduate student in anthropology and the daughter of a Radcliffe vice president, was found dead in her apartment at 2 University Road. Someone had repeatedly bludgeoned her over the head with a sharp instrument, possibly an archaeological artifact.

There were a number of marked similarities between the murder of Jane Britton and that of Beverly Samans almost six years before: both had admitted their killer to their apartments very late at night; both were wearing nightclothes (Jane a nightgown, Beverly a housecoat); both had been killed on their beds and found lying dead there; both had suffered multiple bloody wounds and been killed with extreme sadistic violence; the heads of both were covered by an article of clothing; and the lower bodies of both had been left exposed.

Both were discovered by close men friends who were concerned about them because they had failed to keep important appointments.

Jane had kept her apartment door unlocked, so neighbors could store food in her refrigerator. Beverly had inadequate locks on her door, and was fatalistic about any danger they might fail to prevent.

Independent of the circumstances of the killings, there were likenesses between the two victims: Both were attractive, dark-haired, ambitious, intelligent, gregarious, venturesome, and highly social graduate students in their middle twenties. Both were as rigorous in their intellectual habits as they were careless housekeepers. Both were casual in their lifestyles. Both were open-minded and openhanded in their approach to people. Both had a sympathy for outcasts and pariahs. Both had trouble attracting men whose personalities were as strong and vital as their own.

There was an eerily ritualistic aspect to both murders. The upper part of Jane's body was buried beneath a mound of coats and blankets that in its conformation suggested a burial cairn. Someone had also sprinkled an ocher powder around the room—a funeral rite observed by some of the primitive cultures Jane had studied.

Beverly was stabbed in a circular pattern around and in the left breast. The injury that killed her was inflicted directly to the heart. The ligatures around her neck were not functional—they seemed rather to constitute a grotesque decoration.

Was University Road a focal point for psychotic killers obsessed with a certain type of prey?

The murder of Jane Britton, like that of Beverly Samans, is considered officially unsolved. Both case files remain open today in the Criminal Investigation Division of the Cambridge Police Department.

On Saturday, May 4, 1963, Beverly attended what would be her final class—in educational research—at Boston University. Idly commenting to herself on the burden of being compelled to listen to a dull lecture, she scrawled in her course notebook, "What sins in my life did I ever commit to deserve this?"

She did not know it, but she had just composed her own epitaph.

32

The Murders of Evelyn Corbin and Joann Graff

Retired Lieutenant John Moran of the Salem Police Department bears a pleasant resemblance to actor Andy Griffith. Six feet one inch tall and white-haired, he has a round, high-colored face with a small powder burn mark on the left cheek. The mark is a souvenir of the time Moran was shot at point-blank range by a sixteen-year-old boy he caught trying to break into the coin-changing machine of a Salem laundromat. The bullet grazed his face; if the trajectory it followed had been a millimeter to the right, Moran probably would have been killed.

Moran was one of the principal investigators of the murder of Evelyn Corbin, of 224 Lafayette Street in Salem, on September 8, 1965.

At 9:15 that morning Flora Manchester, also a resident of that apartment building on Lafayette Street, heard someone at her door. She didn't answer, but a few minutes later phoned her good friend Evelyn. Evelyn reported that *she* had heard someone at *her* door at about 9:20.

Evelyn went over to Flora's apartment for breakfast. At around 10:30, using Flora's phone, she called her sister Edna Harney. Then she returned to her own apartment to dress for church.

It was customary for her to tap on Flora's door at 11:10, as she was on her way to an 11:30 mass. This morning she didn't do so. Flora, a little concerned, called Evelyn. The phone went unanswered.

At 12:30 P.M., Flora telephoned Eaton's Drug Store across the street to find out if Evelyn had been in to pick up her Sunday paper. She hadn't.

Evelyn was supposed to join Flora and her forty-one-year-old son, Robert, for dinner that day. Robert had left for his office at 9:00 to attend to a backlog of paperwork.

Flora hung up from her phone call to the druggist and went to the apartment of another neighbor, Marie L'Horty. Had Marie seen Evelyn? Marie hadn't.

Now extremely worried, Flora decided to go into Evelyn's apartment and check for herself. She asked Marie to accompany her.

Using the key Evelyn had given her (Evelyn had a key to Flora's place), Flora unlocked her friend's front door and opened it. Uneasily, she peered inside the apartment.

Then she shrieked, "My God, she's been attacked."

"I'm going to call the police," Marie L'Horty said.

At that moment, Robert Manchester, who had been having an affair with Evelyn, arrived home from work. He went into his lover's apartment. Just last night they had been on a date to Revere Beach, a waterfront amusement park.

A few moments later Robert emerged from the apartment, his hands to his face. "She's gone," he said to his mother.

Evelyn was indeed gone. Her body lay faceup on a disordered bed, its lower half completely exposed. There were two stockings knotted around her neck and one around her left ankle—her feet may have been tied together by her attacker, who cut the bond before he left the apartment.

She was wearing white ankle socks, a torn nightgown, and a housecoat from which three buttons were missing.

There was blood in both her ears and semen in her mouth.

The bed and floor were littered with crumpled lipstick and semen-stained tissues. A pair of underpants, lipstick-stained just above the crotch, lay at the foot of the bed. They had been used to gag Evelyn; Robert had yanked them from her mouth in a frantic but futile effort to resuscitate her.

The blond divorcée, who everyone thought had looked twenty years younger than her true age, had performed, or been forced to perform, oral sex before being strangled.

Evelyn, whose marriage had broken up three decades earlier, had worked for Sylvania Electric as a lamp assembler. She had moved to 224 Lafayette Street in 1959, after the death of her mother. She was known as a quiet and pleasant woman who, despite her friendliness, was somewhat timorous. She would never admit a strange man to her apartment—especially not if she were clad only in a nightgown and bathrobe.

She had written a letter to a relative—never finished and never mailed—in which she spoke of her dream that she and Robert Manchester would be married in the spring of 1964. Robert, like his mother, was apparently unaware that his fiancée was seventeen years older than he.

And there was one other secret Evelyn kept from Manchester: While she was involved with him, she was also seeing another man.

May 7, 1992, was a gorgeous day, sunny and far warmer than the weather forecasters had predicted.

John Moran, ten years retired from the Salem Police Department, spent it taking a visitor on a guided tour of the murder scene of Evelyn Corbin.

He remembers the day of Evelyn's death well. He was one of the first to arrive at 224 Lafayette Street in response to Marie L'Horty's phone call.

Moran believes that he knows who killed Evelyn Corbin, and that person was not Albert DeSalvo. "It was just impractical for DeSalvo to come down and pick out a house on a foggy Sunday morning in Salem."

Another factor had always niggled at Moran: In his confession to Evelyn's murder, Albert said that he'd gotten her to admit him to the apartment because the "super" (superintendent) of the building wanted him to check a leak.

The handyman who took care of such matters at 224 Lafayette Street did not refer to himself by this term. It isn't one that is used in Salem, according to Moran. In any case, Evelyn knew the handyman and also knew that he didn't work Sundays. And there were no emergencies in the building—certainly not in Evelyn's apartment—that would have caused him to disrupt his normal schedule.

Albert DeSalvo told Bottomly that he had come to Evelyn's front door.

Moran knew exactly how Evelyn's killer had entered her apartment: He had climbed the fire escape and crawled in through a window.

He had left evidence of his presence on the fire escape.

Evelyn, a nervous woman, had called the police on a number of occasions before her death to report prowlers in the neighborhood or outside her building. She may have imagined some of these menacing presences, mistaking the rustle of leaves or the creak of a tree branch in the wind for the sound of someone trying to break into her home. Then again, she may not have. In the days before her murder, other people in nearby buildings had complained of men acting suspiciously in the area.

On the morning of Evelyn's murder, a tall, gray-haired man in a dark suit was observed loitering inside as well as outside 224 Lafayette Street.

The previous evening, at 9:00, a man who lived at 233 Lafayette Street answered a knock on his door. A tall gray-haired man, a stranger, asked to see the man's wife. She wasn't in, the apartment dweller replied. The stranger said that he'd heard that the woman was looking for a new job, and that he had a lead on one for her. He promised to return when the wife was home. He never did.

The woman in question did not recognize the description her husband gave of the visitor. Nor was she looking for different work.

At around 11:00 in the morning on September 7, someone had rung the doorbell of Yvonne Michaud, who also lived at 233 Lafayette Street.

That address would shortly assume enormous importance in the investigation of Evelyn's murder.

On Monday, September 9, 1963, a man who lived on Dunlap Street in Salem reported to the police that his sixteen-year-old daughter had run off with a twenty-five-year-old married man from Lynn. Moran, who would spend the next three weeks, day and night without interruption, probing Evelyn's murder, took the complaint.

Moran knew who the Lynn man was, and what he knew he didn't like. The man was a thief. And he was a psychotic. His name was Robert Cambell, and he had been thrown out of his own home by his wife after she had witnessed him kicking their toddler daughter in the face. The child had wandered into a room Cambell was painting and disturbed him at his labors.

He had gone thereafter to live in a boardinghouse in Lynn, from which he was expelled for nonpayment of rent.

On his uppers, he sought refuge in Salem. On the Saturday night before Evelyn's murder, Cambell and the acquaintance he bunked with at 233 Lafayette Street bought a box of doughnuts for their Sunday breakfast. That morning, Cambell woke up, put some of the doughnuts in his pockets, and left 233 Lafayette—about an hour and a half before Evelyn's death.

Later that day, Salem police found a doughnut on the fire escape outside Evelyn's window. She did not eat doughnuts, nor was she in the habit of tossing stale baked goods out her window to feed the birds.

Cambell and his teenage companion left Salem during the early afternoon on September 8. Cambell was adamant about not listening to the radio as he drove; he did not want to hear any news reports.

He told the girl with him that he had five or six dollars. That amount was missing from Evelyn's handbag.

Cambell and his partner in flight had picked up a stray puppy before leaving Salem. After their car broke down, they holed up in a small town in New York State. The girl deserted Cambell after he abused the dog so badly it required veterinary treatment. She went to Hudson, New York, with another man. Cambell followed her in a stolen car and was arrested for auto theft.

A few months later, having served a short prison sentence, he was back in Salem. He moved in with a woman who shortly ejected him from her house because of his violent behavior and nonstop demands for oral sex. Cambell's wife had made a similar complaint.

Evelyn had fellated her killer, probably under extreme duress.

On the corner of Roslyn and Lafayette streets one night, Cambell assaulted a fifty-two-year-old woman. He had rape in mind: He punched his victim, gouged at her eyes, and shoved his fingers down her throat to gag her. He left her bleeding and semiconscious on the sidewalk.

He had done exactly the same thing to another woman in Peabody, a town adjacent to Salem, the previous night.

Both victims positively identified Cambell as their attacker. Charged with the assaults, he was tried, convicted, and imprisoned for eight years.

His whereabouts today are unknown.

When Albert DeSalvo began confessing to the stranglings, Moran asked his chief, City Marshal John Tully, to seek permission from the attorney general's office to interview DeSalvo. Moran had some very specific questions he wanted to ask about the murder of Evelyn Corbin.

Tully made the request several times. It was never granted. It was never even acknowledged.

Moran says he never received back from the Strangler Bureau the information he submitted to it on the Corbin killing—although he had been wise enough to keep copies of the files for himself.

There is an echo here of the Beverly Samans case. John Grainger, captain of detectives for the Cambridge Police Department, had prepared a list of questions relevant to the Samans murder and submitted it to the Strangler Bureau. Those questions were never asked of DeSalvo, a former Cambridge detective maintains today.

Moran interviewed Robert Cambell concerning his whereabouts on the morning of Evelyn's death. Cambell lied, demonstrably so, in saying that he had left 233 Lafayette Street at 11:00 A.M., when it was known that he had departed there at least an hour and a half earlier. "He went into tantrums and had rages," Moran says, adding with considerable understatement, "he was a pretty unstable character."

Moran, convinced that Cambell had slain Evelyn when she interrupted him burglarizing her apartment, forcing her to fellate him before killing her, was never able to collect the one final piece of evidence that would justify Cambell's arrest on a homicide charge.

Thirty years later, Moran is philosophical about the situation. "There are," he says, "a lot more murderers walking the streets than there are behind bars."

Attorney General Edward Brooke's 1964 report on the coordination of the stranglings characterized Joann Graff, who was raped and strangled in Lawrence, Massachusetts, the weekend of the assassination of John F. Kennedy, as "an inhibited, obsessively neat, and insular personality." After her death, some newspaper reports described her as "a statuesque blonde," a phrase that bestowed on her a creamy aura of Marilyn Monroe–like sensuality. The truth, at it usually does, probably lay somewhere in the middle.

Twenty-three-year-old Joann Graff had graduated from the University of Chicago Downtown in June of 1963. There she had been a member of the Art League Paper and the Zion Lutheran Senior Choir and Concert Orchestra. She had attended the Chicago Art Institute and, prior to that, the Chicago Vocational School.

She had come to Lawrence in the summer of her graduation year; she had taken a job as an industrial designer for Bolta Products. For a short while she lived at the YWCA. What she wanted, ideally, was to board with a nice family in the Lawrence area. She even asked the pastor of her church if he could help her locate one within reasonable commuting distance of her job.

He couldn't. On July 23, she moved into a second-floor apartment at 54 Essex Street in Lawrence, although not without trepidation. She wanted assurance from her landlord that the neighborhood was safe. He told her it was.

Exactly four months later she would die there, in considerable pain and terror.

Before that point, however, she had decided that she liked the independence of living alone. And perhaps also the peace and quiet and privacy; she had grown up in a large family.

People who spoke publicly about her after her death described her as a retiring, though pleasant, young woman. Elsie Hartung of Methuen, the town next door to Lawrence, who often had Joann to dinner, told reporter Richard Remmes of the *Boston Herald* that Joann "had no boyfriends and would not even wear a flashy print dress. She was a member of the Missouri Synod which is much stricter [than the mainstream Lutheran church]."

She was certainly a devout practitioner of Lutheranism. Evidence found in her apartment after her murder suggests that her killer had interrupted her while she was reading and making notes on a religious tract. This may have been in preparation for the Sunday school class she was to teach the following morning.

She kept her small apartment, with its linoleum floors and heavy, depressing furniture, impeccably clean. She was a fanatic about staying within the limits of the weekly budget she had set for herself, skipping a meal if she felt she had overspent in some other area.

Her pastor referred to her as "a quiet girl with few friends."

Other reports suggested that she was not quite as prim and repressed as she appeared to be. She was not averse to taking a drink at a party, and after she had, she could giggle and flirt quite charmingly with an attractive male guest. She even developed a crush on a man, one who was unavailable to her for the simple reason that he was gay. She may have been too naive to realize this.

She did socialize with some of the men at Bolta Products. Police administered lie detector tests to thirty-five of the company's employees. Six days after her death, the *Herald* reported that at least fifty men had been questioned or given polygraphs in connection with it.

Other than her killer, the last person to see Joann alive was one of her landlords, George Privitera, who came to collect the rent on Sunday, November 23, 1963. On that day Massachusetts was still staggering in the concussive wake of the murder of John F. Kennedy twenty-four hours earlier.

At 3:35 that afternoon, someone knocked on the door of Kenneth Rowe and his wife at 54 Essex Street. Rowe opened the door to a man in his mid to late twenties, with slicked-back hair, wearing a brown jacket, a dark shirt, and dark green pants. The man asked for "Joan" Graff. Rowe told him she lived upstairs.

Rowe's wife had complained previously that for the past few days, someone had been wandering the halls of their building. The description she gave of this man differed from that her husband provided of the man who had come to their door Saturday afternoon.

Earlier in the day, Joann had been noticed chatting with a blond man outside the apartment building.

At 4:30, Joann was supposed to have dinner with her friends from the Lutheran church, Mr. and Mrs. John Johnson of Andover. Mrs. Johnson had begun telephoning her guest at 3:30. She called several times over the next hour and got no answer. Nonetheless, John Johnson drove over to Lawrence to pick up Joann at the appointed time. He knocked at her door and got no response, then went home.

At that very same time, an agitated and disheveled man entered Martin's Tavern, a short walk from 54 Essex Street, glanced around nervously, used the men's room, and left.

When he'd walked into the bar, he'd held the door open behind him and looked over his shoulder, as if trying to spot someone in pursuit.

At 9:30 on Sunday morning, Mr. and Mrs. Johnson drove to Joann's apartment to pick her up for church. She didn't answer her door. Nor did she show up to teach her Sunday school class. Alarmed, Mr. and Mrs. Johnson consulted with their pastor. Then they called the police.

At 11:35 A.M., Lawrence police officer F. T. O'Connor and Joann's other landlord, Sebastian Corzo, entered the second-floor apartment at 54 Essex Street.

Joann lay on her back across her bed, nude except for an opened blouse. Her ripped bra was blood-stained, as was the bedspread beneath her. Her right breast had been bitten; her left jaw and neck were contused, as was her right thigh.

Two brown nylon stockings and the leg of a black leotard were drawn tightly around her neck.

There was a slight injury to her genitalia and her vagina was loaded with sperm.

Several odd facts and anomalies cropped up during the long investigation of Joann's death.

It was discovered that Kenneth Rowe, the Northeastern University engineering student who had been Joann's neighbor, had previously lived at 84 Gainsborough Street in Boston, just across from Anna Slesers.

Joann's pastor was friendly with Juris Slesers, Anna's son. A Latvian refugee like Mrs. Slesers, the pastor had attended her funeral.

Bradley Schereschewsky, a suspect in the deaths of Anna Slesers, Nina Nichols, Helen Blake, and Jane Sullivan, had been deinstitutionalized the weekend of Joann's death. His parents lived in Andover, just three miles from the murder scene.

The man who had argued with Beverly Samans at the Second Unitarian Church Choir audition in September 1962 owned a cottage in Rockport. Joann and a male coworker had visited that picturesque seacoast town the evening before her death.

Albert DeSalvo, working for the Highland Construction Company, had been building a retaining wall in Andover on Friday, November 22, 1963.

Neither Jules Vens, the proprietor of Martin's Tavern, nor Kenneth Rowe recognized DeSalvo's photograph when shown it by authorities.

33

The Murder of Mary Sullivan

At 5:00 P.M. on January 4, 1964, twenty-five-year-old Christine Tracy and her sixteen-year-old sister, Elizabeth, both of Belmont, were about to get into their car, which they had parked in the Boston Common Underground Garage off Charles Street. At that moment they were confronted by a young man wielding a knife.

"I'm desperate," he said. "I'm wanted for murder. I gotta get out of Boston fast."

He forced Christine and Elizabeth to drive him to Newton Highlands, about eight or nine miles southwest of Boston. There he robbed them of five dollars and fled.

At 6:00 P.M., Pamela Parker and Patricia Delmore returned home from a day's work at Filene's department store in downtown Boston where both were employed. The door to their three-room apartment at 44A Charles Street was locked, so they rang the bell. No one answered.

"Mary must be asleep," said Patricia, referring to their new roommate, Mary Sullivan. "Let's use the key."

Inside the apartment, Pamela opened the bedroom door and glanced into its darkened interior. She saw Mary on the bed. Her assumption that Mary had been napping apparently confirmed, Pam went to the kitchen to help Pat fix dinner.

About fifteen minutes later, Pam yelled to Mary that the meal was ready. Pat banged on the bedroom door. "Gee, she won't wake up," Pat said.

Pam opened the door, switched on the light, and took a good look at what lay on the bed. She backed from the room, stumbling, and gasped at Pat, "Look, look."

Pat did. "My God," she said. "She's been raped; get the police."

The two young women flung themselves down the stairs and out onto Charles Street, screaming.

A Boston police motorcycle officer, John Vadeboncour, heard them. Barely coherent, Pam and Pat told him of their discovery. Vadeboncour sprinted up the steps of 44A Charles Street and into the apartment. He cast an appalled look at the scene in the bedroom and called for detectives.

This, from the official report, is what met the horrified gaze of Pam, Pat, and Officer Vadeboncour:

The body of the deceased was on one of two twin beds, the one nearer the door leading to the kitchen of the apartment. The body was in a sitting position at the head of the bed, leaning against the headboard. The thighs and knees are flexed, and spread apart. The neck is flexed, the chin resting on the upper chest, and the head leaning toward the right . . . The body is nude except for the partial cover of the shoulders by a blouse and bra. The breasts are bare. The mouth contains mucoid sticky secretions, a dried strand of this extending from the mouth towards a dried streak of similar material on the skin of the right breast, and on the right anterior chest wall. A broom handle is present in the vagina [to the extent of $3\frac{1}{2}$ inches], the whole broom extending out flat on the bed in front of the body . . . About the neck are tied three ligatures consisting of (A) a charcoal-colored nylon stocking, (B) a pink silk scarf, and (C) a pink and white scarf with floral design . . . The only clothing present, and this about the shoulders, is a white bra and a yellow and beige striped blouse . . . [The first ligature] is extremely tight causing a deeply depressed furrow, completely encircling the neck . . . [There are] acute traumatic injuries of both breasts.

Her killer had moved her body from one bed to another.

Propped up against the left foot of the victim was a card that read "Happy New Year!"

Mary Sullivan would have turned twenty on January 11. On that day, those who knew and loved her did not attend her birthday party. They received condolence calls.

She was buried on January 8 after the celebration of a solemn high requiem mass in Saint Francis Xavier Church in Hyannis, her hometown.

Police estimated that shortly after Pam and Pat had run screaming into the night, perhaps four hundred spectators jammed Charles Street outside the building in which the murder had taken place. Extra officers had to be called to restore the flow of traffic on the narrow thoroughfare that was one of the main routes in and out of Boston.

One of the spectators was nineteen-year-old William Robert Evans of Arlington, Patricia Delmore's fiancé. He informed the police that Mary, whom he had only recently met, had been frightened because someone had been on the fire escape outside the apartment a few nights previously. He added, "The girls have been worried about a defective window in the kitchen for about a month."

That night Newton police arrested nineteen-year-old Richard Brunette for the kidnapping and armed robbery of Christine and Elizabeth Tracy.

The victims' statement that their attacker had wanted to flee Boston because he was "wanted for murder" resonated with the Boston Homicide Unit. The Boston Common Garage, where Brunette had initiated the kidnapping, was barely three blocks from Mary Sullivan's apartment. And she probably had died close to 5:00, when Brunette was trying to escape the city.

The detectives questioned Brunette well into Sunday. He denied killing Mary Sullivan.

Mary Anne Sullivan, the second of six children of Mr. and Mrs. John T. Sullivan of Sea Street in Hyannis, was a small girl, no more than five-foot-three, with dark chestnut hair and an olive complexion. She was considered attractive as well as high-spirited, although the principal photograph of her published in the newspapers after her death conveys neither of these attributes: It shows, rather, a young woman who looks much older than her age, her expression somber, her lips clamped together in a prim, almost sour line.

Diane Sullivan Dodd remembers her sister as "cute and chubby." Popular as well. "Everybody liked her," says Mrs. Dodd. "She didn't have any enemies." Although her manner was quiet, her sense of humor was abundant. "She was the funniest person in the world." She fretted about her weight. "Mary would go to church at lunch instead of eat," recalls Mrs. Dodd, "because she was always on a diet."

Mary grew up on Cape Cod and attended Barnstable High School. In the summer of 1961, while she was working with her best friend, Meredith (Merry) Ward, at the Hyannis A & P, she acquired her first boyfriend, Nathan Ward, Meredith's brother. Nate was on leave from the army.

Mary's mother disapproved strongly of Nate; he was, she felt, a bad influence on her sixteen-year-old daughter. An honors student in high school, he had turned down a scholarship to divinity school to go into the service. Perhaps he had made this decision because he was, according to one of Mary's sisters, "a terrible atheist." He also gave Mary Communist tracts to read, and a copy of *Lady Chatterley's Lover,* which Mrs. Sullivan promptly confiscated and burned.

Mary adored Nate. Possibly part of his appeal for her was the disfavor in which her mother held him. More likely she was simply swept away by the emotional tide of a first romance. While Nate was away on duty, he sent her poems as well as letters. She kept them in a box; she still had them at the time of her death.

Nate left the army at around the same time that Mary graduated from high school, in June 1962. On July 9, Mary moved out of the family home and into a local rooming house. Mrs. Sullivan felt that she had done so under pressure from Nate. Mary said she wanted privacy. With her she took the hope chest and the set of luggage Nate had given her, the former as a graduation present.

The romantic idyll soon went bad. Mary and Nate began to argue almost constantly, Mary's sister Diane would later tell police. Another witness maintained that he was verbally abusive, yelling insults at her in the presence of their friends. He played on her the kind of practical jokes that verge on torture, such as going into her apartment to turn up the thermostat on hot days.

There was an even darker undercurrent to Mary's life in the summer of 1962 than simply her troubled relationship with Nate. She had possibly become wildly, in fact dangerously, promiscuous. It is impossible now to judge whether this was the cause, the effect, or the symptom of her problems with Nate.

She began to frequent a cottage in South Dennis occupied by a large group of young men. After her death, police interviewed as many of these youths as could be traced. What they had to say about Mary was profoundly disturbing:

> First time I met Mary Sullivan was in late June or early July at the cottage. I think that the other girls, Sharon and Natalie, brought her down. Within two or three weeks I knew she was a pushover, but I was afraid to get involved. One night when Mary was taking on most of the guys, when my turn came, she jerked me off. I'm not sure if it was the night of the gangbang or if it was just me. I had a few drinks . . . Even though she and I were alone in the bedroom I was apprehensive, and now as I think back even though Mary Sullivan gave me a hand job, I could have had a blow job. There were other nights in the cottage during the summer when I was there that Mary would have relations with the guys, but as I told Officer Daly, I was always afraid if I tried there would be serious consequences.

Another youth "stated there was a party in the cottage [in the last week of June] and that he danced with her and then went outside in a car, owner unknown . . . she was grabbing his private and he then let her commit an unnatural act (oral intercourse) on him."

The dreary and revolting litany continued. Several young men openly referred to Mary as "a pig" when describing her to police. "No one wanted to bother with her," said another, meaning that she was fine as a vessel for sexual release but not good enough to be taken to the movies or to dinner. Yet another youth told police that one night, as he lay in a chair in a drunken stupor, he regained consciousness to find Mary attempting to fellate him.

With no shame or guilt, or even embarrassment, a fifth young man described to police how he had tried to rape Mary one evening after she had passed out from heavy drinking. But first, he cut off her clothing with a razor—"all but her panties, those I took off." The rest of the assault—the boy himself called it a rape—came to nothing. The youth was so intoxicated he fell asleep on top of Mary. "When I woke up, she was gone." He thinks she drove home nude; she had at any rate left her shredded clothing behind her. He later burned it in the cottage fireplace, he thought.

The incident became a local joke.

All these heroes marveled over the fact that Mary, who dressed so neatly and demurely, and who wore so little makeup, could behave so sluttishly. None of them seemed to feel that their own behavior had been anything but entirely acceptable.

Only one young man, Christopher Sweeny, manifested a shred of decency when speaking of Mary. "She appeared to be a very nice, quiet girl . . . I never had anything to do [sexually] with her; [I] felt sorry for her. Every week she would come to the cottage and guys would be getting to her."

How much of the above was true, and how much the invention—or the braggadocio—of a locker room mentality, will never be known. One of Mary's girlfriends, Paula Houle, said that Mary was "above reproach morally." One of Mary's sisters, however, told police that Mary was "irresponsible and capable of anything and not a person who could be judged according to the norms of normal people."

Paula Houle counterclaimed that this sister was a troublemaker, a heavy drinker, "a nut," and the real problem child in the Sullivan family.

Carola Blume analyzed Mary's handwriting for the Strangler Task Force. What she found was a young woman who "had sexual satisfaction. She possessed a womanly kindness. Mary would go along with any kind of abnormal tendencies just to please a person, but had no abnormal tendencies herself. It is believed that Mary would have made a good wife for somebody, that she was the passive type, typically feminine, accepting. She would not give any resistance. Perversion was not in her personality, but she would go along with it."

The caption beneath Mary's high school yearbook photo read that she was "of more than common friendliness . . . happy-go-lucky with a cheerful attitude toward life." To this "bright-eyed girl," the encomium added, parties, dancing, and singing "bring many happy hours."

There must have been precious few "happy hours" in the desperate summer of 1962.

In October of that year, Mary moved to the Sun Dial Village cottages in Hyannis, taking a second-floor apartment. Her "official" boyfriend Nate was already living downstairs with a few other young men who were attending Cape Cod Community College. He and Mary were still involved, although how closely is difficult to say. He continued to berate her. When the weather got cold, he'd pull the reverse of his summertime trick and turn off the heat in her apartment. Mary probably fought back a lot less hard than she could—or should—have. The passivity that Carola Blume would later comment on might have been, in the most literal sense possible, her ultimate fatal flaw.

There was, however, one hopeful sign.

With her change of residence, Mary also suddenly—and drastically—changed her sexual habits for the better. She went to a dance held at a youth club in West Roxbury on October 26. There she encountered several of the young men who had used her over the summer. Said one of them, "I tried to make out. She refused to let me put my hands under her clothing. She said the summer was over and she was trying to change."

Another youth confirmed this statement. According to the police report, he "was under the impression that nobody made out with [Mary] on this particular night because she appeared to have reformed; also, that she was not the push-over she had been before."

Also attending this dance, in Mary's company, was the sister who called her "irresponsible." The sister, according to the police report, introduced herself to the other guests with a phony surname.

In the second half of her senior year in high school, Mary had been a food service worker at Cape Cod Hospital. During her stay in Hyannis, she worked as a door-to-door seller of encyclopedias and for the telephone company. Jerrell Wilcox, a phone company co-worker, thought highly of Mary, describing her as "very sentimental."

She was also very generous. In December of 1962, she took in a pregnant and unmarried friend, Jean. Jean, in addition to her other difficulties, was unemployed and broke. Mary let her live in the Sun Dial Village apartment for three months without paying rent.

Mary's generosity was all the more impressive in view of the fact that she herself was unemployed from January to April of 1963. To pay the rent and buy groceries, she took in ironing. Her clients were male students at Cape Cod Community College.

Jean moved out in March, and in June, Mary acquired another roommate, Wendy, who because she had a job at a local nursing home was able to contribute to the household upkeep. Wendy was also a student at the community college, as was her boyfriend Mike— who lived downstairs with Nate Ward for a short while.

In August of 1963, Mary and Nate finally parted. The breakup was probably acrimonious; Mrs. Sullivan later stated that Mary's defection had sent Nate into "a wild rage." However it came about, the split was long overdue. Mrs. Sullivan said that Mary had instigated the parting, which if true shows that she was finally developing some healthy spirit. It is possible that Mary had wanted out of the relationship long before, but had procrastinated for fear of insulting Merry Ward.

Perhaps it was simply that she had found a more appealing man. In the late summer of 1963 she became friendly with Tommy Bahr, who was working as an assistant manager of the Barnstable Howard Johnson's. They went to church together every Sunday at Saint Francis Xavier. They began dating in mid-September.

Tommy had just moved in downstairs with Nate, who was also a waiter at the Howard Johnson's. The tension must have been considerable.

Nate found himself a new girlfriend, Betty. Mary's sister Diane thought he had done so solely to make Mary jealous. He had not lacked for female companionship prior to that; in July he had impregnated a young woman from Connecticut.

Wendy, Mary's new roommate, disliked Nate intensely. She thought him cowardly, a game player. And he eyed her in a way she considered "perverted."

He was certainly not stable in his employment. Between the summer of 1962 and that of 1963 he held four jobs: at a dredging company, at a gas station, at a trading stamp redemption center, and at Howard Johnson's. He also enrolled in the community college but soon dropped out.

In the fall of 1963, Mary left the Sun Dial apartment and went to live in Whitman, near Cape Cod, with Merry Ward, now married to a man named Frank Lombardi. She commuted to Boston, where she had taken a job at Filene's—and where she would meet Pat Delmore and Pam Parker. She continued to date Tommy Bahr.

Nate's new girlfriend, Betty, moved in with Wendy.

A week before her death, Mary quit Filene's and took a receptionist's position with a Boston finance company. She went to work there on Friday, January 3, 1964. Her first day at work would be her last.

Just two days before that, she had moved in with Pam and Pat at 44A Charles Street.

By the winter of 1963, Mary was again having boyfriend problems. Tommy was not sufficiently attentive; she took up with a man named Clyde in order to make Tommy jealous, or so her friend Wendy said. Furthermore, someone identified only as "Don, a steeplejack [who] was staying at the Reindeer Motel in West Yarmouth," had been badgering Mary to date him. She would have nothing to do with this man, succinctly described by Wendy's boyfriend Mike as "a creep." Don was so desperate for Mary's favor that he pleaded with Mike to intercede for him. Mike declined.

On January 4, 1964, the day of Mary's death, Wendy received a letter from her. It had been written just before Mary's move to Boston. She had gone, she informed Wendy, to a New Year's party in Whitman, which had been "lousy." At 1:00 A.M. on January 1, she drove to Sun Dial Village. There she saw Tommy with another woman.

Patricia Delmore would later tell police that she thought Mary had shown up at 44A Charles Street sometime between 2:00 and 3:00 A.M. on January 1, in the mistaken belief that either Pam or Pat would be there.

Wendy seemed sure that after leaving Sun Dial Village, Mary had driven to Clyde's place in Centerville.

Diane Sullivan Dodd says today that Mary spent the

predawn hours of New Year's Day sitting in Saint Anthony's Shrine in Boston.

Mary moved into 44A Charles Street on January 1, a Wednesday. On January 2, Pat's boyfriend William Robert Evans and one of his buddies visited the apartment. All three young women had been present; Evans was introduced to Mary. He and his friend stayed from 7:30 until 11:00 that night.

The next day, the last full day of Mary's life, Pam noticed that her apartment key had been removed from the case in which she normally kept it.

Mary went to work. She left the finance company at 5:30 and drove to a service station, where she had the license plates on her blue Vauxhall—bought with a loan cosigned by Merry Ward Lombardi's husband—changed.

At 7:30 that night, Evans returned to 44A Charles. Speaking through a closed door, Mary informed him that Pat had gone to visit her parents in Lowell. Evans would tell police that he thought he heard a man's voice, low but nasal, inside the apartment. It had stopped as soon as he had knocked. It might have been the voice of a radio announcer. Evans was curious enough, he said, to check later whether any programs broadcast at that hour featured a host or a disk jockey who spoke in such a fashion. He could find none that did.

Just fifteen minutes after Evans's aborted visit, another young man appeared in search of Pat. Again, Mary told him she was away.

Pat was extremely popular. At 9:00 P.M., two more young men, Robert Tole and Richard Leveroni, came to the apartment looking for her.

At midnight, two young women dropped in to chat with Pat and Pam, who were home at that point. Mary was asleep.

Despite the fact that she didn't have to work, Mary was up early Saturday morning. Bleary-eyed, she shuffled into the kitchen as Pat and Pam were preparing breakfast at 7:30. She had cleaning and errands to do, Mary explained, and she wanted to get a jump start on those chores.

At five that afternoon, another resident of the building heard a noise that reminded him of a baby crying. There were no infants at 44A Charles Street.

Then Pam and Pat got home from work.

Five pieces of physical evidence—other than the broom handle thrust into Mary's vagina—were found at the crime scene. The first was a small metal object like a washer; the second was a charred scrap of paper that later proved to be the corner of a page torn from the 1962 West Suburban telephone directory; the third was the cigarette butts (of a brand neither Mary, Pat, nor Pam smoked) found in an ashtray near the bed in which the victim had been left, and the fourth was a piece of label from a dustpan not owned by any of the young women.

The fifth piece of evidence had to be fished from the toilet, down which someone had tried and failed to flush it. It was a red ascot, cut in three pieces.

In January of 1965, Albert DeSalvo told his then attorney, Jon Asgeirsson, that he had gagged Mary, put a sweater over her head, had intercourse with her, and left a knife on the bed.

None of this was true.

When Albert first spoke to Asgeirsson, he didn't know about the broom and what had been done to Mary with it. By—or perhaps at—the time he confessed to her murder to Bottomly, he had been filled in on this salient detail.

As had been the case in the murder of Ida Irga, a single never-identified fingerprint was lifted from the crime scene. If either print had been Albert DeSalvo's it would have been recognized as such by the FBI. Long before Mary or Ida had been murdered, Albert's prints were on file not only with the police but with the military.

In early August 1965, a Bridgewater State Hospital inmate told authorities that Albert DeSalvo had confided to him that he had met Mary Sullivan in the summer of 1963 at Sun Dial Village, and that he had also formed an acquaintance with Nate Ward, who bragged to Albert that he too was a rapist.

The story was a total fabrication.*

Mary's sister told police that Mary had bought Nate Ward ascots as gifts. Mary had shown her a red plaid one. "She said that Nathan Ward loved these ties," according to the investigation report, "and Mary would say how good he looked in them."

The police found this information interesting in view of the evidence that had been found at the murder scene, even though the red ascot that had been thrown down the toilet had belonged to Pam.

And the cops questioned whether Mary's sister was totally credible.

Nate married his girlfriend Betty on Valentine's Day, 1964.

Tommy Bahr did not go to work on the day of Mary's murder. He told police that he spent it with two friends

---

* See pp. 212–13.

in Provincetown viewing the scenery. Between 6:00 and 7:00 that evening he was at an ice rink in Hyannis, watching a hockey game. It was there that he was informed, by a Howard Johnson's coworker, that his girlfriend was dead.

Later he went to Saint Francis Xavier Church, possibly to offer a prayer for the soul of Mary Sullivan. Mrs. Sullivan asked him to be a pallbearer at the funeral. He refused.

On Sunday, January 5, Tommy wanted to drive Mary's sister to Boston to pick up Mary's clothing. He insisted several times that he be allowed to do so. He made the same demand four days later. Mrs. Sullivan would not permit it.

In Mary's jewelry box, police found a note that read: "DON'T LEAVE FRIDAY AFTERNOON OR NIGHT. I'll see you. Tom."

It was undated.

Later in 1964, Tommy would move into Mary's old apartment in Sun Dial Village.

Police showed the page from the West Suburban telephone directory to one of Mary's sisters. She thought she recognized a name on it as one Mary had mentioned to her. She had the impression this man drove a Cadillac.

The page fragment had been found by the toilet; presumably whoever had disposed of the ascot had accidentally dropped it there.

Or it might have been planted, a false clue designed to lead the police from the trail of the real killer.

One month after Mary's death, her mother and her sister Diane went to Saint Anthony's Shrine in Boston, where Mary may have spent the early hours of New Year's Day. They were looking for a small suitcase belonging to Mary, one in which she'd kept cosmetics and personal papers, most notably the Christmas cards she'd received. The suitcase was not found in the apartment on Charles Street, so Mrs. Sullivan thought Mary might have accidentally left it behind in the church.

Mrs. Dodd recalls that there were a number of priests—"maybe twenty or so"—present, all of whom seemed "nervous and upset" to see the two women. Searching for the lost and found booth, Mrs. Sullivan and Diane ended up in the office of an individual Mrs. Dodd describes as the head of the church. The ensuing scene confused and frightened her. The priest pushed his chair back from the desk, rose, and exclaimed to Mrs. Sullivan, "Who are you to accuse anyone of murder?"

Mrs. Sullivan's jaw dropped in shock. Diane was equally dumbfounded. Certainly no accusations of murder against anyone had been lodged. "All we were trying to do was get to the lost and found department," Mrs. Dodd reiterates.

The two were hustled from the church.

Equally troubling to Mrs. Dodd is the memory of an earlier incident also involving Saint Anthony's. "It was one of the priests from there who gave Mary the last rites," says Mrs. Dodd. "The day after [the murder] my mother sent him a thank you gift, a communion plate, the kind you put under your chin." The priest never acknowledged Mrs. Sullivan's expression of gratitude.

Ultimately she learned that he had indeed received the plate. But almost immediately afterward—within a da or so, Mrs. Dodd is sure—he went to a monastery in New Jersey. Upon his arrival, he took the vow of silence required of all members of the order.

Suffolk County Medical Examiner Michael Luongo tested the mucoid substance that had dripped from

Mary's mouth onto her breast and found it to contain "great masses of spermatozoa." The substance was reexamined in the spring of 1965, however, by a New York pathologist, Alexander Wiener, who not only found no spermatozoa in the sample but no presence of semen in it, either—only the epithelial cells normally present in saliva.

The thick white stains found on the blanket on which Mary's body had lain were apparently not semen, either. They contained no spermatozoa.

On February 11, 1965, one Robert Eugene Pennington, alias J. C. Lundy, was arrested in Gary, Indiana. Pennington, thirty-four, had escaped from the Iowa State Penitentiary on March 12, 1963, where he had been confined since 1959. As a fugitive he had traveled around the country, employed sometimes by moving companies and sometimes by circuses. A short man of stocky build, he had curly brown hair, gray eyes, a tattoo on his upper right arm that said "Ruby," and the tattoo of a cross on his left palm. A deformed leg caused him to walk with a limp.

Following his arrest in Indiana, he was rendited to California, which had outstanding warrants on him for kidnapping, child molestation, and at least two counts of murder.

Pennington—or Lundy, to use his circus name—wanted to die. He was quoted as saying, "I am definitely going to the gas chamber even if I have to kill a guard."

On Thursday, March 18, 1965, Pennington was being interrogated by a police captain in Indio, California. In the middle of the questioning, Pennington passed the captain a slip of paper. "Check this out," he said.

The captain looked at what was written on the paper. It read: "In apartment—Mary—Charles St., Boston—strangled her, young, white, January 3 or 4, 1964."

On February 21, 1965, Pennington had informed the same police official that he had had "an operation preventing his production of spermatozoa."

Pennington would not elaborate on the contents of the note.

On March 19, 1965, he was sentenced to one year to life on the child molestation charge. He was sent to an institution similar to Bridgewater; the state of California was positive it had the evidence needed to convict him for at least two of the murders of which he had been accused.

Incarcerated, Pennington talked no further—except to vow that if he had to kill again in order to be executed, he would do so.

On July 7, 1964, Beacon Hill resident Sims Murray was hypnotized and questioned about what he had noticed at noon on a day very early in January when he had taken his dog for a walk on Charles Street:

> . . . I see a girl with records (LPs), a bundle of them, carrying them with both hands, tied with a string. There was a car with someone helping her move. He is average, little under 6 feet, darkish hair, a little bald, face always away from me; not attractive, just average, wearing a jacket . . . The girl had on a raincoat, she is shorter than I am, brownish hair, loafers. Can't see his feet, no hat, he is in back of car, no glasses, clean shaven, fat nose, not pointed . . . Never saw the man before or since . . . He was wearing blue corduroy pants, Canadian warm-up jacket . . .

The only problem was, Murray couldn't remember if this event had occurred on January 1 or January 4. Thinking it wasn't important, he did not report the incident to the police until the very end of the month, after he'd seen Mary's photo in the paper and decided she was the young woman who had been carrying the bundle of records.

Sims Murray, shown a photograph of Albert DeSalvo, did not recognize it. What he had probably seen was Pam Parker's father helping her unpack her car on January 1.

William Robert Evans, Patricia Delmore's principal boyfriend, assured a member of the Strangler Task Force several times that he would do whatever he could to help it in its investigation.

After Mary's death, a Boston University student claimed that not only had he known her, but that he was the Strangler. (He also claimed to know who had committed the Plymouth mail robbery.) His friends and acquaintances thought him an "oddball," "a leech as well as a liar," a manipulator who was always seeking sympathy. He was a kleptomaniac. He also had a criminal record: a conviction for breaking and entering.

He had worked on Cape Cod in the summer of 1963. Employed by the Cotuit Cemetery, he had been fired for breaking into the storage house, stealing a bag of fertilizer, and dumping it into a mailbox.

The Boston police had received an anonymous call from a man who claimed to be the Strangler. For a number of reasons, they thought the caller might be this BU student, trying to draw attention to himself.

In 1964, he sued the Boston Police Department for false arrest—not, however, on any murder charge. The suit was, his friends thought, just another one of the illicit money-making schemes he was forever devising.

No evidence appeared to exist to link him further with Mary Sullivan.

* * *

Meanwhile, the authorities were growing more and more interested in the ever-helpful and cooperative William Robert Evans. At the end of November 1964, they asked him to take a polygraph examination. The relevant question here would be the whereabouts of Pam Parker's apartment key, the one that had vanished during Evans's visit to 44A Charles Street on January 2, 1964. Whoever had killed Mary had not broken into the apartment—he had either been admitted to it or unlocked the door.

Evans was, according to case records, a rather troubled person: a product of a broken home who fought violently with his mother. He had never had any sexual experience. He knew of Mary's checkered past, although he claimed to find her unappealing. It was his belief that the killer had really been after his girlfriend Pat, whom Evans considered gorgeous and sexy.

The polygraph results were not favorable to Evans.

A little before noon on December 4, 1964, exactly eleven months after the murder of Mary Sullivan, Pam Parker received a phone call at the home of her parents in Malden.

She picked up the phone and said, "Hello?"

There was a brief silence. Then a male voice said, "Who's this, Pamela?"

"Who is this calling?" she replied.

The person on the other end of the line didn't identify himself. Instead, he said, "I'm going to do the same thing to you that I did to Mary. I'm going to take that broom and shove it right up your cunt."

The caller was breathing heavily. His voice was deep, nervous, and vibrant with hatred. He sounded as if he meant every word of his dreadful threat.

"Who is this?" Pam said. "Who is this?"

"I'm even going to take your underwear off, even your underpants, I'll use those," the caller continued.

"How would you like that, how would you like that? I'll get you sooner or later like I got Mary. Would you like that, would you really like that? Well, you won't have to wait. Would you like that?"

He broke the connection.

Aghast, Pam dialed the number of the Malden bridal shop where her mother worked. Mrs. Parker immediately called the police.

There was one other peculiarity about the caller's voice, Pam told the detectives. He stuttered. Did she know anyone who did? the investigators asked. Yes, Pam answered, two people.

One of them was William Robert Evans.

That very afternoon, Evans was scheduled to take another polygraph examination. These were its results:

Based on the examinations conducted, it is the considered opinion of this examiner that Evans:

1. Is not telling the truth concerning the extent of his knowledge and/or involvement in the death of MARY SULLIVAN.

2. Cannot be eliminated from this investigation.

It would be no surprise to this examiner if Evans turns out to be the person who caused Mary SULLIVAN's death.

Note: The charts were examined by other examiners . . . who confirmed the findings as outlined in the report.

On December 22, 1964, John Bottomly requested from Edward Brooke permission to seek a court order to tap Evans's mother's home telephone. Said Bottomly's memo, "He has 'failed' two polygraph tests. These is considerable circumstantial evidence which places him in the position of No. 1 suspect. Among other things his statement suggested the possibility that he may have an accomplice or be an accomplice to the murder."

* * *

No one in the Sullivan family ever really recovered from Mary's death, perhaps because for all of them the case was never closed, the mystery never solved. Casey Sherman, Diane Dodd's son, attributes his uncle David's premature death in early 1995 to an anguish that never faded and essentially crippled his existence.

Nor was there ever any surcease for Mrs. John Sullivan, who died in 1994. At the time of her death, she had in her possession some of Mary's personal effects. They now belong to Mrs. Dodd, who refers to them as "artifacts."

Like all of Mary's survivors, Mrs. Dodd believes that the killer was never caught. It galls her that he is quite probably still alive and very likely free, enjoying the life of which he so brutally deprived Mary.

And what are her feelings about the man who confessed to Mary's murder? "What would I say to Albert DeSalvo if he were still alive?" Diane Dodd repeats the question and ponders it. Then she sighs, "I would say to him: You didn't do it. You're a creep, but you didn't do it."

PART SIX

34

Final Thoughts

That many of the Boston stranglings were copycat crimes is beyond doubt. Starting with the death of Anna Slesers on June 14, 1962, the circumstances of the killings were so thoroughly and so well documented in the newspapers that anyone who wanted to rid himself of an inconvenient woman, or kill one for the thrill of it, or for any other reason, had a blueprint to do so. The killer could also be assured that the press—particularly the *Record American*—would attribute the crime to the Phantom Fiend, as would public opinion, which then, as now, was shaped by the media.

The police always knew better.

The press contention was that the murders were identical in method. They were not: No similarity whatever exists between the relatively delicate killing of Patricia Bissette, whose murderer tucked her into bed, and the ghastly homicidal violation inflicted on Mary Sullivan, whose killer's intent was not just to degrade his victim by shoving a broom handle into her vagina but to taunt the discoverer of her corpse by placing a greeting card against her foot. Beverly Samans was stabbed but not sexually assaulted; Joann Graff was raped vaginally and strangled. Evelyn Corbin had performed—probably under duress—oral sex on her killer. Jane Sullivan was dumped facedown to rot in a bathtub. Ida Irga was left in the living room with her legs spread out and propped up on a chair.

These are hardly identical modi operandi.

Nor does the fact that the women who died by strangulation were garroted by articles of their own clothing point to a single killer. Virtually every adult woman owns hosiery, brassieres, blouses, scarves, or bathrobes with tie belts. All of these provide excellent and readily available ligatures for a killer—particularly one who doesn't wish to be observed carrying a murder weapon to the crime scene.

The copycat factor is vividly demonstrated in the case of Mabel St. Clair, an elderly woman who was found dead in the bathroom of her Lynn apartment on the afternoon of October 27, 1964. She had been strangled to death; the murder weapon was the stocking found around her neck. The immediate suspect in the case was the young Boston woman who was found standing in the hall outside Mrs. St. Clair's apartment shrieking hysterically.

The name of this young woman, a long-term mental patient, had cropped up in police files in the days after the murder of Patricia Bissette. An anonymous phone caller had informed police that this young woman had attempted to strangle a nurse while a patient at Boston State Hospital; she therefore might well be the Phantom Fiend.

After being taken into custody, this suspect was briefly questioned by Andrew Tuney of the Strangler Task Force. He reported to John Bottomly, who in turn wrote to Edward Brooke: "She was asked about the possibility of complicity in the other stranglings. She denied any connection with them. She recognizes that having confessed to this murder [of Mabel St. Clair] it would make little difference to her to admit involvement in other murders. She offered the opinion that the publicity about the Strangler probably influenced the method by which Mabel St. Clair was murdered."

The same publicity—and the template for homicide provided by the *Record American*'s "Strangle Work-sheet"—no doubt influenced others as well, including the person who murdered Effie MacDonald in Bangor, Maine, in March of 1965.

Serial killers tend to stick to a certain type of victim: Ted Bundy murdered young, white, very attractive college women who wore their hair long and parted in the center; John Wayne Gacy and Dean Corll murdered young white boys; Anthony Jackson chose young white female hitchhikers. Wayne Williams murdered young black males. Even Jack the Ripper confined himself to prostitutes. A serial killer still at large* in Tennessee victimizes only redheaded women.

The Boston strangling victims were young, middle-aged, old, white, black, Catholic, Protestant, and Jewish. The only similarity between them was that most had some connection, however tenuous, with the medical world, either as patient or practitioners. And virtually everyone falls into one category or the other—mostly the former—at some point in life.

Did Albert DeSalvo kill anyone? Possibly Mary Mullen, a name that does not appear on the roster of strangling victims but to whose murder he confessed anyway. DeSalvo told Bottomly that the eighty-five-year-old woman had admitted him to her apartment at 1435 Commonwealth Avenue in Brighton on June 28, 1962 after he explained he had been sent to do some work there.

Albert was not quite sure how it happened, but suddenly his arm was around her neck—prior to that they

---

* As of this writing.

had been chatting quite pleasantly—and then Mrs. Mullen was dead. He hadn't choked her (and indeed there were no marks of violence on her body); she had simply expired of heart failure.

Her death was attributed to natural causes.

When Virginia Thorner testified at Albert's 1967 Green Man trial, she claimed that he had stated to her in 1964 that he had killed an elderly woman, but that the authorities weren't aware of it.

His use of the singular here is important, because the deaths of six women over the age of fifty-five (counting the youthful-appearing Evelyn Corbin) were attributed to the Strangler. If Albert had killed them all, why cite just one—especially if his purpose in making this claim was to terrorize Mrs. Thorner into submission?

In the case of Mary Mullen, it seems most likely that Albert broke into her apartment with the intent to burglarize it, encountered Mrs. Mullen, and simply frightened her to death by his very presence. Overwhelmed by guilt—and Albert was prone to severe attacks of guilt*—he set Mrs. Mullen's body on the couch and fled without removing any valuables from her apartment.

And why would a man who had treated with such savage disrespect the corpses of Ida Irga, Jane Sullivan, and Helen Blake be so delicate in his treatment of the body of Mary Mullen? There is a logic even to extreme pathology—often a very rigid one—that does not exist here.

Albert's feeling of responsibility for the death of Mary Mullen—and if he *did* break into her apartment and inadvertently frighten her to death, he was under Massachusetts law technically guilty of a homicide com-

---

* A quality that again radically distinguishes him from the typical serial killer.

mitted in the perpetration of a felony—may have been one of the factors that drove him eventually to confess to the stranglings.

Mary Brown, who was raped, stabbed, strangled, and beaten to death in Lawrence sometime on the evening of March 5 or during the day on March 6, 1963, was not on the Strangler Task Force's original list of victims—she had, in fact, specifically been discounted. Her name was put back on the roster when Albert mentioned it, although Bottomly was not very interested in taking his confession to that crime. This was possibly because Albert's confession was not a very good one—he got many of the salient details wrong.

A number of authorities believe that Albert was given sketchy information about the murder of Mary Brown from the Bridgewater inmate who had actually committed that crime.

Mary Brown lived on Park Street in Lawrence, where Domenic Kirmil, the man shot to death by George Nassar in 1948, kept his shop.

For some former high-ranking Boston Police Department officials, the prime suspect in the death of Anna Slesers was someone very close to her, an individual who had the motive, means, and opportunity to kill her.

Anna's son, who had discovered her body and told police that he thought she had committed suicide, stated that although his mother would have considered herself presentable clad in a bathrobe, she would never have admitted a stranger to her apartment when she wasn't wearing her dentures.

She was without them when her body was found.

There were odd codas to three other of the murders. The agitated and disheveled man who had entered

Martin's Tavern in Lawrence at 4:30 on the afternoon of Joann Graff's murder had visited the bar two and a half hours earlier. He had asked then for a "Lucky" beer. Jules Vens, the proprietor of the tavern, had never heard of that brand. The man remarked that it was sold on the West Coast.

Fourteen months later, while interviewing strangling suspect Peter Burton at Bridgewater State Hospital, Ames Robey asked his patient if he drank. Burton replied, "Yeah, you know, beer." Robey asked him what his favorite brand was. Burton replied that it was Lucky Lager, sold only in California.

At the time of Joann's murder, Burton was living in New Hampshire. Lawrence is five miles from the state line.

On January 4, 1964, the day of Mary Sullivan's death, a young, light-haired man with a hysterical laugh walked into a bar on Charles Street, a few blocks down from the murder scene, and asked for a Lucky Lager.

On that same day, Peter Burton was getting married in Troy, New York.

On May 6, 1963, Arthur W. Barrows, a prime suspect in the murders of the elderly women, was freeloading in Harvard Square. A priest at Saint Paul's church recalls giving him $1.50 for food.

Beverly Samans, who took in waifs and strays and mental patients, had died only hours earlier.

An inmate of Bridgewater State Hospital, incarcerated there during the same period as were George Nassar, Albert DeSalvo, Peter Burton, and Arthur Barrows, states firmly that Albert DeSalvo was coached for his role as the Boston Strangler by another inmate who had actually committed the crimes, or some of them: "I was there when all of this was being put together," the man claims. "I was there in the prison yard sitting next to a tree as DeSalvo and [the other inmate] would talk each day. They would come out to the prison yard and sit next to a tree and [the other inmate] would tell DeSalvo things, like how he had inserted a bottle in one of the victims, what color a room was, or how the victim looked, or how old she was . . . Bottomly put two and two together and he knew then that [the other inmate] was his man. He wanted to save the public the money trying anyone, and what the hell, both [the other inmate] and DeSalvo were not going anyplace."

Dan Doherty, DeSalvo's social worker during his Walpole incarceration, says today that Albert never showed the slightest sign of violence: "He was a delightful rogue. There's no way he could have killed a girl." Doherty has had a lot of experience working with hard cases. "I had the Brink's guys and the wiseguys from the North End [members of the New England Mafia based in Boston] and Albert didn't fit in with them."

Doherty remembers asking one of the imprisoned Cosa Nostra soldiers if *he* believed DeSalvo was the killer of eleven women.

The curt response: "The Strangler's not Italian."

Doherty put the same question to another wiseguy and got the same answer.

The upper echelon of the Mafia held similar views. Speaking two years after Albert's death, Joseph "The Baron" Barboza commented disgustedly to an associate that some fool down at Walpole State Prison had taken the rap for being the Boston Strangler.

35

Last Moments

On a Sunday night in late November 1973, a few hours before he was stabbed to death in his quarters in the infirmary of the state prison at Walpole, Albert DeSalvo made at least two telephone calls. One of them, to his brother Richard, was lighthearted. The other was not.

Between the time he hung up the phone after speaking with Richard and the time he made his next call, something bad had happened—something that had terrified Albert. Either that, or he had been feigning his earlier jollity with Richard.

Ames Robey, who in 1973 was director of forensic psychiatry for the state of Michigan, had come back to Massachusetts the weekend after Thanksgiving to testify at a criminal trial unrelated to the stranglings. That Sunday night, he received a phone call from Albert. Albert had heard through the prison grapevine that Robey was back in the area.

It was ironic that the last known telephone call that DeSalvo would ever make would be to Ames Robey, whom DeSalvo had once despised for his refusal to

believe that he was the Strangler. DeSalvo obviously
had a change of heart, because he told Robey that he
wanted to see him as soon as possible. The matter was
one of great urgency.

"He was really scared," says Robey.

Robey agreed to meet Albert at the prison at 9:00
A.M. the following day.

It was never to be. Early Monday morning, as Robey
was finishing shaving and dressing, he flipped on the
radio. A news bulletin reported that Albert DeSalvo,
forty-two, had been found stabbed to death in his bed
at Walpole.

One story has it that Albert was killed in a fight over
two pounds of institutional bacon.

Another has it that Albert died in the aftermath of
a quarrel over drugs. Says a Walpole* inmate, "The
things in prison that are important to some cons are
dope, sex, and money. The cons that ran Walpole back
in the seventies used Mr. DeSalvo . . . They made him
the dope man. To a con that didn't know what was
going on, he was a big shot."

The inmate observes that the hard cases wielded tremendous power. "One word from one of these prisoners and you could end up hurt or dead. Sometimes,
they don't hurt you; they break you or use you." De-
Salvo, who enjoyed his illusory role as a big shot, wasn't
aware that he was actually being used.

"Most cons didn't like Albert to start with," the inmate continues, "even though we all knew he wasn't
the Strangler. One night one of the so-called tough
guys went to see Albert in his cell in the hospital unit
and asked Albert for some dope."

---

* The prison is now officially designated MCI-Cedar
  Junction.

DeSalvo's role as drug kingpin had gone to his head. "He reminded this guy that he had not paid his bill from the last few times. This con that wanted the drugs was a tough s.o.b., and had killed before, so he took out a knife and stabbed Albert and left him laying on the bed as if he fell asleep reading a book."

According to Ames Robey, Albert had asked one other person to meet him at Walpole that Monday morning—a reporter.*

Why?

"He was going to tell us who the Boston Strangler really was, and what the whole thing was about," says Robey.

And why had Albert been so frightened when he'd spoken to the doctor?

"He had asked to be placed in the infirmary under special lockup about a week before," Robey says. "Something was going on within the prison, and I think he felt he had to talk quickly. There were people in the prison, including guards, that were not happy with him."

And how had Albert's murder been arranged?

If it was an inmate who did the killing, Robey, who is very familiar with the prison layout, says the murderer "would have had to get out of one block, out of his cell, out of his corridor, out of his section, out of his whole ward down a hallway with two or three doors into the infirmary, in through the administration area, into the patient area, through that into the inner area, and then into Albert's room. All of which was always supposed to be kept locked. Somebody had to leave an awful lot of doors open, which meant,

---

* Robey never knew who this might be; Albert did not give a name.

because there were several guards one would have to go by, there had to be a fair number of people paid or asked to turn their backs or something. But somebody put a knife into Albert DeSalvo's heart sometime between evening check and the morning."

Bill O'Donnell, a senior corrections officer at Walpole during the time of DeSalvo's imprisonment, is another who is convinced the murder was drug-related: "The reason Albert was killed was because he was attempting to run a drug operation out of the hospital."

O'Donnell continues: "I knew Albert because the warden at Walpole felt he had been handed a hot potato [when DeSalvo was transferred there after his 1967 escape from Bridgewater]. He ordered DeSalvo to be kept in a cell in the hospital area, with a twenty-four-hour guard."

O'Donnell was the day guard. He got to know De-Salvo very well. "Albert was examined by many doctors," says O'Donnell. All of them concluded that Albert didn't have the personality of a psychopath typical of a serial killer.

One day DeSalvo and O'Donnell had the following conversation:

Out of the blue, Albert asked, "Do you believe I'm who they say I am?"

"Who's that?" O'Donnell replied, knowing full well but feigning innocence.

"The Boston Strangler," Albert said.

"Oh, Albert," O'Donnell said. "For Chrissake, you're no more the Boston Strangler than I am."

"Well, who do you think it was?" Albert asked.

O'Donnell named a name, that of DeSalvo's very close associate in prison.

Albert nodded. Neither he nor O'Donnell ever again raised the subject.

O'Donnell was off-duty the night DeSalvo was slain.

* * *

Three men were charged with Albert's murder and tried twice. Both times the trials ended in hung juries.

Says the Walpole inmate, "The man who killed Mr. DeSalvo has been free for years now and is still running around someplace out there . . . I can't give you his name. It wouldn't bring Albert back."

Other sources remain convinced that Albert's murderer is still incarcerated within the prison system.

The manuscript DeSalvo told his brother Richard that he was writing, the biographical document that would finally set straight the record of his life, was never found.

One of Albert's literary efforts, a poem, survives. It was composed several years before his death:

> Here is the story of the Strangler, yet untold,
> The man who claims he murdered thirteen women,
>   young and old.
> The elusive Strangler, there he goes,
> Where his wanderlust sends him, no one knows.
> He struck within the light of day,
> Leaving not one clue astray.
> Young and old, their lips are sealed,
> Their secret of death never revealed.
> Even though he is sick in mind,
> He's much too clever for the police to find.
> To reveal his secret will bring him fame,
> But burden his family with unwanted shame.
> Today he sits in a prison cell,
> Deep inside only a secret he can tell.
> People everywhere are still in doubt,
> Is the Strangler in prison or roaming about?

"Albert," says Ames Robey with a sigh, "was a showman."

Epilogue

This is what has happened to some of the principal actors in the Strangler drama:

Jon Asgeirsson practices law in Stoneham, Massachusetts.

F. Lee Bailey has law offices in Boston and West Palm Beach, Florida. In 1973 he was indicted for mail fraud and successfully defended by Alan M. Dershowitz. In 1976, after being found guilty on bank robbery charges, Patricia Campbell Hearst retained a new lawyer to challenge her conviction. Ms. Hearst maintained that Bailey had failed to represent her fully because his interests were engaged elsewhere. Although a lower court dismissed the claim, the Ninth U.S. Circuit Court of Appeals in San Francisco noted that Bailey had "created a potential conflict of interest" in seeking a publishing contract for a book about the Hearst case while it was ongoing. After his February 1982 arrest on drunken driving charges in San Francisco, charges against which he was successfully defended by Robert Shapiro, he wrote *How to Protect Yourself from Cops in California and Other Strange Places.*

Bailey is a commentator for *Court TV.* With Robert Shapiro, he participated in the defense of O. J. Simpson, accused of the double murder of Nicole Brown Simpson and Ronald Goldman.

John S. Bottomly was suspended in 1980 for six months from the practice of law in Massachusetts for mismanaging a trust. In 1968, he discovered that sixty thousand dollars' worth of bearer bonds was missing from his office, a fact that Bottomly did not bother to report to any of the trust's principals until several years later. In 1981, he was indicted for and found guilty of state tax evasion committed in 1973. The judge presiding over the disposition of both cases was Hiller Zobel, who in March 1967 had been appointed by the Boston Bar Association to investigate the professional conduct of F. Lee Bailey.

Bottomly died in 1984. Although he and his wife made restitution for the missing bearer bonds, the bonds themselves were never recovered.

Edward Brooke lost his Senate seat in 1978. He has a law office in Warrenton, Virginia.

Phillip J. DiNatale resigned from the Boston Police Department to accept an offer from Twentieth Century-Fox to serve as technical consultant on the 1968 film *The Boston Strangler.* He later became president of his own private detective agency. He died in 1987.

John Donovan, retired from the Boston Police Department, was most recently head of security for the College of the Holy Cross in Worcester, Massachusetts.

James McDonald, the Boston Police Department detective sergeant who investigated a number of the strangling murders, remains convinced that Albert De-

Salvo committed none of them. He is retired from security work in the private sector.

Edmund McNamara, who served ten years as Boston Police Commissioner, is retired from law enforcement.

John Moran is enjoying his leisure after thirty-two years with the Salem Police Department.

George Nassar, whose long association with Albert De-Salvo ended a month before the latter was slain, is an inmate at the Massachusetts Correctional Institution in Norfolk, Massachusetts. In 1968, the United States Supreme Court rejected his appeal for a new trial in the 1964 murder of Irvin Hilton.

Francis C. Newton, Jr., brought an action against F. Lee Bailey in 1971 to recover monies owed Albert De-Salvo as a result of the release he had signed to Gerold Frank. Over the next six years, Newton scheduled numerous appointments with Bailey in order to take the latter's deposition; unfortunately, Bailey always had to cancel these appointments at the last minute because of trial commitments. In 1977, four years after Albert's murder, Newton received a payment from Bailey of $47,761.37, which, less an eight-thousand-dollar fee to Bailey and a two-thousand-dollar fee to Newton (for six years' work) and other expenses, went into Albert's estate.

Mr. Newton practices law in Boston and pursues his avocation of Civil War studies.

Ames Robey practices psychiatry in Stoneham, Massachusetts, and consults on various criminal cases.

Thomas Troy practices law in Reading, Massachusetts.

Andre Tuney is chief investigator of the Kuhn Bureau of Investigation, Inc., in Lynn, Massachusetts. He has taught for the Learning Adventure in Boston a course called "Be Your Own Private Detective."

Update

On July 9, 1999, a front-page story in the *Boston Globe* reported that the Boston Police Department had announced it was searching for DNA evidence to establish whether Albert H. DeSalvo had actually committed the strangling murders that had terrorized the greater Boston area over three decades previously.

The probe had actually begun in the summer of 1998, when the BPD's Cold Case Squad examined fourteen boxes of evidence taken from the scenes of the crimes. "The Strangler case is one of the most notorious in the country," said Captain Timothy Murray to the *Globe*. "If we can solve this, it might just spark other cities to use DNA to solve old crimes. There's no statute of limitations on murder."

As of July 9, 1999, the police had been unable to locate some of the physical evidence known to have been preserved. Among these missing items were semen samples taken from some of the victims as well as the knife that had been used to stab Albert DeSalvo to death.

On November 7, 1999, Albert DeSalvo's son Michael gave an interview to the Boston CBS television news affiliate in which he called for Massachusetts law enforcement authorities to perform the DNA testing that might exonerate his father.

The Boston Police Department, however, seemed to have lost its enthusiasm for the project since the past July. A spokesperson for the department told the *Boston Herald* that "There is no biological evidence (from the women) that could give us a suspect. Things (evidence) get contaminated if you leave them out in the air."

Timothy Murray was promoted out of the Cold Case Squad.

In February 2000, Elaine Whitfield Sharp, a British-born Massachusetts attorney who, with her lawyer husband Dan, ran a practice out of Marblehead, received an e-mail from Professor James Starrs of George Washington University. Professor Starrs wondered if Sharp would be interested in working on the Boston Strangler case. Starrs added that if she would prefer not to be involved, she should notify him.

Sharp knew next to nothing about the Boston Strangler case. A vague recollection suggested to her that it might have taken place around the turn of the twentieth century. (She comments that as someone English-bred, she might have confused the Boston Strangler with Jack the Ripper.) Sharp did, however, know a great deal about Starrs, an internationally famous expert in forensic science. Sharp, a bulldog litigator with an interest in medico-legal work and a specialization in traumatic brain injury and police misconduct cases, also shared Starrs's professional interests: she had cocounseled or consulted in about sixty murder trials. Her highest-profile case to date was Commonwealth vs. Louise Woodward, in which she prepared the medical defense for the British au pair charged with the beating death of Matthew Eappen, infant son of Drs. Deborah and Sunil Eappen of Newton, Massachusetts. The trial made international headlines for nearly two years.

In October 1999, Sharp attended the annual meeting of the American Academy of Forensic Sciences in Reno, Nevada, where Starrs gave a talk on expert testimony and scientific evidence. After the speech Starrs, Sharp, Sharp's assistant, and a mutual friend had dinner, and later made a day trip to Virginia City, Nevada, to one of the city's famous graveyards. "A place which held an equal and mutual fascination," Sharp remarks.

Starrs, a relaxed man with a quick dry wit, had in his career undertaken to solve some of American history's great puzzles. He had spearheaded the effort to exhume the remains of explorer Meriwether Lewis, long thought to have died by his own hand, maintaining that the description of the gunshot wounds Lewis had died of—one in the head, the other in the chest— pointed to murder rather than suicide. Starrs led the team of scientists who performed the DNA testing on the body exhumed from the Kearney, Missouri, grave of Jesse James and concluded that the remains were 99 percent likely to be those of the legendary outlaw. This was disappointing news to Texas author Betty Duke, who claimed the real Jesse James was her great-grandfather James Lafayette Courtney, who died in 1943 at age ninety-six. In 1998, Starrs was granted access to the Washington, D.C., medical examiner's records to determine exactly how FBI Director J. Edgar Hoover had died. Starrs was dubious that Hoover— whose body had never been autopsied—died of a heart attack, since nothing in his medical history warranted such a diagnosis. "Hoover had numerous enemies in all walks of life," Starrs told the Associated Press. "The man's life was marked for death by all sorts of people."

Ambling about the Virginia City cemetery, Sharp told Starrs she'd like to work with him on an exhumation project. They agreed to join forces on the repatriation of an American member of the Abraham Lincoln Brigade killed during the Spanish civil war and buried in a mass grave. Starrs entered negotiations with the Spanish government to proceed with the exhumation while Sharp, a journalist before she entered law school, used her press contacts to publicize the effort.

"Given the events that follow[ed]," Sharp comments, "the repatriation project has not moved forward much."

She agreed to work with Starrs on the Strangler project. At Starrs's behest, she telephoned a relative of Mary Sullivan, the eleventh Strangler victim. This individual was having difficulty obtaining information about the Sullivan homicide from the Massachusetts Attorney General's office and from the Boston Police Department. Sharp received from him a copy of the hardcover edition of this book, read it, and decided on the basis of the information the book contained that the case should be reinvestigated, putting to use current forensic technology such as DNA testing.

Sharp met with Mary Sullivan's relatives and explained their rights to them under the Freedom of Information Act/Massachusetts Public Records Law (FOIA) and the Fair Information Practices Act (FIPA). She then decided that an alliance between the Sullivan survivors and the DeSalvo family might prove a powerful force in persuading the authorities to release the information about the homicide of Mary Sullivan. With this in mind, Sharp telephoned Timothy DeSalvo, Albert DeSalvo's nephew, who was resistant to her idea but nonetheless eventually suggested she call his father Richard.

Richard DeSalvo was, at first, Sharp says, "a bit hostile." Sharp understands why, given the previous experience Richard had had with some of the lawyers involved in the matter of Albert DeSalvo. As Sharp explained what she wanted to do, Richard seemed to soften. He spoke of his brother's murder, and of how Albert's corpse had been found hours after the commission of the crime.

"When a person dies, they stop bleeding, right?" Richard asked Elaine.

She said yes, that was indeed what happens.

"Well, there was blood all over the mattress and I think they [the prison authorities] left my brother to bleed to death," Richard replied bitterly.

At that moment, Sharp says, she knew she would do whatever was necessary to ease Richard's decades-old anguish.

She and Dan Sharp, who would serve as her cocounsel, visited Richard and Rosalie DeSalvo and their son Timothy at the DeSalvos' home in April 2000. A vital order of business was to have Richard and Rosalie sign a waiver of conflict of interest: the Sharps were representing the family of Albert's alleged victim Mary Sullivan as well; and suppose, after a thorough investigation was completed, it should emerge that Albert had indeed killed Mary? Insistent that all they wanted was the truth, Richard and Rosalie signed the waiver.

On May 11, 2000, the Sharps, the DeSalvos, and members of the Sullivan family held a press conference in Boston to announce their intent to reopen the Sullivan homicide. The goal, as Elaine Sharp explained to the media, was to exonerate Albert DeSalvo and, ideally, establish the identity of Mary's true killer. Timothy DeSalvo stepped forward and, in a statement prepared for him by Elaine, threw down the gauntlet: "Let the investigation begin and let the chips fall where they may."

The Sharps distributed copies of letters they had written to various law enforcement agencies, including the Suffolk County District Attorney's Office and the Massachusetts Attorney General's Office, requesting the release of materials these agencies held relating to the murder of Mary Sullivan.

Following the press conference, Massachusetts Attorney General Thomas Reilly told a reporter from the

Boston CBS news affiliate that he sympathized with the Sullivan and DeSalvo families and was inclined to grant their request for access.

On May 12, 2000, the Boston Police Department issued the following statement: "Due to the passage of time, the deterioration of the evidence, and the likelihood that successful testing cannot be performed on the evidence which remains in Boston Police custody, the Boston Police Department has declined to participate in further investigation into the Boston Strangler case."

On September 14, 2000, the families of Mary Sullivan and Albert DeSalvo announced that they had filed suit against Massachusetts Attorney General Thomas Reilly, the Boston Police Department, and other law enforcement agencies to compel the release of old evidence collected during the investigation of the murder of Mary Sullivan. Elaine and Dan Sharp would serve as cocounsel for the two families in the suit. James Starrs was on hand to oversee the scientific testing on whatever evidence was released. This did not appear likely to happen soon, if ever. According to Attorney General Reilly, Mary Sullivan's murder was unsolved—despite Albert DeSalvo's confession to it—and thus was an open case.

Nonetheless documents pertaining to it had leaked all over the place. Elaine Sharp obtained a copy of Mary Sullivan's autopsy report. She read it and compared it to DeSalvo's confession. The report stated that no spermatozoa had been found in Mary's vagina, nor had the hyoid bone in her neck been broken.

If Albert DeSalvo had strangled Mary manually, as he said in January 1965 he had, the hyoid bone would have been fractured. If he had penetrated her vagina with his penis, that too would have left its traces.

The Sullivan family had Mary's body exhumed in October 2000. At a funeral home in Marstons Mills,

Michael Baden reautopsied the corpse, a process that took more than eight hours. Elaine Sharp watched the procedure, which was recorded by a videographer.

No sign of trauma could be observed on Mary's skull. Albert DeSalvo had confessed to knocking her unconscious with a blow to the head before he strangled her.

Baden removed sixty-eight samples of hair, tissue, and possible semen from the body.

Subsequently Attorney General Reilly ordered DNA tests to be conducted on the evidence in the Sullivan homicide the A.G.'s office had retained in its custody. Investigators had found some long-missing case files, as well as semen samples taken from the crime scene.

In mid-November 2000 a Christmas card signed by Albert DeSalvo sold for $202.50 on the E-Bay Internet auction site. A letter written by DeSalvo sold for $600 at the same site, and, in late November, yet another letter went up for bid. The author, who so desperately wanted to be world-famous, could never have imagined such a thing happening.

U.S. District Court Judge William Young attempted, on December 14, 2000, to mediate between the Sullivan family and the DeSalvos and the law enforcement authorities of Massachusetts. "Why don't you give [the families the evidence] or at least share it with them?" Young asked Judy Kalman, Senior Counsel for the Attorney General's Office. "They want to hire their own people. Why not let them do that?"

Said Dan Sharp to the Boston Herald: "We have met with the Attorney General's Office and we have been given zip, zilch, zero, zed."

Kalman maintained the need for the A.G.'s office to

hold on to the evidence in the Sullivan case: "This is an open, ongoing criminal investigation."

Young urged Kalman and the Sharps to get together and work out their differences amicably. Negotiations were attempted; the attempts did not prove fruitful.

On February 20, 2001, Attorney General Reilly announced that DNA testing of the evidence in the Sullivan case had been "nonproductive." A second group of tests was being conducted, from which, Reilly told the press, he would expect results in another four weeks. The Sharps filed a motion in U.S. District Court demanding a halt to the state's testing. "The defendants are in the process of destroying evidence even as we speak," Dan Sharp stated.

James Starrs was attending the annual meeting of the American Academy of Forensic Science in Seattle, Washington. On Friday, February 23, he had called a press conference to discuss the results of the tests he had performed on the samples taken from Mary Sullivan's body. The announcement he made to the two hundred people gathered to hear him speak was, however, something no one in the audience anticipated. He said that he had been ordered by Judge Young not to talk.

Elaine Sharp was present. Masking her frustration, she turned to the members of her team and stated formally, "It is my duty to inform you that you are gagged." Young's order covered the attorneys as well as Starrs.

On February 28, 2001, Judge Young held a session at the Harvard Law School. During this proceeding he rejected the major counts in Attorney General Reilly's motions for dismissal of the lawsuit brought by the DeSalvo and Sullivan families.

The litigation continues. It appears nowhere near a speedy resolution.

How do the relatives of Albert DeSalvo and Mary Sullivan—other than those behind the lawsuit—feel about the reopening of the Strangler case? Distinctly unhappy, in several instances. Helen Sullivan Rapoza, Mary Sullivan's sister, was quoted in *Newsweek* (March 5, 2001) as telling Diane Sullivan Dodd, the sister behind the litigation, that "I hate what you've done. I don't want to talk about it." Albert DeSalvo's children are in favor of the effort to exonerate their father; most of Albert DeSalvo's siblings are unwilling to join in Richard's quest to clear his brother's name, although one brother, Joseph, has softened his opposition to the idea.

Kathleen Johnson, sister of Patricia Bissette, told *Newsweek* she could see no happy outcome to a reinvestigation of the murders: "I feel it can only cause more hurt. I wish they'd leave it alone."

In mid-April 2001 I received a letter from a man living in northern New England. He began the letter by asking if I were the Susan Kelly who had written *The Gemini Man,* and went on to hint that a close friend of his had information that might bear on the Strangler case. He provided his business address, voice-mail number, and e-mail address. He ended the letter by requesting that I e-mail him if I happened to be the Susan Kelly he sought.

For several days, I debated whether to do so. Over the years I had received a lot of mail from individuals claiming to know something crucial about the Strangler case. Almost none of them did. A good number of the writers appeared to be demented. Some were demented and venal: one correspondent demanded "a lot of money" before he would divulge a tale of how the FBI, the CIA, and a certain famed attorney conspired (in a Manhattan hotel room) to frame Albert DeSalvo for the stranglings. Interestingly, the late father of this person was an ex-police officer suspected by some of his colleagues of feeding details of the killings to DeSalvo while the latter was incarcerated at Bridgewater in later 1964 and early 1965.

I had also been harassed and threatened with a law-suit, although the harassment and threats came by tele-phone, and the harasser was a member of a news organization. This person felt I had secret information about the identity of the real killers, and wanted it.

The memory of such nonsense made me reluctant to make contact with the man who'd written to me in mid-April. Writer's curiosity being what it is, though, I finally did e-mail him. I should add that the letter I received from him was clearly the product of someone not only sane, literate, and intelligent but averse to personal publicity. And he didn't want money in ex-change for a story.

I sent him an e-mail letting him know he'd found the right Susan Kelly. He replied immediately. The cap-sule information he gave was, to say the least, intrigu-ing. Ultimately I agreed to meet him and his friend, at a restaurant in western Massachusetts of my choos-ing. I picked the place because I knew the people who owned it. If someone tried to kidnap me out of the parking lot, at least there'd be reliable witnesses to re-cord the license plate numbers and furnish accurate descriptions of the kidnappers. I let a good friend know where I was going and what I was going to be doing. I also told the friend I'd telephone when I re-turned from the meeting. Which I did.

Since they wish to remain anonymous, for the pre-sent, I'll call the people I met that Sunday afternoon Sarah and David. David was the letter writer. Sarah, his good friend, was the person who had the actual story to tell. Sarah, like David, was intelligent, highly edu-cated, articulate, and possessed of a sharp memory and an eye for detail. In other words, the perfect witness. The three of us hit it off immediately.

Here is Sarah's story.

In the summer of 1964 she was living in Cambridge,

Massachusetts, sharing an apartment with three other young women. That season a professional acquaintance of Sarah's father, like him a prominent Boston psychoanalyst, warned her to be careful: whatever party was responsible for the strangling murders that had taken place from June 1962 to January 1964 was still at large. Sarah—very young, very attractive, a student—fit the prototype of the second group of victims. So she should certainly take care.

I will refer to this psychoanalyst, whose identity is known to me, as Dr. G.

Sarah vividly recalls the warning he gave her. According to Dr. G., the strangler was a Harvard professor who had been arrested by the Cambridge police for beating his wife. Although unspecified authorities were positive he was the killer, there was insufficient evidence to pin the eleven murders on the man. Thus he was no longer in custody. So said Dr. G.

In the autumn of 1964, in conversation with Dr. G., Sarah raised the subject of the Harvard professor. To her shock, he denied ever discussing it with her. He denied it, she recalls, quite vehemently.

On March 30, 2001, David had done some intensive research of his own. He visited the Cambridge Police Department and asked to inspect their journals from late 1963 to August 1964. He was seeking the record of an arrest for wife-beating (it wasn't called domestic violence back then) that might have corresponded to the one described—and subsequently denied—by Dr. G. What David found was that the journal was meticulously kept. With the following exception: some of the pages for November and December 1963 were loose rather than bound, and out of chronological order. Some had been tucked beneath the front cover of the journal.

There were no entries for arrests or incidents happening between November 29, 1963, and December 20, 1963. In David's words: "Considering how meticulously these records were kept and the fact that their current availability at the time must have required that they be sequentially bound each day, this is unlikely to be an error by the clerk who typed the archival version of the pages. It seems like a good hypothesis that pages were excised at the time, and, after that occurred, the dutiful record keeper started the next day's December entry on the last available clean page, which in this case happened to be on the back of a finished November day." David, someone naturally endowed with investigative ability, adds that "the missing pages could be historically important since they fall between the murders of Joann Graff and Mary Sullivan."

David also noted that in March 1964 the journal notes a case marked "confidential" and assigned to the Bureau of Criminal Investigation. No hint of what crime the case might involve, who victim and perpetrator might be, is provided.

I explained to Sarah and David that cases thus marked, where no public information is given, usually involve sex crimes.

A point to bear in mind: Albert DeSalvo, who confessed to eleven murders and claimed to have committed two thousand rapes, never confessed to a sexual assault in Cambridge in March 1964. Nor was he charged with such an offense.

One wonders why the Cambridge police journal entries from the November–December period are missing. It is possible they were removed by the state police. At my request, the matter is being investigated. Perhaps the missing pages will reappear, as well as the confidential file from March 1964. Probably not. Except for unsolved homicides, the Cambridge Police Department, like virtually all police departments, routinely destroys the records of all cases after a certain period of time.

Since no one on the Cambridge police force ever seriously believed that Albert DeSalvo murdered Cambridge resident Beverly Samans in May 1963, that case remains officially open. As I've mentioned before, the principal suspect in that murder has long since died.

Final note: Sarah has been a lifelong friend of one of Albert DeSalvo's sexual assault victims. Many years ago, Sarah reports, this woman had a dream in which DeSalvo appeared to her and asked her forgiveness. She gave it. The following morning she learned from the news that he had been stabbed to death in prison.

Since 1995, the following people, who contributed so much to this book, have died:

Former Boston Police Department Commissioner
    Edmund McNamara
Attorney Thomas Troy
Former Massachusetts and United States Attorney
    General Elliot Richardson
Former Massachusetts Governor Endicott Peabody
Former Cambridge Police Detective James Roscoe
George Higgins

F. Lee Bailey has suffered some serious reversals since 1995. In March 1996 he was sentenced by U.S. District Court Judge Maurice Paul to six weeks in a Tallahassee, Florida, jail on a contempt of court charge, specifically for failing to turn over to the government 400,000 shares of stock owned by one of the lawyer's former clients, international drug trafficker Claude DuBoc. In January 2000, in Orlando, Florida, U.S. Magistrate James Glazebrook recommended that Bailey be held in contempt on a similar matter: a refusal to hand over to the federal government two million dollars in legal fees from client William McCorkle, infomercial king and convicted swindler. Said Judge Glazebrook: "[Bailey] has no right to accept fraudulently obtained and laundered money in payment of a fee." Glazebrook further stated that while Bailey was being cross-examined, he "rarely gave a straight answer. The privilege to practice law is not a license to share in the proceeds of fraud."

From May 30 to June 5, 2000, Collier County (Florida) Circuit Court Judge Cynthia Ellis refereed disciplinary proceedings against Bailey. The complainant was the Florida Bar. In her Amended Report of Referee, Judge Ellis recommended that Bailey be disbarred from practicing law in Florida on the grounds that he had committed the following violations:

- Commingling of Client Funds which were to be held in trust with the Lawyer's personal funds and failure to maintain the client funds in a specifically identified lawyer's trust account.
- Misappropriation of Client trust funds and failure to maintain said funds in a separate trust account.
- Misuse and misappropriation of client funds and disobedience of a court order and dishonest conduct before a tribunal.
- Violation of the rules prohibiting dishonesty and false statements to a tribunal.
- Violation of the rules proscribing conduct which creates a conflict of interest with the client.
- Disclosure of confidential communication without authorization of the client.
- Use of information obtained during the course of representation to the disadvantage of the client.

—In the Supreme Court of Florida (Before a Referee); Case No. SC96767, TFB Number 1996-51,085 (15B), 1997-50, 110 (15A). Complainant: The Florida Bar vs. Respondent: F. Lee Bailey, p. 20.

Furthermore, Judge Ellis wrote,

The Court finds the following aggravating factors to be present under Standard 9.22 of the Florida Standards for Imposing Lawyer Sanctions

- 9.22(b) dishonest or selfish motive
- 9.22(c) a pattern of misconduct
- 9.22(d) multiple offenses
- 9.22(f) submission of false statements
- 9.22(g) refusal to acknowledge the wrongful nature of conduct
- 9.22(i) substantial experience in the practice of law
    Ibid., pp.20–21

Ellis concluded her withering assessment by writing that "Indeed, since the disciplinary actions noted above, Chief Judge Paul and Magistrate Judge Glazebrook and this Referee have had numerous opportunities to assess and characterize the demeanor and credibility of the Respondent. In each instance, the various Judges and Justices have employed circumspect and eloquent ways of saying the same thing: The Respondent is a liar . . . At the end of the day, the Respondent has forfeited his privilege to practice law in the state of Florida. Frankly, it is difficult for this referee to conceive of a more egregious set of circumstances than those which Mr. Bailey has brought upon himself."
Ibid., p. 23.

The day before Thanksgiving 2001, F. Lee Bailey was disbarred in Florida.

What of Albert DeSalvo's other attorneys?
Jon Asgeirsson has told Elaine Sharp that he is suffering from Alzheimer's disease.
Francis C. Newton, Jr., is a judge.

In the spring of 2001 someone gave me a copy of an interesting document: a transcript of an "interrogation" of Albert DeSalvo conducted at Bridgewater State Hospital on March 6, 1965. This was not an interrogation made by a police officer or other law enforcement official. March 6, 1965, was one of the days F. Lee Bailey visited Albert DeSalvo at Bridgewater. At the top of the document is a handwritten note partially cut off by the photocopying process. What is visible of the inscription reads "Bai Tape."

The transcript consists of a series of questions posed to DeSalvo about the murders of Anna Slesers, Ida Irga, Nina Nichols, Helen Blake, and Sophie Clark. The document is jumbled and oddly annotated: next to the typed heading of a portion of the transcript that identifies it as detailing the murder of Nina Nichols is handwritten "Ida Irga." Whether this is a correction is difficult to determine. A footnote to the dialogue about Helen Blake states that the "rest of the tape did not record."

The Helen Blake discussions preserved in the transcript contain, nonetheless, some striking passages. One occurs when Albert DeSalvo describes his rape of Blake: "She was a well-built woman, and I picked her up, took off her clothes, and rather than doing anything more to her, took off her clothes and had intercourse with her."

The autopsy of Helen Blake found no spermatozoa present in either her vagina or her rectum.

The autopsy additionally found that the ligatures around Blake were a bra, tied in front, and two stockings tied at the nape. DeSalvo was quite clear on March 6, 1965, that the reverse was true.

The Sophie Clark portion of the March 1965 transcript contains equally interesting details. The interrogator asks DeSalvo what he did with Sophie's half-slip.

A: I put it around her throat.
Q: What color was it?
A: A white one, if I'm not mistaken.

Q: Okay, that's it.
Q: Is that it? Is that right?

Surely a killer with a much-vaunted photographic memory should have recalled such a detail. And not have demanded assurance that his memory hadn't played him false.

On page eighteen of John Bottomly's personal transcript of Tape One of DeSalvo's confession to the murder of Sophie Clark, recorded on August 24, 1965, Bottomly notes that Albert has already viewed the police photographs of the crime scene.* The March 6, 1965, transcript of the interrogation of DeSalvo at Bridgewater records the following dialogue about the murder of Helen Blake.

Q: If you stand in the middle of the bedroom door looking in, where would the bed be?
A: To your right.
Q: What kind of bed was it? Now c'mon . . .
A: Let's see. The bed would be . . . yes, the bed would be to your right. I've got the picture now. I've got the picture now, and the dresser would be to your left. The dresser to your left, the bed to your right, and there was windows there, because one was half open.

A distinct picture forms in the mind of whoever reads the above passage, and the picture is not a pretty one.

---

* No experienced ethical professional interrogator would ever show photos of a crime scene to the suspect and then take the suspect's confession.

The lawsuit of the DeSalvo and Sullivan families against the Attorney General of Massachusetts is set for trial in June 2002. Elaine Sharp considers using the following quote from Shakespeare's *Rape of Lucrece* in her closing argument.

> Time's Glory is to calm contending kings
> To unmask falsehood and bring truth to light
> To stamp the seal of time in aged things
> To wake the morn and sentinel the night
> To wrong the wronger till he render right
>   To ruinate proud buildings with thy hours
>   And smear with dust their glitt'ring golden
>   towers.

Shortly after eight on the morning of October 26, 2001, the body of Albert DeSalvo was exhumed from a cemetery in Peabody, Massachusetts. I was present, as were Elaine Sharp, Richard and Rosalie DeSalvo, and Timothy DeSalvo. James Starrs oversaw the procedure; he and his daughter-in-law and assistant Traci Starrs recorded data as the grave was opened and the coffin raised. Videographer Mitchell Calhoun and photographer Gaetan Cotton documented every step of the process.

Kevin Watts and Leo Barry of the John-Lawrence Funeral Home in Marstons Mills, Massachusetts—the funeral home that had provided, free of charge, the facilities for the autopsy of Mary Sullivan—loaded the casket into the back of a black SUV. Just before the door of the SUV was closed, Timothy DeSalvo kissed his right hand and laid it on the casket to wish the earthly remains of his uncle Godspeed.

There was no way to tell that the SUV was a hearse except by looking at its license plate. The choice of an innocuous vehicle was deliberate: Elaine Sharp and the DeSalvos wanted to attract as little attention as possible.

After some business was finished at the cemetery office, the convoy—the hearse in the lead, Gaetan Cotton, Elaine Sharp, and I in a bright red SUV loaded with photographic equipment, and James Starrs, Traci Starrs, and Mitchell Calhoun in a black pick-up truck equally loaded with photographic equipment—set off for Pennsylvania. The autopsy of Albert DeSalvo would be performed at York College of Pennsylvania.

The purpose of the autopsy would be twofold: to recover physical evidence that might lead to the solution of the 1973 murder of DeSalvo and the 1964 murder of Mary Sullivan. The York College site for the procedure had been chosen because it was convenient for the many experts being called in from various parts of the country to participate.

There was already considerable certainty that Albert DeSalvo had not—as he insisted he had—murdered Mary Sullivan. Tests on the samples of material taken from her body compared with samples of mitochondrial DNA taken from Richard DeSalvo indicated this. Tests run on nuclear DNA extracted from the tissue of Albert DeSalvo himself would merely affirm those results.

The mood of everyone in the convoy—we communicated vehicle to vehicle by walkie-talkie—was tense, punctuated by moments of hilarity. The drive south through Massachusetts had everyone a little on edge. Would the press find out and follow us? Would we be stopped by law enforcement? The latter possibility was remote, but hovered nonetheless. In exhuming DeSalvo's corpse and transporting it out of state, could we be said to be tampering with the evidence in an ongoing criminal investigation?

We crossed the border into Connecticut and stopped for breakfast to celebrate. "It's like a road trip with friends," Leo Barry remarked. "And then you remember what we're doing." That knowledge was with us every time we made a rest stop during the ten-hour journey. We would glance at tourists in their RVs, stretching their legs, walking their dogs, eating burgers, and think, "You have no idea of what's in the cargo bay of that black SUV."

One of the convoy vehicles ran low on gas in New York and made an urgent plea by walkie-talkie to get off at the next exit and seek a service station. The exit we took led to the Poughkeepsie airport. "There has to be a gas station around here somewhere," someone said. After a half mile we ran into a traffic jam. As the cars ahead of us inched along, I noticed a huge roadside sign. It read HIGH SECURITY AREA. ALL VEHICLES SUBJECT TO SEARCH. I looked over at Gaetan Cotton, who was driving. Judging by the expression on his face, he had also noticed the sign. So had the passengers in the other two vehicles. As one, the hearse, the truck, and our SUV pulled out of line, U-turned, and sped back to the highway. When we did stop for gas twenty minutes later everyone rolled out of the cars laughing uncontrollably. It was the hysteria of relief.

"What would you have done?" I asked Kevin Watts. "If the police had told you to open the . . ."

He closed his eyes and shook his head slowly. "I don't want to think about it."

Night had fallen by the time we drove up to the rear entrance of the York College building where the autopsy would take place. John (Jack) Levisky, a professor of anthropology, was waiting to admit us. Kevin Watts and Leo Barry rolled the casket on a wheeled gurney into the building and onto an elevator. Gaetan Cotton and Mitchell Calhoun swarmed like paparazzi with their cameras. It was essential that every step of the process be photographed. Cotton and Calhoun would indeed film the autopsy from beginning to end.

There was a Halloween moment when the casket was brought into the biology laboratory. The doorway was too narrow to accommodate the steel box horizontally; it had to be upended and tilted slightly sideways. "Oh,

God," someone said, echoing everyone's fear. "I hope it doesn't pop open." It didn't. The casket was settled in the lab. Everyone grouped around and stared at it for a moment.

Leaving the building, we followed a Hansel and Gretel trail of fluid that had dripped from the casket—a combination of ground water, formaldehyde, and other substances no one particularly wished to identify closely. The stench made me gag; I yanked the turtleneck of my dress up over my nose to filter out the smell.

We piled back into our cars and went to a restaurant. Some of the other members of the forensic team joined us: Major Timothy Palmbach, a crime scene specialist from the Connecticut State Police; Professor Michael Warren, Deputy Director of the C.A. Pound Human Identification Laboratory at the University of Florida; and James (Jack) Frost, Deputy Chief Medical Examiner for the State of West Virginia. Just after the first round of drinks had arrived, a pleasant man named Scott Koscevic, the sales manager of Yorktowne Caskets, appeared. In his van he had a Ziegler container (a sealed metal case) in which what would be left of DeSalvo after the autopsy would be placed and sealed in the casket for reburial. The company had been kind enough to donate the container. A moment before the salad course was served, Kevin Watts, Leo Barry, and Koscevic went to the parking lot to transfer the container to the hearse. Another Halloween moment.

The autopsy began at eight on Saturday morning, October 27. I was present for most of it.

Richard DeSalvo, convinced from the start that his brother was not the Boston Strangler, had taken great pains to insure that Albert's body was preserved against the day when an exhumation might prove necessary—

as it had twenty-eight years later. The embalmed corpse had been placed in a twelve-gauge steel casket and then into a plastic-lined concrete vault. Despite these precautions, the body had deteriorated in the course of nearly three decades. The face was unrecognizable as such, except for the thrust of Albert's protuberant nose; it was a mask of some crusty black substance shortly afterward identified as the husks of maggots. Along with ground water, beetles had entered the casket and done their work. Ironically, the suit in which DeSalvo had been buried was in nearly perfect condition.

Starrs had assembled an all-star team to perform the autopsy and tests on materials extracted from the corpse. In addition to Frost, Levisky, Warren, Palmbach, and Traci Starrs were forensic specialists Michele Hamburger, Sherry Brown, and Barbara Hanbury; pathologists Michael Baden and Patricia Aronica-Pollak; odontologist John McDowell; geophysicist George Stephens; radiographers Michael and Susan Calhoun (brother and sister-in-law of videographer Mitchell Calhoun); toxicologist Bruce Goldberger; microscopist Walter F. Rowe; radiologist G. Brogden; entomologist Neal Haskell; researcher Matthew Mantel; and attorney Linda Kenney as well as Sean Brebbia, Starrs's legal assistant.

After pausing for a brief two P.M. lunch break—catered from a local McDonald's by Elaine Sharp, who removed her scrubs long enough to make the food run—the autopsy continued until six that evening. It was an exquisitely choreographed ballet of necrosis: Frost and Aronica-Pollak performing the actual autopsy, the others receiving and readying the materials removed from the corpse for further testing.

The day's work ended at six P.M. At that moment the energy and purpose that had buoyed each member of the forensic team seemed to escape like air from a leaky balloon. I stood next to one of the team members as she slumped back against a counter and stripped off her surgical mask. "I want a shower," she said. "Then a restaurant. And a bar, and a bar, and a bar . . ."

It was a sentiment echoed by everyone else on the team.

We went to an Italian restaurant and consumed large quantities of food and wine. Afterward, most team members returned to their motels and collapsed into bed. A few went to a pre-Halloween celebration in York. One of them danced with a fellow costumed as the Frankenstein monster. It seemed, under the circumstances, quite appropriate.

At eleven on Sunday morning, the forensic team held a press conference on a lawn outside the York College Music, Arts, and Communications Center. James Starrs, wearing a white medical coat and a George Washington University baseball cap, took center stage. He promised the assembled reporters "blockbuster" results from the Albert DeSalvo autopsy and "many rewards" for the DeSalvo family.

Back in Massachusetts, Attorney General Thomas Reilly, asked to comment on the weekend events, termed the autopsy "a macabre stunt." George Burke, the retired Norfolk County (Massachusetts) District Attorney who had twice prosecuted Carmen Gagliardi, Robert M. Wilson, and Richard L. Devlin for DeSalvo's 1973 prison murder, told the *Boston Globe* that there was no mystery about Albert's homicide. Both trials ended in hung juries and mistrials. According to Burke, authorities decided not to pursue the matter further because Gagliardi, Devlin, and Wilson were already serving long prison sentences. Gagliardi would in fact die of a heroin overdose shortly after the second trial.

And why had DeSalvo been murdered? Again according to Burke, to prevent him from muscling in on the drug trade flourishing in Walpole State Prison.

* * *

On Monday, October 29, 2001, Albert DeSalvo's remains were reinterred at the Puritan Lawn Cemetery in Peabody, Massachusetts. Elaine Sharp bought flowers for the service and located a minister to perform it—the Reverend Patricia Long of the United Church of Christ in Marblehead.

Like the day of the exhumation, the day of the reburial was a beautiful one, warm and sunny with a panoply of autumn foliage spread out against a lapis sky. Present were Richard and Rosalie DeSalvo; Timothy DeSalvo, his wife Cheryl, and their children; Richard and Rosalie's other son, daughter, and son-in-law; James Starrs; British journalist Noel Young; Mitchell Calhoun; Gaetan Cotton; Elaine Sharp; Dan Sharp; Michael DeSalvo, the only son of Albert DeSalvo; and me.

The service was brief, dignified, and very moving. Reverend Long read two psalms, a prayer of her own composition for the repose of the soul of Albert DeSalvo, and asked the mourners to join her in the Lord's Prayer.

Timothy and Cheryl's four children each carried a single rose. At the end of the service, they approached the casket and set the flowers atop. Elaine Sharp followed with the bouquets she had purchased earlier that morning. The casket was lowered into the ground. Cemetery attendants began immediately to fill the hole with earth.

"Daddy," piped one of Timothy's sons, "what did Albert DeSalvo do?"

Timothy looked at the boy for a moment and then rested a hand on his head.

"Someday," he said. "When you're older."

On December 6, 2001, James Starrs held a press conference in Washington, D.C., to announce the final results of the tests that had been conducted on the materials taken from the remains of Mary Sullivan and Albert DeSalvo. Accompanying Starrs were George Washington University Professor David Foran, who, with his post-graduate team of assistants, had done the DNA profiling; Michael Baden, who had compared the Sullivan autopsy report with DeSalvo's confession to the murder; and University of Florida Professor Bruce Goldberger, who had performed toxicological studies.

Goldberger's findings indicated that no drugs or alcohol were present in Mary Sullivan's system when she died. Baden outlined the discrepancies in DeSalvo's confession. Foran's test results showed the presence of two different DNA samples—one taken from Mary Sullivan's pubic area, the other from the underwear put on the body at the funeral home. Neither sample matched the DNA of Albert DeSalvo.

Since 1928, the Times Square ticker has kept New Yorkers informed of all major news—the end of World War II, the death of John F. Kennedy, the moon landing, etc. On December 7, 2001, the 369-foot moving sign carried a message that surely startled many viewers. It read ALBERT DESALVO NOT THE BOSTON STRANGLER.

The old showman would have loved seeing his name in lights.

Update: 2013

June 14, 2012, marked the fiftieth anniversary of the murder of Anna Slesers. Her death was the first in a series of homicides that would come to be attributed in the press, and in popular imagination, to the "Boston Strangler."

Since this book was last updated in 2002, after the exhumation of Albert DeSalvo in October 2001 to be autopsied again and for DNA testing, a number of events important to the case have occurred. Not one of these events remotely suggests that DeSalvo was the Boston Strangler. In fact, most of them strongly indicate that he was innocent of the crimes for which he was charged and convicted only in the court of public opinion.

First, though, I have to note the passing of some of the principal actors in the Strangler drama, which has played out over five decades and still continues to run.

Ames Robey, the forensic psychiatrist who first met Albert DeSalvo when the latter was held at Bridgewater State Hospital after his November 1964 arrest, died on September 23, 2004. Dr. Robey, who was one of the last people—if not the last person—to speak with DeSalvo before DeSalvo's death, maintained to the end of his own life that the Malden, Massachusetts, handyman who had gained worldwide notoriety by confessing to the stranglings never committed a single murder. The doctor always recalled that DeSalvo, who had called Robey from prison, sounded terribly frightened about something. There was good reason, given that he was stabbed to death several hours later.

Jon A. Asgeirsson, who became DeSalvo's lawyer in November 1964, died on December 9, 2009. To my knowledge, Asgeirsson declined to speak publicly about the Strangler case after I interviewed him in December 1991. Whatever his private thoughts were about his client's guilt or innocence, he took them to his grave. He and his most famous client are buried in the same cemetery—though not in proximity.

Daniel Sharp, who with his wife and law partner, Elaine Whitfield Sharp, spent a substantial part of the last ten years of his life trying to establish in the courts the facts of the Boston Strangler case, died on February 13, 2010. Elaine Sharp continues to work on behalf of the DeSalvo family.

The Honorable Francis C. Newton Jr., DeSalvo's last lawyer, died on February 6, 2012. After a thirty-year career in the United States Army, the Massachusetts Army National Guard, and the U.S. Army Reserve, he retired as a colonel. In 2011, he retired from the legal field as an administrative law judge in the Social Security Administration. Judge Newton was always firm in stating his belief that Albert DeSalvo was innocent of committing any murders.

On July 25, 2012, I spoke with former FBI agent Mark Safarik. After twenty-three years with the Federal Bureau of Investigation, Safarik retired in 2007 as a senior member of the Behavioral Analysis Unit (BAU). He was also a supervisory special agent at the National Center for the Analysis of Violent Crime (NCAVC) at the FBI Academy. At present, he is a partner with Robert Ressler in Forensic Behavioral Services, a consulting firm in Virginia.

In the course of his career, Safarik has researched the

rape-murders of over five hundred elderly women. He has published several scholarly papers on the subject in the *Journal of Forensic Sciences,* the *Journal of Forensic Nursing, Homicide Studies: An Interdisciplinary & International Journal,* and elsewhere.

The first four women to be murdered in the summer of 1962, whose deaths came to be attributed to a putative Boston Strangler, ranged in age from fifty-five to seventy-five. Safarik has established a profile of the kind of man who sexually assaults and kills older women.

"Despite age, race, and culture, the offenders who sexually assault and murder older women—the mean age of these offenders is twenty-seven," Safarik said. "After the age of thirty, they really drop off sharply. The most violent offenders are fifteen to twenty-four years of age. They likely have a substance abuse problem. Most of their previous crimes are misdemeanor crimes—burglary, drug possession, larceny, public disturbance, and prowling. They generally live close to the crime scene, so that they can stay in their neighborhoods, their comfort zones. Eighty-one percent of them come to the crime scene on foot, and they leave on foot."

Safarik continued: "Ninety-three percent are unskilled. Seventy percent are unemployed. Seventy percent were never married. They don't have wives and girlfriends. They rarely engage in postmortem activity with the victim that would be described as ritual in nature, posing her, adding clothing items to her. These offenders generally leave the woman in whatever position they last interacted with them, usually when they finish interacting with them sexually. Socially, they're not competent. Sexually, they're not competent, with investigators finding semen at the crime scene less than fifty percent of the time. They often live with a mother or grandmother, and they resent that loss of control that comes from being dependent on an older woman for shelter, food, and money."

Did Albert DeSalvo match this profile? According to Safarik, "DeSalvo does not fit the template. If he was the

Boston Strangler, he would be an extreme outlier for this type of offender."

Indeed, he would be. DeSalvo was married, had children, had no substance abuse problems, was generally employed or seeking work, and lived with his family miles from any of the crime scenes. And, by 1962, he had aged well out of the cohort most responsible for the rapes and murders of elderly women.

Safarik pointed out another fact that undermines the belief that the Boston stranglings were serial killings committed by the same person. "White offenders offend almost exclusively against white females. They don't cross the racial barrier. Black females who are killed are—again, almost exclusively—killed by black men."

Sophie Clark, the sixth strangling victim, was a student. She was very young, she was beautiful, and she was of African ancestry. The possibility that she was murdered by the man or men responsible for the stranglings of the four older white women who preceded her in death is virtually nonexistent.

George Nassar, who first met Albert DeSalvo while the two were held at Bridgewater State Hospital, and remained a strong and influential presence in DeSalvo's life thereafter, continues to serve his sentence on the first-degree murder charge of which he was convicted in 1967. His appeals for a new trial have been turned down by the courts.

As I noted in the first update to this book, F. Lee Bailey was disbarred in Florida in 2001. In June 2002, the Supreme Court of the United States issued the following opinion: *F. Lee Bailey, having been suspended from the practice of law in this Court by order of March 18, 2002; and a rule having been issued and served upon him requiring him to show cause why he should not be disbarred; and the time*

*to file a response having expired; It is ordered that F. Lee Bailey
is disbarred from the practice of law in this Court. (IN THE
MATTER OF DISBARMENT OF F. LEE BAILEY, D-2291,
SUPREME COURT OF THE UNITED STATES, 536 U.S. 936,
122 S. Ct. 2650; 153 L. Ed. 2d 827; 2002 U.S. LEXIS 4674.
Judges: Rehnquist, Stevens, O'Connor, Scalia, Kennedy, Souter,
Thomas, Ginsburg, Breyer.)*

On December 3, 2001, a petition for reciprocal disci-
pline regarding Bailey was filed in the Supreme Judicial
Court of Massachusetts for Suffolk County. One justice
of the Massachusetts SJC judged that Bailey be disbarred
in Massachusetts. On April 11, 2003, the SJC affirmed this
judgment, pointing out: *[T]he fact that Bailey had committed such grave misconduct despite his vast experience as a seasoned
litigator only serves to heighten the seriousness of his offenses.*

Among the instances of what the Florida court termed
Bailey's "egregious and cumulative misconduct" were the
following: offering false testimony, violating a client's
confidences, violating two federal court orders, engaging
in ex parte communications, and trust account violations. The latter entailed the commingling and misappropriation of funds. The Florida court also concluded that
such offenses, in "the absence of any mitigating factors,"
necessitated disbarment. Said the Massachusetts court: "We
agree." (*IN THE MATTER OF F. LEE BAILEY, SJC-08764,*
SUPREME JUDICIAL COURT OF MASSACHUSETTS,
439 Mass. 134; 786 N.E.2d 337; 2003 Mass. LEXIS 268.)

Bailey requested of the United States District Court for
the District of Massachusetts an evidentiary hearing on
this matter. On November 5, 2005, his request was denied,
and he was disbarred. On June 9, 2006, the United States
Court of Appeals for the First Circuit affirmed this judgment: *The court held that, even assuming that the attorney could
prove that the stock was not transferred to him in trust, such
proof would not adequately undermine the states' rationale for
disbarment because the disbarment hinged on a finding that the
attorney appropriated the funds without prior court approval.*

(*IN RE: F. LEE BAILEY, Appellant. No. 05-2779,* UNITED STATES COURT OF APPEALS FOR THE FRIST CIRCUIT, 450 F.3d 71; 2006 U.S. App. LEXIS 14189.)

In February 2009, Bailey was invited to speak on the topic of ethics and the law at Wellesley College. At present, he lives in Maine, where he and his girlfriend, Debbie Elliott, a former cosmetologist, operate a consulting firm. Bailey & Elliott Consulting offers a variety of services, including expert advice on financial matters.

Edward Brooke, attorney general of Massachusetts during the Boston Strangler case, and later United States senator from Massachusetts, lives in Virginia with Anne, his second wife. A breast cancer survivor, he has advocated for awareness of the disease in men.

On June 20, 2000, the Edward W. Brooke Courthouse in Boston, a Massachusetts trial court, was dedicated. A Boston charter school was founded in his name in 2002. In 2004, Brooke was awarded the Presidential Medal of Freedom by George W. Bush. In 2006, the Massachusetts Republican Party instituted the Edward Brooke Award for distinguished service. Its first recipient was Andrew Card, the former White House chief of staff for the forty-third president. In 2009, Brooke received the Congressional Gold Medal.

In an article published in the *Boston Globe* on June 14, 2012—fifty years to the day since Anna Slesers was murdered—reporter Martine Powers quoted Brooke as saying: *"Even to this day, I can't say with certainty that the person who ultimately was designated as the Boston Strangler was the Boston Strangler."* He added, *"I'll probably go to my grave not knowing for sure."*

In June 2012, several news agencies reported that 139 Blue Hill Avenue in Roxbury—the house in which sixty-year-old Margaret Davis, a purported Strangler victim, had been murdered and found dead—was due for demolition. These press reports were inaccurate on two counts.

According to the initial police reports and follow-up investigative reports on the case, Margaret Davis died in room 7 of the Hotel Roosevelt on Washington Street in Boston. She had checked into the hotel on July 10, 1962. She and her male companion had used the names "Mr. and Mrs. Byron Spinney." Chambermaid Eva Day found Davis's body the following day. Byron Spinney, who had given a false name and a false address to the hotel clerk, was nowhere to be found. Davis herself had a number of pseudonyms or street names, among them "Anne Cunningham," "Annie Oakley," "Winnie Hughes," and "Tobey." An itinerant, she may have spent some time at the house on Blue Hill Avenue, but she certainly didn't die there.

In some ways, the second issue is an even larger one. Was Davis even a Strangler victim? The police working on her case didn't think she was. An August 18, 1964, progress report by the Strangler Task Force, working out of Edward Brooke's office, noted that Davis most likely died as a result of a fight with her companion, Byron Spinney. Spinney himself had vanished back into whatever netherworld from which he'd briefly emerged on July 10, 1962.

Again, the Davis case was another illustration of the way in which any unsolved murder of a woman in the Boston area during the early and mid-1960s would come, in the public mind, to be attributed to a single killer—and later to Albert DeSalvo.

During an autopsy, the internal organs are removed from the body, examined for visible disease, defect, or injury, and weighed. Samples may be taken for microscopic analysis or other tests. The organs are then placed in a plastic bag and returned to the body cavity, or bagged and placed in the coffin. By law, the body of the decedent and all its parts belong to the survivors.

Albert DeSalvo's first autopsy took place after his November 1973 murder in the infirmary of what was then known as Walpole State Prison (now Massachusetts Correctional Institution–Cedar Junction). At his second autopsy, in York, Pennsylvania, in October 2001, it was discovered that all of DeSalvo's internal organs—but for the bladder—were missing. So was his brain.

On December 18, 2001, Elaine and Daniel Sharp, lawyers for Richard DeSalvo, Albert's brother, sent a letter to Thomas Reilly, attorney general of Massachusetts:

> The tort claims we are presenting on behalf of our clients, Richard DeSalvo and the Estate of Albert DeSalvo, include but are not limited to the grossly negligent loss of Albert DeSalvo's internal organs upon autopsy by state agencies, including but not limited to the Office of the Attorney General, the Massachusetts State Police, and the Office of the Medical Examiner. . . . The relatives of Albert DeSalvo had no idea whatsoever that his internal organs (including the heart, liver, kidneys, lungs, and spleen) had been removed from the body and never replaced for burial by one of the above-named agencies until Albert DeSalvo was exhumed on October 26, 2001. We are also claiming that the above-named state agencies negligently failed to return the personal property of Albert DeSalvo to his representative, Richard DeSalvo, upon both his written and oral request. . . . If, in the course of your investigation, you determine that individuals other than public employees—or government entities other than the state agencies described—have caused or contributed to the claimants' injuries, we would appreciate it if you would so advise us, and provide the identity of such individuals or entities.

* * *

The Sharps subsequently filed a complaint on behalf of Richard DeSalvo in the Suffolk Division of the Superior Court of Massachusetts. The defendants were Attorney General Thomas Reilly, Chief Medical Examiner Richard J. Evans, M.D., and Colonel Thomas Robbins, superintendent of the Massachusetts State Police. In addition to the general allegations, the complaint listed five counts: negligent infliction of emotional distress, tortuous mutilation of a corpse, negligent failure to return personal items, violations of the Fair Information Practices Act, and request for equitable relief.

What Richard DeSalvo really wanted to know was why the organs had been taken, and who had taken them. Albert DeSalvo had been stabbed to death. During the second autopsy of the body, his heart, lungs, liver, and spleen might have provided further information about the murder.

Richard DeSalvo would also like to have returned to the DeSalvo family the autobiography his brother told him he was writing shortly before his death. Albert had said the document would reveal the truth about his life. As of this writing, its whereabouts are unknown. It was just one of Albert DeSalvo's personal possessions—perhaps the most important one—that vanished after he died in prison.

As of 2012, the litigation is ongoing. Elaine Sharp is seeking to negotiate a global settlement, in which the DeSalvo family would drop the suit for the return of the organs in exchange for the state's agreement to test the samples taken from the Strangler crime scenes for traces of Albert DeSalvo's DNA, and furnish the results of those tests to the DeSalvo family.

No matter what you think about the Boston Strangler case, or whom you believe might be guilty of some or all of the murders that took place between June 1962 and January 1964, keep in mind this one irrefutable fact: The Commonwealth of Massachusetts never intended to charge Albert DeSalvo with murder, for the very good reason that no physical or circumstantial evidence, nor any eyewitness testimony, ever existed to connect him with any of the crimes. (It is worth repeating that DeSalvo's DNA was not found on the body of the final Strangler victim.) All authorities had was an unsubstantiated and, in numerous instances, wildly inaccurate confession that, to be blunt, many of them never believed in the first place.

And that is why, to this day, the case files for the murders that took place between 1962 and 1964 remain packed away in archival boxes labeled "unsolved homicides."

Bibliography

Newspaper Articles

Gerhart, Ann, "An honor for a Senate pioneer," *Washington Post*, October 29, 2009.

Powers, Martine, "Memories of the Strangler," *Boston Globe*, June 14, 2012.

Court Documents and Police Reports

Casebook on Homicide of Margaret Davis: Code 04.

COMMONWEALTH OF MASSACHUSETTS, THE TRIAL COURT, SUPERIOR COURT, SUFFOLK DIVISION, CIVIL ACTION: 04-4647F.

COMMONWEALTH v. *GEORGE NASSAR, SJC-09951,* SUPREME JUDICIAL COURT OF MASSACHUSETTS, 450 Mass. 1031; 880 N.E.2d 793; 2008 Mass. LEXIS 128.
COMMONWEALTH v. *GEORGE H. NASSAR, SJC-10349,* SUPREME JUDICIAL COURT OF MASSACHUSETTS, 454 Mass. 1008; 908 N.E.2d 371; 2009 Mass. LEXIS 318.

GEORGE NASSAR v. *DISTRICT ATTORNEY FOR THE EASTERN DISTRICT & OTHERS [The Commonwealth and the Attorney General], SJC-10629,* SUPREME JUDICIAL COURT OF MASSACHUSETTS, 456 Mass. 1006; 922 N.E.2d 140; 2010 Mass. LEXIS 40.

IN THE MATTER OF DISBARMENT OF F. LEE BAILEY, D2291, SUPREME COURT OF THE UNITED STATES, 536 U.S. 936; 122 S. Ct. 2650; 153 L. Ed. 2d 827; 2002 U.S. LEXIS 4674.

IN THE MATTER OF F. LEE BAILEY, SJC-08764, SUPREME JUDICIAL COURT OF MASSACHUSETTS, 439 Mass. 134; 786 N.E2d 337; 2003 Mass. LEXIS 268.

IN RE: F. LEE BAILEY, M.B.D. No. 02-10093, UNITED STATES DISTRICT COURT FOR THE DISTRICT OF MASSACHUSETTS, 2005 U.S. Dist. LEXIS 26528.
IN RE: F. LEE BAILEY, Appellant. No. 05-2779, UNITED STATES COURT OF APPEALS FOR THE FIRST CIRCUIT, 450 F.3d 71; 2006 U.S. App. LEXIS 14189.

Tort Claims Presentment Letter Pursuant to M.G.L.C. 258 Section 1, ET Seq., December 18, 2001.

Telephone Interview

Mark Safarik, July 25, 2012.

Miscellaneous

www.wellesley.edu/PublicAffairs/WellesleyWeek/archiveweek.html

Sources

Those people who were kind enough to be interviewed by letter, by telephone, or in person are mentioned in the Acknowledgments to this book.

COURT DOCUMENTS

Commonwealth vs. Albert H. DeSalvo. Docket Number 71789. Criminal Numbers 71789, 71790, 71841, 72032, 72034, 72097-8-9.

Commonwealth vs. Albert H. DeSalvo. Superior Court Numbers 71841-2-3.

Commonwealth of Massachusetts: Middlesex Superior Court; Probate Court Number 70560. Decree Nisi of Divorce; Sonja Marie Anderson, Libellant, and Albert DeSalvo, Libellee. November 22, 1966.

Commonwealth of Massachusetts: Suffolk Superior Court; Superior Court Civil Action No. 93223, Richard E. DeSalvo, Administrator of the Estate of Albert DeSalvo, Plaintiff, vs. F. Lee Bailey, Defendant.

Massachusetts Reports: Decisions of the Supreme Judicial Court of Massachusetts. Commonwealth vs. Albert H. DeSalvo. Vol. 353 (1968).

Massachusetts Reports: Decisions of the Supreme Judicial Court of Massachusetts. Commonwealth vs. Anthony Jackson. Vol. 370 (1976), Vol. 376 (1978), Vol. 384 (1981), Vol. 388 (1983), Vol. 391 (1984).

Massachusetts Reports: Decisions of the Supreme Judicial Court of Massachusetts. Commonwealth vs. George H. Nassar. Vol. 351 (1966), Vol. 354 (1968).

Massachusetts Reports: Decisions of the Supreme Judicial Court of Massachusetts. Commonwealth vs. Roy Smith. Vol. 350 (1966).

Massachusetts Reports, Papers, and Briefs. Vol. 353. CivCom v. DES, 4.

Massachusetts Reports, Papers, and Briefs. Vol. 354. BucNas, 5.

United States Court of Appeals for the First Circuit: Albert DeSalvo, Plaintiff, Appellant vs. Twentieth Century-Fox Film Corp., Defendant, Appellee. Order of Court Entered Feb. 19, 1970.

United States District Court: District of Massachusetts; Civil Action Number 68-882-G. Albert H. DeSalvo, Plaintiff vs. 20th Century Fox Film Corp. and Reade Organization, Defendants. October 10, 11; December 20, 24, 30, 1968.

United States District Court: District of Massachusetts; Civil Action Number 68-1114-G. Albert DeSalvo, Plaintiff vs. Twentieth Century Fox Film Corp. and Walter Reade Organization, Inc., Defendants. June 16, 1969.

LAW ENFORCEMENT AGENCY REPORTS

Casebook on Homicide of Anna Slesers: Code 01
Casebook on Homicide of Nina G. Nichols: Code 02
Casebook on Homicide of Helen E. Blake: Code 03
Casebook on Homicide of Margaret Davis: Code 04
Casebook on Homicide of Ida Irga: Code 05
Casebook on Homicide of Jane Sullivan: Code 06
Casebook on Homicide of Sophie Clark: Code 07
Casebook on Homicide of Patricia Bissette: Code 08

Casebook on Homicide of Evelyn Corbin: Code 09
Casebook on Homicide of Joann Graff: Code 10
Casebook on Homicide of Mary Sullivan: Code 11
Casebook on Homicide of Jennie Woronowski: Code 12
Casebook on Homicide of Mary M. Brown: Code 13
Casebook on Homicide of Bessie Goldberg: Code 14
Casebook on Homicide of Beverly F. Samans: Code 15
Casebook on Homicide of Modeste Freeman: Code 16
Casebook on Attempted Homicide of Erika Wilsing: Code 17
Casebook on Homicide of Effie MacDonald
Interrogations of Albert DeSalvo Conducted by John S. Bottomly, August–September 1965 (Transcripts of Tapes)
Preliminary Notes for the Project to Establish a "Psychiatric Profile of the Boston Strangler," Donald P. Kenefick, M.D.
Report of Attorney General Edward W Brooke: Coordination of Investigations of "Stranglings," (August 18, 1964)

CORRESPONDENCE

Nathan Cobb to Albert DeSalvo: 11/30/72
Albert DeSalvo to F. Lee Bailey: 7/21/68
Albert DeSalvo to L. Burke: 9/2?/70
Albert DeSalvo to Clerk of Court, Middlesex Probate Court: 3/11/71
Albert DeSalvo to Massachusetts Bar Association Grievance Committee: 12/24/69
Albert DeSalvo to Francis C. Newton, Jr.: 8/29/70; 9/2/70; 10/6/70; 10/7/70; 7/27/70
Albert DeSalvo to Frederick H. Norton, Jr.: 1/11/70
Albert DeSalvo to P. J. Piscitelli: 1/13/73
Albert DeSalvo to Robert Quinn: 10/12/70
Albert DeSalvo to Paul Reardon: 2/15/71
John J. Keane to Albert DeSalvo: Undated
George Nassar to Richard and Rosalie DeSalvo: 6/24/73; 7/1/73

George Nassar to P. J. Piscitelli: 6/24/73

Francis C. Newton, Jr., to Albert DeSalvo: 9/4/70; 9/23/70; 10/7/70; 10/27/70; 11/5/70; 11/21/70; 2/8/71

Francis C. Newton, Jr., to Sheldon Newman: 12/27/76

P. J. Piscitelli to Nathan Cobb: 12/17/72

P. J. Piscitelli to Albert DeSalvo: 1/22/73

P. J. Piscitelli to Sheldon Newman: 7/18/75

NEWSPAPERS

"After Three Stranglings . . . MCNAMARA'S APPEAL! To Public: Help Us Find the Killer. TO WOMEN: Keep Doors Locked," *Traveler,* June 3, 1962.

"Albert DeSalvo Found Stabbed to Death in Cell," Stephen Wermiel, *Boston Globe,* November 27, 1973.

"Another Silk Stocking Murder; Lynn Nurse, 65, Strangled Same Day as Brigthon Woman, 68," Boston Globe, July 3, 1962.

"An Appeal to Reason Paid Off," Ray Richard, *Boston Globe,* February 25, 1967.

"Arrested Twice for Burglaries at Age of 12," Jack Kendall, *Record American,* February 25, 1967.

"Atty. John Bottomly of Holliston, a Former Assistant State Attorney," *Boston Globe,* August 16, 1980.

"Back Bay Girl Found Strangled; Hospital Worker-Student 7th Victim; Painter Sought," Frank Mahoney, *Boston Globe,* December 12, 1962.

"Back Bay Killer Known in Building," Stanley Eames, *Boston Herald,* December 8, 1962.

"Back Bay Secretary, 23, Slain, Hunt Clues in Date Book, Cards," Jim Murray and Frank McGrath, *Record American,* January 1, 1963.

"Bailey Begs Client to Give Himself Up," Ken O. Botwright, *Boston Globe,* February 25, 1967.

"Bailey Charges Double-Cross," Jack Wharton and Tom Downey, *Record American,* February 25, 1967.

"Bailey Does It—Again!" *Record American*, February 25, 1967.

"Bailey May Let DeSalvo Testify," Jonathan Klarfeld, *Boston Globe*, January 16, 1967.

"Bailey Wins Case for A.F. Captain," *Boston Globe*, February 25, 1967.

"Beacon Hill Girl Slain; Strangled in Apartment," Michael Bennett, *Boston Sunday Herald*, January 5, 1964.

"Beverly, Too, Liked Music," *Record American*, May 9, 1963.

"Bloodstained Paring Knife Reportedly Killed Student," *Boston Sunday Herald*, May 12, 1963.

"Boston's Own Strangler," George Frazier, *Boston Herald*, January 12, 1964.

"Bottomly Fined $1000 for Tax Return Charge," *Boston Globe*, July 22, 1981.

"Brooke Names Top Assistants," *Boston Advertiser*, January 13, 1963.

"Brooke: Patient Strangle Suspect," Jean Cole, Jack Wharton, and Frank Thompson, *Record American*, March 12, 1965.

"B.U. Coed Slain by Knife Fiend," James B. Ayers, *Boston Globe*, May 9, 1963.

"Burke and Nassar Counsel Confer," *Lawrence Eagle-Tribune*, October 22, 1964.

"Cambridge Choir Girl Strangled," Dan Gould, Ed Martin, and Warren Walworth, *Record American*, May 9, 1963.

"Cambridge Girl Murdered; B.U. Singer's Death Follows Terror Pattern," Robert Hassett, *Boston Herald*, May 9, 1963.

"Case Rests on MD's Conflicting Stories," Bill Duncliffe, *Record American*, January 19, 1967.

"Check Dates of Throttled Back Bay Girl," *Record American*, January 1, 1963.

"Chief Strangler Prober Bottomly Set to Take Stand," Ed Corsetti, Jean Cole, Tom Berube, and Bill Duncliffe, *Record American*, January 18, 1967.

"Co-Ed Worked With Handicapped," Ed Gillooly, *Record American*, May 9, 1963.

"Conn Calls DeSalvo Cunning Criminal," *Record American*, January 19, 1967.

"Cop Laxity Charged in Slain Girl Case," Joe Guilotti and Frank McGrath, *Record American*, January 9, 1963.

"Correct Bin Sought for Vegetable," W.J. McCarthy, *Boston Herald*, January 13, 1967.

"Defendant 'Satisfied' With Bailey's Work," Ed Corsetti and Harold Banks, *Record American*, January 17, 1967.

"Defendant's Hopes Rest on Two Medics," Harold K. Banks, *Record American*, January 13, 1967.

"DeSalvo Believed Headed for Mexico; Two Pals Nabbed," Ken Powers, Tom Riley, and Ed Gillooly, *Record American*, February 25, 1967.

"DeSalvo Branded Boston Strangler," Arthur Stratton, *Boston Herald*, January 13, 1967.

"DeSalvo Curable, Dr. Robey Says," Ed Corsetti, Jean Cole, Tom Berube, and Bill Duncliffe, *Record American*, January 17, 1967.

"DeSalvo Death Probe Near End in Walpole," *Boston Globe*, November 29, 1973.

"DeSalvo 'Discussions' Belong in the Proper Hands," Mike Barnicle, *Boston Globe*, November 29, 1973.

"DeSalvo Is 'Boston Strangler'; Defense Says He Killed 13," Robert J. Anglin, *Boston Globe*, January 13, 1967.

"DeSalvo Is Pictured by Bailey as Killer of 13 in 18 Months," Jean Cole, Ed Corsetti, and Frank Thompson, *Record American*, January 13, 1967.

"DeSalvo Pal Started Pill Riot at Walpole," Ollie Brennan and Frank Thompson, *Record American*, March 14, 1967.

"DeSalvo Picked for Jury," *Chelsea Record*, March 7, 1967.

"DeSalvo Psychiatrists Split; Experts Attack 'Impulse' Claim," Robert J. Anglin, *Boston Globe*, January 17, 1967.

"DeSalvo Seeks Ban Against Boston Strangler Label," Joseph M. Harvey, *Boston Globe*, April 1, 1971.

"DeSalvo Stabbed to Death at Walpole," Jerome Sullivan, *Boston Globe*, November 26, 1973.

"DeSalvo Sues Bailey for Film, Book Cash," *Boston Herald*, April 1, 1971.

"DeSalvo Sues Maker of Strangler Film," *Boston Globe*, December 4, 1968.

"DeSalvo Tapes Found in Vault," Ronald A. Wysocki, *Boston Globe*, February 14, 1968.

"DeSalvo's Brother Faces Gun Charge," *Boston Globe*, February 25, 1967.

"DeSalvos Get Continuance," *Record American*, March 14, 1967.

"Doctor Says DeSalvo 'Conned' Him: Now Thinks Insanity Symptoms Faked," *Boston Herald*, January 17, 1967.

"Door Unlocked Briefly, Killer Ambushed Her," Loretta McLaughlin and Jean Cole, *Record American*, January 15, 1963.

"The Doubting Detective," *Salem Evening News*, April 3, 1992.

"An Earlier Serial Killer Remembered," Peggy Hernandez, *Boston Globe*, May 8, 1989.

"Early Knockout," Jimmy Breslin, *Boston Herald*, January 13, 1967.

"18 Get Lie Detector Tests in Girl's Strangler Hunt," *Boston Herald*, January 9, 1964.

"Eldest Strangling Victim, Ida Irga, Least Likely Quarry," Jean Cole and Loretta McLaughlin, *Record American*, January 23, 1963.

"Elusive Killer Focused on Easy-Access Buildings," Jean Cole and Loretta McLaughlin, *Boston Sunday Advertiser*, January 13, 1963.

"Entire Boston Police Force on the Alert," *Boston Globe*, August 31, 1962.

"Epitaph for Beverly," Gloria Negri, *Boston Globe*, May 10, 1963.

"Escape Plot Hatched a Year Ago," John O'Neill, *Record American*, February 25, 1967.

"Ex-Convict Booked for Murder; Paroled Killer Suspected in No. Andover Slaying," Raymond L. Poirer, *Lawrence Eagle-Tribune*, October 2, 1964.

"Fay in the Middle of the Action," *Boston Globe*, February 25, 1967.

"FBI Grads Hunt for Strangler," *Boston Globe*, August 23, 1962.

"Fernald School Loved Warm, Outgoing Girl," *Boston Herald*, May 9, 1963.

"50 More Detectives Hunt Strangle Killing Clues," *Boston Globe*, January 2, 1963.

"1st and 7th Stranglings Only a Few Blocks Apart," *Boston Globe*, December 6, 1962.

"First Defense Witnesses Testify at Nassar's Trial," Raymond Maynard, *Lawrence Eagle-Tribune*.

"First Witness on Stand for Trial," Raymond Maynard, *Lawrence Eagle-Tribune*.

"5 Medics Can't Agree Whether He's Dangerous," Harold Banks, *Record American*, February 25, 1967.

"$5,000 Reward by Record American-Advertiser," *Record American*, February 25, 1967.

"Former Assistant Attorney General Fined for Failing to File Income Tax," *Boston Globe*, July 22, 1981.

"Former Mass. Official Guilty of Tax Evasion in 1973," Alan H. Sheehan, *Boston Globe*, July 7, 1981.

"Former Neighbor Sought in Slaying," Michael Bennett, *Boston Herald*, September 11, 1963.

"Friendly, Pretty, Popular, Not Afraid of Being Alone," Gloria Negri, *Boston Globe*, January 1, 1963.

"Girl Positively Identifies Nassar as Hilton's Killer," *Lawrence Eagle-Tribune*, June 18, 1965.

"Girl Seen With Youth Before Death," Irene Michalek, John Wade, and Tom Downey, *Record American*, January 7, 1963.

"Girl Strangled in Boston," *Boston Globe*, January 5, 1964.

"Girl Victim in City's 7th Strangle Murder," *Boston Herald*, December 6, 1962.

"Girl's Stricken Parents Here," *Boston Globe*, May 9, 1963.

"Girls: Keep Doors Shut 'Til DeSalvo Again in Custody," Jean Cole, *Record American*, February 25, 1967.

"'He May Head for Germany,'" Sara Davidson, *Boston Globe*, February 25, 1967.

"How They Died," *Boston Globe*, January 1, 1963.

"Hub Man Booked in Andover Murder," *Boston Globe*, October 2, 1964.

"I Abused Her Body in the Tub . . . !" *Tatler*, vol. 6, no. 23, June 4, 1967.

"Intruder Slugs Woman; Police Sift 4 Slayings," *Boston Globe*, July 13, 1962.

"Is Albert DeSalvo Really Boston Strangler?" Bill Duncliffe, Tom Sullivan, and Eddie Corsetti, *Record American*, August 17, 1971.

"Jennings Special Assistant to Oppose Nassar Appeal," *Lawrence Eagle-Tribune*, October 29, 1968.

"Jittery Homeowners Turn to Locksmiths," Gary Kayakachoian, *Boston Globe*, August 22, 1962.

"John S. Bottomly, at 63, Former Mass. Assistant Attorney General," *Boston Globe*, August 21, 1984.

"Jury Finds Nassar Guilty of First Degree Murder," George J. Gelineau, *Lawrence Eagle-Tribune*, June 26, 1965.

"Jury Hears Nassar Plead Innocent as Trial Nears End," Raymond Maynard, *Lawrence Eagle-Tribune*, August 23, 1967.

"Jury Sees Hilton Death Site," *Lawrence Eagle-Tribune*, June 15, 1965.

"Jury Weighs Fate of Albert DeSalvo in Four Sex-Robbery Cases," Ed Corsetti, Jean Cole, Tom Berube, and Bill Duncliffe, *Record American*, January 19, 1967.

"Keenan, Nassar—Twice in 16 Years," Joseph A Marois, *Lawrence Eagle-Tribune*, October 2, 1964.

"Killer Hurled Girl's Body to Ice," Irene Michalek and Tom Downey, *Record American*, January 6, 1963.

"Killer Ransacked Home; Religious Items Untouched," Loretta McLaughlin and Jean Cole, *Record American*, January 14, 1963.

"Lawrence Girl Says Nassar 'Killer,'" Raymond Maynard, *Lawrence Eagle-Tribune*, August 11, 1967.

"Lawrence Girl Says She Saw Nassar Shoot Hilton," Raymond Maynard, *Lawrence Eagle-Tribune*, August 18, 1967.

"Lawrence Woman Found Strangled," Richard Remmes, *Boston Herald*, November 25, 1963.

"Lawyers Clash Over Cross Examination of Mrs. Buote," *Lawrence Eagle-Tribune,* June 22, 1965.

"The Lee Baileys at Home," Harold Banks, *Boston Sunday Advertiser,* January 15, 1967.

"Lie Tests Given in Girl Strangling," Wendell Colton, *Boston Herald,* November 26, 1963.

"Live Alone? Here's Advice Worth Taking," *Boston Globe,* August 22, 1962.

"Male Friend Hunted in Eighth Strangling," Douglas S. Crocket, *Boston Globe,* January 1, 1963.

"A Man Here Says He's the Strangler," Jeremiah V. Murphy, *Boston Globe,* February 25, 1967.

"Married Man Admits Dating With Slain Girl," Robert L Hassett, *Boston Herald,* January 2, 1963.

"McCann Seeks Nassar Parole Explanation," *Lawrence Eagle-Tribune,* October 2, 1964.

"M'Namara Spurs Hunt for Vicious Strangler," Ed Corsetti and Bill Duncliffe, *Boston Sunday Advertiser,* January 6, 1963.

"Merrimac Man Nassar Jury Foreman," Raymond Maynard, *Lawrence Eagle-Tribune,* August 16, 1967.

"Met Audition Was Victim's Highest Hope," *Boston Herald,* May 9, 1963.

"Mom Found Strangled in Back Bay Apartment," *Traveler,* June 15, 1962.

"Mother-Daughter Witnesses to Vicious Murder are Hidden," *Boston Globe,* October 1, 1964.

"Mother of Strangled Girl Helps Sleuths," Ed Corsetti, Al Salie, and Bill Duncliffe, *Record American,* January 1, 1963.

"'Mystery Tour' Takes Boston's Dark Past," William A Davis, *Boston Globe,* July 18, 1992.

"Nassar Appeals Conviction in Andover Murder Case," *Lawrence Eagle-Tribune,* August 30, 1967.

"Nassar Begins Life Term; Retrial Ends in Conviction—Appeal Planned," Raymond Maynard, *Lawrence Eagle-Tribune,* August 24, 1967.

"Nassar Case Goes to U.S. High Court," *Lawrence Eagle-Tribune,* October 21, 1968.

"Nassar Case to Jury Today," *Lawrence Eagle-Tribune,* June 25, 1965.

"Nassar Conviction Before High Court," *Lawrence Eagle-Tribune,* March 7, 1968.

"Nassar Conviction Set Aside," *Lawrence Eagle-Tribune,* June 8, 1966.

"Nassar Council [sic] Satisfied With Pre-Trial Publicity," *Lawrence Eagle-Tribune,* November 24, 1964.

"Nassar Defense Money Sought," *Lawrence Eagle-Tribune,* November 12, 1964.

"Nassar Freeing Probe OK With Parole Board; Parole Chief Denies Foot-Dragging," *Lawrence Eagle-Tribune,* October 9, 1964.

"Nassar Has Rare Mental Condition," *Lawrence Eagle-Tribune,* February 20, 1965.

"Nassar Hearing Again Continued," *Lawrence Eagle-Tribune,* October 28, 1964.

"Nassar Held for Grand Jury in Hilton Murder," *Lawrence Eagle-Tribune,* November 6, 1964.

"Nassar Identified As Killer; Trial Recessed Until Monday," Raymond Maynard, *Lawrence Eagle-Tribune,* August 19, 1967.

"Nassar In Court Admits Lie To Parole Officer; Previous Murder Sentence Revealed," *Lawrence Eagle-Tribune,* June 24, 1965.

"Nassar Murder Trial Starting," Raymond Maynard, *Lawrence Eagle-Tribune,* August 14, 1967.

"Nassar Retrial Opens; Judge Instructs Prospective Jurors," *Lawrence Eagle-Tribune,* August 15, 1967.

"Nassar Takes the Stand But Trial Jury Excluded," *Lawrence Eagle-Tribune,* June 6, 1965.

"Nassar Trial June 14," *Lawrence Eagle-Tribune,* April 10, 1965.

"Nassar Trial June 14," *Lawrence Eagle-Tribune,* June 9, 1965.

"Nassar Trial Jury Hears State Case," *Lawrence Eagle-Tribune,* June 17, 1965.

"Nassar Wanted to Be Reporter," Michael J. Carney, *Lawrence Eagle-Tribune,* October 2, 1964.

"Nassar's Counsel Claims Murder Alibi," *Lawrence Eagle-Tribune,* October 14, 1964.

"Nassar's Fate Now Rests With Essex County Jury," Raymond Maynard, *Lawrence Eagle-Tribune,* August 23,1967.

"Nassar's Lawyer Denied $1000 Fee," *Lawrence Eagle-Tribune,* September 20, 1967.

"Naval Officer Says 2 Guns in Auto on Day of Murder," Raymond Maynard, *Lawrence Eagle-Tribune,* August 18, 1967.

"Neighbors Tell of Coed's Singing," Irene Michalek, *Record American,* May 10, 1963.

"New Police Squad Hunts Strangler," Stanley Eames, *Boston Herald,* December 7, 1962.

"New Strangle Suspect," Ed Corsetti and Bill Duncliffe, *Boston Sunday Advertiser,* January 20, 1963.

"New Trial for Nassar on August 14," *Lawrence Eagle-Tribune,* April 6, 1967.

"No New Strangler Clues—McNamara," *Boston Herald,* January 14, 1964.

"No Screams, So Strangler Attack Swift," Michael Bennett, *Boston Herald,* September 9, 1963.

"Phantom Strangler Kills Sixth Woman," Seymour Linscott, *Boston Globe,* August 31, 1962.

"Phantom Strangler Strikes Again, Back Bay Secretary 8th Victim," Irene Michalek, Jack Wharton, and Bill Duncliffe, *Record American,* January 1, 1963.

"Phillip DiNatale, Top Investigator in Boston Strangler Case," John Maddock, *Boston Globe,* January 27, 1987.

"Phone Call to Mother Bad Omen," Jack Kendall, *Record American,* January 1, 1963.

"Police Doubt Hub Stranglings Related," Frank Mahoney, *Boston Globe,* January 8, 1964.

"Police Hint Strangler Killed the Wrong Girl," Frank Mahoney, *Boston Globe,* January 10, 1964.

"Police Hunt Mad Triple Killer; Warn Women Living Alone: Keep Door Locked," *Boston Globe,* July 4, 1962.

"Police Probe Pattern in Girl Slaying," *Boston Herald,* January 7, 1964.

"Police Quiz Break Suspect in Strangling of 3 Women," *Boston Globe,* July 5, 1962.

"Police Quiz 60 in Killing of Refuge," *Boston Globe,* June 16, 1962.

"Police Quiz Two Men in Knife Slaying," *Boston Globe,* May 9, 1963.

"Posse of 250 Men on Trail of Hub Strangler DeSalvo," Ed Corsetti, Ollie Brennan, and Bill Duncliffe, *Record American,* February 25, 1967.

"Prints Clue in Latest Beacon Hill Strangle," *Record American,* January 6, 1964.

"Prints Seen As Clue in Girl's Strangling," Jeffrey A. Osoff, *Boston Globe,* January 5, 1964.

"Protection Do's, Don'ts," *Record American,* February 25, 1967.

"Psychiatrist Duels Bailey's Verbal, Electronic Lashes," Arline Grimes, *Boston Herald,* January 17, 1967.

"Psychiatrist Seen Key to Killer Hunt," Richard Remmes, *Boston Herald,* May 11, 1963.

"Psychiatry Rapped in Final Argument," *Record American,* January 19, 1967.

"'Real Truth Has Never Been Told,'" Bill Duncliffe and Tom Sullivan, *Record American,* August 12, 1971.

"'Real Truth' of DeSalvo Left Untold," Richard Connolly, *Boston Globe,* November 26, 1973.

"Record Lifted by Hospital Inmate," Jean Cole and Harold Banks, *Record American,* January 18, 1967.

"Report Hub Gunman Out to Kill Bailey," Tom Berube, Ed Corsetti, and Frank Thompson, *Record American,* January 12, 1967.

"Richardson Asks Prosecutor Conn to Aid in Pursuit," Joe Albano and Al Horne, *Record American,* February 25, 1967.

"Richardson Asks Prosecutor's Aid," Joe Albano and Al Horne, *Record American,* February 25, 1967.

"Roadblocks Bristle, Guns at the Ready," Robert J. Anglin, *Boston Globe,* February 25, 1967.

"Salem Man Found Strangled In Bed," Frank Thompson, *Record American,* January 7, 1963.

"Salem Woman Strangled With Nylon Stocking; Boston Police Seek Link to Recent Scenes," *Boston Herald,* September 9, 1963.

"Search Pressed for Coed's Slayer," Frank Mahoney, *Boston Globe,* December 8, 1962.

"Second Witness Pinpoints Nassar as Hilton's Slayer," *Lawrence Eagle-Tribune,* June 21, 1965.

"Sensations Eagerly Awaited at Trial," Jean Cole, *Record American,* January 12, 1967.

"Sidelights on Arraignment of Hilton Murder Suspect," *Lawrence Eagle-Tribune,* October 2, 1964.

"Similarity Found in Strangle Knots," *Boston Globe,* January 7, 1964.

"Six Given Lie Tests in Lawrence Strangling," *Boston Herald,* November 29, 1963.

"Slaying Climaxes Year of Torment," Bryant Rollins, *Boston Globe,* December 7, 1962.

"Sleuths Probe Mystery Date in Patricia's Killing," Al Salie and Bill Duncliffe, *Record American,* January 9, 1963.

"Solid Clues Found in Strangling of Coed; Police Get Photo, Prints of Suspect," Frank Mahoney, *Boston Globe,* December 7, 1972.

"Stark Fear Grips Three States," John Sullivan, *Record American,* February 25, 1967.

"Strangle Case at 'Impasse'; Suspect Clears Lie Detector Tests," Robert L. Hassett, *Boston Herald,* January 3, 1963.

"Strangle Victim Was Deaf," Jean Cole, *Record American,* May 10, 1963.

"Strangled Girl's Book Reveals Suspects," Ed Corsetti, Al Salie, and Bill Duncliffe, *Record American,* January 3, 1963.

"Strangled Sophie, Patsy Told of Death Dreams," Loretta McLaughlin and Jean Cole, *Record American,* January 12, 1963.

"Strangler Clues to Be Compared," *Boston Herald,* January 13, 1964.

"Strangler Escape Flayed," *Record American,* January 15, 1963.

"Strangler Fear Spreads After Latest Killing," *Boston Globe,* August 22, 1962.

"Strangler Knew Victim, Police Say," Michael Bennett, *Boston Herald,* January 6, 1964.

"Strangler of Two Mother-Hater?" *Boston Globe,* July 12, 1962.

"Strangler Strong, Calm, Cold Killer," Jean Cole and Loretta McLaughlin, *Record American,* January 10, 1963.

"Strangler Used Surprise to Slay 2 Hub Women," Loretta McLaughlin and Jean Cole, *Record American,* January 22, 1963.

"Strangler Victim's Mother Waits," Jonathan Klarfeld, *Boston Globe,* January 17, 1967.

"Sullivan Slaying Second on Hill," *Boston Herald,* January 5, 1964.

"Sullivan Strangling 11th in Greater Boston," *Boston Herald,* January 5, 1964.

"Surprise State Witness Places Nassar in Andover," Raymond Maynard, *Lawrence Eagle-Tribune,* August 20,1967.

"Terror Grips Girls in Area of Strangling," Al Salie and Bill Duncliffe, *Record American,* January 5, 1963.

"Test Ordered for Strangler," Ronald A. Wysocki, *Boston Globe,* March 11, 1965.

"Texans Commend DeSalvo," (Boston) *Herald Traveler,* April 2, 1971.

"Three Men Quizzed in Eight Stranglings," Al Salie, Loretta McLaughlin, and Bill Duncliffe, *Record American,* January 2, 1963.

"3 of 10 Victims NOT Linked to One Killer," Jean Cole and Loretta McLaughlin, *Boston Sunday Advertiser,* January 27, 1963.

"The Facts on Girl Reporters' Strangle Worksheet," *Record American,* January 23, 1963.

"Time Softens Terror for Strangle Victim's Son," Jean Cole and Loretta McLaughlin, *Boston Sunday Advertiser,* January 20, 1963.

"Top Court Upholds Nassar's Conviction," *Lawrence Eagle-Tribune,* May 7, 1968.

"Tortured DeSalvo Tried to Seek Help in Church," *Record American,* January 18, 1967.

"Trial Lawyers to Hear Bailey," *Boston Herald,* January 13, 1967.

"A Twisted, Driven, 'Vegetable,'" Jonathan Klarfeld, *Boston Globe,* January 13, 1967.

"Twisted Nylons Use Bared After Patsy Stranglings," Loretta McLaughlin and Jean Cole, *Record American,* January 11, 1963.

"Two Escapers Captured, But DeSalvo Still at Large," Robert J. Anglin and Richard J. Connolly, *Boston Globe,* February 25, 1967.

"2 Girl Reporters Analyze Strangler," Jean Cole and Loretta McLaughlin, *Record American,* January 9, 1963.

"Two Greater Lawrence Men Chosen Nassar Trial Jurors," *Lawrence Eagle-Tribune,* August 15, 1967.

"2 Men Face Lie Tests in Cambridge Killing," Stanley Eames, *Boston Herald,* May 10, 1963.

"2 Take Lie Tests in Coed Slaying," James B. Ayres, *Boston Globe,* May 10, 1963.

"Unidentified Print Is Slim Strangle Clue," Michael Bennett, *Boston Herald,* January 8, 1964.

"Unknown Footsteps . . . And A Girl in Fear," *Boston Globe,* January 10, 1964.

"Unlocked Gate Let Someone in to Kill DeSalvo," Stephen Wermiel, *Boston Globe,* November 28, 1973.

"U.S. Supreme Court Turns Down Nassar," *Lawrence Eagle-Tribune, January 15, 1969.*

"Victim 12th in Past Year; 3 Just Miss," *Record American,* May 9, 1963.

"Visitor Hunted in Strangling," Richard Connolly, *Boston Herald,* January 1, 1963.

"Volpe 'Shocked,'" *Boston Globe,* February 25, 1967.

"Walpole Inmate Suspect in DeSalvo Murder," Robert Ward and Seymour Linscott, *Boston Globe,* November 27, 1973.

"Wellesley Girls and Harvard Men: 'Better Than Reading a Racy Book'," Gloria Boykin, *Record American,* January 17, 1967.

"When Fear Was in Season," Loretta McLaughlin, *Boston Globe,* June 6, 1992.

"Widow 5th Victim of Strangler," *Boston Globe,* August 22, 1962.

"With the Keys Rest Was Easy," Ray Richard, *Boston Globe,* February 25, 1967.

"Woman Found Strangled in Back Bay Apartment," *Boston Herald,* June 15, 1962.

"Woman Slain in Back Bay Home," *Boston Globe,* June 15, 1962.

"Women Beware! He's a Smoothie," Jean Cole, *Record American,* February 25, 1967.

"Women Lock Up, Wait for News," Jonathan Klarfeld, *Boston Globe,* February 25, 1967.

BOOKS

Bailey, F. Lee, and Harvey Aronson. *The Defense Never Rests.* Stein and Day: New York, 1971.

Dershowitz, Alan M. *The Best Defense.* Random House: New York, 1982.

Frank, Gerold. *The Boston Strangler.* NAL: New York, 1966; Signet/NAL: New York, 1967. All quotes taken from the 1967 edition.

Hearst, Patricia Campbell, with Alvin Moscow. *Every Secret Thing.* Pinnacle Books: New York, 1982. (Previously published by Doubleday.) All quotes taken from the 1982 edition.

Rae, George William. *Confessions of the Boston Strangler.* Pyramid Books: New York, 1967.

MAGAZINE ARTICLES

Cameron, John, "That Fatal Silk Stocking Caress," *Inside Detective,* June 1963.

Higgins, George V., "The Wrong Man?" *Memories,* Spring 1968.

Kahn, Ric, "The Toughest S.O.B.'s in Town," *Boston,* December 1983.

Kelly, Susan, "The Untold Story Behind the Boston Strangler," *Boston,* April 1992.

Linn, Edward, "F. Lee Bailey: Renegade in the Courtroom," *Saturday Evening Post,* November 5, 1966.

Russell, Dick, "True Crime Stories." *Boston,* September 1982.

Index

GREAT BOOKS, GREAT SAVINGS!

When You Visit Our Website:
www.kensingtonbooks.com
You Can Save 30% Off The Retail Price
Of Any Book You Purchase

- All Your Favorite Kensington Authors
- New Releases & Timeless Classics
- Overnight Shipping Available
- All Major Credit Cards Accepted

Visit Us Today To Start Saving!
www.kensingtonbooks.com

All Orders Are Subject To Availability.
Shipping and Handling Charges Apply.